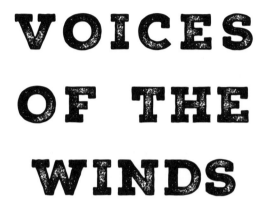

# VOICES OF THE WINDS

BY THE SAME AUTHORS

by Margot Edmonds and Ella E. Clark
*Sacagawea of the Lewis and Clark Expedition*

by Ella E. Clark
*Poetry: An Interpretation of Life*
*Indian Legends of the Pacific Northwest*
*Indian Legends of Canada*
*Indian Legends of the Northern Rockies*
*Guardian Spirit Quest*
*In the Beginning*

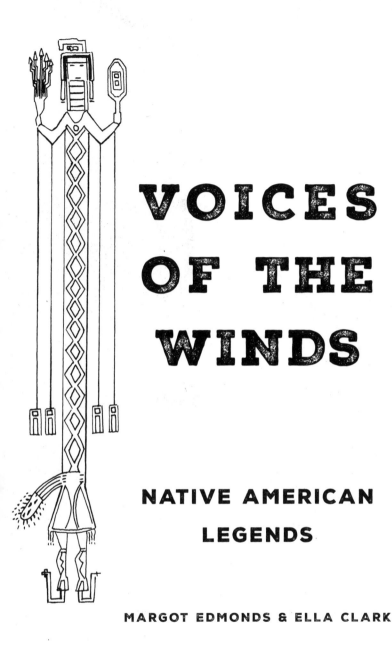

# VOICES
# OF THE
# WINDS

## NATIVE AMERICAN
## LEGENDS

**MARGOT EDMONDS & ELLA CLARK**

chartwell
books

Inspiring | Educating | Creating | Entertaining

Brimming with creative inspiration, how-to projects, and useful information to enrich your everyday life, Quarto Knows is a favorite destination for those pursuing their interests and passions. Visit our site and dig deeper with our books into your area of interest: Quarto Creates, Quarto Cooks, Quarto Homes, Quarto Lives, Quarto Drives, Quarto Explores, Quarto Gifts, or Quarto Kids.

This edition published in 2021 by Chartwell Books,
an imprint of The Quarto Group,
142 West 36th Street, 4th Floor,
New York, NY 10018, USA
**T** (212) 779-4972  **F** (212) 779-6058
**www.QuartoKnows.com**

Voices of the Winds by Margot Edmonds © 1989
Published under license from
Facts on File, Inc.
132 West 31st Street 17th Floor
New York, NY 10001

Chartwell titles are also available at discount for retail, wholesale, promotional, and bulk purchase. For details, contact the Special Sales Manager by email at specialsales@quarto.com or by mail at The Quarto Group, Attn: Special Sales Manager, 100 Cummings Center, Suite 265D, Beverly, MA 01915, USA.

10 9 8 7 6 5 4 3 2

ISBN: 978-0-7858-3975-0

Library of Congress Control Number: 2021933423

Text Design by Stein & Ehn
Composition by Facts on File
Cover Design by Beth Middleworth
Cover Image: Haida double thunderbird, American School, (19th century) (after) / Look and Learn / Elgar Collection / Bridgeman Images

Printed in China

# Contents

*To the original North American Indians,
and to their descendants, who have preserved
Indian oral literature through the centuries,
since the last Ice Age, translating their wisdom
about this Universe for all its peoples.*

# Acknowledgments

The authors gratefully acknowledge the sources of assistance given in the preparation of this anthology of Indian legends:

The Bureau of American Ethnology, Smithsonian Institute, Washington, D.C.

The American Folklore Society, Washington, D.C., for its *Journal of American Folklore.*

The historical societies of Oregon, Washington, and Montana.

The U.S. Bureau of Indian Affairs, Washington, D.C.

AMS Reprints Press, Kraus Reprints, Gale Press Reprints, Johnson Corporation Reprints, and Reader's Digest Association.

The University of Washington State Libraries, Pullman. Mr. John Guido, Archival Head. The librarians at the University of California, San Diego, CA. The librarians at San Diego Central Library and its La Jolla Branch Library.

Grateful acknowledgment is also made to the original authors and publishers of these tales. Sources for legends appear in footnotes; see Bibliography for complete citation.

After diligently searching and using every effort to seek permissions from copyright proprietors, the authors regret any omissions.

Aleuts
Makah
Salish
Okanagon
Sanpoil
Chelan
Columbia
Wasco
Shasta
Pomo
Washo
Miwok
Yosemite
Mariposa
Yokut
Luiseno
Diegueno
Papago
Pima
Paiute
Hopi
Navaho
Apache
Zuni
Acoma
Apache
Ute
Yellowstone
Shoshone
Cheyenne
Flathead
Blackfeet
Piegan
Chipewyan
Hidatsa
Mandan
Arikara
Dakota-Sioux
Pawnee
Arapaho
Wichi's
Iowa
Illini
Winnebago
Chippewa
Ottawa
Shawnee
Yuchi
Cherokee
Tuskegee
Creek
Natchez
Alabama
Seminole
Micmac
Wabanaki
Passamaquoddy
Penobscot
Abnaki
Seneca
Iroquois
Wampanoag

■

# AS IT WAS

■

Long, long ago, as all good stories begin, man first appeared upon the North American continent from eastern Asia. He followed the trails of the caribou, elk, reindeer, camels, and bear who were seeking food, as was he. They crossed over the ice-covered Bering Strait land bridge long before the end of the last Ice Age disappeared, over 10,000 years ago. These early humans became the first inhabitants of the area, and along with their children and descendants became known as the North American Indians.

These Indians established colonies of tribes along the coastal region of what has now become Alaska. Eventually, still in search of food, they migrated eastward across what we today call Canada. They then moved southward along the West Coast and the East Coast. Later, they spread inland to the Central and the Great Plains regions of the present United States of America.

A few thousand years later the North American Indians were found in the southern areas of the continent from west to east, all of them descendants of those first Asians who crossed the Bering Strait land bridge, before the end of the last Ice Age.

Since the very beginning, North American Indians mostly communicated their beliefs through oral history, as well as through their paintings, carvings, the body movements in their expressive dances, and with rhythmic sounds produced on drumlike instruments.

Indians told their history using all of these methods. Most notable, of course, has been the oral transmission of myths and legends from one generation to the next, through tribal historians. From early childhood, these historians were trained by their elders to learn the tales and mimic the characters in the stories.

Traditionally, storytelling was reserved for the cold seasons, as people gathered around winter fires. Storytelling at any other season was taboo among the tribal ancients who maintained traditions for their people. During the other seasons more important activities for the tribal members were hunting, fishing, harvesting, and making clothes for all members in the tribal family. If violations of tribal rules occurred, offenders were certain to suffer great misfortune at the hands of evil spirits, according to tribal traditions.

To help us learn and understand more about the life of the North American Indians, their myths and legends are a rich source of their oral tradition, comparable to reading European folklore and fairy tales.

Classical Greek and Latin stories of giants, monsters, and other supernatural heroes provided a similar oral account of their time and people.
So superbly trained were North American Indian tribal historians from
generation to generation that their acting and the mimicry of sounds
portraying human and animal characters were limited only by the
imagination of the storytellers.

The Indian myths and legends collected in this volume represent most
of the tribes of longtime North American Indian cultures in the six major
regions of the United States of America: Northwest, Southwest, Great
Plains, Central, Southeast, and Northeast. We hope to introduce these
stories to the general reader, stories that were generally accessible only
to the specialists in folklore.

American Indian legends originated from a variety of experience.
Some describe the beauty and power of the landscape. Others reflect
themes of natural phenomena, creation myths, the origin of fire, historical events and customs, and the mystical beliefs of North American
Indians.

We have chosen representative legends from various sources,
preserved in government documents, old histories, periodicals, and
reports from anthropologists in the field. Also included are a few tales
from manuscripts treasured by early pioneers in the Northwest region.

Some of the legends from printed material have been rewritten slightly for clarity and grammatical expression, and to make them more
suitable for the general reader.

Ella E. Clark spent many summers on fifteen North American Indian
reservations, listening to elder tribal historians and recording their
stories. Several of these are included in *Voices of the Winds*. You will find
all of our sources for the material included in this book listed in the
extensive bibliography.

We have considered as our underlying theme in this volume the way
North American Indians believed that spirit life dwelled in all of nature.
So very much of the North American Indian's way of life was related to
their spiritual beliefs and to the rituals of daily life for each tribe. They
believed that everything in nature possessed a life or spirit within, even
the sky, earth, mountains, trees, waters, animals, birds—and man.

The North American Indian believed all rain or hail from the sky
contained its own special spirit song for his sensitive ear, a challenge to
him for further endeavor or perhaps a warning of things to come.
Indians believed every wind breathed forth the spirit of the one who
made the wind blow, however far away, and they had their own special
names for the many spirit *Voices of the Winds*. "Indians heard them in
every sigh, whisper, bluster, roar, moan, or whistle of the wind—each

filled with spirit life and power for the one who listened," described Martin Sampson, an Indian grandfather.

The Indians believed the happenings in every river, waterfall, echo, thunder, and even the changing positions of stars in the sky resulted from actions by their indwelling spirits. They believed these spirits of nature controlled nature itself, the way good or bad spirits living in man seem to control much of his behavior.

North American Indians judged spirits as good or bad according to how they treated Indians, naturally favoring those that protected them from wrath or evil. Indians believed that angered spirits caused crop failures or caused fish and game to vanish, and were responsible for other catastrophies of nature that might endanger all life.

Evil spirits associated themselves with darkness in caves and deep underground caverns. From these they emerged periodically and performed horrendous deeds, or so thought the North American Indians. Spirits of swamplands and dark forests, inadvertently overheard by Indians, could cause them to lose their way home— forever. Indian children were taught *never* to listen to these kinds of misleading spirits for fear of kidnapping and separation from their tribes.

Enormous Thunderbird ruled over all as chief spirit of storms. North American Indian tales relate that his large flapping wings caused the frightening sounds of roaring thunder. His flashing eyes emitted lightning. Thunderbird lived in a black cloud high above the tallest mountain, or sometimes Thunderbird rested in an enormous cave of a mammoth mountain. When he became terribly hungry, he charged westward to the Pacific Ocean and devoured a whole whale. Thunderbird's homeward trip was accompanied by thunder and lightning, frightening Indians in his path.

Did the North American Indians think certain spirits in nature seemed more powerful than others? Many of their legends tell about the Great Spirit, probably meaning their most awesome spirit. Other Indians also speak of the Chief of the Sky Spirits. The coming of the white man to the Northwest followed the Lewis and Clark Expedition, from 1804 to 1806. Is it possible that both the Great Spirit and the Chief of the Sky Spirits was the Indians' interpretation of the white man's God or Supreme Being?

North American Indians believed that the mysterious power of spirits in nature was stronger than human power. Consequently, an Indian searched to discover for himself the strong spirit of a supernatural power to become his guardian spirit for life. For a young Indian, a Guardian Spirit Quest became the most important event of his life. To accomplish his feat, an Indian youth isolated himself from his family and tribe. He built a small shelter, then fasted and thirsted for many days and nights alone.

Usually in a dream, a strong animal spirit in human form appeared to the boy. The dream spirit taught him his own sacred song, his family duties, his tribal duties, and gave him a special gift to become a hunter, or a leader, or even a healer for his tribe. The young Indian was given a token, or talisman, usually by his father or his tribal Medicine Man to wear always. His newly acquired spirit power and his gifts became his "Medicine" for life.

He hid his "Medicine" in his own self-decorated animal skin bag. This became his power, or "sacred bundle," that he brought forth at ceremonials and for his meditation as long as he lived.

Medicine Men and Medicine Women of the tribes possessed phenomenal powers to help their people, and had a wide knowledge of medicinal herbs and potions. They also officiated at ceremonies and celebrations of their tribes. Their position in the tribe was equivalent to that of a high priest or high priestess.

Ella E. Clark wrote in her book, *Indian Legends of the Northern Rockies*, "My ideals of style have been simplicity, sincerity, a conversational tone or one of oral quality, and the variety of rhythms in everyday speech. In my opinion, these qualities are appropriate to the folk literature of any people." The authors of this volume have endeavored to use these ideals in *Voices of the Winds*.

You will discover here through Indian oral histories how tribal traditions and cultures have been preserved from generation to generation from their earliest beginnings in Alaska during the last Ice Age. Included in this collection of North American Indian myths and legends are some from the 1800s and early 1900s as well. From these, general readers can gain greater understanding of the long heritage of Indian tribal life.

Through these Indian legends from ancient times you can listen to the voices of the North American Indians. *Never* would they have opened their hearts to *strangers* in the past! Here, together, we are fortunate to hear an echo of these voices of the winds.

Margot Edmonds and
Ella E. Clark

# VOICES
## OF THE
# WINDS

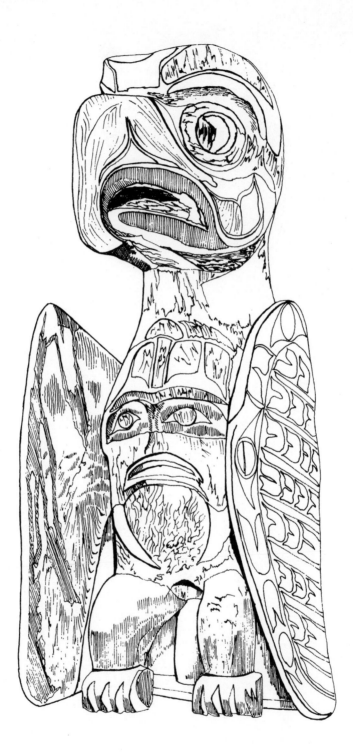

*Thunderbird*

# PART ONE

# FROM
# THE
# NORTHWEST

*The saga of the Northwest Indians probably began millenniums ago when hunting families in search of food set out from Siberia, walked across a land bridge, the Bering Strait, to a new country that became known as Alaska.*

*Later, many Indian tribes lived south of the Arctic Circle and divided into two distinct language groups: the Algonquians extended eastward to below Hudson Bay, and the Athapascans stayed in northwest Canada. Gradually, some of each group moved southward into the United States.*

*The Lewis and Clark explorers of 1803 to 1806 probably were the first white men to be seen by some descendants of those ancient Athapascan tribes. Mainly they lived on the north side of the Columbia River; on the south side of the river tribes of the Salishan language family located. Salishan Indians derived their name from the Salish, another name for the Flathead tribes of Montana.*

*Hunting and fishing provided the chief occupation and food supply of the Northwest Indians. When trading posts developed, commerce increased with white emigrants. The traditions and ceremonies of the tribes, however, continued from one generation to the next.*

■

# THE CREATION OF THE FIRST INDIANS
## *Chelan*

This story was told by the Chelan Indians, who used to live beside a long lake in the central part of the state of Washington. The lake is still called Lake Chelan (pronounced shȧ-lăn), meaning "Beautiful Water."

■

Long, long ago, the Creator, the Great Chief Above, made the world. Then he made the animals and the birds and gave them their names— Coyote, Grizzly Bear, Deer, Fox, Eagle, the four Wolf Brothers, Magpie, Bluejay, Hummingbird, and all the others.

When he had finished his work, the Creator called the animal people to him. "I am going to leave you," he said. "But I will come back. When I come again, I will make human beings. They will be in charge of you."

The Great Chief returned to his home in the sky, and the animal people scattered to all parts of the world.

After twelve moons, the animal people gathered to meet the Creator as he had directed. Some of them had complaints. Bluejay, Meadowlark, and Coyote did not like their names. Each of them asked to be some other creature.

"No," said the Creator. "I have given you your names. There is no change. My word is law.

"Because you have tried to change my law, I will not make the human being this time. Because you have disobeyed me, you have soiled what I brought with me. I planned to change it into a human being. Instead, I will put it in water to be washed for many moons and many snows, until it is clean again."

Then he took something from his right side and put it in the river. It swam, and the Creator named it Beaver.

"Now I will give you another law," said the Great Chief Above. "The one of you who keeps strong and good will take Beaver from the water some day and make it into a human being. I will tell you now what to do. Divide Beaver into twelve parts. Take each part to a different place and breathe into it your own breath. Wake it up. It will be a human being with your breath. Give it half of your power and tell it what to do. Today I am giving my power to one of you. He will have it as long as he is good."

When the Creator had finished speaking, all the creatures started for their homes—all except Coyote. The Great Chief had a special word for Coyote.

"You are to be head of all the creatures, Coyote. You are a power just like me now, and I will help you do your work. Soon the creatures and all the other things I have made will become bad. They will fight and will eat each other. It is your duty to keep them as peaceful as you can.

"When you have finished your work, we will meet again, in this land toward the east. If you have been good, if you tell the truth and obey me, you can make the human being from Beaver. If you have done wrong, someone else will make him."

Then the Creator went away.

It happened as the Creator had foretold. Everywhere the things he had created did wrong. The mountains swallowed the creatures. The winds blew them away. Coyote stopped the mountains, stopped the winds, and rescued the creatures. One winter, after North Wind had killed many people, Coyote made a law for him: "Hereafter you can kill only those who make fun of you."

Everywhere Coyote went, he made the world better for the animal people and better for the human beings yet to be created. When he had finished his work, he knew that it was time to meet the Creator again. Coyote thought that he had been good, that he would be the one to make the first human being.

But he was mistaken. He thought that he had as much power as the Creator. So he tried, a second time, to change the laws of the Great Chief Above.

"Some other creature will make the human being," the Creator told Coyote. "I shall take you out into the ocean and give you a place to stay for all time."

So Coyote walked far out across the water to an island. There the Creator stood waiting for him, beside the house he had made. Inside the house on the west side stood a black suit of clothes. On the other side hung a white suit.

"Coyote, you are to wear this black suit for six months," said the Creator. "Then the weather will be cold and dreary. Take off the black suit and wear the white suit. Then there will be summer, and everything will grow.

"I will give you my power not to grow old. You will live here forever and forever."

Coyote stayed there, out in the ocean, and the four Wolf brothers took his place as the head of all the animal people. Youngest Wolf Brother was was strong and good and clever. Oldest Wolf Brother was worthless. So the Creator gave Youngest Brother the power to take Beaver from the water.

One morning Oldest Wolf Brother said to Youngest Brother, "I want you to kill Beaver. I want his tooth for a knife."

"Oh, no!" exclaimed Second and Third Brothers. "Beaver is too strong for Youngest Brother."

But Youngest Wolf said to his brothers, "Make four spears. For Oldest Brother, make a spear with four forks. For me, make a spear with one fork. Make a two-forked spear and a three-forked spear for yourselves. I will try my best to get Beaver, so that we can kill him."

All the animal persons had seen Beaver and his home. They knew where he lived. They knew what a big creature he was. His family of young beavers lived with him.

The animal persons were afraid that Youngest Wolf Brother would fail to capture Beaver and would fail to make the human being. Second and Third World Brothers also were afraid. "I fear we will lose Youngest Brother," they said to each other.

But they made the four spears he had asked for.

At dusk, the Wolf brothers tore down the dam at the beavers' home, and all the little beavers ran out. About midnight, the larger beavers ran out. They were so many, and they made so much noise, that they sounded like thunder. Then Big Beaver ran out, the one the Creator had put into the water to become clean.

"Let's quit!" said Oldest Wolf Brother, for he was afraid. "Let's not try to kill him."

"No!" said Youngest Brother. "I will not stop."

Oldest Wolf Brother fell down. Third Brother fell down. Second Brother fell down. Lightning flashed. The beavers still sounded like thunder. Youngest Brother took the four-forked spear and tried to strike Big Beaver with it. It broke. He used the three-forked spear. It broke. He used the two-forked spear. It broke. Then he took his own one-forked spear. It did not break.

It pierced the skin of Big Beaver and stayed there. Out of the lake, down the creek, and down Big River, Beaver swam, dragging Youngest Brother after it.

Youngest Wolf called to his brothers, "You stay here. If I do not return with Beaver in three days, you will know that I am dead."

Three days later, all the animal persons gathered on a level place at the foot of the mountain. Soon they saw Youngest Brother coming. He had killed Beaver and was carrying it. "You remember that the Creator told us to cut it into twelve pieces," said Youngest Brother to the animal people.

But he could divide it into only eleven pieces.

Then he gave directions. "Fox, you are a good runner. Hummingbird and Horsefly, you can fly fast. Take this piece of Beaver flesh over to that place and wake it up. Give it your breath."

Youngest Brother gave other pieces to other animal people and told them where to go. They took the liver to Clearwater River, and it became the Nez Perce Indians. They took the heart across the mountains, and it became the Methow Indians. Other parts became the Spokane people, the Lake people, the Flathead people. Each of the eleven pieces became a different tribe.

"There have to be twelve tribes," said Youngest Brother. "Maybe the Creator thinks that we should use the blood for the last one. Take the blood across the Shining Mountains and wake it up over there. It will become the Blackfeet. They will always look for blood."

When an animal person woke the piece of Beaver flesh and breathed into it, he told the new human being what to do and what to eat.

"Here are roots," and the animal people pointed to camas and kouse, and to bitterroot, "You will dig them, cook them, and save them to eat in the winter.

"Here are the berries that will ripen in the summer. You will eat them, and you will dry them for use in winter."

The animal people pointed to chokecherry trees, to serviceberry bushes, and to huckleberry bushes.

"There are salmon in all the rivers. You will cook them and eat them when they come up the streams. And you will dry them to eat in the winter."

When all the tribes had been created, the animal people said to them, "Some of you new people should go up Lake Chelan. Go up to the middle of the lake and look at the cliff beside the water. There you will see pictures on the rock. From the pictures you will learn how to make the things you will need."

The Creator had painted the pictures there, with red paint. From the beginning until long after the white people came, the Indians went to Lake Chelan and looked at the paintings. They saw pictures of bows and arrows and of salmon traps. From the paintings of the Creator they knew how to make the things they needed for getting their food.

Note: The paintings (or pictographs) on the lower rocks have been covered by water since a dam was built at the foot of the lake. Surprisingly high on the rocks that are almost perpendicular walls at the north end of the lake, the paintings remained for a long, long time. Then white people with guns and little respect for the past ruined them—for fun.

Clark, *In the Beginning*, 5.

■

# COYOTE AND MULTNOMAH FALLS
## *Wasco*

The Big River, or Great River, in the stories of the Northwest Indians is the Columbia. The Big Shining Mountains are the Rockies.

■

"Long, long ago, when the world was young and people had not come out yet," said an elderly Indian years ago, "the animals and the birds were the *people* of this country. They talked to each other just as we do. And they married, too."

Coyote (ki-o'-ti) was the most powerful of the animal people, for he had been given special power by the Spirit Chief. For one thing, he changed the course of Big River, leaving Dry Falls behind. In some stories, he was an animal; in others he was a man, sometimes a handsome young man.

In that long ago time before this time, when all the people and all the animals spoke the same language, Coyote made one of his frequent trips along Great River. He stopped when he came to the place where the water flowed under the Great Bridge that joined the mountains on one side of the river with the mountains on the other side. There he changed himself into a handsome young hunter.

When traveling up the river the last time, he had seen a beautiful girl in a village not far from the bridge. He made up his mind that he would ask the girl's father if he might have her for his wife. The girl's father was a chief. When the handsome young man went to the chief's lodge, he carried with him a choice gift for the father in return for his daughter.

The gift was a pile of the hides and furs of many animals, as many skins as Coyote could carry. He made the gift large and handsome because he had learned that the man who would become the husband of the girl would one day become the chief of the tribe.

The chief knew nothing about the young man expect that he seemed to be a great hunter. The gift was pleasing in the father's eyes, but he wanted his daughter to be pleased.

"She is my only daughter," the chief said to the young hunter. "And she is very dear to my heart. I shall not be like other fathers and trade her for a pile of furs. You will have to win the heart of my daughter, for I want her to be happy."

*Plateau Indian carved skeleton figure*
Wasco

So Coyote came to the chief's lodge every day, bringing with him some small gift that he thought would please the girl. But he never seemed to bring the right thing. She would shyly accept his gift and then run away to the place where the women sat in the sun doing their work with deerskins or to the place where the children were playing games.

Every day Coyote became more eager to win the beautiful girl. He thought and thought about what gifts to take to her. "Perhaps the prettiest flower hidden in the forest," he said to himself one day, "will be the gift that will make her want to marry me."

He went to the forest beside Great River and searched for one whole day. Then he took to the chief's lodge the most beautiful flower he had found. He asked to see the chief.

"I have looked all day for this flower for your daughter," said Coyote to the chief. "If this does not touch her heart, what will? What gift can I bring that will win her heart?"

The chief was the wisest of all the chiefs of a great tribe. He answered, "Why don't you ask my daughter? Ask her, today, what gift will make her heart the happiest of all hearts."

As the two finished talking, they saw the girl come out of the forest. Again Coyote was pleased and excited by her beauty and her youth. He stepped up to her and asked, "Oh, beautiful one, what does your heart want most of all? I will get for you anything that you name. This flower that I found for you in a hidden spot in the woods is my pledge."

Surprised, or seeming to be surprised, the girl looked at the young hunter and at the rare white flower he was offering her.

"I want a pool," she answered shyly. "A pool where I may bathe every day hidden from all eyes that might see."

Then, without accepting the flower that Coyote had searched for so many hours, she ran away. As before, she hurried to play with her young friends.

Coyote turned to her father. "It is well. In seven suns I will come for you and your daughter. I will take you to the pool she asked for. The pool will be for her alone."

For seven suns Coyote worked to build the pool that would win the heart of the girl he wished to marry. First he cut a great gash in the hills on the south side of Great River. Then he lined that gash with trees and shrubs and ferns to the very top of a high wall that looked toward the river.

Then he went to the bottom of the rock wall and slanted it back a long way, far enough to hollow out a wide pool. He climbed up the wall again and went far back into the hills. There he made a stream come out of the earth, and he sent it down the big gash he had made, to fall over the slanting rock wall. From the edge of that wall the water dropped with spray and mist. And so the water made, at the bottom, a big screen that hid the pool from all eyes.

When he had finished his work, Coyote went to the village to invite the chief and his daughter to see what he had made. When they had admired the new waterfall, he showed them the pool that lay behind it and the spray. He watched the eyes of the girl.

She looked with smiling eyes, first at the pool and the waterfall in front of it, and then at the young hunter who had made them for her. He could see that she was pleased. He could see that at last he had won her heart. She told her father that she was willing to become the wife of the young hunter.

In that long ago time before this time, two old grandmothers sat all day on top of the highest mountains. One sat on the top of the highest mountain north of Great River. The other sat on the highest mountain south of it. When the one on the north side talked, she could be heard eastward as far as the Big Shining Mountains, westward as far as the big water where the sun hides every night, and northward to the top of the world.

The grandmother on the south side of the river also could be heard as far west as the big water and as far south as anyone lived. The two old women saw everything that was done, and every day they told all the people on both sides of the river.

Now they saw the chief's daughter go every morning to bathe in the pool, and they saw Coyote wait for her outside the screen of waterfall and spray. The old grandmothers heard the two sing to each other and laugh together. The grandmothers laughed at the pair, raised their voices, and told all the people what they saw and heard.

Soon the chief's daughter knew that all the people were laughing at her—all the people from the big water to the Big Shining Mountains, all the people from the top of the world to as far south as anyone lived.

She was no longer happy. She no longer sang with joy. One day she asked Coyote to allow her to go alone to the pool. The old grandmothers watched her go behind the waterfall. Then they saw her walk from the pool and go down into Great River. Her people never saw her again.

Coyote, in a swift canoe, went down Great River in search of her. He saw her floating and swimming ahead of him, and he paddled as fast as he could. He reached her just before she was carried out into the big water where the sun hides at night.

There the two of them, Coyote and the girl, were turned into little ducks, little summer ducks, floating on the water.

That was a long, long time ago. But even today, when the sun takes its last look at the high cliff south of Great River, two summer ducks swim out to look back at the series of waterfalls that dash down the high mountain. They look longest at the lowest cascade and the spray that hides the tree-fringed pool behind them.

If those who want to understand will be silent and listen, they will hear the little song that the chief's daughter and Coyote used to sing to each other every morning after she had bathed in the pool. The song begins very soft and low, lifts sharply to a high note, and then fades gently away.

Ella E. Clark.

■

# WHEN THE ANIMALS AND BIRDS WERE CREATED
## *Makah*

The Indians who live on the farthest point of the northwest corner of Washington State used to tell stories, not about one Changer, but about the Two-Men-Who-Changed-Things. So did their close relatives, who lived on Vancouver Island, across the Strait of Juan de Fuca.

■

When the world was very young, there were no people on the earth. There were no birds or animals, either. There was nothing but grass and sand and creatures that were neither animals nor people but had some of the traits of people and some of the traits of animals.

Then the two brothers of the Sun and the Moon came to the earth. Their names were *Ho-ho-e-ap-bess,* which means "The Two-Men-Who-Changed-Things." They came to make the earth ready for a new race of people, the Indians. The Two-Men-Who-Changed-Things called all the creatures to them. Some they changed to animals and birds. Some they changed to trees and smaller plants.

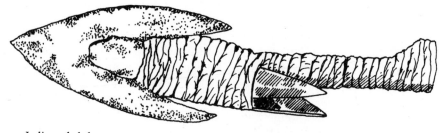

*Indian whale harpoon*
Makah

Among them was a bad thief. He was always stealing food from creatures who were fishermen and hunters. The Two-Men-Who-Changed-Things transformed him into Seal. They shortened his arms and tied his legs so that only his feet could move. Then they threw Seal into the Ocean and said to him, "Now you will have to catch your own fish if you are to have anything to eat."

One of the creatures was a great fisherman. He was always on the rocks or was wading with his long fishing spear. He kept it ready to thrust into some fish. He always wore a little cape, round and white, over his shoulders. The Two-Men-Who-Changed-Things transformed him into Great Blue Heron. The cape became the white feathers around the neck of Great Blue Heron. The long fishing spear became his sharp-pointed bill.

Another creature was both a fisherman and a thief. He had stolen a necklace of shells. The Two-Men-Who-Changed-Things transformed him into Kingfisher. The necklace of shells was turned into a ring of feathers around Kingfisher's neck. He is still a fisherman. He watches the water, and when he sees a fish, he dives headfirst with a splash into the water.

Two creatures had huge appetites. They devoured everything they could find. The Two-Men-Who-Changed-Things transformed one of them into Raven. They transformed his wife into Crow. Both Raven and Crow were given strong beaks so that they could tear their food. Raven croaks "Cr-r-ruck!" and Crow answers with a loud "Cah! Cah!"

The Two-Men-Who-Changed-Things called Bluejay's son to them and asked, "Which do you wish to be—a bird or a fish?"

"I don't want to be either," he answered.

"Then we will transform you into Mink. You will live on land. You will eat the fish you can catch from the water or can pick up on the shore."

Then the Two-Men-Who-Changed-Things remembered that the new people would need wood for many things.

They called one of the creatures to them and said "The Indians will want tough wood to make bows with. They will want tough wood to

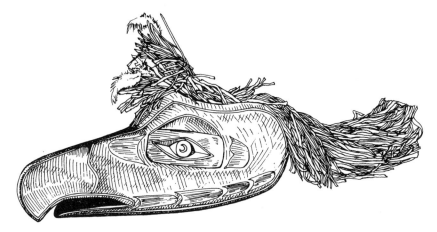

*Black raven mask*
Makah

make wedges with, so that they can split logs. You are tough and strong. We will change you into the yew tree."

They called some little creatures to them. "The new people will need many slender, straight shoots for arrows. You will be the arrowwood. You will be white with many blossoms in early summer."

They called a big, fat creature to them. "The Indians will need big trunks with soft wood so that they can make canoes. You will be the cedar trees. The Indians will make many things from your bark and from your roots."

The Two-Men-Who-Changed-Things knew that the Indians would need wood for fuel. So they called an old creature to them. "You are old, and your heart is dry. You will make good kindling, for your grease has turned hard and will make pitch. You will be the spruce tree. When you grow old, you will always make dry wood that will be good for fires."

To another creature they said, "You shall be the hemlock. Your bark will be good for tanning hides. Your branches will be used in the sweat lodges."

A creature with a cross temper they changed into a crab apple tree, saying, "You shall always bear sour fruit."

Another creature they changed into the wild cherry tree, so that the new people would have fruit and could use the cherry bark for medicine.

A thin, tough creature they changed into the alder tree, so that the new people would have hard wood for their canoe paddles.

Thus the Two-Men-Who-Changed-Things got the world ready for the new people who were to come. They made the world *as it was* when the Indians lived in it.

Swan, *The Indians of Cape Flattery*, 64-65.

■

# RAVEN'S GREAT ADVENTURE
## *Alaska*

Early North American Indians living along the Alaska and North Pacific coast carved the stories of their people on trees, as they had no written language.

They carved strange and beautiful figures, representing people, animals, birds, fish, and supernatural characters, then painted them with bright colors. The tallest red cedar trees were selected for totem poles, and were used for landmarks as well as illustrating the legends told from generation to generation.

On one of these poles was carved a stunning Raven, but he had no beak!

The Raven in Alaska was no ordinary bird. He had remarkable powers and could change into whatever form he wished. He could change from a bird to a man, and could not only fly and walk, but could swim underwater as fast as any fish.

■

One day, Raven took the form of a little, bent-over old man to walk through a forest. He wore a long white beard and walked slowly. After a while, Raven felt hungry. As he thought about this, he came to the edge of the forest near a village on the beach. There, many people were fishing for halibut.

In a flash, Raven thought of a scheme. He dived into the sea and swam to the spot where the fishermen dangled their hooks. Raven gobbled their bait, swimming from one hook to another. Each time Raven stole bait, the fishermen felt a tug on their lines. When the lines were pulled in, there was neither fish nor bait.

But Raven worked his trick once too often. When Houskana, an expert fisherman, felt a tug, he jerked his line quickly, hooking something heavy. Raven's jaw had caught on the hook! While Houskana tugged on his line, Raven pulled in the opposite direction. Then Raven grabbed hold of some rocks at the bottom of the sea and called, "O rocks, Oplease help me!" But the rocks paid no attention.

Because of his great pain, Raven said to his jaw, "Break off, O jaw, for I am too tired." His jaw obeyed, and it broke off.

Houskana pulled in his line immediately. On his hook was a man's jaw with a long white beard! It looked horrible enough to scare anyone. Houskana and the other fishermen were very frightened, because they thought the jaw might belong to some evil spirit. They picked up their feet and ran as fast as they could to the chief's house.

Raven came out of the water and followed the fishermen. Though he was in great pain for lack of his jaw, no one noticed anything wrong because he covered the lower part of his face with his blanket.

The chief and the people examined the jaw that was hanging on the halibut hook. It was handed from one to another, and finally to Raven, who said, "Oh, this is a wonder to behold!" as he threw back his blanket and replaced his jaw.

Raven performed his magic so quickly that no one had time to see what was happening. As soon as Raven's jaw was firmly in place again, he turned himself into a bird and flew out through the smoke hole of the chief's house.   Only then did the people begin to realize it was the trickster Raven who had stolen their bait and been hooked on Houskana's fishing line.

On the totem pole, Raven was carved, not as the old man, but as himself without his beak, a reminder of how the old man lost his jaw.

Brindze, *The Totem Pole*, 43-44.

■

# YELLOWSTONE VALLEY AND THE GREAT FLOOD

## *Yellowstone*

"I have heard it told on the Cheyenne Reservation in Montana and the Seminole camps in the Florida Everglades, I have heard it from the Eskimos north of the Arctic Circle and the Indians south of the equator.  The legend of the flood is the most universal of all legends.  It is told in Asia, Africa, and Europe, in North America and the South Pacific."  Professor Hap Gilliland of Eastern Montana College was the first to record this legend of the great flood.

This is one of the fifteen legends of the flood that he himself recorded in various parts of the world:

He was an old Indian.  his face was weather beaten, but his eyes were still bright.  I never knew what tribe he was from, though I could guess. Yet others from the tribe whom I talked to later had never heard his story.

We had been talking of the visions of the young men. He sat for a long time, looking out across the Yellowstone Valley through the pouring rain, before he spoke.  "They are beginning to come back," he said.

"Who is coming back?" I asked.

"The animals," he said.  "It has happened before."

"Tell me about it."

He thought for a long while before he lifted his hands and his eyes.  "The Great Spirit smiled on this land when he made it.  There were mountains and plains, forests and grasslands. There were animals of many kinds—and men."

■

The old man's hands moved smoothly, telling the story more clearly than his voice.

The Great Spirit told the people, "These animals are your brothers. Share the land with them. They will give you food and clothing. Live with them and protect them.

"Protect especially the buffalo, for the buffalo will give you food and shelter. The hide of the buffalo will keep you from the cold, from the heat, and from the rain. As long as you have the buffalo, you will never need to suffer."

For many winters the people lived at peace with the animals and with the land. When they killed a buffalo, they thanked the Great Spirit, and they used every part of the buffalo. It took care of every need.

Then other people came. They did not think of the animals as brothers. They killed, even when they did not need food. They burned and cut the forests, and the animals died. They shot the buffalo and called it sport. They killed the fish in the streams.

When the Great Spirit looked down, he was sad. He let the smoke of the fires lie in the valleys. The people coughed and choked. But still they burned and they killed.

So the Great Spirit sent rains to put out the fires and to destroy the people.

The rains fell, and the waters rose. The people moved from the flooded valleys to the higher land.

Spotted Bear, the medicine man, gathered together his people. He said to them, "The Great Spirit has told us that as long as we have the buffalo we will be safe from heat and cold and rain. But there are no longer any buffalo. Unless we can find buffalo and live at peace with nature, we will all die."

Still the rains fell, and the waters rose. The people moved from the flooded plains to the hills.

The young men went out and hunted for the buffalo. As they went, they put out the fires. They made friends with the animals once more. They cleaned out the streams.

Still the rains fell, and the waters rose. The people moved from the flooded hills to the mountains.

Two young men came to Spotted Bear. "We have found the buffalo," they said. "There was a cow, a calf, and a great white bull. The cow and the calf climbed up to the safety of the mountains. They should be back when the rain stops. But the bank gave way, and the bull was swept

*Buffalo robe*
Cheyenne

away by the floodwaters.  We followed and got him to shore, but he had drowned.  We have brought you his hide."

They unfolded a huge white buffalo skin.

Spotted Bear took the white buffalo hide.  "Many people have been drowned," he said.  "Our food has been carried away.  But our young people are no longer destroying the world that was created for them. They have found the white buffalo. It will save those who are left."

Still the rains fell, and the waters rose. The people moved from the flooded mountains to the highest peaks.

Spotted Bear spread the white buffalo skin on the ground. He and the other medicine men scraped it and stretched it, and scraped it and stretched it.

Still the rains fell. Like all rawhide, the buffalo skin stretched when it was wet. Spotted Bear stretched it out over the village. All the people who were left crowded under it.

As the rains fell, the medicine men stretched the buffalo skin across the mountains. Each day they stretched it farther.

Then Spotted Bear tied one corner to the top of the Big Horn Mountains. That side, he fastened to the Pryors. The next corner he tied to the Bear Tooth Mountains. Crossing the Yellowstone Valley, he tied one corner to the Crazy Mountains, and the other to Signal Butte in the Bull Mountains.

The whole Yellowstone Valley was covered by the white buffalo skin. Though the rains still fell above, it did not fall in the Yellowstone Valley.

The waters sank away. Animals from the outside moved into the valley, under the white buffalo skin. The people shared the valley with them.

Still the rains fell above the buffalo skin. The skin stretched and began to sag.

Spotted Bear stood on the Bridger Mountains and raised the west end of the buffalo skin to catch the West Wind. The West Wind rushed in and was caught under the buffalo skin. The wind lifted the skin until it formed a great dome over the valley.

The Great Spirit saw that the people were living at peace with the earth. The rains stopped, and the sun shone. As the sun shone on the white buffalo skin, it gleamed with colors of red and yellow and blue.

As the sun shone on the rawhide, it began to shrink. The ends of the dome shrank away until all that was left was one great arch across the valley.

The old man's voice faded away; but his hands said "Look," and his arms moved toward the valley.

The rain had stopped and a rainbow arched across the Yellowstone Valley. A buffalo calf and its mother grazed beneath it.

Gilliland, *The Flood*, 1, 38-44.

■

# COYOTE AND THE MONSTERS OF THE BITTERROOT VALLEY
## *Flathead or Salish*

This story was recorded from a great-great-grandmother whose name means "Painted-Hem-of-the-Skirt." In the summer of 1955, she was the only person on the Flathead Reservation in western Montana that even an interested interpreter could find who knew the old stories of their people.

The Bitterroot Valley is in western Montana.

■

After Coyote had killed the monster near the mouth of the Jocko River, he turned south and went up the Bitterroot Valley. Soon he saw two huge monsters, one at each end of a ridge. Coyote killed them, changed them into tall rocks, and said, "You will always be there."

There the tall rocks still stand.

Then he went on. Someone had told him about another monster, an Elk monster, up on a mountain to the east. Coyote said to his wife, Mole, "Dig a tunnel clear to the place where that monster is. Dig several holes in the tunnel. Then move our camp to the other side."

Coyote went through the tunnel Mole had made, got out of it, and saw the Elk monster. The monster was surprised to see him.

"How did you get here?" he asked. "Where did you come from?" The monster was scared.

"I came across the prairie," lied Coyote. "Don't you see my trail? You must be blind if you didn't see me."

The monster became more scared. He thought that Coyote must have greater powers than he himself had.

Coyote's dog was Pine Squirrel, and the Elk monster's dog was Grizzly Bear. Grizzly Bear growled at Pine Squirrel, and Pine Squirrel barked back.

"You'd better stop your dog," said the monster. "If you don't, he'll lose his head."

The dogs wanted to fight. Grizzly Bear jumped at Coyote's dog. Pine Squirrel went under him and killed him with the flint he wore on his head. The flint ripped Grizzly Bear. Bones and flesh flew everywhere.

"Look down there," said Coyote to the Elk monster. "See those people coming along that trail? Let's go after them."

He knew that what he saw was Mole moving their camp, but the monster could not see clearly in the tunnel. Elk monster picked up his shield, his spear, and his knife. "I'm ready," he said.

After they had gone a short distance along the trail, the monster fell into the first hole. Coyote called loudly, as if he were calling to an enemy ahead of them. The monster climbed out of the hole, tried to run, but fell into one hole after another. At last Coyote said to him, "Let me carry your shield. Then you can run faster."

Coyote put the shield on his back, but the monster still had trouble. "Let me carry your spear," Coyote said. Soon he got the monster's knife, also—and all of his equipment. Then Coyote ran round and round, shouting, "This is how we charge the enemy."

*Plateau Indian antler adze handle*
Flathead

And he jabbed the monster with the monster's spear. "I have the enemy's warbonnet!" he yelled. He jabbed the monster four times, each time yelling that he had taken something from the enemy. The fifth time he jabbed the monster, he yelled, "I have stripped the enemy." Then he said to the Elk monster, "You can never kill anyone again."

Coyote went on up the Bitterroot Valley. He heard a baby crying, up on a hill. Coyote went up to the baby, not knowing it was a monster. He put his finger in the baby's mouth, to let it suck. The baby ate the flesh off Coyote's finger, then his hand, and then his arm. The monster-baby killed Coyote. Only his skeleton was left.

After a while, Coyote's good friend Fox came along. Fox stepped over the dead body, and Coyote came to life. He began to stretch as if he had been asleep. "I've slept a long time," he said to Fox.

You've been dead," Fox told him. "That baby is a monster, and he killed you."

Coyote looked around, but the baby was gone. He put some flint on his finger and waited for the baby to come back. When he heard it crying, he called out, "Hello, baby! You must be hungry."

Coyote let it have his flinted finger to suck. The baby cut himself and died.

*Plateau Indian sheep horn bowl*
Flathead or Salish

"That's the last of you," said Coyote. "This hill will forever be called Sleeping Child."

And that is what the Indians call it today.

After Coyote had left Sleeping Child, Fox joined him again and they traveled together. Soon Coyote grew tired of carrying his blanket, and so he laid it on a rock. After they had traveled farther, they saw a storm coming. They went back to the rock, Coyote picked up his blanket, and the two friends moved on. When the rain began to fall, he put the blanket over himself and Fox. While lying there, covered by the blanket, they looked out and saw the rock running toward them.

Fox went uphill, but Coyote ran downhill. The rock followed close on Coyote's trail. Coyote crossed the river, sure that he was safe. Spreading his clothes out on a rock, he thought he would rest while they dried. But the rock followed him across the river. When he saw it coming out of the water, Coyote began to run. He saw three women sitting nearby, with stone hammers in their hands.

"If that rock comes here," Coyote said to the women, "you break it with your hammers."

But the rock got away from the women. Coyote ran on to where a creek comes down from the mountains near Darby. There he took some vines—Indians call them "monkey ropes"—and placed them so that the rock would get tangled up in them. He set fire to the monkey ropes. The rock got tangled in the burning ropes and was killed by the heat.

Then Coyote said to the rock, "The Indians will come through here on their way to the buffalo country. They will play with you. They will find you slick and heavy, and they will lift you up."

In my childhood, the rock was still there, but it is gone now, no one knows where.

Coyote left the dead rock and went on farther. Soon he saw a mountain sheep. The sheep insulted Coyote and made him angry. Coyote grabbed him and threw him against a pine tree. The body went clear through the tree, but the head stayed on it. The horns stuck out from the trunk of the tree.

Coyote said to the tree, "When people go by, they will talk to you. They will say, 'I want to have good luck. So I will leave a gift here for you.' They will leave gifts and you will make them lucky—in hunting or in war or in anything they wish to do."

The tree became well known as the Medicine Tree. People from several tribes left gifts in it when they passed on their way to the buffalo country that is on the rising-sun side of the mountains.

In my childhood, the skull and face were still there. When I was a young girl, people told me to put some of my hair inside the sheep's horn, so that I would live a long time. I did. That's why I'm nearly ninety years old.

As the interpreter and I were leaving Painted-Hem- of-the-Skirt, she bent low and made a sweeping movement around her ankles and the hem of her long skirt. Then she said a few words and laughed heartily. The interpreter explained: "She says she hopes that she will not find a rattlesnake wrapped around her legs because she told some of the old stories in the summertime."

She had laughed often as she told the tales, but I feel sure that her mother would not have related them in the summertime. "It is good to tell stories in the wintertime," the Indians of the Northwest used to say. "There are long nights in the wintertime."

Ella E. Clark.

■

# CREATION OF THE RED AND WHITE RACES
## *Flathead or Salish*

The Salish or Flatheads, belonging to the Salishan language family, early in the 1800s were driven from the Plains into western Montana by the Blackfeet tribes, who had begun to use guns and horses. The Flathead name applied because they left their hair up-standing, flat on top. Other bands of Crow, Arapaho, Cheyenne, and Chippewa in the same area similarly "flattened their heads." Salish relations with whites were always friendly and they were missionized by Father De Smet. Most of these tribes and bands settled on the Flathead Reservation in Montana and still live there today.

■

Among the people of long, long ago, Old Man Coyote was the symbol of good. Mountain Sheep was the symbol of evil.

Old-Man-in-the-Sky created the world. Then he drained all the water off the earth and crowded it into the big salt holes now called the oceans. The land became dry except for the lakes and rivers.

Old Man Coyote often became lonely and went up to the Sky World just to talk. One time he was so unhappy that he was crying. Old-Man-in-the-Sky questioned him.

"Why are you so unhappy that you are crying? Have I not made much land for you to run around on? Are not Chief Beaver, Chief Otter, Chief Bear, and Chief Buffalo on the land to keep you company?

"Why do you not like Mountain Sheep? I placed him up in the hilly parts so that you two need not fight. Why do you come up here so often?"

Old Man Coyote sat down and cried more tears. Old-Man-in-the-Sky became cross and began to scold him.

"Foolish Old Man Coyote, you must not drop so much water down upon the land. Have I not worked many days to dry it? Soon you will have it all covered with water again. What is the trouble with you? What more do you want to make you happy?"

"I am very lonely because I have no one to talk to," he replied. "Chief Beaver, Chief Otter, Chief Bear, and Chief Buffalo are busy with their families. They do not have time to visit with me. I want people of my own, so that I may watch over them."

"Then stop this shedding of water," said Old-Man-in-the-Sky. "If you will stop annoying me with your visits, I will make people for you. Take this *parfleche*. It is a bag made of rawhide. Take it some place in the mountain where there is red earth. Fill it and bring it back up to me."

Old Man Coyote took the bag made of the skin of an animal and traveled many days and nights. At last he came to a mountain where there was much red soil. He was very weary after such a long journey, but he managed to fill the parfleche. Then he was sleepy.

"I will lie down to sleep for a while. When I waken, I will run swiftly back to Old-Man-in-the-Sky."

He slept very soundly.

After a while, Mountain Sheep came along. He saw the bag and looked to see what was in it.

"The poor fool has come a long distance to get such a big load of red soil," he said to himself. "I do not know what he wants it for, but I will have fun with him."

Mountain Sheep dumped all of the red soil out upon the mountain. He filled the lower part of the parfleche with white solid, and the upper part with red soil. Then laughing heartily, he ran to his hiding place.

Soon Old Man Coyote woke up. He tied the top of the bag and hurried with it to Old-Man-in-the-Sky. When he arrived with it, the sun was going to sleep. It was so dark that the two of them could hardly see the soil in the parfleche.

Old-Man-in-the-Sky took the dirt and said, "I will make this soil into the forms of two men and two women."

He did not see that half of the soil was red and the other half white. Then he said to Old Man Coyote, "Take these to the dry land below. They are your people. You can talk with them. So do not come up here to trouble me."

Then he finished shaping the two men and two women—in the darkness.

Old Man Coyote put them in the parfleche and carried them down to dry land. In the morning he took them out and put breath into them. He was surprised to see that one pair was red and the other was white.

"Now I know that Mountain Sheep came while I was asleep. I cannot keep these two colors together."

He thought a while. Then he carried the white ones to the land by the big salt hole. The red ones he kept in his own land so that he could visit with them. That is how Indians and white people came to the earth.

Clark, *In the Beginning*, 17.

■

# THE WARM WIND BROTHERS VS. THE COLD WIND BROTHERS
## Moses Band of Columbia River Indians

This story was recorded in 1961 at the request of George Nanamkin, who lived near the Grand Coulee Dam. In the early 1950s, he was not living on the Colville Reservation when I collected stories for *Indian Legends of the Pacific Northwest*. But he knew the book and several of the storytellers.

In his letter asking me for an interview, he wrote that the story he wanted recorded had been told by his people for many, many years. "It shows that we had an Ice Age." Scientists now believe that the last Ice Age ended over 10,000 years ago.

■

This is a story about two tribes that lived during the last Ice Age, many years ago. One of these tribes was called the Tribe of the Warm Wind. The people lived in the Dry Falls-Vantafe area. Wherever they camped, they were in warm country. The chief of the Warm Wind people had five sons.

The second tribe was the Tribe of the Cold Wind. The chief of this tribe also had five sons. Wherever the Cold Wind people settled, cold weather followed. All the lakes and rivers froze, and snow fell.

When the Tribe of the Cold Wind tried to move south, they were stopped by the Tribe of the Warm Wind. The Cold Wind people held council and decided that if they would kill the five brothers in the Warm Wind tribe, they could go south whenever they wished.

They asked Coyote to deliver a challenge for a duel between the five brothers in the Warm Wind tribe and the five brothers in the Cold Wind tribe. The challenge was accepted, and the date was set. Then Coyote traveled around to tell all the people in both tribes about the contest.

When the day arrived, both tribes gathered at the place for the duel. Two warriors fought at a time, one Warm Wind brother against one Cold Wind brother. The young warriors of the Cold Wind people were much stronger than their rivals. Soon all the Warm Wind brothers had been killed.

The Tribe of the Cold Wind now had the power to rule, and they ruled strongly and severely. The country became cold. The rivers and lakes froze solid, and snow fell until the lodges were nearly covered. As far south as Dry Falls, the ice was piled as high as mountains.

Coyote was cruelly treated, and his work was never done. The Warm Wind people were miserable. They were made the slaves of the Cold Wind people. Any food they found was taken from them. They had to eat the scraps of food the Cold Wind people did not want.

Not long before the struggles, the youngest son of the Warm Wind chief had married a girl from a tribe farther south. She decided to go back to her people. Before she left, she told her husband's people, "I am expecting a child. Pray that it will be a boy. If I have a son, I will train him to be the greatest warrior in the world. When he is grown, I will send him to you. Watch for him. He will avenge the defeat of his father and uncles."

A few moons later the woman gave birth to a son. When he was about three months old, he was given baths in cold water to make him strong. As soon as he was old enough, his mother and her brothers had him follow a training course that would make him a strong warrior.

For years he trained. He became so strong that he could uproot trees and throw them over hills. He could throw large boulders many miles. At this time he believed himself the strongest man in the world.

Then his mother told him about the duel between the Warm Wind brothers and the Cold Wind brothers. The young man felt that he was ready to avenge the death of his father and uncles, and to set their people free. But his mother insisted that he train for one more year.

By the end of that year he could move small mountains. Then his mother told him that he was ready to go north to help his people. She told him just what he should do and what he should ask his grandparents to do to help him.

The young warrior started north, and a warm south wind went with him. As he neared the home of his grandparents, the ice on their lodgepoles began to melt for the first time since they became slaves. They were glad and asked each other, "Do you think that our grandson is coming?"

Before the sun set that day, the young man reached them. They saw that he was strong, and they believed him when he said that he had come to free them and their people from the Cold Wind tribe. He was sorry that they had been treated unkindly.

Coyote was sent to the camp of the chief of the Cold Wind tribe to deliver a challenge from the grandson of the chief of the Warm Wind tribe. It was accepted. The day and the place were decided upon.

In the camp of the defeated people, the grandson asked them to follow his mother's instructions: "Boil some salmon, and put the broth in five containers."

On the morning of the duel, the people of both tribes gathered at the river at the chosen place. The grandson fought with the oldest brother from the Cold Wind tribe. The ice was very slick. But the grandson's people threw down a bucket of hot salmon broth, and the ice became rough. So the young warrior defeated the first of the five brothers.

Then the second brother stepped forth, and the grandson fought him. The Cold Wind people threw water on the ice, hoping to make it slick. Then the Warm Wind people threw another bucket of hot broth on the ice, and it became rough. So the young warrior defeated the second brother.

The third, fourth, and fifth brothers he struggled with, each in turn. Each time he was helped by the hot salmon broth. When he had defeated the youngest brother, the Warm Wind people were free. They drove the rest of the Cold Wind people so far north that they could never find their way back. Soon the warm wind came in and melted all the ice.

When the young grandson travels north in the spring, warm weather follows. If he had not defeated the five brothers of the Cold Wind tribe, we still would be living in the Ice Age.

Ella E. Clark.

*Plateau Indian*
Flathead

■

# COYOTE'S ADVENTURES IN IDAHO
## *Flathead*

North American Indians of the Flathead, Salish, Pend d'Oreilles (named by Europeans because they wore large shell earrings) or Kalispel tribes in Montana were all visited by Lewis and Clark in 1805. A Post was established in Pend d'Oreille Lake in 1809 by the North West Company and another Post at Clark Fort called Salish House. In 1844, these Indians were converted by the Roman Catholic church. By 1855, all of the tribes in the area had surrendered their lands, except those around Flathead Lake, which became the Jocko Reservation.

In 1700 the Indian population of that area ranged from 5,000 to 6,500. Lewis and Clark estimated about 1,600 when they visited in 1805. Tribal names have been preserved in countries, cities, banks, lakes, mountains, and rivers in the Northwest region.

■

Near Spokane one day, Coyote and Fox were traveling together on their way north. When they reached a river, Coyote said to Fox, "I believe I'll get married. I'd like to take one of those Pend d'Oreille women for my wife."

So they decided to go in search of the Chief of the Pend d'Oreilles. They soon located him with his tribe, and Coyote approached him with a gift of salmon.

"Chief, I would very much like to have one of your tribal women for my wife. Can we talk about which one you would choose for me?"

"Now Coyote, you know we do not approve that our women intermarry with other tribal members. So you cannot have one of our Pend d'Oreille women for your wife."

Coyote and Fox left the Chief. Coyote became so disappointed with the Chief's decision, he began to rage to his partner, Fox.

"Soon the Chief will be sorry for his refusal. I'll make a big waterfall here in his big river. Forevermore, salmon will not be able to get over the falls to feed the Pend d'Oreilles."

Since Coyote had the power for his wishes to be granted, the great falls immediately formed as he had proclaimed. That is how the Spokane Falls began.

From there, Coyote walked north to Ravalli. Soon he met an Old Indian Woman camped close by. Old Woman said to Coyote, "Where are you going?"

"I am on my way to travel all over the world."

"Well, you had better go back and not stay here," Old Woman said to Coyote.

"Why should I turn back and not stay here for a while? I am looking for a wife."

"Because there is a Giant here who kills everyone passing through this valley," replied Old Woman.

"But I am strong, I will fight him and kill him instead."

So Coyote did not heed Old Woman's warning and started walking on the trail again. He noticed a large tamarack tree nearby on a hillside.

"I'll put an end to the Giant with a hard blow from this tree. That's the way I'll kill him," Coyote said to himself. So he pulled the tamarack tree from the ground and swung it onto his shoulder and continued his search for the Giant.

Soon Coyote saw a woman who seemed nearly dead. He asked, "What is the matter, are you sick?"

"No, I am not sick," she replied.

"I am going to kill the Giant with this tamarack tree," said Coyote.

"You might as well throw the tree away. Don't you know the Giant already sees you and you are already a tasty bite in the Giant's belly?" said the woman.

Coyote took her advice and threw the tamarack tree up on a hillside where it is still growing near Arlee, a little station on the Northern Pacific Railroad. All of what was Jocko Valley now fills the Giant's belly.

As Coyote traveled on from there, he observed many people lying here and there. Some were already dead, others seemed about to die, or were nearly dead.

"Tell me what is the trouble with all of you people," asked Coyote of an Old Woman with her eyes open.

"We are all starving to death," she answered.

"How can that be, when I can see plenty to eat here, lots of meat and fat?" said Coyote.

Then Coyote attacked the Giant and cut away large chunks of grease and fat from the sides of the Giant and fed all of the people. Soon all became well again.

"All of you people prepare to run for your lives. I am going to cut out the Giant's heart. When I start cutting, you must all run to O'Keef's Canyon or to Ravalli," called out Coyote.

With his stone knife, Coyote cut out the Giant's heart. The Giant called out, "Please, Coyote, let me alone. Go away from here. Get Out!"

"No I won't go away. I'm going to stay right here until I kill you," said Coyote.

Then he cut out the Giant's heart. As he was dying, the Giant's jaws began to close tightly. Woodtick was the last one to escape from the Giant's belly when Giant's jaws closed. But Coyote caught hold of him, and with all his strength pulled Woodtick out of the Giant's mouth.

"We can't help it but you will always be flatheaded from your experience," said Coyote as he left and started again on his world trip.

From there the traveler continued on to what is today Missoula, Montana. Coyote walked along between Lolo and Fort Missoula when he thought he heard someone call his name. But he could not see anyone. He trotted forward again, and heard his name called again. He stopped and when he looked into the woods, he saw two women sitting down beside a river.

Coyote swam across the river, and went up the embankment to the women. They were very good-looking women, thought Coyote, maybe he could marry one of them. He sat down between them, but they stood up and danced down to the river.

"Wait for me," called Coyote. "I'll go swimming with you." He took off his jacket beaded with shells, denoting that he was a great Chief.

"We don't want to wait, we are having a good time dancing," replied the two women as they danced on into the river. When Coyote joined them, they pushed him down into the water and tried to drown him.

Later, Coyote's partner, Fox, appeared from around a bend in the river, looking for something to eat. When he looked into the river and saw something lying on the bottom, he said, "This must be my partner, Coyote!"

Fox pulled out the object, and when he was sure it was Coyote, he made a magical jump over him and brought Coyote back to life.

Coyote said, "Oh, I must have had a long sleep."

"You were not asleep, you were dead," replied Fox. "Why did you go near those women, you had no right to be near them, they are from the Shell tribe."

Coyote climbed partway up the hill and set the grass on fire. Later, it was discovered that the women could not escape, and died in the fire. Today some shells have a black side, because they had been burned at the same time.

McDermott, "Coyote's Adventures in Idaho."

■

# THE ORIGIN OF CAMAS ROOTS
## *Okanagon*

Camas (pronounced căm-ăs) is a flowering plant of the lily family, somewhat like the blue hyacinth in appearance. Its root was an important vegetable food for the Northwest Indians.

The Wishing Stone in the following story used to stand not far from Oroville, Washington, near the Canadian border. Whenever Indians passed it, they left gifts, believing that to do so would bring them good luck.

■

Long ago, a great sickness came upon the Indians who lived in the country near the Wishing Stone. So many people died that it seemed as if the whole nation would soon pass away. Every day the oldest and wisest of the medicine men talked to the Great Chief Above. One day the Great Chief Above said to him: "Tell your people that I will send a messenger to them. On the day after the moon is full, gather all the people together at the Wishing Stone. Tell them to bring all the sick ones."

The medicine man sent out runners, and on the morning after the moon was full, Indians for hundreds of miles came together at the Wishing Stone. All were dressed in their best robes. The sick people were with them.

Before the sun reached the middle of the sky, the medicine man pointed toward the highest mountain in sight. Hundreds of eyes looked where he pointed. They saw a white light, and then they saw a figure appear in the sky. As they watched, they saw that the figure was a woman, young and beautiful.

She floated toward them, came down slowly from the sky, and rested on the Wishing Stone. There she spoke to the people gathered round her.

"The Great Chief Above has heard your prayers and has sent me to help you. Come near and be healed of your sickness."

The people crowded round her, touched her, and soon all were well. They shouted with happiness. Lifting her hand to quiet them, the spirit woman spoke again.

"I will come again some time. But you must do what I tell you to do. You must plant the seed that I shall give you. It is camas seed. Plant it everywhere. In the spring it will have blue flowers. There will be so many that they will look like a blue lake. In the fall, gather the roots. If you eat the roots of the camas, the sickness will never return."

Then she gave them the seed. When she had put some in every hand, she was caught up by the breeze and carried back to the sky. The people watched until she could no longer be seen among the clouds. They called her the Spirit of the Camas.

Even after, when they drew near the Wishing Stone on which she had stood, they left gifts for the Spirit of the Camas.

Steele, *History of Northern Washington*, 529-530.

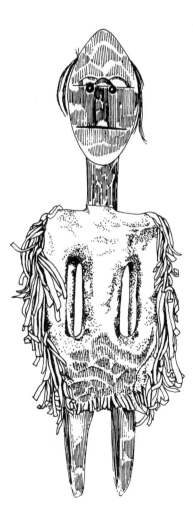

*Shaman's wand*
Flathead

■

# COYOTE'S SALMON

## *Sanpoil*

While *sanpoil* is a native American word meaning "unknown,"
the Sanpoil tribe has flourished since 1600 in Washington State with
a large number of villages along the Sanpoil River, and the Columbia
River below Big Bend, Oregon. Sanpoils belonged to the Salishan
linguistic group. Later they lived on the Sanpoil and Colville Reservations in Washington State.

■

Long ago on the Sanpoil River that flows southward into the Columbia River, Old Man and old Woman lived with their tribe, the Sanpoils.
They were so stooped that it appeared they were walking on their knees
and their elbows. Their very pretty granddaughter lived with them.

One day Coyote came along and saw the old couple with the beautiful
girl. Immediately, he decided that he wanted the girl for his wife. But
he knew better than to ask for her then. He thought he would wait until
evening. So during the day he sat around, becoming better acquainted
with the family.

The old couple watched him, noting that his long hair was braided
neatly and his forelocks were carefully combed back. They noticed too
that he was tall and strong. Old Man and Old Woman talked between
themselves about Coyote, wondering if he could be a Chief.

In the late afternoon, Coyote asked Old Man, "What is that thing
down in the stream?"

"Why, that is my fish trap," Old Man replied.

"A fish trap? What is that? What do you do with it?" asked Coyote,
pretending he did not know.

"Oh, occasionally I catch a few bullheads and sunfish," Old Man said.

"Is that what you eat? I never heard of them. Are they big enough
for a meal?" asked Coyote.

"They are not much, but what else can we eat?" replied Old Man.

"I think I will go up the hill and look around," said Coyote. It was
then about an hour before sunset.

On top of the hill, Coyote saw some grouse roosting in a tree. He
threw some stones at them, killing five. He carried the grouse back to
Old Man and said, "Let's eat these for supper."

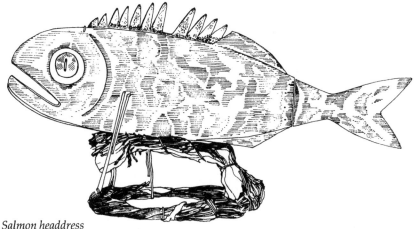

*Salmon headdress*
Sanpoil

After removing the feathers, Old Man roasted the game over the fire, and when they were done, everyone sat down to eat the wonderful meal. To Old Man and his family, it seemed like a feast.

"Is this the kind of food you eat every day?" the Old Man asked Coyote.

"Sometimes I eat berries, roots, and I catch some real big fish, as long as your arm," Coyote said.

Later, Coyote announced that he would like to stay there if they wanted him, otherwise he would move on.

"What do you mean?" asked Old Man.

"Well, it is like this. I would like to marry your granddaughter," said Coyote.

Old Man and Old Woman looked at each other but said nothing. Coyote went for a little walk to allow the old couple to talk privately.

While Coyote was gone Old Man said to his wife, "What do you think of this fellow? You saw what he did, bringing good food for our supper. If we let him marry our granddaughter, maybe they will stay here and we will have such good food always. Surely our girl will marry someone soon, perhaps some man not as good as this young fellow."

"Well, husband, I'll leave it entirely up to you."

Soon Coyote returned. He decided to let Old Man open the conversation. Old Man held his pipe in one hand and said, "How I wish I had a smoke. My tobacco ran out some time ago."

"Have some of mine," said Coyote, reaching into his jacket pocket. He pulled out a large bunch of tobacco and gave it to Old Man, who filled his pipe, feeling very much surprised that Coyote would have real tobacco.

After a while Old Man spoke, "My wife and I have talked over your proposal and she left the decision up to me. I have decided to let you marry our granddaughter and live here. If you go away, we want you to take her with you. How are we to know that you will do this?"

"You need not worry," said Coyote. "I am tired of traveling. I want to settle down here for the rest of my life, if you wish."

Old Man was pleased with Coyote and believed what he said. So Coyote took the pretty granddaughter for his wife.

Early that evening Coyote stayed with his wife and later said, "I am going out for a few minutes and when I return we will go to bed."

"All right," answered his wife.

Coyote went downstream to where Old Man had his fish trap. He changed it into a basket-type trap, piling rows of rocks to guide fish into the basket. When finished he called out, "Salmon, I want two of you in the basket trap tomorrow morning, one male and one female." Then he returned to his bride.

Next morning Coyote asked Old Man to go to his fish trap early. "I think I heard a noise in the night that sounded like fish caught in a trap," he said.

Old Man went downstream to see his fish trap. Sure enough, he saw two big fish in the trap. Old Man was so excited, he stumbled up the trail toward Coyote.

"You were right, there are two great fish in the trap—bigger than I have ever seen," reported Old Man.

"You must be dreaming," said Coyote.

"Come down with me and see for yourself," Old Man said.

When the two reached the trap, Coyote exclaimed, "You are so right. These are salmon, chief among all fish. Let us take them over to that flat place, and I will show you what to do with them."

When they reached the open field, Coyote sent Old Man up the hill to gather sunflower stems and leaves.

"Those are salmon plants," Coyote explained. "Salmon must always be laid on sunflower stems and leaves."

Old Man spread the sunflower plants upon the ground. Coyote placed the salmon on them, and proceeded to show Old Man how to prepare the salmon.

"First, put a stick in the salmon's mouth and bend it back to break off the head. Second, place long sharp poles inside the salmon lengthwise to hold for roasting over your campfire," said Coyote.

"Now remember this," he continued. "The first week go down to the trap and take out the salmon every day. But when fixing it, never use a knife to cut it in any way. Always roast the fish over the fire on sticks, the way I have shown you. Never boil salmon the first week. After the salmon is roasted, open it carefully and take out the backbone without breaking it. Also, save the back part of the head for the sacred bundle—never eat that.

"If you do not do these things as I have told you, either a big storm will come up and you will be drowned, or you will be bitten by a rattlesnake and you will die.

"After you have taken out the salmon's backbone, wrap it and the back of the head carefully in tules, the marsh grasses, to make a sacred bundle, then place it somewhere in a tree, where it will not be bothered. If you do as I tell you, you will always have plenty of salmon in your trap.

"I am telling you these sacred things about the salmon because I am going to die sometime. I want you and your tribe to know of the best way to care for and use your salmon. After this, your men will always place their fish traps up and down the river to catch salmon. The man having the first trap will be Chief of the Salmon, and the others should always do anything he tells them to do.

"After the first week of the salmon season, you can boil your salmon or cook it any way you wish. But remember to always take care of the bones, wrapping them in a sacred bundle—never leaving them where they can be stepped upon or stepped over."

For the next few days each time Old Man went down to his fish trap in the morning, he found twice as many salmon as on the day before. Coyote showed him how to dry fish to prepare them for winter use. Before long they had a large scaffold covered with drying fish.

People of the Sanpoil tribe saw the fish and noticed how well Old Man and Old Woman were doing. They went to their hogans and told others about the big red fish called salmon, and about the tall young stranger who taught Old Man about caring for the salmon.

Soon thereafter, all the people came to see for themselves. Old Man and Old Woman invited them to feast on their roasted salmon. The old couple explained how their new grandson-in-law had shown them how to trap the salmon and dry them for winter food.

To this day, the Sanpoils say their tribe harvests the salmon in exactly the way that Coyote taught their ancestors long, long ago.

Ray, "Coyote Introduces Salmon," 167.

■

# WOODPECKER AND THE THEFT OF FIRE
## *Sanpoil*

Probably every North American Indian tribe told a myth about the origin of fire, as did early people in all parts of the world.

The following story was a favorite among several tribes of the West. Woodpecker's part in it was sometimes taken by Chickadee, sometimes by Sapsucker, sometimes by Wren.

■

Long, long ago, in the days of the animal people, there was no fire on the earth. There was fire in the sky, but none on the earth.

One day the chief of the animal people said to those near him, "Let us go up to the sky country and try to get some fire. Tell all the people to gather here. Then I will tell you what to do."

When the animal people had gathered together, the chief said to them, "Each of you will make a bow and many arrows. Then come together again and shoot at the sky. We'll see if we can hit the sky. If we can, we'll make a chain of arrows down to the earth. Then we'll climb up to the sky country and steal some fire from the sky people."

The people obeyed the chief's orders—all except Woodpecker. They made long, strong bows, and they made many arrows. Then all the people came together again at one place. Everyone shot at the sky, but no one could hit it with his arrows.

Then Woodpecker decided to get busy. First he made a bow from the rib of Elk. Then he made some arrows from the stems of serviceberry bushes.

"Where can I get some feathers for my arrows?" Woodpecker asked himself.

He saw Golden Eagle, and then he saw Bald Eagle.

Woodpecker said to Bald Eagle, "Golden Eagle has been saying mean things about you."

Bald Eagle flew straight at Golden Eagle and began to fight him with his strong bill. That was just what Woodpecker wanted. Soon feathers were dropping from the two eagles fighting high in the air. Many feathers dropped.

Woodpecker spread out a mat and gathered all of them. He took all of the feathers home with him and fastened them to his arrows. Soon he had two big bags full of nice, feathered arrows.

"Now where can I get some points for my arrows?" Woodpecker asked his grandmother.

"Go to see Flint Rock and Hard Rock," his grandmother told him.

Woodpecker went. And he said to Flint Rock, "Hard Rock has been saying mean things about you."

Then Hard Rock and Flint Rock began to fight. That was just what Woodpecker wanted. Hard Rock broke Flint Rock into little pieces. Woodpecker took all the flint chips home with him and used them as arrowheads.

*Plateau Indian warclub*
Sanpoil

Woodpecker knew that in two days the animal people were going to have another meeting. They would try again to reach the sky with their arrows. So after two days Woodpecker went toward the shooting place with his two bags of arrows. When he got there, he saw Coyote.

"Why have you come?" asked Coyote. "You can't shoot."

"I came to look on."

Coyote looked at Woodpecker's bow and said, "That won't shoot anywhere."

All the people laughed at Woodpecker. "You can't shoot as far as the sky," they said.

The chief was a wise and kind chief. "Don't make fun of Woodpecker," he said. "He may shoot better than you think. I will call him when his time comes."

Then the chief called on each animal, one at a time, to shoot at the sky. But no one's arrow reached that far. At last Woodpecker's turn came. When the chief called him, Woodpecker dropped his two bags of arrows on the gound and put a string in his bow.

"Watch me," he said, and he shot an arrow toward the sky. It went so high it disappeared from sight. Everyone watched and waited. The arrow did not come down. Woodpecker shot another arrow. It disappeared from sight and did not come down. He kept on shooting until he had emptied one bag of arrows. By that time the animal people could see the end of the chain of arrows.

Then Woodpecker started to shoot the second bag of arrows. The people could see that each arrow stuck in the neck of the preceding arrow. When Woodpecker had emptied his second bag, the last arrow was still a long distance from the ground.

"Take some of the other people's arrows," said the chief.

Woodpecker shot from the other animals' bags until the chain reached the ground. Then, one by one, all the animals started up the arrow chain toward the sky. Golden Eagle was the first. The others followed him. Grizzly Bear was the last.

I'll take some food along with me," said Grizzly Bear. "We don't know what we are getting into."

So he filled a large bag with food and fastened it across his back. Then he took hold of the bottom arrow of the chain. He and his bag of food were so heavy that the arrow broke in two. He took hold of the second arrow. It broke in two. He broke the first five arrows that way. He could not reach the sixth one, so Grizzly Bear did not go up to the sky country.

By sunset all the other animal people were in the sky world.

"Let's all look around," said Woodpecker. "Let's not stay bunched together. If we go one by one, some of us will be sure to find fire."

So the animals separated, and each one got some fire. As they started back toward the arrow chain, they saw the sky people coming after them. And they found that the chain of arrows was broken.

"Quick!" said Eagle. "Each bird will take an animal on his back and fly down to earth with him."

That is the way the animals got down to earth again. Sapsucker was afraid to fly and so jumped instead. He hit the ground with his mouth. Ever since then, sapsuckers have had flat mouths and have to suck their food.

Fish slipped and fell down from Magpie's back. He was carrying his arrows with him, and when he hit the ground, the arrows went right through his body. Ever since then, fish have had many bones.

The animal people laid the fire down in front of their chief, "You can tell us what to do with it," they said.

The chief said to his people, "It is best to divide the fire, so that people all over the world can use it."

So he and Grizzly Bear gave pieces of the fire to Horsefly and Hummingbird. They carried the fire into all parts of the country.

People have had fire ever since.

Ray, "Sanpoil Folk Tales," 152-53.
Ella E. Clark.

■

# PAH-TO, THE WHITE EAGLE
## Wasco

When the first white people came to the Northwest, Indians of several tribes told them about a great bridge of rocks and earth that once spanned the lower Columbia River. When the bridge fell, they said, the rocks made numerous rapids and little waterfalls in the Columbia, near the present city of Hood River. Now the rocks and rapids are covered by the waters above Bonneville Dam.

Here is one of many stories that Indians used to tell about the fall of this natural bridge.

■

In the days of our grandfathers' grandfathers, the peaks now called Mount Hood and Mount Adams stood much closer to the Columbia River than they do today. Mount Hood, called Wy-east, stood on the south bank, facing Mount Adams, Pah-To, on the north bank.

Between the two peaks was a bridge, where big rocks formed an arch. One base of the bridge rested on Wy-east, the other on Pah-To. For many years the rock bridge stood there. Beneath it, the waters of the great river flowed peacefully. Canoes went up and down the river without danger from the rocks and rapids that have been there in our time.

Some people in the canoes admired the big arch over their heads and were proud of the Great Power Above that had made it. Other people were afraid. When they were traveling up or down the river, all except the oarsmen would get out of the canoes when they neared the spot. They would walk to the opposite side of the bridge and reenter the canoes there. All would pray for the oarsmen, because the medicine men of the tribe prophesied that some day the bridge would fall.

Our grandfathers and our great-uncles tell us about the long, dark journey under the bridge. They tell us that the river used to be peaceful where we now see rapids and waterfalls.

But mountains did not let the river remain at peace. Each peak was the home of a powerful spirit, and the spirits were jealous of each other. Each was proud of its beautiful home, and each envied the beauty and grandeur of the other. Sometimes they became so jealous and so angry that they threw hot rocks at each other.

The Great Power Above was made unhappy by their frequent quarrels. But he thought that he would let them fight until they grew weary

*Wasco basket*
Wasco

of fighting. Then they would become friends and would stay at peace with each other.

Instead, the mountain spirits became more and more quarrelsome. They became angry more and more often. They shook the earth. They sent forth fire and smoke, and they threw hot rocks across the river. At last the mountain peaks were set on fire, and a lake near the bridge was drained into the river.

Once more the fighting mountains made the earth tremble. This time they shook it so hard that the earth and the trees along the banks of the river slid into the water. The foundations of the bridge were loosened, the arch lost its balance, and the rocks fell into the river. There they made rapids and many waterfalls.

The Great Power Above was so angry that he determined to punish the mountain spirits. He came down from the sky and stood by the river. There he picked up Pah-To and hurled it as far as he could northeast of where he stood. Then he lifted Wy-east and hurled it as far as he could southwest of where he stood.

The mountain peaks stand there today, watching from a distance the Columbia River on its way to the sea.

McWhorter Papers.

■

# THE BRIDGE OF THE GODS
## *Wasco*

This story was told to McWhorter in 1914 by a Wasco Indian woman who was about 100 years old.

The Klickitat Indian custom was added in a note by McWhorter. He was a rancher in the Yakima Valley of Washington, and he employed native Americans for many summers. He recorded much of their history and folklore. Some of their history he had published.

■

In the days of the animal people, a great bird lived in the land of the setting sun. It was Thunderbird. All of the animal people were afraid of it. Thunderbird created five high mountains and then said to the animal people, "I made a law that no one is to pass over these five high mountains. If any one does, I will kill him. No one is to come where I live."

Wolf did not believe the law. "I will go," declared Wolf. "I will be the first to see what Thunderbird will do to me."

"I will go with you," said Wolf's four brothers.

So the five Wolf brothers went to the first mountain. They stood in a row, and each stepped with his right foot at the same time. Immediately the five wolf brothers were dead.

When the animal people heard that the five Wolf brothers were dead, Grizzly Bear, the strongest of the animals, decided that he would go.

"I will cross over the mountains," announced Grizzly Bear. "I will not die as the Wolf Brothers have died."

"We will go with you," said Grizzly Bear's four brothers.

So the five Grizzly Bear brothers went to the first mountain. They stood in a row, and each stepped with his right foot, all at the same time. Then each stepped with his left foot, all at the same time. Immediately the five Grizzly Bears were dead.

"I will go now," said Cougar. "I will take a long step and leap over the mountain."

Cougar's four brothers went with him. They made one leap together, and then all were dead.

"We will go next," said the five Beaver brothers. "We will go under the mountain. We will not be killed. We will not be like the Wolf brothers, the Grizzly brothers, and the Cougar brothers."

But as they tried to cross under the mountains, all five Beaver brothers were killed.

Then Coyote's oldest son said, "I will talk to the mountains. I will break down the law so that people may live and pass to the sunset."

His four brothers went with him, and two of them talked to the five mountains. They made the mountains move up and down; they made the mountains dance and shake. But the five sons of Coyote were killed. The five mountains still stood. No one could pass over or under them to the sunset.

Coyote's sons had not told their father their plans. He had told them that they must never stay away from home overnight. When they did not return, he knew that they had been killed by Thunderbird. Coyote was wiser than the others. He had been instructed in wisdom by the Spirit Chief.

After his sons had been gone five nights, Coyote was sure that they were dead. He cried loud and long. He went to a lonely place in the mountains and rolled on the ground, wailing and howling with grief.

*Bear mask*
Wasco

Then he prayed to the Spirit Chief for strength to bring his five sons back to life.

After Coyote had cried and prayed for a long time, he heard a voice. "You cannot break the law of the Thunderbrid. You cannot go over the five mountains. Thunderbird has made the law."

Coyote continued crying and praying, rolling on the ground in a lonely place in the mountains. After a time he heard the voice again.

"The only thing you can do is to go up to the Above-World. It will take you five days and five nights. There you will be told how you can bring your five sons to life again."

So for five days and five nights Coyote traveled to the Above- World. There he told his troubles to the Spirit Chief.

"Give me strength," he ended. "Give me so much strength that I can fight Thunderbird. Then the people can cross over the mountains to the sunset."

At last the Spirit Chief promised to help.

"I will blind the eyes of Thunderbird," he promised. "Then you can go over the five mountains and kill him.

"I will tell you what you must do," continued the Spirit Chief. "When you get back to the earth, find the big bird called Eagle. He has great strength. Ask him for a feather from his youngest son. Ask for a feather, a small feather from under his wing. This feather is downy and has great strength. It has power running out from the heart because it grows near the heart. Return now to the earth."

After five days and five nights, Coyote reached the earth again. He found Eagle and told him all that the Great Spirit had said. Then he asked, "Will you give me the feather that grows nearest the heart of your youngest son?"

"I will do as the Spirit Chief bids," replied Eagle. "If he told you to come to me, then I will give you my power to fight Thunderbird."

So Eagle picked a feather from under the wing of his youngest son. It was such a small downy feather that it could not be seen when it floated through the air. The coyote followed the next commandment the Spirit Chief had given him.

"Fast for ten days and ten nights," he had said. "If you will go without food and drink for ten days and nights, you will be changed to a feather. You will then be able to go anywhere."

So Coyote fasted. After ten days and ten nights, he was turned into a feather, like the one Eagle had given him. He floated through the air toward the five mountains. At a distance from them, he made a noise like thunder, as the Spirit Chief had told him to do. Three times he made a slow, deep rumbling, off toward the sunrise.

Thunderbird heard the rumble and asked, "Who is making this noise? I alone was given the power to make that rumbling sound. This noise must be coming from the Above-World. I am dead! I am dead! I am dead!"

A fourth time Coyote rumbled, this time closer to Thunderbird. Thunderbird became angry. "I will kill whomever this is that is making the noise. I will kill him! I will kill him!" he repeated angrily.

Thunderbird made a mighty noise, a greater thunder than Coyote had made. Coyote, in the form of a feather, went into the air, higher and higher and ever higher. He darted and whirled, but could not be seen.

Thunderbird was afraid. He knew that if a fifth rumble of thunder came he would be dead. He sought the deep water of Great River, to hide himself there. He heard Coyote far above him.

Coyote prayed to the Spirit Chief. "Help me one more time, just one more time. Help me kill Thunderbird so that the people may live, so that my sons will come to life again."

The Spirit Chief heard Coyote and helped him. Thunderbird sank deeper into the water, terrified. Coyote, still invisible above him, made a greater noise than ever, a noise like the bursting of the world. The five mountains crumbled and fell. Pieces of the mountain, floating down the Great River, formed islands along its course.

Thunderbird died, and his giant body formed a great bridge above the river. The five sons of Coyote and all the other animal people who had been killed by Thunderbird came back to life.

Though many hundreds of snows had passed, the great bridge formed from the rocks that had been made out of Thunderbird's body still stood above the river. It was there long after the first Indians came to the earth. The Indians always called it "the Bridge of the Gods." No one must look at the rocks of the bridge. People knew that some day it would fall. They must not anger the Spirit Chief by looking at it, their wise men told them.

The Klickitat Indians had a different law. Only a few men necessary to paddle the canoes would pass under the bridge. All the others would land when they approached the Bridge of the Gods, walk around to the opposite side of it, and there reenter the canoes. The oarsmen always bade their friends good-bye, fearing that the bridge would fall while they were passing under it.

After many snows, no one knows how many, the prophecy of the wise men came true. The Bridge of the Gods fell. The rocks that had once been the body of Thunderbird formed the rapids in the river that were long known as Cascades of the Columbia.

McWhorter Papers.

■

# RAVEN AND HIS GRANDMOTHER
## *Aleuts*

These stories were obtained by F. A. Golder on Kodiak, Alaska, during his three year residence there at the end of the 1890s. They were told in the Russian language by Mrs. Reed, Nicoli Medvednikoff, and Corneil Panamaroff, all natives of Kodiak Island. The natives of Kodiak speak Russian as freely as they do their own tribal language. They call themselves "Aleuts," and that refers distinctly to them and not the "real Aleut" to the west on the Aleutian Islands.

■

In her *barrabara* (a native home) at the end of a large village, lived an old grandmother with her grandson, a raven. The two lived apart from the other villagers because they were disliked. When the men returned from fishing for cod, the raven would come and beg for food, but they would never give him any of their catch. But when all had left the beach, the raven would come and pick up any leftover refuse, even sick fish. On these, raven and his grandmother lived.

One winter was extremely cold. Hunting was impossible; food became so scarce the villages neared starvation. Even their chief had but little left. So the chief called all his people together and urged them to use every effort to obtain food enough for all, or they would starve.

The chief then announced that he wished for his son to take a bride, and she would be selected from the girls of the village. All the girls responded to the excitement of the occasion and dressed in their very best costumes and jewelry.

For a short time hunger was forgotten as the girls lined up for the contest and were judged by the critical eye of their chief, who selected the fairest of the fair for his son's bride. A feast was given by the chief following their marriage ceremony. But soon after hunger began again.

The raven perched on a pole outside his barrabara, observing and listening attentively to all that had happened. After the feast, he flew home and said to his grandmother, "I, too, want to marry." She made no reply, so he went about his work, gathering what food he could for his little home. Each day he flew to the beach and found dead fish or birds. He always gathered more than enough for two people. While he was in the village, he noted that the famine seemed worse. So he asked the chief, "What will you give me, if I bring you food?"

The chief looked at him in great surprise and said, "You shall have my oldest daughter for your wife." Nothing could have pleased raven more. He flew away in a joyful mood and said to his grandmother, "Let's clean out the barrabara. Make everything clean for my bride. I am going to give the chief some food, and he has promised to give me his oldest daughter."

"Ai, Ai, Y-a-h! You are going to marry? Our barrabara is too small and too dirty. Where will you put your wife?"

"Caw! Caw! Caw! Never mind. Do as I say," he screamed at his grandmother, and began pecking her to hurry.

Early next morning raven flew away, and later in the day returned with a bundle of *yukelah* (dried salmon) in his talons. "Come with me to the chief's house, grandmother," he called to her. Raven handed the fish to the chief and received the chief's oldest daughter for his bride.

Raven preceded his grandmother as she brought the bride to their little home. He cleared out the barrabara of old straw and bedding. When the two women arrived, they found the little home empty, and the grandmother began to scold him and said, "What are you doing? Why are you throwing out everything."

"I am cleaning house, as you can see," raven curtly said.

When night came, raven spread wide one wing, and asked his bride to lie on it, and then covered her with the other wing. She spent a miserable night, as raven's fish odor nearly smothered her. So she determined she would leave in the morning.

But by morning, she decided to stay and try to become accustomed to him. During the day she was cheerless and worried. When raven offered her food, she would not eat it. On the second night, raven invited her to lay her head on his chest and seek rest in his arms. Only after much persuasion did she comply with his wish. The second night was no better for her, so early the next morning she stole away from him and went back to her father's house, telling him everything.

Upon waking and finding his wife gone, raven inquired of his grandmother what she knew of his wife's whereabouts. She assured raven that she knew nothing. "Go then to the chief and bring her back to me," called raven. Grandmother feared him and left to do his bidding. When she came to the chief's house, she was pushed out of the door. This she promptly reported to her grandson.

The summer passed warm and pleasant, but a hard winter and another famine followed. As in the previous winter, the grandmother and the raven had plenty of food and wood, while others suffered greatly from lack of food. Raven's thoughts again turned to marriage. This time she was a young and beautiful girl who lived at the other end of the village. He told his grandmother about her and that he wanted to marry her.  He asked, "Grandmother, will you go and bring the girl here, and I will marry her."

"Ai, Ai, Y-a-h!  And you are going to marry her?  Your first wife could not live with you because you smell strong.  The girls do not wish to marry you.

"Caw! Caw! Caw!  Never mind my smell!  Never mind my smell! Go— do as I say."

To impress his commands and secure her obedience, he started pecking at her until she was glad to go.  While his grandmother was gone, raven became restless and anxious.  He hopped about the barrabara and nearby hillocks, straining his eyes for a sight of his expected bride.

Hurriedly he began cleaning out the barrabara, throwing out old straw, bedding, baskets, and all.  The grandmother upon her return scolded raven, but he paid no attention to her.

The young bride, like her predecessor, was enfolded tightly in his wings, and likewise she had a wretched and sleepless night.  But she was determined to endure his odor if possible.  She thought at least with him she would have plenty of food to eat.  The second night was as bad as the first, but she stayed on and secretly concluded she would do her best to stay until spring.

On the third day the raven, seeing that his wife was still with him, said, "Grandmother, tomorrow I will go and get a big, fat whale.  While I am gone, make a belt and a pair of *torbarsars* (native shoes) for my wife."

"Ai, Ai, Y-a-h!  How will you bring a big, fat whale?  The hunters cannot kill one, how will you do it?"

"Caw! Caw! Caw!  Be quiet and do what I tell you: make the belt and torbarsars while I go and get the whale," he angrily exclaimed, using his most effective method of silencing her.

Before dawn next morning the raven flew away to sea.  In his absence the old woman was busily engaged making the things for the young bride, who watched and talked to her.  About midday, they saw raven flying toward shore, carrying a whale.

The grandmother started a big fire, and the young woman tucked up her *parka* (native dress), belted it with her new belt, put on the new torbarsars, sharpened the stone knife, and went to the beach to meet her husband.  As he drew near he called, "Grandmother, go into the village and tell all the people that I have brought home a big, fat whale."

She ran as hard as she could and told the joyful news. The half-dead people suddenly became alive. Some sharpened their knives, others dressed in their best clothes. But most of them just ran as they were and with such knives as they had with them to the beach to see the whale.

His sudden importance was not lost on the raven, who hopped up and down the whale's back, viewing the scene of carnage, as the people gorged themselves on the whale.

Every few moments raven would take a pebble out of his bag, then after some thought put it back. When the chief and his relatives came near, raven drove them away. They had to be content just watching the people enjoy their feasting, and carrying off blubber to their homes. Later, in the village, the people did share with the chief.

The raven's first wife, the chief's daughter, had a son by him, a little raven. She had it in her arms at the beach and walked in front of raven,

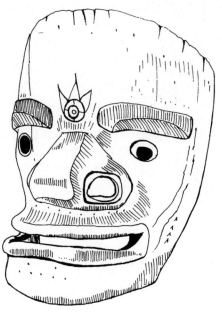

*Wooden burial mask*
Aleuts

where he could notice her. "Here is your child, look at it," she called. But he ignored her. She called to him several times and continued to show him the baby. At last he said, "Come closer—nearer still." But when she could not stand his odor any longer, she left him without a word.

Death occurred as a result of the feast. Many of the people ate so much fat on the spot that they died soon after. The rest of the people had eaten so much and filled their barrabaras so full, that during the night they all suffocated. Of the entire village, only three were left—the raven, his new wife, and the grandmother. There they lived on as their descendants do to this day.

Golder, "Raven and His Grandmother," 26.

———, "Kodiak Island Legends," 16-19, 26.

# THE WHITE-FACED BEAR
## Aleuts

In a tribal village there lived a mighty bear-hunter. For more than three years, he had been constantly successful in killing so many that his friend tried to persuade him to stop hunting.

"If you insist upon hunting one more bear, you will come across a huge bear who might kill you," he said. The hunter ignored his friend's advice and replied, "I will attack every bear I come across."

A few days later the hunter started out and saw a bear with two cubs. He decided this was not the huge bear he had been worried about, so he attacked the mother bear, and after some difficulty killed her. The cubs ran away. After the hunter dragged the bear home for his tribe, his friend continued to urge him to give up the bear hunt, but without success.

On another hunt, after a few days on the trail, the hunter met a stranger who informed him that near his village were a great many bears. "Every year many are killed by our hunters, but always there is an invincible one that has destroyed many of our hunters. Each time he kills a man, the bear tears him apart, examines him carefully as if searching for a special body mark. He is different because his feet and head are white."

They parted, and the hunter started out to look for that hunting ground. On his way, he stopped near a fish creek looking for game, but after a long night none appeared. Next morning he moved onward andcame to a high bluff; below it he saw many bears on the tundra. He waited until some separated and looked over the remainder.

Among those, he saw the white-faced bear with white feet and concluded that this must be the ferocious, huge bear he sought. First he would keep an eye on it and wait for a favorable opportunity to kill it.

Now it seems that at one time, the white-faced bear was a human being and a very successful bear-hunter, too successful for his own good. His friends were envious and plotted to kill him. So they went to a medicine-man deep in the woods, and begged him to transform the successful hunter into a beast.

"Shoot a bear, skin it and place the skin under the pillow of your successful hunter," advised the shaman.

After the bear-skin had been prepared, the shaman and his friends quietly went to the man's hut and placed the skin under the man's pillow. They hid themselves to see what would happen when the man went to bed. Upon waking, the man found that he had become a huge bear with a white face and white feet.

"The white marks will show you which bear he is," said the shaman, who disappeared into the woods.

Now our bear-hunter still sat at the edge of the bluff. Toward evening he saw the bears begin to leave, all except the white-faced bear. He was the last to get up, and he shook himself three times and acted as if he was deeply enraged. He moved toward the bluff where the hunter sat perfectly still. But the bear approached, and when he was almost face to face, asked, "What are you doing here?"

"I came out to hunt," he replied.

"Is it not enough that you have killed all my family, and recently killed my wife, and now you want to take my life? If you had injured my children the other day, I would now tear you to pieces. I will, however, spare your life this time on your promise that you will never hunt bears again. All the bears you saw today are my children and of my brother. Should I ever see you hunting bear, I will tear you apart."

Relieved to get away so easily, the hunter headed homeward. His friend met him and inquired about the white-faced bear, and when told what had happened, he urged the hunter to give up hunting. A whole week passed before the hunter set forth again, taking along six hunting friends.

For two days they hunted without luck, then came to the fish creek where they camped overnight. Next morning their leader took the six to the edge of the bluff where they could look down at the tundra and see many bears. But they could not see the white-faced bear and, encouraged, followed their leader toward the animals.

"Look at that strange-looking beast with white paws and a white face!" exclaimed one man.

The hunter-leader caught sight of that special bear and ordered his followers to retreat at once. So they went around another mountain where they saw many bears. They killed seven, one for each man.

Loaded with their spoil they took the homeward trail, but a short distance behind them they heard a commotion. They saw the white-faced bear rapidly approaching them. The hunter aimed, but his bowstring broke. The others shot and missed. The white-faced bear spoke up and said, "Why do you shoot at me? I never harm you. Your leader killed my wife and nearly all my family. I warned him that if I found him hunting again, I would tear him apart. And this I shall do now, piece by piece. The rest of you can go. I'll not harm you because you have not harmed me."

Hurriedly, as fast as possible, the six men fled. The white- faced bear turned to the bear-hunter.

"I had you in my power once and I let you go on your promise not to hunt bear again. Now you are back at it and brought more bear-hunters along. This time I will do to you as you have done to mine."

The hunter pleaded to be allowed to live one more night so he could go home. At first the bear refused outright. The white-faced bear then relented, and would even spare his life entirely, if the hunter would tell him who had transformed him from a man into a beast. The hunter agreed to meet him the next night and go to the home of the shaman.

When the bear-hunter reached home and found his six companions talking excitedly about the day's experience, they were surprised to see the hunter-leader alive.

The hunter told them his plan to meet the white-faced bear at the home of the shaman next evening and asked the six to go with him. They refused and tried to dissuade their leader. But the bear-hunter kept his word and met the white-faced bear at the appointed place. A light shone from every hut except that of the shaman.

"This is the place," said the man.

"I will remain here," ordered the bear. "You go inside and tell him there is a man outside wishing to speak with him."

The man advanced and found the skin-door tied, so he reported to the bear that the shaman must be out. The bear ordered him back to cut the door, then walk in. Upon entering, the man heard someone call, "Who dares come into my lodge?"

"It is I," said the bear-hunter.

"What do you wish?"

"There is a man outside who wishes to speak to you."

Had the shaman not been so sleepy, he might have been suspicious. Under the circumstances, his mind was not clear and he fell into the trap.

When the shaman came near the white-faced bear, the old man became frightened and was ready to run away. But the bear blocked his way and said, "For years you have tortured me and made my life a burden in this condition. I demand you give me back my human form immediately, otherwise I shall tear you to pieces."

The shaman promised to do so if the bear would follow him into his hut. Before going in, the bear said to the hunter, "Meet me here when I come out."

All night the shaman worked hard with the bear, and by next morning succeeded in pulling off the bear-skin, and a human form appeared. The shaman asked to keep the white-faced bear's skin, but the man kept the white-face and the white claws, which he cut off at once, giving the rest of the skin to the shaman.

"If you ever again try to transform a man into a beast, I will be back and kill you dead, dead, dead," said the man.

The next day when the bear-man met the bear-hunter he said, "I caution you against ever going out to hunt bear. You may even hear people say I've become a bear again, and they will hunt me. Don't you joint them. If I find you in their company, I will kill you dead, dead, dead."

For about four weeks the hunter remained at home with every intention of keeping his promise to the transformed man. But one day two young men from the neighboring tribal village came to beg his assistance. They asked his help to kill a ferocious bear with a white face and four white feet.

Of course the hunter knew the bear they feared, but decided to disguise himself and go help them. They gathered all of the village warriors and set out to find the white-faced bear. The bear saw them coming. He rose and shook himself three times, giving the impression of great anger, which frightened the warriors. Their chief said, "We are in great danger, so we must stand and fight."

Madly, the white-faced bear jumped, landed in front of the hunter and tore him to pieces. Then it pawed a hole in the ground and covered up the parts. The terrified warriors tried to escape, but the white-faced bear chased them back to their village, tearing them apart, killing all of them, including the old shaman. Finished, the white-faced bear turned back into the woods to rest undisturbed forever.

Golder, "The White-Faced Bear," 296–299.

■

# THE TWO INQUISITIVE MEN
## *Aleuts*

■

There were two men in the old days by the names of Acha-yuongch and Ach-goyan. They lived together, but spoke and looked at each other only when they were compelled to do so. They were curious about anything happening nearby and they usually went to investigate.

One day, as they were sitting in their barrabara around the fire, their backs toward each other, eating shellfish, Ach-goyan pulled out a feather from his hair, threw it in front of him and said, "Acha-yuongch, what shall we do? There is a man living over there on the other side of the village. He hunts every day with his sling."

Acha-yuongch was silent for a while, then he scratched his ear and said, "I do not know what is the matter with me. There is much whistling in my ear."

Silence followed for some time, then Ach-goyan pulled out another feather from his hair and threw it up in front of him and said, "Acha-yuongch, what shall we do? There is a man living over there who hunts every day with his sling."

Acha-yuongch again replied, "There is very much whistling in my ear." A third time Ach-goyan threw a feather into the air and said, "There is a man living on the other side whose name is Ploch-goyuli. He hunts every day with his *plochgo* (sling). Let's go and see him." So they prepared for the trip, piling their barrabara and all their other possessions on their canoe, including the grave with the remains of their wife.

But on launching, they discovered that the load was too heavy on one side. So they dug up a small hillock and placed it on top to equalize their load. They filled hollow reeds with fresh water and started on their trip. When they arrived on the other shore they saw Ploch-goyuli hunting ducks with his sling. He saw them, too, and knew the nature of their visit, so he threw rocks at them. The first rock hit close to the canoe. Ach-goyan exclaimed, "Ka! Ka! Ka! It nearly hit me."

The second rock hit closer, and he exclaimed louder, "Ka! Ka! Ka!" Rocks kept coming, and they turned their damaged canoe around and headed homeward, where they replaced their barrabara and all of their things.

A few days later, sitting around the fire in their barrabara, Ach-goyan pulled out a feather from his hair, tossing it in the air and said, "Let's visit the man on the island who heats a bath and catches codfish every day."

"My ear is still whistling," replied Acha-yuongch. After tossing another feather into the air, Ach-goyan said, "Let's visit the man living on an island in the middle of the sea, who heats his bath and catches codfish every day. His name is Peting-yuwock."

Again they loaded the canoe with all of their things and started off. They reached the island, beached their canoe, and went to the old man's barrabara. He cried out, "Where is the man-smell coming from?"

"We came to visit you because we heard you heat your bath and catch codfish every day."

"The hot bath is ready," said Peting-yuwock and directed the two inquisitive men to it. While they were bathing, the old man tied together a lot of thin, dried kelp, which he had kept to make clothes. Out of it, he made a long rope and fastened one end of it to the canoe. He then roasted a codfish and gave it to the two men after their bath.

"There is a strong wind blowing. You had better hasten to your barrabara before it becomes too strong," suggested the old man.

*Kayak*
Aleuts

The two men heeded his warning and shoved off into the sea. When they were about halfway across, the old man pulled the rope and brought the two men back to his shore. He came out and called to them, "Why have you come back. I warned you how strong the wind was."

Again the two men started off, and again were halfway home when the old man pulled on the rope and hauled them back to the beach. "Why are you back here? Get on with you or you will never make it," he shouted at them against the wind.

The third time when the old man pulled on the rope, it broke, and the canoe upset and the two men were lost with all of their belongings.

The grave of their wife became a beautiful porpoise. Acha-yuongch and Ach-goyan were cast upon the shore, where they became two capes of land, jutting into the sea like two peninsulas.

They had been so inquisitive about everything that they became prominent landmarks, two safe harbors for fishermen and others at sea, forever.

Golder, "The Inquisitive Men," 19-21.

■

# THE GIRL WHO SEARCHED FOR HER LOVER

## *Aleuts*

■

A terrible misfortune befell the people of a very large tribe. Of all the hunters that left the village, not one came back alive, nor was it known what had happened to them. In that tribe lived a beautiful young girl, who loved and was beloved by a brave hunter. She had joyfully consented to be his wife, but her parents objected.

The disappointed hunter had decided to drown his grief by going with the warriors to hunt. Older men cautioned against his hunting, but the young lover departed with the warriors. A month passed, but he did not return and was given up for lost by his tribe. Not so the young girl, who could not believe him dead. She felt she must go and search for him.

Secretly she made preparations, and one night she stole away quietly, taking her father's one-hatch kayak and a waterproof elk skin shirt. After some distance from her village, she ceased paddling, closed her eyes, and began singing. After a verse, she opened her eyes. Noticing the kayak drifting with the current, she closed her eyes again and sang some more. At the end of the second verse, she looked again and found the kayak drifting faster than before. Then she closed her eyes and sang for a long time.

When she looked again, the kayak was going so fast that she became alarmed but could not change her course. Her speed increased by the moment, then she heard the mighty roar of waterfalls. Since life without her lover was not worth living, she closed her eyes to await her fate.

Very swiftly the boat rushed forward. The roaring waters became powerful. Her heart nearly stopped beating from fright when she felt herself going down, down, down, then come suddenly to a standstill.

She was not hurt, but could neither get out of the kayak nor move it. The boat was stuck fast. Dawn approached as she lay there, wondering what would become of her and what had happened to her lover. At sunrise, she saw a kayak coming toward her with one man paddling.

The man exclaimed aloud, "Ha! Ha! I have another victim," as he placed a bow and arrow beside him with a two-edged knife attached to the tip. But as he drew nearer, he put away his weapons, thinking, "That is a woman." Then he called out, "If you are a woman, speak up, and I will not kill you, for I never kill women." She assured him that she was a woman, and he came and helped her out of her boat and seated her in his kayak. He paddled off with her.

They reached his own barrabara where he lived alone. She noticed many human heads scattered about. One she recognized as her lover's. She said nothing, but to herself she pledged vengeance. The man asked her to be his wife, and ordered her to cook deer and seal meat for them to eat. At bedtime, he pointed to a corner for her to sleep, while he slept in an opposite corner. She obeyed without questioning him.

Next morning, he led her to a smaller barrabara and showed her a number of headless bodies. He said, "These I do not eat; but I have three sisters living some distance from here, who eat human flesh only. It is for them I have killed these people. Each day I take one body to a different sister." He then picked up a corpse and his bow and arrow and walked away.

The young girl followed him to the place where the road forked. One path led to the right, one led to the left, and one led straight ahead. She noticed which one he took, then returned to his barrabara, where she busied herself, removing two posts from one of the walls. She dug out an underground passage for escape.

All of the extra dirt she carried to the sea, then cunningly concealed the passage. Toward evening, she cooked a good supper for him when he returned, eating in silence, then they retired, each to their own corner.

After breakfast next morning, he carried away another corpse. She took the bow and arrow, which he left behind, following him secretly. He took the left fork while she took the middle one. She hurried on, then cut across to the left fork and managed to reach the home of his sister before he arrived, killing her with the bow and arrow.

From there she ran to the homes of the other two sisters, killing them, before running back to the barrabara. He found all three sisters dead and was suspicious.

She was sitting on the barrabara when he returned. "You killed my sisters, now I will kill you," he cried out angrily, rushing for his bow and arrow. They were not in their usual place and he discovered them in her hands. He begged her to give them to him, promising to do her no harm. At first she refused, but he pleaded and promised until she trusted him and gave them to him.

As soon as they were his again, he shouted, "Now you shall die," and shot at her. She suddenly dropped through the smoke hole, out of sight, before the arrow could reach her. While he looked for the arrow, she

*Wood hat*
Aleuts

crawled out through the underground passage and perched herself anew on top of the barrabara.

Her disappearance and sudden reappearance was a mystery to him. he shot at her again and again, but she disappeared each time mysteriously. At least, since he could not kill her, he said, "Take this bow and arrow and kill me."

"I do not want to kill you," she told him. "But I'm afraid you will kill me someday."

He swore never to hurt her, and she came down from the roof. Together they ate their supper and retired in the usual manner. But as he was about to fall asleep, she moved closer to him and began talking to him, keeping him awake the entire night.

For five days and five nights she tormented him in this way, giving him no time to sleep. On the sixth day, in spite of all she could do, he fell into a deep, deep sleep. Although she pinched him and pulled at him, she could not arouse him. She brought a block of wood from outside and placed it under his neck. Then, with a knife she had stolen from one of his sisters, she beheaded him.

In his kayak, she put his bow, arrow, and knife, then seated herself and paddled homeward by way of the falls. But there were no falls, as they had existed only through the evil of that man. When he died, the river flowed smoothly and steadily in its own original channel. She found her kayak, which had drifted onto the beach, and she tied it to his and paddled to her home.

Her people learned of her adventures and the evil man. The older men decreed his weapons be burned on the trash pile. Then the people rejoiced in the young girl's safe return and the safety of their tribe.

Golder, "Girl Searches for Her Lover," 26-28.

■

# THE GIRL WHO MARRIED THE MOON
## *Aleuts*

■

Long ago there were two girl cousins who lived in a large tribal village. Those evenings when the moon was out, they liked to go to the beach and play. Claiming the moon as their husband, they spend the night gazing and making love to the man in the moon.

For shelter they had propped up a *bidarka* (large skin boat), and during the night they changed positions several times, so they could always face the moon. In the morning, upon returning home, their parents always questioned them about their whereabouts. The girls told them how they had watched the moon until it passed from sight. Many of their family heard them tell how much they loved the moon, always wishing they were moons.

One evening, with other young people of their tribe, they amused themselves on the beach. Night came and the others returned to their homes, but the two girls remained. When the moon went away out of their sight, one complained, "Why does the moon hide so suddenly? I like to play with him and enjoy his moonlight." "I, too," said the other. It was not yet midnight, and the moon was already behind the clouds.

Up to now they had not noticed how disheveled their appearance was from playing. They became startled when they heard the voice of a young man as he approached them. "You have been professing your love for me," he said. "I have observed you and know you love me, therefore, I have come for you. But since my work is very hard, I can only take one of you—the more patient one."

Each begged to be chosen. He said, "I have decided to take both of you. Now close your eyes and keep them closed." So he grabbed each by the hair, and the next moment they were rushing through the air. The patience of one wore thin. As she opened her eyes, she felt herself drop down, down, down, leaving her hair behind in his hands. She found herself beside the bidarka where she had left it.

The patient cousin kept her eyes closed the entire time, and in the morning found herself in a comfortable barrabara, the home of the moon. There she lived as the wife of the moon, happy in loving him. Generally he slept during the day, as he worked all night.

Frequently he went away in the morning and returned in the evening. Sometimes he was gone from mid-day until midnight. His irregular schedule puzzled his wife. But he never offered an explanation to her of what he did in his absence.

His silence and indifference piqued the young bride. She waited as long as she could, until one day she said, "You go out every day, every evening, every night, and you never tell me what you do. What kinds of people do you associate with, while I am left behind?"

"I am not with other people, for there are not my kind of people here," he said. "I have important work to do, and I cannot be with you all the time."

"If your work is so hard, can you take me with you to help you sometimes?" she asked.

"My work is too hard for you," he replied. "I brought you up here, because I had no rest when you were down there. You and your lovely cousin were constantly staring at me and teasing me. Now stop your foolishness, you cannot help me. Stay home and be happy for me when I do return."

"Surely, you don't expect me to stay home all the time." She began to weep. "If I cannot go with you, can I go out by myself occasionally?"

"Of course, go anywhere you like, except in the two homes you see yonder. In the corner of each there is a curtain, under which you must never look." After this warning, he left his barrabara, and that night he looked paler than usual.

Later, she went out for a walk. Although she went far and in different directions, she saw no people. She tried several short trails, and on each saw a man lying face down. It gave her pleasure to kick them to disturb them. Each would turn and look at her with his one bright, sparkling eye and cry out, "Why do that to me? I am working and busy." She kicked all of them until she tired and ran home.

On her way she saw the two forbidden barrabaras, and she just had to look inside. A curtain hid a corner in the first. She couldn't resist the desire to look under the curtain. There she beheld a half-moon, a quarter-moon, and a small piece of moon. In the second barrabara, she found a full moon, one almost full, and another more than half-full.

Thinking about the beautiful pieces, she decided it would be such fun and no harm to try on one to see how she would feel. The one almost full pleased her most, so she placed it on one side of her face and there it stuck. She cried, "Ai, Ai, Y-a-h, Ai, Ai, Yah!" She tugged and pulled but the moon would not come off. For fear her husband would soon arrive, she hastened home, threw herself on the bed, and covered that side of her face.

There he found her, complaining that her face pained her. He suspected the real cause and went out to investigate. Upon his return he asked her about the missing moon. "Yes," she admitted. "I tried it on for fun, and now I cannot take it off." He laughed and laughed at her. Gently he pulled it off for her.

Seeing his good humor, she told him of her eventful day, especially the sport she had with the one-eyed people scattered about the sky.

"They are stars," he said reprovingly. "Since of your own free will you put on this moon, you can wear it from now on and help me in my hard work. I will finish my rounds with the full moon, and after that you can start in and finish out the month while I rest."

To this happy arrangement she consented gladly. Since that time the two have shared the hard work between them—the man in the moon and his lady in the moon.

Golder, "The Girl Who Married the Moon," 28-31.

*Painted Cape*
Apache

# PART TWO

# FROM THE SOUTHWEST

*In early times, the states of this area nurtured great Indian tribes who gave us these stories from the Southwest.*

*The Apache, a name that means "enemy," is an extensive Athapascan language family located mostly in New Mexico, Arizona, Texas, and southeast Colorado. Coming from the north in prehistoric times, the Apache traveled along the east side of the Rocky Mountains. Francisco Vasquez de Coronado, with his Spanish explorers, met them in 1540 in eastern New Mexico, where they became cliffdwellers. These Indians did not reach Arizona until 100 years later. The Jicarilla (whose name means "little basket" because of their expert women basket makers), became a strong band of the Apache, one group extending west into Colorado permanently and another east into Texas.*

*Frequent skirmishes occurred between the Navaho, Pueblo, Apache, and Zuñi over territorial rights, and later against the whites. The name Pueblo ("town") indicated those tribes who lived in community stone cliff-houses perched along the canyon walls of New Mexico. These Indians descended from the prehistoric Anasazi culture.*

*The Hopi, the "peaceful ones," a group from the north and east, became a Pueblo culture living on the Three Mesas in northern Arizona. When the gold rush began in 1849, these tribes guided and protected prospectors on their way to California.*

*The Yuma and Maricopa tribes were related closely to each other and lived along the Gila River and on both sides of the Colorado River. The Ute, Paiute, and Arapaho spread over Colorado, Nevada, and Utah, and the Pima, Papago, Navaho, and Chipewyan, tribes expanded and extended mostly throughout New Mexico and Arizona.*

*The many tribes of California mainly followed their sources of water. Several landscape myths and legends are included here.*

■

# THE FLOOD ON SUPERSTITION MOUNTAIN
## *Pima*

In the state of Arizona, the Pima Indian tribe declares that the father of all men and animals was Great Butterfly—Cherwit Maké, meaning the Earth-Maker.

■

One day long ago, Great Butterfly fluttered down from the clouds to the Blue Cliffs, where two rivers met, later called the Verde and Salt rivers. There he made man from his own sweat.

From that day on the people multiplied, but in time they grew selfish and quarrelsome. Earth-Maker became annoyed with their behavior and decided it might be best to drown all of them.

But first, he thought to warn them through the *voices of the winds*.

"People of the Pima tribe," called North Wind. "Sky Spirit warns you to be honest with one another and to live in peace from now on."

Suha, Shaman of the Pimas, interpreted to the people what North Wind had warned them about.

"What a fool you are, Suha, to listen to the voices of the winds," taunted his tribesmen.

On the next night, the same warning from Earth-Maker was repeated by East Wind, who added, "Chief Sky Spirit warns that all of you will be destroyed by floods if you do not live nobler lives."

Again, the Pimas mocked the winds and ignored their warnings. Next night, West Wind spoke, "Reform, people of the Pimas, or your evil ways will destroy you."

Then South Wind breathed into Suha's ear, "Suha, you and your good wife are the only people worth saving. Go and make a large, hollow ball of spruce gum in which you and your wife can live a long as the coming flood will last."

Because Suha and his wife believed the warnings and were obedient, they set to work immediately on a high hill, gathering spruce gum and shaping it into a large hollow ball. They stocked it with plenty of nuts, acorns, water, and bear and deer meats.

Near the appointed time, Suha and his good wife looked down sadly upon the lovely green valley. They heard the songs of the harvesters. They sighed to think of the beauty about them that would be destroyed when the flood came because of the people's selfishness. Suddenly, a bright lightning flash and loud thunder rocked the Blue Cliffs. It was a signal for the flood to begin.

Suha and his wife went into the gum-ball ark and closed the door tightly. Swirling, dark clouds surrounded them. Torrents of rain poured down everywhere. For many days, the ark rolled and tossed about on the deepening sea.

After many, many moons, the downpour of rain stopped. The ark settled upon the land again, high on a mountaintop. Suha opened the door and stepped forth to see a tuna cactus growing near his feet. He and his wife ate some of the red fruit of the cactus plant. Below them, they saw water everywhere.

*Basket*
Pima

That night they retired again to the ark. They must have slept a very long time, because when they awoke the water had disappeared, the valleys were green, and the bird songs rang forth again.

Suha and his wife descended from Superstition Mountain, a name later given to the mountain upon which the ark had landed. They went down into the fertile valley and lived there for a thousand years. The forthcoming people prospered, becoming known as the Pima tribe.

These Pimas later believed a story that an evil one named Hauk lived behind Superstition Mountain. He was also called the "Devil of Superstition Mountain" because he tried to steal daughters from the Pimas.

One day, Hauk secretly descended into Pima valley, where the women were busy weaving. He stole one of Suha's daughters. Suha followed Hauk to his home behind Superstition Mountain, where he observed his daughter treated as a servant-girl by Hauk.

Suha poisoned the cactus wine that his daughter served Hauk. When he drank it, Hauk died instantly. After that the world seemed less wicked, but always the Pimas feared that Hauk's evil spirit still lurked behind Superstition Mountain.

Suha, Shaman and inspired leader of the Pima tribe, taught his people to build adobe houses, to dig gardens with bones and stones, to irrigate their lands from the rivers; to raise sheep, horses, and cattle, and, above all, to live in peace with one another.

On his dying day, Suha gathered his people and foretold:

"If you ever grow arrogant with wealth, if you ever become covetous of others' lands, if you ever make war for gain, if you ever disgrace yourselves before Chief of the Sky Spirits—another flood will come upon you.

"If that happens again, bad persons will never be saved; only good persons will eventually live with the Sun-God."

Since that time, Pimas have believed Suha's prophecies; and they never, never go onto Superstition Mountain.

But their people love to tell the story of why and how the gum-ball ark landed on Superstition Mountain, saving Suha and his good wife, who became the beloved ancestors of their large and important Pima Tribe.

Skinner, *Myths and Legends of Our Own Land*, vol. II, 215-218.

■

# HOW THE HOPI INDIANS REACHED THEIR WORLD
## *Hopi*

Hapitu or Hopi meaning the "peaceful ones" were the only Shoshones to adopt a pueblo culture, located on the Three Mesas in Northeastern Arizona.

Their first European contact was with the Spanish explorer Coronado in 1540. In 1598, the Governor of New Mexico territory made them swear allegiance to the King of Spain. In 1529, a Franciscan Mission was established at several Hopi settlements, however they were destroyed in 1680 at the general Pueblo uprising. The present Hopi Reservation became a reality by presidential order on December 16, 1882.

The performance of their spectacular Snake Dance attracts a huge public, and they remain one of the largest and best known of the North American tribes.

■

When the world was new, the ancient people and the ancient creatures did not live on the top of the earth. They lived under it. All was darkness, all was blackness, above the earth as well as below it.

There were four worlds: this one on top of the earth, and below it three cave worlds, one below the other. None of the cave worlds was large enough for all the people and the creatures.

They increased so fast in the lowest cave world that they crowded it. They were poor and did not know where to turn in the blackness. When they moved, they jostled one another. The cave was filled with the filth of the people who lived in it. No one could turn to spit without spitting on another. No one could cast slime from his nose without its falling on someone else. The people filled the place with their complaints and with their expressions of disgust.

Some people said, "It is not good for us to live in this way."

"How can it be made better?" one man asked.

"Let it be tried and seen!" answered another.

Two Brothers, one older and one younger, spoke to the priest-chiefs of the people in the cave world, "Yes, let it be tried and seen. Then it shall be well. By our wills it shall be well."

The Two Brothers pierced the roofs of the caves and descended to the lowest world, where people lived. The Two Brothers sowed one plant after another, hoping that one of them would grow up to the opening through which they themselves had descended and yet would have the strength to bear the weight of men and creatures. These, the Two Brothers hoped, might climb up the plant into the second cave world. One of these plants was a cane.

At last, after many trials, the cane became so tall that it grew through the opening in the roof, and it was so strong that men could climb to its top. It was jointed so that it was like a ladder, easily ascended. Ever since then, the cane has grown in joints as we see it today along the Colorado River.

Up this cane many people and beings climbed to the second cave world. When a part of them had climbed out, they feared that that cave also would be too small. It was so dark that they could not see how large it was. So they shook the ladder and caused those who were coming up it to fall back. Then they pulled the ladder out. It is said that those who were left came out of the lowest cave later. They are our brothers west of us.

After a long time the second cave became filled with men and beings, as the first had been. Complaining and wrangling were heard as in the beginning. Again the cane was placed under the roof vent, and once more men and beings entered the upper cave world. Again, those who were slow to climb out were shaken back or left behind. Though larger, the third cave was as dark as the first and second. The Two Brothers found fire. Torches were set ablaze, and by their light men built their huts and kivas, or traveled from place to place.

While people and the beings lived in this third cave world, times of evil came to them. Women became so crazed that they neglected all things for the dance. They even forgot their babies. Wives became mixed with wives, so that husbands did not know their own from others. At that time there was no day, only night, black night. Throughout this night, women danced in the kivas (men's "clubhouses"), ceasing only to sleep. So the fathers had to be the mothers of the little ones. When these little ones cried from hunger, the fathers carried them to the kivas, where the women were dancing. Hearing their cries, the mothers came and nursed them, and then went back to their dancing. Again the fathers took care of the children.

These troubles caused people to long for the light and to seek again an escape from darkness. They climbed to the fourth world, which was this world. But it too was in darkness, for the earth was closed in by the sky, just as the cave worlds had been closed in by their roofs. Men went from their lodges and worked by the light of torches and fires. They found the tracks of only one being, the single ruler of the unpeopled world, the tracks of Corpse Demon or Death. The people tried to follow these tracks, which led eastward. But the world was damp and dark, and people did not know what to do in the darkness. The waters seemed to surround them, and the tracks seemed to lead out into the waters.

With the people were five beings that had come forth with them from the cave worlds: Spider, Vulture, Swallow, Coyote, and Locust. The people and these beings consulted together, trying to think of some way of making light. Many, many attempts were made, but without success. Spider was asked to try first. She spun a mantle of pure white cotton. It gave some light but not enough. Spider therefore became our grandmother.

Then the people obtained and prepared a very white deerskin that had not been pierced in any spot. From this they made a shield case, which they painted with turquoise paint. It shed forth such brilliant light that it lighted the whole world. It made the light from the cotton

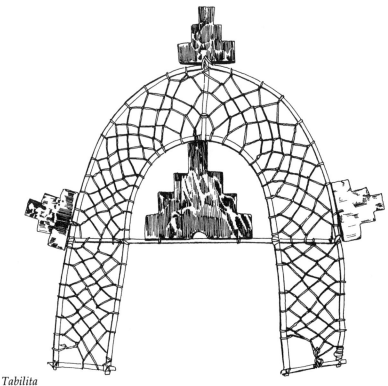

*Tabilita*
Hopi

mantle look faded. So the people sent the shield-light to the east, where it became the moon.

Down in the cave world Coyote had stolen a jar that was very heavy, so very heavy that he grew weary of carrying it. He decided to leave it behind, but he was curious to see what it contained. Now that light had taken the place of darkness, he opened the jar. From it many shining fragments and sparks flew out and upward, singeing his face as they passed him. That is why the coyote has a black face to this day. The shining fragments and sparks flew up to the sky and became stars.

By these lights the people found that the world was indeed very small and surrounded by waters, which made it damp. The people appealed to Vulture for help. He spread his wings and fanned the waters, which flowed away to the east and to the west until mountains began to appear.

Across the mountains the Two Brothers cut channels. Water rushed through the channels, and wore their courses deeper and deeper. Thus the great canyons and valleys of the world were formed. The waters have kept on flowing and flowing for ages. The world has grown drier, and continues to grow drier and drier.

Now that there was light, the people easily followed the tracks of Death eastward over the new land that was appearing. Hence Death is our greatest father and master. We followed his tracks when we left the cave worlds, and he was the only being that awaited us on the great world of waters where this world is now.

Although all the water had flowed away, the people found the earth soft and damp. That is why we can see today the tracks of men and of many strange creatures between the place toward the west and the place where we came from the cave world.

Since the days of the first people, the earth has been changed to stone, and all the tracks have been preserved as they were when they were first made.

When people had followed in the tracks of Corpse Demon but a short distance, they overtook him. Among them were two little girls. One was the beautiful daughter of a great priest. The other was the child of somebody-or-other. She was not beautiful, and she was jealous of the little beauty. With the aid of Corpse Demon the jealous girl caused the death of the other child. This was the first death.

When people saw that the girl slept and could not be awakened, that she grew cold and that her heart had stopped beating, her father, the great priest, grew angry.

"Who has caused my daughter to die?" he cried loudly.

But the people only looked at each other.

"I will make a ball of sacred meal," said the priest. "I will throw it into the air, and when it falls it will strike someone on the head. The one it will strike I shall know as the one whose magic and evil art have brought my tragedy upon me."

The priest made a ball of sacred flour and pollen and threw it into the air. When it fell, it struck the head of the jealous little girl, the daughter of somebody-or-other. Then the priest exclaimed, "So *you* have caused this thing! You have caused the death of my daughter."

He called a council of the people, and they tried the girl. They would have killed her if she had not cried for mercy and a little time. Then she begged the priest and his people to return to the hole they had all come out of and look down it.

"If you still wish to destroy me, after you have looked into the hole," she said, "I will die willingly."

So the people were persuaded to return to the hole leading from the cave world. When they looked down, they saw plains of beautiful flowers in a land of everlasting summer and fruitfulness. And they saw the beautiful little girl, the priest's daughter, wandering among the flowers. She was so happy that she paid no attention to the people. She seemed to have no desire to return to this world.

"Look!" said the girl who had caused her death. "Thus it shall be with all the children of men."

"When we die," the people said to each other, "we will return to the world we have come from. There we shall be happy. Why should we fear to die? Why should we resent death?"

So they did not kill the little girl. Her children became the powerful wizards and witches of the world, who increased in numbers as people increased. Her children still live and still have wonderful and dreadful powers.

Then the people journeyed still farther eastward. As they went, they discovered Locust in their midst.

"Where did you come from?" they asked.

"I came out with you and the other beings," he replied.

"Why did you come with us on our journey?" they asked.

"So that I might be useful," replied Locust.

But the people, thinking that he could not be useful, said to him, "You must return to the place you came from."

But Locust would not obey them. Then the people became so angry at him that they ran arrows through him, even through his heart. All the blood oozed out of his body and he died. After a long time he came to life again and ran about, looking as he had looked before, except that he was black.

The people said to one another, "Locust lives again, although we have pierced him through and through. Now he shall indeed be useful and shall journey with us. Who besides Locust has this wonderful power of renewing his life? He must possess the medicine for the renewal of the lives of others. He shall become the medicine of mortal wounds and of war."

So today the locust is at first white, as was the first locust that came forth with the ancients. Like him, the locust dies, and after he has been dead a long time, he comes to life again—black. He is our father, too. Having his medicine, we are the greatest of men. The locust medicine still heals mortal wounds.

After the ancient people had journeyed a long distance, they became very hungry. In their hurry to get away from the lower cave world, they had forgotten to bring seed. After they had done much lamenting, the Spirit of Dew sent the Swallow back to bring the seed of corn and of other foods. When Swallow returned, the Spirit of Dew planted the seed in the ground and chanted prayers to it. Through the power of these prayers, the corn grew and ripened in a single day.

So for a long time, as the people continued their journey, they carried only enough seed for a day's planting. They depended upon the Spirit of Dew to raise for them in a single day an abundance of corn and other foods. To the Corn Clan, he gave this seed, and for a long time they were able to raise enough corn for their needs in a very short time.

But the powers of the witches and wizards made the time for raising foods grow longer and longer. Now, sometimes, our corn does not have time to grow old and ripen in the ear, and our other foods do not ripen. If it had not been for the children of the little girl whom the ancient people let live, even now we would not need to watch our cornfields whole summers through, and we would not have to carry heavy packs of food on our journeys.

As the ancient people traveled on, the children of the little girl tried their powers and caused other troubles. These mischief-makers stirred up people who had come out of the cave worlds before our ancients had come. They made war upon our ancients. The wars made it necessary for the people to build houses whenever they stopped traveling. They built their houses on high mountains reached by only one trail, or in caves with but one path leading to them, or in the sides of deep canyons. Only in such places could they sleep in peace.

Only a small number of people were able to climb up from their secret hiding places and emerge into the Fourth World. Legends reveal the Grand Canyon is where these people emerged. From there they began their search for the homes the Two Brothers intended for them.

These few were the Hopi Indians that now live on the Three Mesas of northeastern Arizona.

Cushing, "Origin Myth from Oraibi," 163-169.
James, "How the Hopi Indians Reached Their Country," 12.

■

# HOW THE GREAT CHIEFS MADE THE MOON AND THE SUN
## Hopi

"Haliksai" was the usual beginning when a Hopi told a story in his own language. "Once upon a time" was his beginning when he told it in English.

■

Once upon a time, when our people first came up from the villages of the underworld, there was no sun. There was no moon. They saw only dreary darkness and felt the coldness. They looked hard for firewood, but in the darkness they found little.

One day as they stumbled around, they saw a light in the distance. The Chief sent a messenger to see what caused the light. As the messenger approached it, he saw a small field containing corn, beans, squash, watermelons, and other foods. All around the field a great fire was burning. Nearby stood a straight, handsome man wearing around his neck a turquoise necklace of four strands. Turquoise pendants hung from his ears.

"Who are you?" the owner of the field asked the messenger.

"My people and I have come from the cave world below," the messenger replied. "And we suffer from the lack of light and the lack of food."

"My name is Skeleton," said the owner of the field. He showed the stranger the terrible mask he often wore and then gave him some food. "Now return to your people and guide them to my field."

When all the people had arrived, Skeleton began to give them food from his field. They marveled that, although the crops seemed so small, there was enough food for everyone. He gave them ears of corn for roasting; he gave them beans, squashes, and watermelons. The people built fires for themselves and were happy.

Later, Skeleton helped them prepare fields of their own and to make fires around them. There they planted corn and soon harvested a good crop.

"Now we should move on," the people said. "We want to find the place where we will live always."

Away from the fires it was still dark. The Great Chiefs, at a council with Skeleton, decided to make a moon like the one they had enjoyed in the underworld.

They took a piece of well-prepared buffalo hide and cut from it a great circle. They stretched the circle tightly over a wooden hoop and then painted it carefully with white paint. When it was entirely dry, they mixed some black paint and painted, all around its edge, completing the picture of the moon. When all of this was done, they attached a stick to the disk and placed it on a large square of white cloth. Thus they made a symbol of the moon.

Then the Great Chiefs selected one of the young men and bade him stand on top of the moon symbol. They took up the cloth by its corners and began to swing it back and forth, higher and higher. As they were swinging it, they sang a magic song. Finally, with a mighty heave, they threw the moon disk upward. It continued to fly swiftly, upward and eastward.

As the people watched, they suddenly saw light in the eastern sky. The light became brighter and brighter. Surely something was burning

*Eagle kachina*
Hopi

there, they thought. Then something bright with light rose in the east. That was the moon!

Although the moon made it possible for the people to move around with less stumbling, its light was so dim that frequently the workers in the fields would cut up their food plants instead of the weeds. It was so cold that fires had to be kept burning around the fields all the time.

Again the Great Chiefs held a council with Skeleton, and again they decided that something better must be done.

This time, instead of taking a piece of buffalo hide, they took a piece of warm cloth that they themselves had woven while they were still in the underworld. They fashioned this as they had fashioned the disk of buffalo hide, except that this time they painted the face of the circle with a copper-colored paint.

They painted eyes and a mouth on the disk and decorated the forehead with colors that the Great Chiefs decided upon according to their desires. Around the circle, they then wove a ring of corn husks, arranged in a zig zag design. Around the circle of corn husks, they threaded a string of red hair from some animal. To the back of the disk, they fastened a small ring of corn husks. Through that ring they poked a circle of eagle feathers.

To the top of each eagle feather, the old Chief tied a few little red feathers taken from the top of the head of a small bird. On the forehead of the circle, he attached an abalone shell. Then the sun disk was completed.

Again the Great Chiefs chose a young man to stand on top of the disk, which they had placed on a large sheet. As they had done with the moon disk, they raised the cloth by holding its corners. Then they swung the sun disk back and forth, back and forth, again and again. With a mighty thrust, they threw the man and the disk far into the air. It traveled fast into the eastern sky and disappeared.

All the people watched it carefully. In a short time, they saw light in the east as if a great fire were burning. Soon the new sun rose and warmed the earth with its kindly rays.

Now with the moon to light the earth at night and the sun to light and warm it by day, all the people decided to pick up their provisions and go on. As they started, the White people took a trail that led them far to the south. The Hopis took one to the north, and the Pueblos took one midway between the two. Thus they wandered on to the places where they were to live.

The Hopis wandered a long time, building houses and planting crops until they reached the mesas where they now live. The ruins of the ancient villages are scattered to the very beginnings of the great river of the canyon—the Colorado.

James, *Haliksai* 10-11.

■

# FIRST JOURNEY THROUGH GRAND CANYON
## *Hopi*

Long ago, on the enormous far rim of the Grand Canyon in Arizona, lived the ancestors of the Snake Clan, who belonged to the Hopi Indian tribe.

■

Chief of the Hopis had a very wise son, who liked to sit and meditate on the edge of the canyon rim. He tried many times to imagine where the powerful river far below finally ended.

Experienced ancient men of their tribe did not know the answer for Wise Son. Their council leaders had different ideas among themselves. One thought the river took a secret course through enormous underground passages. Another thought it entered the middle of the world and there it nurtured large and dangerous reptiles.

Impatient, Wise Son said to his father, the Chief, "Is it not time for me to seek my quest? I wish to go down the great river and find the place where it ends."

Proud of his son's desire for accomplishment, the Chief gladly granted him permission to follow his quest. Wise Son, overjoyed with his coming venture, planned specifically for every need. His family and tribal friends helped him to design and to build a waterproof boat that could be closed entirely, like a cocoon.

He constructed a long pushing-pole to help him navigate the waters. The Shaman tied prayer sticks at the top of the pole, with special blessings for a safe journey.

Finally, the day arrived for Wise Son to launch his special canoe. The Chief and his braves arrived with supplies of food, good wishes, and more prayer sticks.

Week after week, Wise Son drifted with the river. He was happy. He learned to keep his boat in the main current, though it carried him through several turbulent side routes, including rapids and tunnel-like caves. He victoriously came though these experiences with joy in his heart.

On and on Wise Son traveled, winding his way out of steep canyons and through flat meadowlands. He caught fresh fish for his main food supply. One day, Wise Son noticed a change in the taste of the water. It was salty and he knew that he should not drink it. Then to his surprise, he suddenly floated into a great body of water that extended as far as he could see. He had discovered the place where the mighty river ended, in the ocean where the sun sleeps!

He saw an island and guided his boat to its shore. There was a house nearby. Upon investigation, he found only a very small entrance door. He knocked and asked, "Please, will you let me come in and see you?"

Spider Woman, who possessed supernatural power, lived there and answered, "Please make the hole large enough and enter." This, Wise Son did and sat down inside. He presented to Spider Woman one of his prayer sticks and told her of his adventure to find the place where the river ended.

"When I return to my tribe, I wish to take with me a gift that might be helpful to my people," he said.

"There is a neighboring house where there are many beautiful ornament-like beads and rocks. These might be gifts that you can take to your people," she replied. "But I must caution you to be careful of the vicious animals on the path. I will give you some of my magic lotion to protect you."

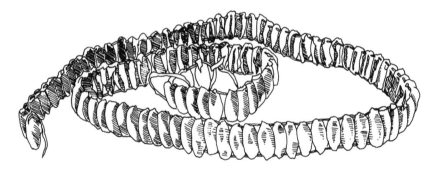

*Cocoon sash*
Hopi

Together they started for the treasure house. To guide him, Spider Woman sat upon Wise Son's ear, where she could whisper to him.

Immediately, Wise Son sprinkled some magic lotion on the marshy path. A colorful bridge appeared instantly, guiding them across the marsh to the treasure house.

First, they encountered an enormous lionlike animal showing its fangs. Wise Son tossed him a prayer stick and sprinkled magic lotion, which calmed the creature.

Second, they met a bearlike animal; third, a mad catlike creature; fourth, a ferocious wolf-like beast; fifth, a huge angry-looking snake with rattles on its tail. Wise Son quieted all of them with Spider Woman's magic lotion.

The treasure house had steps leading to the roof, and from there steps took them down into a large room. Men squatted around the inside walls. The braves wore handsome, bright-colored beads hanging about their necks. They had painted their faces tribal fashion.

Wise Son squatted by the fire. All remained quiet for some time. The men gazed at Wise Son constantly. Finally, their Chief arose and lighted his pipe. After smoking four times, he passed the pipe to the stranger. Wise Son smoked the magic number of times that seemed to please the Chief and the others. They then greeted him in a friendly manner, as if he were one of their own.

In return for their warm welcome, Wise Son gave to each man a prayer stick tipped with special feathers made by ancient Hopi tribesmen.

"Now it is time to put on our snake costumes," announced the Chief.

Wise Son observed that skins of enormous serpents were suspended from the ceiling, around all four walls. He was asked to face about, so that he would not see how the braves got into their snakeskin costumes.

When Wise Son was asked to turn back, he saw snakes of many sizes and colors, hissing and writhing over the dirt floor. Spider Woman remained on Wise Son's ear.

"Be strong," she whispered to him. "The snakes will not hurt you, only frighten you. Do whatever I tell you." The Chief of the Snake People had made his daughter become a yellow-snake-with-rattles. Wise Son did not know this, and he was asked to choose the Chief's daughter. If he could choose correctly, the Snake People would show him their ceremonial dance. They also would give him many beads and gem-rocks to take to his tribe.

Wise Son tried very hard to guess which snake was the Chief's daughter. Spider Woman whispered in his ear, "Choose the yellow one with rattles." Wise Son did, and yellow-snake-with-rattles suddenly became the loveliest and fairest of Indian maidens. He knew immediately that he could easily fall in love with her.

That evening the Chief and his braves gave to Wise Son all the secrets of the Snake Ceremony. They taught him the words of praise and thanksgiving, which they sang for him. They showed him the ceremonial steps, which they danced for him. They showed him how they put on their snake costumes. Finally, they showed him their religious altar.

After Wise Son learned all that he should know, he and Spider Woman re-crossed the bridge and returned to her house. He presented her with another prayer stick, as he thanked her for her help. In return,

The young men of Zuñi village gathered in a Kiva, a ceremonial lodge, saying to the Bow Chief, "Please announce that in four days we will go on a parrot hunt. Say, also, that anyone who does not join us will lose his wife."

Later, Kia's brother returned home and reported, "In the village, they are saying that on the hunt for young parrots, the young hunters will throw my new brother-in-law from the mesa and kill him. they will then claim his wife."

"They are just loud-mouth talking," said Chief Kya-ki-massi.

But Hoya believed that whe he heard from younger brother. He quickly put on his hummingbird coat and flew away to Parrot Woman's Cave.

"What have you to say?" she asked.

"I wish to warn you to protect your young parrots from harm. I also ask your help for myself," Hoya said, telling her of the plot to kill him. In a few minutes, he returned to Kia's home.

Next day, the parrot hunt began, with Hoya bringing up the rear. He secretly wore his magic coat beneath his buckskin shirt. At the high mesa, a yucca rope was let down toward the parrot's cave.

Hoya was instructed by the group to go down the rope to the nest of the young parrots. When he was halfway down, the village hunters let go of the rope. Parrot Woman was waiting for him, spreading her large fanlike tail outside her cave entrance. She caught Hoya in time.

Upon returning to the village, the young men reported that the rope broke, letting hoya fall to his death. In Kia's lodge, there was much sadness at the loss of Kia's new husband.

Parrot Woman took her two young birds and, with Hoya in his magic coat, flew up to the mesa.

"Please keep my two children with you," she said. "But bring them back to me in four days."

Hoya took the two young parrots to his new home and, from the roof, he heard Kia crying inside.

"I hear someone on our roof," her father said. "Perhaps, it is your new husband."

"Impossible," said his son. "Hoya is dead. But Kia ran up the ladder and to her great joy, she discovered her husband with the two parrots.

At dawn, Hoya placed the two young parrots on the tips of the ladder poles. A village youth came out of the Kiva and saw the birds. He ran back inside calling, "Wake up everyone! Hoya is not dead. He has come back to his home with two young parrots!"

When the Zuñi villagers saw the two parrots, they decided to make another plan to rid themselves of Hoya.

"Please, Bow Chief, give us permission to hunt the Bear's children. If anyone does not come along with us, he will lose his wife."

Hoya heard the terrible news, so he went to the cave of the Bear Mother.

"What do you wish of me?" she asked Hoya.

"The young hunters of Zuñi village are going on a hunt for your children. I have come to warn you and to ask you for your help in protecting me," replied Hoya. Then he told her of the plot to kill him.

Four days later, the young hunters charged toward Bear Mother's cave. Hoya again secretly wore his magic hummingbird coat beneath his buckskin shirt. He was forced by the young men to lead the attack at the cave entrance. Then the others pushed him inside the Bear's cave!

Mother Bear grabbed him but she shoved him behind her. She chased the young Zuñi hunters, killing a few of the young tribesmen. Later, Hoya flew home with two bear cubs and at dawn he placed them on the roof. When the villagers discovered the bears on Kia's roof, they knew that Hoya was sitll alive.

Hoya decided to fly to his beloved grandmother's home near Rainbow Cave to seek her wisdom about a new plan of his. She helped him paint a bird cage with many colors and they filled it with birds of matching colors. Back to Zuñi village he flew, carrying the cage, which he placed in the center of the plaza. Around it, he planted magic corn, bean, squash, and sunflower seeds.

That very evening welcome rains came down gently. Next morning the sun shone brightly and warmly. When the Zuñi villagers came out of their hogans, they were amazed at the sight before them! In the plaza center, growing plants surrounded the beautiful cage of colorful, singing birds!

From that moment on, all of the happy, dancing Zuñi tribe accepted Hoya and his gifts. They learned to love him as one of their own. His wife they called Mother, and they called him Father of their tribe for many contented years.

Curtis, *The North American Indians*, vol. 17, 179-81.

■

# THE FOUR FLUTES
## Zuñi

■

How the Zuñis wished for new music and new dances for their people when they participated in ceremonials! But they knew not how to create their wishes into realities.

Their Chief and his counselors decided to ask their Old Grandfathers for help. They journeyed to the Elder Priests of the Bow and asked, "Grandfathers, we are tired of the same old music and the old dances. Can you please show us how to make new music and new dances for our people?"

After much conferring, the Elder Priests arranged to send our Wise Ones to visit the God of Dew. Next day the four Wise Ones set out upon their mission.

Slowly climbing a steep trail, they were pleased to hear music coming from the high Sacred Mountain. Near the top, they discovered that the music came from the Cave of the Rainbow. At the cave's entrance, vapors floated about, a sign that within was the god Paíyatuma.

When the four Wise Ones asked permission to go in, the music stopped; however, they were welcomed warmly by Paíyatuma, who said, "Our musicians will now rest while we learn why you have come."

"Our Elders, the Priests of the Bow, directed us to you. We wish for you to show us your secret in making new sounds of music. Also with the new music, we wish to learn how to create new ceremonial dances.

"As gifts, our Elders have prepared these prayer sticks and special plume-offerings for you and your people."

"Come sit with me," responded Paíyatuma. "You shall now see and hear."

Before them appeared many musicians with beautifully decorated long shirts. Their faces were painted with the signs of the gods. Each held a lengthy tapered flute. In the center of the group was a large drum, beside which stood its drum-beater. Another musician held the conductor's wand. These were men of age and experience, graced with dignity.

Paíyatuma stood and spread some magic pollen at the feet of the visiting Wise Ones. With crossed arms, he then strode the length of the cave, turning and walking back again. Seven beautiful young girls, tall and slender, followed him. Their garments were similar to the musicians, but were of various colors. They held hollow cottonwood shafts from which bubbled dainty clouds when the maidens blew into them.

"These are not the maidens of corn," Paíyatuma said. "They are our dancers, the young sisters from the House of Stars."

Paíyatuma placed a flute to his lips and joined the circle of dancers. From the drum came a thunderous beat, shaking the entire Cave of the Rainbow, signaling the performance to begin.

Beautiful music from the flutes seemed to sing and sigh like the gentle blowing of the winds. Bubbles of vapor arose from the girls' reeds. In rhythm, the Butterflies of Summerland flew about the cave, creating their own dance forms with the dancers and the musicians. Mysteriously, over all the scene flooded the colors of the Rainbow throughout the cave. All of this harmony seemed like a dream to the four Wise Ones, as they thanked the God of Dew and prepared to leave.

Paíyatuma came forward with a benevolent smile and symbolically breathed upon the four Wise Ones. He summoned four musicians, asking them to give each one a flute as a gift.

"Now depart to your Elders," said Paíyatuma. "Tell them what you have seen and heard. Give them our flutes. May your people the Zuñis learn to sing like the birds through these woodwinds and these reeds."

In gratitude the Wise Ones bowed deeply and accepted the gifts, expressing their appreciation and farewell to all of the performers and Paíyatuma.

Upon the return of the four Wise Ones to their own ceremonial court, they placed the four flutes before the Priests of the Bow. The Wise Ones

*Dance mask*
Zuñi

described and demonstrated all that they had seen and heard in the Cave of the Rainbow.

Chief of the Zuñi tribe and his counselors were happy with their new knowledge, returning to their tribe with the gift of the flutes and the reeds. Before their next ceremonial, many of their tribesmen learned to make new music and to create new dances for all their people to enjoy.

Nusbaum, *Zuñi Indian Tales*, 125-132.

■

# THE YELLOW HAND
## *Papago*

The Papago tribe's native word *papáh*, beans, is the source for being called the "bean people." They belong to the Piman branch of the Uto-Aztecan linquistic family, and are closely related to the Pima tribe southeast of the Gila River and south of Tucson, Arizona, and extending west and southwest across the desert Papaguería on into Sonora, Mexico. In 1694, Father Kino became the first white man to visit the Papago nation, finding a very large population into the thousands. Census figures in 1937 listed 6,305 members of the Papago tribe. They have their own Papago printed alphabet and language studies.

■

Years ago, but not nearly so many years ago as in most of our stories, said an old Papago Indian, a man who lived in this village owned much land and worked very hard. He was always getting fields from someone who did not work so hard.

Sometimes his wife scolded him. "Both of us do nothing but work," she would say to him. "We already have more than we need and more than our daughter needs." Their daughter was their only child.

Her husband kept on working and trading until he had the very best land in all this valley. He had the best horses. He had the greatest number of cattle.

Then he began to collect yellow stones.

And his wife began to scold more and more. "It is time to choose a husband for our daughter," she told him, "but you do not know anyone. You are always too busy to go with other men on hunts or to feasts. The people of the village do not like you and are afraid of you." But her scolding had no effect.

One day a Stranger appeared from the south, riding a burro. He went to the place where the man I am telling you about was working. There Stranger emptied a sack of rocks. Then the two men pounded some of these rocks, pounded them, and burned them. After doing this a long time, the man brought Stranger to his home for food. His wife and daughter served them. The mother was very cross and scolded a great deal. Stranger watched the girl closely.

When Stranger left, the wife asked her husband, "What did you trade this time?"

Her husband only laughed and showed her a pile of stones.

When the woman had decided upon a husband for her daughter, the father would not lsiten to her. He paid no attention to anything that she said. She was very sad and quiet and worried.

But one morning, everything seemed to change. When the woman looked far south, she saw several burros with baskets on their sides. The burros came to the house. Driving them was the Stranger who had been there before. He asked the woman for her husband, who soon came from his fields. He helped Stranger unload the baskets. When they finished, the girl's father came to the house and said to his wife, "I have found a husband for our daughter. Tell her to get her things together, so that she can go with Stranger."

The mother wept and begged her husband not to give up her daughter to a stranger from a strange land. But her husband paid no attention to her. He was pounding the rocks that Stranger had brought. He paid no attention to his wife or to his daughter.

Next day the girl started south with her husband. Her father pounded the rocks that Stranger had brought to him. Her mother grumbled while she did her work, feeling very heavy and queer inside.

Time passed. The man no longer worked in his fields. He spent all of his time pounding his rocks and washing them and burning them. Again Stranger came with his burros loaded with baskets of rocks. After the baskets had been emptied, he went away.

Now all the people in the village knew that the man had traded his daughter for a pile of rocks. They laughed at him and ignored him. The woman was alone too much and became very sad. She complained that her husband was changing to rock.

When he had almost finished with one pile of rocks, Stranger would appear from the south with more rocks. This would make the man work harder than ever. His wife did not know what he did with the small yellow stones that he got out of the rocks. She thought that he put them in a hole in the ground.

Often she had to carry his meals out to him, where he was working. All day long he pounded, pounded, and pounded the rocks. The pile that he had crushed became larger than three houses. And the man's hands, his wife noticed, were always covered with yellow dust.

After a few years, she became old and very tired all the time. She refused to work in the fields; the man did nothing but pound rocks. So other people plowed and planted his fields and gave the man and his wife a certain portion of the crops.

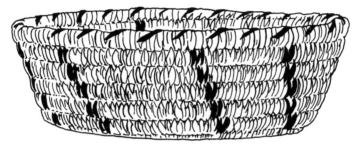

*Basket*
Papago

When the summer rains fell, the man refused to leave the rocks. He worked all day and worked at night by the light of a big fire. Many times he became wet from the rains. Soon he began to cough—very hard. His wife begged him to stop and rest. "If you do not rest, the deer will come," she reminded him.

A certain sickness, the Desert People used to believe, was brought by a deer. When people got sick in that way, there was no hope that they would ever get well. The deer that brings that sickness has a black tail. So when the Desert People eat meat from a deer with a black tail, they are still very careful. If they cough while eating the meat from that kind of deer, some of them believe they will cough until they die.

But the man who pounded rocks all day was not kept from his work by fear that the deer would come. Day after day he sat in the rain and pounded the rocks for which he had traded his only daughter. And his wife noticed that the rain did not wash the yellow from one of his hands.

One morning when the woman looked out, her husband was not pounding rocks. She went to him and found that he was dead.

She called the people living nearest her, and they began to prepare for the burial ceremony. She brought out all the blankets and the other things needed. While the dead man was being wrapped in the blankets, his right hand fell off. Picking it up, his wife found that it was very yellow and heavy and hard—just like a rock.

When everything was ready, the body was taken to the burial hill. The hand was placed beside the body and, according to custom, everything was covered with brush and stones.

That night, some kind women stayed with the widow in her home because she was now all alone. After they had been sleeping for a few hours, they heard a sound of pounding near the house! The dead man's wife was very tired and very sleepy. Hardly half-awake, she said to her friends, "It is only my husband at his rocks." And then she went to sleep again.

But the other women were frightened and could not sleep. The pounding continued until morning. Then the widow realized that her husband could not be working at his rocks. So she went out to find who had made the sound of pounding but came back puzzled, still wondering.

The next night the sounds were heard again. The third night the pounding seemed to be growing louder. The people of the village began to whisper, and they began to keep away from the widow and her home.

Then the woman became so angry that she determined to find out who was making the noise. When night came and she heard the pounding, she went out to the rocks that her husband had been breaking up when he died. As she drew near the pile of rocks, the sound became fainter.

Then she decided to visit her husband's grave. The night was dark. As she drew nearer the burial mound, the sound of the pounding became louder and louder. But everything was so dark that she decided to go home and wait until morning. Then she and some other women went to the place where Man-Who-Pounded-Rocks was buried.

They heard no noise, but they knew that a very restless spirit was there. The widow could not understand. She walked all around the mound of brush and rocks, looking at it keenly and wondering.

Suddenly she saw something bright. She stooped and looked carefully. It was the yellow hand of her husband that had broken off!

Her friends who were with her said that Coyote had tried to take the hand. But the widow felt sure she had a better idea. When they took the yellow hand to the house, one woman kept watching it. When she picked it up, several little pieces of yellow rock fell out. She quickly picked them up and slipped them out of sight. She thought that no one saw her, but the widow of the dead man had noticed her and the tiny bits of yellow rock.

After a long talk about what they should do with the yellow hand, the widow decided to put it in the ground. She and her friends wrapped it, dug a hole near the house, put the hand in it, and covered it with dirt. Then her neighbors went to their homes.

That night the widow was so very tired that she went to sleep early. But she was soon wakened by a tap, tap, tap. When she opened the door, she found no one there. She went back to bed thinking that she had been mistaken. A few minutes later she heard again the tap, tap, tap.

This time she felt sure that the sound came from the yellow hand, and so she started toward the place where they had buried it. In a few minutes she stumbled over something. Feeling around in the dark, she soon found it—the yellow hand!

She sat down to think. She did not know what to do or whom to ask for help. Soon some Little People, who work night and day in the summer, passed by her. She called to them. Quickly the message was passed to all the Little People that a human being needed their help.

The woman remained sitting on the ground, in the dark, waiting for the message that she knew would come from the Little People. They will not always help, but when they are willing, the advice they give is always good. After a time, still in the darkness, the woman heard, or felt, or understood, what she was to do.

She knew now that her dead husband's yellow hand had come back for the little pieces of yellow rock that a woman had taken. Her husband had loved them very much. The sound of pounding in the night had come from the yellow hand working at the rocks as the man was working when he died.

"If the yellow hand is left where others can find it," the woman was made to realize, "those who find it will feel that same intense love for the little pieces of yellow rock that the dead man felt for years. You must hide the yellow hand far away, where no one can ever find it. And you must find all the pieces of yellow rock that the yellow hand wanted, so that it will never come back again."

This was the advice that the woman received, in some way, from the Little People.

When morning came, she went to the home of the friend who, she knew, had kept those pieces of yellow rock. At first, the woman said that she had not taken them, but later she gave them up.

At the place where he had broken many, many rocks, she searched and searched until she had picked up all the little yellow pieces. Late in the day, she put them and those that her friend had picked up—put them all, with the yellow hand, in a blanket. Then she started up the steep side of the mountain, alone. It was a rough, hard climb for an old woman.

She became so tired that she sat down to rest in the twilight. As she sat there, she considered just throwing the yellow hand and the pieces of rock far from her and then going back to her house and her supper. Just as she was feeling sorry for herself, Taw-tawn-ye, Ant, ran over her hand. And Taw-tawn-ye stopped. "Does Taw-tawn-ye have a message for me?" the old woman thought to herself. She sat very still and listened hard, with her inside ears.

"Remember the advice the Little People gave you," Ant reminded her. "And remember what troubles would happend if you left the yellow hand where people could find it."

The woman thought of her lonely years. She thought of her daughter who had been traded for rocks. And she knew that she would never let anyone else live in this way. So she wrapped her blanket around her and slept until the morning light made eveything clear.

Then she picked up the yellow hand and all the pieces of yellow rock and hid them in different places on the mountain.

When she had finished, she returned to her home and lived in peace and happiness ever after, with all her people. Not once did she ever hear the sound of the yellow hand pounding rocks.

The mountain where the woman hid the yellow hand and the pieces of yellow rock is called *Schook Toahk*, which means "Black Mountain." Many people have searched for the place where this gold is hidden, but they have never found it. If the Desert People should learn where gold is, they would not tell anyone. Gold has always brought trouble to Indians, the Desert People of today believe. The gold hand held the beginning of all their troubles.

Wright, *Legends of the Papago Indians*, 277-290.

■

# WHY THE NORTH STAR STANDS STILL
## *Paiute*

The North American Indians told many stories about the stars— individual stars and groups of stars. Often in these legends, the stars are referred to as "the People of the Sky World."

■

Long, long ago, when the world was young, the People of the Sky were so restless and traveled so much that they made trails in the heavens. Now, if we watch the sky all through the night, we can see which way they go.

But one star does not travel. That is the North Star. He cannot travel. He cannot move. When he was on the earth long, long ago, he was known as Na-gah, the mountain sheep, the son of Shinoh. He was brave, daring, sure-footed, and courageous. His father was so proud of him and loved him so much that he put large earrings on the sides of his head and made him look dignified, important, and commanding.

Every day, Na-gah was climbing, climbing, climbing. He hunted for the roughest and the highest mountains, climbed them, lived among them, and was happy. Once in the very long ago, he found a very high peak. Its sides were steep and smooth, and its sharp peak reached up into the clouds. Na-gah looked up and said, "I wonder what is up there. I will climb to the very highest point."

Around and around the mountain he traveled, looking for a trail. But he could find no trail. There was nothing but sheer cliffs all the way around. This was the first mountain Na-gah had ever seen that he could not climb.

He wondered and wondered what he should do. He felt sure that his father would feel ashamed of him if he knew that there was a mountain that his son could not climb. Na-gah determined that he would find a way up to its top. His father would be proud to see him standing on the top of such a peak.

Again and again he walked around the mountain, stopping now and then to peer up the steep cliff, hoping to see a crevice on which he could find footing. Again and again, he went up as far as he could, but always had to turn around and come down. At last he found a big crack in a rock that went down, not up. Down he went into it and soon found a hole that turned upward. His heart was made glad. Up and up he climbed.

Soon it became so dark that he could not see, and the cave was full of loose rocks that slipped under his feet and rolled down. Soon he heard a big, fearsome noise coming up through the shaft at the same time the rolling rocks were dashed to pieces at the bottom. In the darkness he slipped often and skinned his knees. His courage and determination began to fail. He had never before seen a place so dark and dangerous. He was afraid, and he was also very tired.

"I will go back and look again for a better place to climb," he said to himself. "I am not afraid out on the open cliffs, but this dark hole fills me with fear. I'm scared! I want to get out of here!"

But when Na-gah turned to go down, he found that the rolling rocks had closed the cave below him. He could not get down. He saw only one thing now that he could do: He must go on climbing until he came out somewhere.

After a long climb, he saw a little light, and he knew that he was coming out of the hole. "Now I am happy," he said aloud. "I am glad that I really came up through that dark hole."

Looking around him, he became almost breathless, for he found that he was on the top of a very high peak! There was scarcely room for him

*Wickiup*
Paiute

to turn around, and looking down from this height made him dizzy. He saw great cliffs below him, in every direction, and saw only a small place in which he could move. Nowhere on the outside could he get down, and the cave was closed on the inside.

"Here I must stay until I die," he said. "But I have climbed my mountain! I have climbed my mountain at last!

He ate a little grass and drank a little water that he found in the holes in the rocks. Then he felt better. He was higher than any mountain he could see and he could look down on the earth, far below him.

About this time, his father was out walking over the sky. He looked everywhere for his son, but could not find him. He called loudly, "Na-gah! Na-gah!" And his son answered him from the top of the highest cliffs. When Shinoh saw him there, he felt sorrowful, to himself, "My brave son can never come down. Always he must stay on the top of the highest mountain. He can travel and climb no more.

"I will not let my brave son die. I will turn him into a star, and he can stand there and shine where everyone can see him. He shall be a guide mark for all the living things on the earth or in the sky."

And so Na-gah became a star that every living thing can see. It is the only star that will always be found at the same place. Always he stands still. Directions are set by him. Travelers, looking up at him, can always find their way. He does not move around as the other stars do, and so he is called "the Fixed Star." And because he is in the true north all the time, our people call him *Qui-am-i Wintook Poot-see*. These words mean "the North Star."

Besides Na-gah, other mountain sheep are in the sky. They are called "Big Dipper" and "Little Dipper." They too have found the great mountain and have been challenged by it. They have seen Na-gah standing on its top, and they want to go on up to him.

Shinoh, the father of North Star, turned them into stars, and you may see them in the sky at the foot of the big mountain. Always they are traveling. They go around and around the mountain, seeking the trail that leads upward to Na-gah, who stands on the top. He is still the North Star.

Palmer, *Pahute Indian Legends*, 79-81.

■

# A CALIFORNIA CREATION MYTH
## *Yokut*

Yokuts were originally thought to be a distinct linguistic family but are now considered a part of the large Penutian family. They occupy the entire floor of San Joaquin Valley of central California from the mouth of the San Joaquin River to the foot of the Tehachapi Mountains and adjacent to the foothills of the Sierra Nevada range, up to an altitude of a few thousand feet. Their environment lends itself to agriculture and forestry. In 1770 the estimated population of the Yokuts was 18,000 and in 1910 only 600. Today dozens of small bands and villages are spread over a wide area.

■

A Great Flood had occurred upon Earth long, long ago. While Earth was still covered with water, there were no living creatures upon the land.

Then out of the sky one day glided an enormous Eagle with a black Crow riding upon its back, searching for a place to light.

Around and around Eagle flew until he discovered a projecting tree stump, or what appeared to be a stump, upon which he landed to rest. There was a home at last upon the flat surface, which was amply large enough for Eagle and Crow to roost upon.

From here, they surveyed the greenish gray water as far as they could see. The sky was a gorgeous bright blue with a few white drifting clouds, occasionally swirled by a passing breeze. All seemed serene to Eagle and Crow.

Small fish were visible below the water, sometimes leaping out of the sea playfully. Hunger caused Eagle and Crow to swoop down, catching a meal for themselves from time to time. Soon a game developed between the two birds to see which one would be the winner in the fish-catching contest. Upon their return to the stump, however, they always shared the reward.

Because of Eagle's great size and wingspan, he soared to great heights and surveyed widely, as the two birds often flew in opposite directions exploring for land. But no land did they find. No other flying creatures did they see. But they always returned to their home base on the tree stump.

Between them, they wondered "How can we possibly think of a way to make land?"

"We know we cannot dive deep enough to find dirt, and the fish are of no help except to provide food."

Day after day these scenes were repeated, exploring in search of land or wondering how to create land, only to return to their stump and catch more fish.

One morning soon thereafter and much to their surprise, a Duck was swimming around and around their stump. Occasionally, it dived deep in the water, rose to the surface chewing small fish, twisting its head from side to side trying to swallow its meal. One time, Duck emerged with more mud than fish in its mouth.

Eagle and Crow birdtalked excitedly about this! "Can Duck possibly bring up enough mud for us to build land?" they wondered.

How could they let Duck know that mud was what they needed most?

An idea occurred to Eagle, which he birdtalked to Crow, "If we supply fish for Duck, maybe he will bring up more mud than fish."

By trial and error, the two birds caught fish for Duck, placing them at the edge of the stump, until Duck learned that the fish were for him in exchange for mud!

When Duck appeared on the surface after a deep dive, Eagle and Crow brushed off the mud from Duck's bill and his body with their wings. Progress was slow but steady.

Gradually, Eagle had a pile of mud on his side of the stump and Crow had a similar pile on his side. Each placed fish on his own side for Duck, who now responded by carrying more and more mud to Eagle and Crow. This became a great game of fish-and-mud exchange.

Duck worked very hard, consequently he was always hungry. The birds were surprised at how large each one's mud pile grew every day. In birdtalk they said, "Duck is helping us to make a new world. This we will share equally."

Occasionally, Eagle and Crow flew toward the horizon, exploring for any new signs of land. But they returned with nothing new to report; however, they noticed a slight lowering of water around the tree stump.

"Surely, the flood must be coming to an end," Crow and Eagle birdtalked.

Each day they watched for a change in the waterline. Each day their piles of mud seemed higher and higher. Faithful Duck kept up his good work as Eagle and Crow caught fish for him and scraped off mud from him for each side of the new world.

Another time, Eagle flew high and far in search of dry land, not returning until late. The sun set and darkness enveloped his world on the stump. Next morning, to Eagle's surprise, he saw how much more mud he had acquired, and he was pleased. But after looking across at Crow's mud pile, Eagle was astounded to see that Crow had given himself twice as much mud while Eagle was away.

"Was this Crow's idea of sharing the new world equally?" accused Eagle.

Of course, they quarreled all that day and the next over Crow's unfairness. But the following day, they went back to work making their new land. Eagle decided that he must catch up. He caught two fish for Duck and put them in his usual place. Duck responded by bringing up mud twice to Eagle in exchange for his two fish. All three worked very hard for many, many moons.

Gradually, Eagle's half of the new world became taller and taller than Crow's half, even though Crow seemed to work just as hard as Eagle. Duck was faithful to his task, never tiring in his effort to supply mud. Of course, Duck continued to give Eagle twice as much mud for his two fish. Crow never seemed to notice why Eagle's half became higher and higher than his half.

One morning, as the sun rose brightly, the two birds looked down through the water and saw what appeared to be land!

"So that is where Duck finds the mud," they birdtalked. They were pleased to see that the water was subsiding. How they hoped that soon they would be high and dry on their new world.

But all was not so easy, for that very night lightning flashed across the waters and thunder rolled and rolled from one horizon to the other, followed by a heavy, drenching rain. Eagle and Crow sought shelter in holes they dug into the sides of their mud piles. All night long the rain continued to fall, washing away much of the new world into the sea.

As the rain stopped and the sun rose, Eagle and Duck looked out upon the waters and saw an arc of many colors reaching from one edge of the horizon across the sky to the other horizon. This brilliant display held their eyes in wonderment. What did it mean? They marveled at how long the colors lingered in the sky. Eagle flew toward the scene for a closer look, returning when the arc disappeared.

In birdtalk, Eagle and Crow decided that the storm of the night before must have been a clearing shower. They began their land-building project again, hoping that Duck would resume his work as mud-carrier. Soon the sun's rays burned strong and hot, packing the mud until it was hard. Duck appeared and the team of three continued to build the two halves of the new world.

Day by day, the waters subsided and new land began to show above the waterline but far, far below the new creation by Eagle and Crow. Eagle's half became taller and taller and hard packed by the hot sun. Crow's share of the new world was still great, but never could become as large as Eagle's half of the new world.

> In retelling this creation story, Yokut tribal historians always claim that Eagle's half became the mighty Sierra Nevada Mountains. They also tell how Crow's half became known as the Coast Mountain Range.
>
> Yokut historians end their tale by saying that people everywhere honor the brave and strong Eagle, while Crow is accorded a lesser place because of his unfair disposition displayed during the creation of the new world by Eagle and Crow.

Potts, "A California Creation Myth," 73-74.

*Reed boat*
Yokut

■

# WHY MOUNT SHASTA ERUPTED

## *Shasta*

The Shasta tribe probably acquired its name from a long ago chief named Sasti. They are located in California and Oregon, on the Klamath River from Indian and Thompson Creeks to the mouth of Fall Creek; in the drainage areas of two Klamath River tributaries, the Scott and Shasta rivers; and on the north side of the Siskiyou Mountains in Oregon on affluents of the Rogue River. All of these waterways proved rich sources of fish for many tribes through the centuries. Mount Shasta and Shasta County perpetuate the name of the Shasta Indians.

■

Coyote, a universal and mischievous spirit, lived near Mount Shasta in what is now California. Coyote's village had little fish and no salmon. His neighboring village of Shasta Indians always had more than they could use.

Shasta Indians had built a dam that served as a trap for fish, especially the wonderful salmon. They ate it raw, baked it over hot coals, and dried large quantities for their winter food supply. Other tribes came to Shasta Village to trade for salmon, which created wealth and respect for the Shasta tribe.

One day Coyote was dreaming of a delicious meal of salmon. His mouth watered at the thought of a nice freshly cooked, juicy salmon.

"I am so terribly hungry," he said to himself upon waking. "If I visit the Shasteans, maybe I can have a salmon dinner."

Coyote washed and brushed himself to look neat and clean, then started for Shasta Village with visions of fresh salmon swimming behind his eyes. He found the Shasteans at the dam hauling in big catches of salmon. They welcomed him and said that he could have all the fish he could catch and carry.

Hunger and greed caused Coyote to take more fish than was good for him. Finally, he lifted his big load onto his back and began his homeward journey, after thanking the Shasta Indians for their generosity.

Because his load was extra heavy and he still had a long way to go, Coyote soon tired.

"I think I had better rest for a while," he thought. "A short nap will do me good."

He stretched himself full length upon the ground, lying on his stomach, with his pack still on his back. While Coyote slept, swarms and swarms of Yellow Jackets dived down and scooped up his salmon. What was left were bare salmon bones.

Coyote waked very hungry. His first thought was how good a bite of salmon would taste at that moment. Still half-asleep, he turned his head and took a large bite. To his great surprise and anger, his mouth was full of fish bones! His salmon meat was gone. Coyote jumped up and down in a rage shouting, "Who has stolen my salmon? Who has stolen my salmon?"

Coyote searched the ground around him but could not locate any visible tracks. He decided to return to Shasta Village and ask his good friends there if he could have more salmon.

"Whatever happened to you?" they asked when they saw his pack of bare salmon bones.

"I was tired and decided to take a nap," replied Coyote. "While I slept, someone slightly stole all of the good salmon meat that you gave me. I feel very foolish to ask, but may I catch more fish at your dam?"

All of the friendly Shasteans invited him to spend the night and to fish with them in the morning. Again, Coyote caught salmon and made a second pack for his back and started homeward.

Strangely, Coyote tired at about the same place as he had on the day before. Again he stopped to rest, but he decided that he would not sleep today. With his eyes wide open, he saw swarms of hornets approaching. Because he never imagined they were the culprits who stole his salmon, he did nothing.

Quicker than he could blink his eyes, the Yellow Jackets again stripped the salmon meat from the bones and in a flash they disappeared!

Furious with himself, Coyote raged at the Yellow Jackets. Helpless, he ran back to Shasta Village, relating to his friends what he had seen with his own eyes. They listened to his story and they felt sorry for Coyote, losing his second batch of salmon.

"Please take a third pack of fish and go to the same place and rest. We will follow and hide in the bushes beside you and keep the Yellow Jackets from stealing your fish," responded the Shasta Indians.

Coyote departed carrying this third pack of salmon. The Shasteans followed and hid according to plan. While all were waiting, who should come along but Grandfather Turtle.

"Whoever asked you to come here?" said Coyote, annoyed at Grandfather Turtle's intrusion.

Turtle said nothing but just sat there by himself.

"Why did you come here to bother us," taunted Coyote. "We are waiting for the robber Yellow Jackets who stole two packs of salmon. We'll scare them away this time with all my Shasta friends surrounding this place. Why don't you go on your way?"

But Turtle was not bothered by Coyote; he continued to sit there and rest himself. Coyote again mocked Grandfather Turtle and became so involved with him that he was completely unaware when the Yellow Jackets returned. In a flash, they stripped the salmon bones of the delicious meat and flew away!

Coyote and the Shasta Indians were stunned for a moment. But in the next instant, they took off in hot pursuit of the Yellow Jackets. They ran and ran as fast as they could, soon exhausting themselves and dropping out of the race. Not Grandfather Turtle, who plodded steadily along, seeming to know exactly how and where to trail them.

Yellow Jackets, too, knew where they were going, as they flew in a straight line for the top of Mount Shasta. There they took the salmon into the center of the mountain through a hole in the top. Turtle saw where they went, and waited patiently for Coyote and the other stragglers to catch up to him. Finally, they all reached the top, where turtle showed them the hole through which the Yellow Jackets had disappeared.

Coyote directed all the good people to start a big fire on the top of Mount Shasta. They fanned the smoke into the top hole, thinking to smoke out the yellow jackets. But the culprits did not come out, because the smoke found other holes in the side of the mountain.

Frantically, Coyote and the Shasta Indians ran here, there, and everywhere, closing up the smaller smoke holes. They hoped to suffocate the Yellow Jackets within the mountain.

Furiously, they worked at their task while Grandfather Turtle crawled up to the very top of Mount Shasta. Gradually, he lifted himself onto the top hole and sat down, covering it completely with his massive shell, like a Mother Turtle sits on her nest. He succeeded in completely closing the top hole, so that no more smoke escaped.

Coyote and his friends closed all of the smaller holes.

"Surely the Yellow Jackets will soon be dead," said Coyote as he sat down to rest.

What is that rumbling noise, everyone questioned? Louder and louder the noise rumbled from deep within Mount Shasta. Closer and closer to the top came the rumble. Grandfather Turtle decided it was time for him to move from his hot seat.

Suddenly, a terrific explosion occurred within the mountain, spewing smoke, fire, and gravel everywhere!

Then to Coyote's delight, he saw his salmon miraculously pop out from the top hole of Mount Shasta—cooked and smoked, ready to eat!

Coyote, the Shasta Indians, and Grandfather Turtle sat down to a well-deserved meal of delicious salmon.

To this day, the Shasta Indian tribe likes to conclude this tale saying, "This is how volcanic eruptions began long, long ago on Mount Shasta."

Dixon, "The Origin of the Mount Shasta Eruptions," 27-29.

■

# LAND OF THE GHOST DANCE
## *Shasta*

■

Eagle, the supreme spirit of all flying creatures, wanted to create people. So he sent two children to earth, a boy and a girl. They created more children, and in time there were many, many people everywhere on earth. It seems that no one ever died. More and more people were created, and soon the world was becoming much too crowded.

Everyone pondered the question of what could be done about the crowded conditions on earth? Then a boy died! His people were very sad to lose him, and friends gathered to comfort the family of the lost boy. They said to each other, "Let us not die, let us not die!"

Buy Coyote replied, "People must die, people must die!"

Soon thereafter the parents buried the little boy. But in their hearts, they were disturbed about what Coyote kept saying. Now they secretly wished that Coyote's child might die. Perhaps then he would understand somewhat of how they felt about losing their son.

A few moons passed, when Coyote's child became ill and he died. Coyote wanted so much to bring him back to life. He even followed his child's spirit to the land where the Ghosts danced about a fire. There he watched the spectacular cavortings of the Ghosts dancing continuously, enjoying their frolic.

Coyote built his own fire of wild parsnips to attract his child's ghost. When the Ghost clan smelled the burning parsnips, they could not stand the aroma and gave Coyote's child back to him. They returned happily to their homeland.

On their way, Coyote was so very delighted to have his child with him. Coyote asked, "What wish would you like to have me grant you?"

"Father, for ten years you must never scold me," replied the child.

All was happiness for five years, no one scolded Coyote's child. Then someone forgot and scolded him, and he died a second time. Again

*California Indian point*
Shasta

Coyote went to the Land of the Ghost Dance. Again the Ghosts saw Coyote return and said, "Go back, go back to your home and return the day after tomorrow to see your child."

Joyous at the future prospect of seeing his child again, Coyote practically danced all the way home. Because he was tired from the excitement of his journey, Coyote lay down to rest when he reached his home. The very next day, his friends found Coyote dead in his own bed. Coyote's spirit returned for the third time to the Land of the Ghost Dance, and for the third time was welcomed by his child and the other dancing Ghosts.

Shasta Indians used to say that no one should follow the dead to the Land of the Ghost Dance, or soon they, too, would become a new Ghost in the Land of the Ghost Dance!

Gifford, *California Indian Nights' Entertainment.*

■

# A SAN JOAQUIN VALLEY TALE

## *Mariposa*

In the central part of California is a wide level plain about 300 miles long, extending southward from the Sacramento River. This area of about 20,000 square miles is walled in on three sides by the Sierra Nevada and the Coast Ranges.

At one time, the Mariposa Indian tribe occupied a large portion of this land. Today, only remnants of the tribe live along the western slope of the Sierras.

■

Long ago, a Mariposa tribesman named Soho lived in a pleasant canyon with his beautiful wife, Ule, whom he loved very, very much.

They made a comfortable home in a hillside cave with a thatched cover over their doorway.  Soho covered the thatch and the doorway with animal hides to keep them warm in stormy weather.

Nearby, their fenced garden provided them with bountiful supplies of fresh fruits and vegetables.  Beyond the fencing, their domestic animals roamed freely on good grazing land.  Besides horses and a few cows, they had goats, rabbits, and even wild deer joined the herd occasionally, probably for protection from wild coyotes and foxes.  Toward evening, the domestic animals gathered beneath the thatched shelter Soho had built for them.  He was continually enlarging the sheds as the numbers of his stock increased.

The animals gave them a plentiful supply of meat and hides for their food and clothing.  Members of other tribes stopped by to trade with Soho on their migrations north and south.  Consequently, Soho and Ule were content with their home location and with the success they experienced with their crops, stock production, and trading.  They agreed that they could not have been happier with their lives.

Suddenly, Soho's beautiful Ule became ill.  Without any warning, she died.  Soho's grief overwhelmed him.  He felt very, very sad, crying aloud and wailing to himself.  He could find little comfort in his daily living—even his friendly animals were neglected at the end of the day.  He could neither eat nor sleep.

In despair, Soho walked to his wife's grave and lay there beside her mound for three days and three nights.  During the fourth night while he was crying for his wife to come back to him, he noticed a very bright star directly overhead that spread light everywhere.  What did it mean?

Then suddenly Soho felt the ground shake like an earthquake.  The earth on top of his wife's grave moved!  His wife arose from the grave!  She stood and brushed sand and dirt from her clothing!

Soho stared at Ule in silence, because a Mariposa superstition claimed that one who speaks with a ghost will soon die.  As Soho continued to stare speechless, Ule floated swiftly away toward Toxil, the place of the setting-sun.  Soho ran in pursuit of her with tears of joy overflowing his eyes at seeing his wife again.

Ule turned and motioned Soho to go back, go back!  She told him that she was going to Tib-ik-nict, the home of the dead—he must not follow her.

But for four days and four nights Solo pursued Ule, until they reached a large roaring river.  She stepped onto a light bridge, fragile as a spider's web, and started to cross over.

Soho cried aloud and beckoned frantically for Ule to come back!  She turned, stretching her hand toward him as a sign of comfort.  He sprang forward onto the bridge, but she would not let him touch her.  Together they crossed the long bridge where good spirits can cross easily.  Bad spirits somehow unbalance the bridge and fall off into the water. Later, they turn into pike fish that must swim back to feed the living people.

At the far end of the bridge, Soho saw a warm, fruitful land with happy people from all parts of the world. They seemed to live peacefully together and there seemed to be plenty for everyone.

Ule told Soho to observe everything closely, because he must return to the Mariposa tribe and tell them all that he had experienced before he died on the fourth day.

She guided him back over the bridge and said good-bye, until his return. Soho ran fast to his home and reported to his tribe all that he had seen and heard. At the fourth sunrise, Soho's friends came to find him dead, as Ule had foretold. They wrapped his body in a cowhide and carried him to the sacred burial ground, placing him beside the mound where Ule had once lain.

Hudson, "Legend of the San Joaquin Valley," 104-105.

■

# THE QUEEN OF DEATH VALLEY
## *Shoshone*

"Ground Afire" is the meaning of the Indians' name for what is now known as Death Valley. "And in the height of summer there is no better name for this sun-tortured trench between blistered ranges. But when a group of forty-niners [1849] blundered into it, they renamed it Death Valley."

The valley and the high mountain ranges west and east of it are now called Death Valley National Monument. It is located in southeastern California and southwestern Nevada. Many square miles of the valley are below sea level—the lowest level in the Western Hemisphere.

More than 600 kinds of plants thrive in the valley. Its rocks make it a geologists' paradise. And for everyone, "the great charm of the area lies in its magnificent range of color, which varies from hour to hour."

■

Long, long ago, Indians used to say, this valley was beautiful and fertile. The people who lived there were ruled by a beautiful but capri-

*Bear claw necklace*
Shoshone

cious queen. One time she ordered them to build a mansion for her, one that would surpass any mansion ever built by their neighbors, the Aztecs.

For years, her people worked to make a palace that would please her. From places many miles away they dragged stones and logs. The queen, fearing that her age or an accident or an illness might prevent her from seeing her dream come true, ordered many of her people to assist in the work. Gradually, her tribe became a tribe of slaves.

The queen commanded even her own daughter to join those dragging logs and stones. When the noonday heat caused the workers to drag along slowly, with heads bowed, the queen strode angrily among them and lashed their naked backs.

Because royalty was sacred, the people did not complain. But when she struck her daughter, the girl turned, threw down her load of stone, and solemnly cursed her mother and her mother's kingdom. Then, overcome by heat and weariness, the girl sank to the ground and died.

In vain, the queen lamented and regretted. All nature seemed to punish her. The sun came out with blinding heat and light. Vegetation withered. Animals disappeared. Streams and wells dried up. At last the queen had to give up her life; she died with high fever. There was no one to soothe her last moments, for her people, too, were dead.

The mansion, half-completed, stands in the midst of this desolation. Sometimes it seems to rise into view of people at a distance, in the shifting mirage that plays along the horizon.

Skinner, *Myths and Legends of Our Own Lands*, vol. II, 259-260.

■

# THE STORY OF CREATION

## *Diegueños*

The Mission Indians of San Diego County, California, include the Diegueños of Yuman heritage and fragments of Shoshonean tribes related to people of Mexican Baja California. The Diegueños therefore have Aztec influences in their culture.

Though Mission Indians were converted long ago and civilized by Spanish friars, those teachings were not evident in the continuance of their early folklore, passed down from generation to generation. Cinon Duro, the last of long-ago chiefs of the Diegueños, related their traditions of very primitive people in the following legends to Constance Goddard Du Bois in the late 1890s.

■

When Tu-chai-pai made the world, the earth was the woman, the sky was the man. The sky came down upon the earth. The world in the beginning was a pure lake covered with tules. Tu-chai-pai and his younger brother, Yo-ko-mat-is, sat together, stooping far over, bowed down by the weight of the sky. The Maker said to his brother, "What am I going to do?"

"I do not know," said Yo-ko-mat-is.

"Let us go a little farther," said the Maker.

So they went a little farther and sat down to rest. "Now what am I going to do?" said Tu-chai-pai.

"I do not know, my brother."

All of this time the Maker knew what he was about to do, but he was asking his brother's help. Then he said, "We-hicht, we-hicht, we-hicht," three times. He took tobacco in his hand, and rubbed it fine and blew upon it three times. Every time he blew, the heavens rose higher above their heads.

Yonger brother did the same thing because the Maker asked him to do it. The heavens went higher and higher and so did the sky. Then they did it both together, "We-hicht, we-hicht, we-hicht," and both took tobacco, rubbed it, and puffed hard upon it, sending the sky so high it formed a concave arch.

Then they placed North, South, East, and West. Tu-chai-pai made a line upon the ground.

"Why do you make that line?" asked younger brother.

"I am making the line from East to West and name them so. Now you make a line from North to South."

Yo-ko-mat-is thought very hard. How would he arrange it? Then he drew a crossline from top to bottom. He named the top line North, and the bottom line South. Then he asked, "Why are we doing this?"

The Maker said, "I will tell you. Three or four men are coming from the East, and from the West three or four Indians are coming."

The brother asked, "Do four men come from the North, and two or three men come from the South?"

Tu-chai-pai said, "Yes. Now I am going to make hills and valleys and little hollows of water."

"Why are you making all of these things?"

The Maker explained, "After a while when men come and are walking back and forth in the world, they will need to drink water or they will die." He had already made the ocean, but he needed little water places for the people.

Then he made the forests and said, "After a while men will die of cold unless I make wood for them to burn. What are we going to do now?"

"I do not know," replied younger brother.

"We are going to dig in the ground and find mud to make the first people, the Indians." So he dug in the ground and took mud to make the first men, and after that the first women. He made the men easily, but he had much trouble making women. It took him a long time.

After the Indians, he made the Mexicans and finished all his making. He then called out very loudly, "People, you can never die and you can never get tired, so you can walk all the time." But then he made them sleep at night, to keep them from walking in the darkness. At last he told them that they must travel toward the East, where the sun's light was coming out for the first time.

The Indians then came out and searched for the light, and at last they found light and were exceedingly glad to see the Sun. The Maker called out to his brother, "It's time to make the Moon. You call out and make the Moon to shine, as I have made the Sun. Sometime the Moon will die. When it grows smaller and smaller, men will know it is going to die, and they must run races to try and keep up with the dying moon."

The villagers talked about the matter and they understood their part, and that Tu-chai-pai would be watching to see that they did what he wanted them to do. When the Maker completed all of this, he created nothing more. But he was always thinking how to make Earth and Sky better for all the Indians.

Du Bois, "The Story of Creation," 181-183.

*Basket bowl*
Diegueños

■

# THE FLY AT THE COUNCIL

## *Diegueños*

■

Another time, Tu-chai-pai thought to himself, "If all my sons do not have enough food and drink, what will become of them?" He thought about this for a long, long time and said, "Then they will surely die." He then thought, "What do my men want to do? I will give them three choices: to die now forever, or to live for a long time and then return to the heavens or to live forever."

When the Maker had finished his thinking, he called all men together, but none of the women. He said to the men, "I have been thinking, since there is not much food and water now, I want to know what you wish to do? Here are your three choices: to die forever, to live for a long time on Earth, or to live forever."

Some Indians replied, "We want to die forever"; some said, "We want to live for a time and then die"; others said, "We want to live forever." So they talked and talked in a Council meeting, for they did not know how to decide for everyone.

Then the fly arrived and said, "Oh, you men, what are you talking so much about? Tell the Maker you want to die forever." So the people talked and talked a long time and decided upon their choice: to die and be done with life forever.

This is the reason the fly rubs his hands together constantly, because he is begging forgiveness of the Indians for these fateful words of his.

Du Bois, "The Fly at the Council," 183.

■

# THE IMPIETY OF FROG
## *Diegueños*

■

When the moon had grown very little, all the Indian people were running races to keep up with the moon. At the end, the rabbit and the frog agreed to run a race together. The people watched and laughed loudly at the frog, because he had the shape of a man but wore no clothes. Frog became very angry at the Maker and said, "Because you did not make me well, you shall have to pay for my disgrace."

Now Tu-chai-pai had gone away to a very high place and fell asleep. Frog was down in a deep place shaking his fists in defiance of the Maker.

Suddenly the Sun appeared, and the maker came with it. He had a long stick pointed at both ends, which he held over his head. He reached down with it around the deep place and touched the back of the frog, where it left a long white mark.

By this time Frog had become so angry that he thought of a wrong deed to commit. He decided to spit poison into the water where Tu-chai-pai would drink. Thoughts of this evil deed by now had magically entered the Maker's heart, who said to himself, "I shall die." Some boys then came and told the Maker what the frog had done.

Tu-chai-pai told them, "I shall die with the Moon. Watch the Moon and when it becomes very small, then I will die." The boys watched and watched as the Moon grew smaller, and in six large stars, the Maker finished his life.

At that time, since all of the things on this Earth were the children of Tu-chai-pai, they too will die, sometime when the Moon seems right, according to the Maker of long, long ago.

Du Bois, "The Impiety of Frog," 183-184.

■

# FIESTA TU-CHAI-PAI
## *Diegueños*

■

As soon as the Indian villagers found that Tu-chai-pai was dead, all living things came together from the mountains and the valleys—all men and all animals—to mourn for him. The dove that lives here went away to seek her mate upon a high white mountain, and when she came back there was blood on her wings, the blood of her Maker.

Then the people went up on a high mountain and set two stone tablets—one facing East and one facing West. On these tablets were marked the number of days of the fiesta for Tu-chai-pai.

The men wished to bury him, and they made a great funeral pyre. They were about to set fire to it when Coyote appeared and would not agree to this, and the men gave in to him, because they were afraid of him. The villagers sent Coyote far to the East on an errand. He was far away when he saw a plume of smoke rising above the hills, and he came rushing back.

"What are you burning?" he asked.

"We are burning nothing," they told him.

Again the villagers sent Coyote far away toward the sunset. When he looked back, again he saw smoke. By then the people had finished burning the body—all but the heart. Coyote returned and found the Indian warriors standing shoulder to shoulder about the heart of their beloved Tu-chai-pai.

"I see what you are doing," said Coyote. "You are burning the heart." Suddenly, he sprang over the heads of the Indian men and seized the heart and fled to the mountains, where he devoured it. Ever since the Indians have hated Coyote for this dreadful trick he played upon them.

Yo-ko-mat-is, the younger brother, went far away to the West, but when the Indians pray to him for rain, he comes back every time, and their prayers are answered by the great spirits of himself and Tu-chai-pai.

Du Bois, "Fiesta Tu-Chai-Pai," 184-185.

■

# THE ORIGIN OF YOSEMITE
## *Yosemite*
## *(Miwok)*

Long, long ago before the white man came to the West, a large happy tribe of peaceful Indians lived among the trees of beautiful Oak Canyon. This spectacular place is now known as Yosemite Valley, situated in Yosemite National Park, California.

In the beginning these peaceful Indians were called Ah-wah-nees, meaning "Deep Grass Valley," which was the first name given to Yosemite Valley.

It is of interest to note that because of a printer's error at a later date, the spelling of the tribe's name was inadvertently changed to Yosemite. Now Yosemite National Park identifies the original home of the Ah-wah-nee band (Yosemite), southern division of the Miwok Tribe.

Today, the California State flag carries a picture of the grizzly bear as a reminder of the State's official animal, Yo Semitee.

■

Ah-wah-nees were proud of their Chief, a tall and young athletic man. Early one spring morning, he started off with his spears in hand to hunt for trout in the nearby lake known as Sleeping Water.

Imagine his astonishment when he rounded a large boulder and came face to face with an enormous grizzly bear, probably just out of its winter hibernation!

Such an unexpected meeting caused both of them to rear back in stunned surprise. Immediately, however, all of the fighting spirit within each arose. They attacked one another furiously! The Chief realized his fighting power was not equal to the great strength of the grizzly.

"What can I do to help myself?" he wondered.

At that moment, he saw an oak limb within reach and grabbed it for a weapon.

"I must do everything possible to subdue this bear, even if it means my own death," he thought while he fought. "I am determined that future Ah-wah-nee children will always remember the proud and brave blood that flowed in the veins of their ancestors."

*Mush paddle*
Miwok

He pounded heavy blows, one after another, upon the head of the grizzly bear. In return, the young Chief received innumerable cuts from the bear's teeth and claws. They exchanged blows that could have been death blows to either one, if each had not been determined to survive. The grizzly bear's hunger drove him to attack; the Chief's pride, courage, and great height strengthened his defense.

On and on they fought. Then when the Chief saw the eyes of the bear glaze with a cold stare, he knew his great moment had come. With his club raised overhead, the Chief brought down a whopping smash upon the head of the bear, who then slowly slumped to the ground. The Chief charged in to finish the task, making sure the grizzly bear was dead.

Exhausted, the young Chief withdrew a short way to rest, but kept his eyes upon the grizzly bear in case it revived. After some time, when he was certain of the bear's death, the Chief stepped forward and skinned the animal.

Later, dragging the bearskin behind him, the Chief returned to his village and proclaimed his victory. Young and old braves gathered to welcome him and to praise his success. The young braves took off, following the trail where the bearskin dragged upon the ground. They found the grizzly bear before any other wild animal had a chance to claim it. Immediately, they set to work and butchered the bear and then carried the parts back to their camp.

In the meantime, the braves prepared a huge fire and sent young runners to the outlying camps, inviting all the people to an evening of feasting.

The victory of their young Chief over the enormous grizzly bear astounded all of the Ah-wah-nees. They cheered and cheered their admiration for their great Chief. They renamed their hero, Chief Yo Semitee, which means "Grizzly Bear."

Following the feast, the entire tribe gathered for a victory dance, attired in all their fine beads and fine feathers. Chief Yo Semitee sat and overlooked the celebration, smoking the peace pipe with his tribal council. More feasting and dancing continued most of the night, as Ah-wah-nees showed their affection for their young and strong Chief.

Yo Semitee's children, and finally all of the tribe, became known as Yo Semitees in honor of their brave Chief.

Hutchings, *In the Heart of the Sierras, the Yosemite Valley*, 58.

■

# THE ORIGIN OF TU-TOK-A-NU-LA

## *Yosemite*

## *(Miwok)*

■

Two young and curious Indian boys, long ago, lived in Yosemite Valley. They were always exploring faraway places, climbing ledges where later they needed rescue, yet they continued their adventures.

One day, they came upon a new lake and decided to swim across to a large rock. When they reached the opposite shore, they climbed to the top of the huge rock to rest in the sunshine, but soon they fell asleep. On and on they slept through that night, the next, and the next night, until many moons had come and gone.

Can you imagine what happened to that rock? It kept right on growing and growing, rising higher and higher, until the faces of the two Indian boys brushed the sky.

Of course their families were distraught in the beginning, but finally gave up hope of ever seeing their two lost sons again.

Now it happened that many animals had heard from their ancestors about what had happened to the two lost Indian boys. At a council gathering of the animals, they were wondering how they could help bring the boys down as the huge rock had grown into a giant granite mountain.

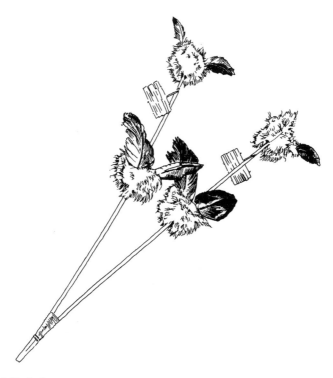

*Ceremonial hairpins*
Miwok

All of the animals decided to have a contest. Every creature would try to jump up to the mountain top. Poor little mouse only jumped a foot, larger rat leaped two feet, strong racoon much higher, grizzly bear made a mighty leap, but he was too heavy, mountain lion took a long run and jumped, but he fell down flat on his back. None could jump high enough.

Insignificant little measuring-worm came late to the contest. Everyone explained to him their predicament. None could leap high enough to the top of the mountain to rescue the two boys.

Measuring-worm decided to try. Step by step, inch by inch, little by little he began measuring his way up the granite wall that reached to the sky. He went so high that he was out of sight!

Up and up he crawled through many sleeps and through many moons, almost through a whole snow. Measuring-worm kept on crawling and at last reached the top of the giant mountain, whose magic somehow allowed the boys to remain boys!

What fun they experienced on the way down! Measuring-worm led them on a continuous, circuitous slide around and around the slippery snowy sides of the mighty mountain. They laughed and screamed with delight at the adventure they were having.

At last, measuring-worm and the two Indian boys were safe on the ground again. Their animal friends gathered to welcome them down from the sky, as well as the elders and braves of the Yosemite tribe.

From that day on to this, the great granite mountain has been called by the Indians *Tu-tok-a-nu-la*, which means "measuring-worm." Later, the Spaniards named the mountain El Capitan, a name that now appears on most maps of the Yosemite National Park.

Powers, *Tribes of California*, 366-367.

■

# How Half Dome Was Formed
## *Yosemite*
## *(Miwok)*

■

Tu-tok, Yosemite Spirit Chief, lived in his castle atop this highest mountain. He was the giver of all creature comforts to his people. He was giver of future enjoyment in the happy hunting grounds of Indian heaven. Tu-tok lived for all the Indians surrounded by the granite range of mountains. He kept vigilant watch that no foreign enemy should invade their homeland.

Long, long ago, when the children of the Sun lived in Yosemite Valley, all was happiness. Tu-tok sat high on his rocky throne overlooking the peaceful people and animals below.

He herded the wild deer and roused the sleeping bear so that the brave Yosemites might have a good hunt. He prayed to the Sky Chief for soft rain and warm sunshine to make the corn grow. He prayed that the harvest be rich for their womenfolk to gather.

When Tu-tok laughed, the winding river rippled with smiles. When he sighed, the wind swept sadly through the pines. When he spoke, the sound was like the deep voice of a roaring waterfall. When he smote the bear, his triumphant whoop rang out and echoed from mountaintop to mountaintop. His feet were swift. His eyes were strong and bright like the rising sun.

One morning a shining vision of the maiden Tis-sa appeared before the eyes of Tu-tok. She was the guardian angel of Yosemite Valley. He saw her sitting on the southern granite Dome, among the highest mountains. She was beautiful. On her shoulders rested two filmy, cloudlike wings.

"Tu-tok," she whispered. Then she vanished over the rounded granite Dome. With his eyes alert, his ears quick, his feet swift, he ran in pursuit. She had left a soft, downlike mist behind. His vision was blurred by it. He could not find her.

"Tis-sa! Tis-sa!" he called every morning as he leaped the stony crests in search of her. Every day he placed acorns and wild flowers upon her granite Dome. Sometimes he seemed to have a vision of her and saw her beautiful eyes. But never did he hear her voice. Never did he speak to her.

Tu-tok's love for Tis-sa grew so strong that he forgot the crops of the Yosemites. The rain did not fall. The corn drooped their heads. The wind whistled mournfully through the wild crops. The flowers lost their blooms. The bees stored no honey in the hollow trees. Green leaves turned brown.

Tu-tok saw none of these changes in the valley, because he was blinded by his love for Tis-sa. But she looked down with sad eyes upon the neglected valley below. Kneeling upon the gray granite Dome, she prayed to the Chief of the Sky spirits. She prayed that the flowers might be bright again; that the grasses and trees might be green again; that the corn might be ripe again.

Then a thundering sound like a giant earthquake split the Dome beneath her. Half the Dome disappeared. Melting snow from the High Sierra Mountains gushed through an opening made by the split. Rushing water, tumbling over rocks, formed a waterfall into Mirror Lake below. The lake overflowed into the beautiful Merced River winding through Yosemite Valley. All was changed!

Birds dipped their bodies into small pools. Fluttering from the water, they burst into songs of delight again. Moisture seeped silently into the parched earth. Flowers lifted their heads with fragrant gratitude. Corn gracefully stood upright. Sap ran upward into all the trees. But the maid, Tis-sa, vanished as strangely as she had first appeared. In memory of her, she left in the hearts of the Yosemites the beautiful falls, the quiet lake, the winding river, the Half Dome. The Yosemite tribe called it Tis-sa-ack.

When Tis-sa flew away, small downy feathers drifted from her shiny wings. Where they fell on the edge of the lake and in the meadows, you can see thousands of little white violets growing today. Some people say they hear whispers that he who sees a white violet and lovingly picks it with a kiss will have happy thoughts and pleasant dreams.

When Tu-tok was certain that Tis-sa was gone, he left his rocky mountain castle. He wandered everywhere in search of the one he loved. Before he left, however, he carved a bold outline of his head upon the rock, El Capitan, which bears his nobel tribal name, Tu-tok-ah-nu-lah.

There in stone, Tu-tok still guards the entrance to Yosemite Valley, which once he cared for tenderly. There the Yosemites remember him, though he wandered for many years. His search for Tis-sa ended without success. He returned alone to his mountaintop home, always looking expectantly toward Half Dome for Tis-sa.

Hutchings, *In the Heart of the Sierras, the Yosemite Valley*, 387.

■

# BRIDAL VEIL FALL

## *Yosemite*

## *(Miwok)*

"Bridal Veil Fall's plume of mist seems to drop out of a lost world. The 620-foot cataract...wears a triple crown: Cathedral Rocks." The base of the fall is surrounded by trees and shrubs.

"The vast ravine of Yo Semitee, formed by tearing apart the solid Sierras, is graced by many waterfalls raining down the mile-high cliffs." The Indians used to tell this legend about the one called Bridal Veil Fall.

■

Hundreds of years ago, in the shelter of this valley, lived Tu-tok-a-nu-la and his tribe. He was a wise chief, trusted and loved by his people, always setting a good example by saving crops and game for winter.

While he was hunting one day, he saw the lovely guardian spirit of the valley for the first time. His people called her Ti-sa-yac. He thought her beautiful beyond his imagination. Her skin was white, her hair was golden, and her eyes were like heaven. Her voice, as sweet as the song of a thrush, led him to her. But when he stretched his arms toward her, she rose, lighter than a bird, and soon vanished in the sky.

From that moment, the Chief knew no peace, and he no longer cared for the well-being of his people.

Without his directions, Yo Semite became a desert. When Ti-sa-yac came again, after a long time, she wept because bushes were growing where corn had grown before, and bears rooted where the huts had been. On a mighty dome of rock, she knelt and prayed to the Great Spirit Above, asking him to restore its virtue to the land.

He granted her plea. Stooping from the sky, the Great Spirit Above spread new life of green on all the valley floor. And smiting the mountains, he broke a channel for the pent-up snow that soon melted. The water ran and leaped far down, pooling in a lake below and flowing off to gladden other land.

The birds returned with their songs, the flowering plants returned with their blossoms, and the corn soon swayed in the breeze. When the Yo Semitee people came back to their valley, they gave the name of Ti-sa-yac to what is now called South Dome. That is where she had knelt.

Then the Chief came home again. When he heard what the beautiful spirit maiden had done, his love for her became stronger than ever. Climbing to the crest of a rock that rises three thousand feet above the valley, he carved his likeness there with his hunting knife. He wanted his tribe to remember him after he departed from the earth.

Tired from his work, he sat at the foot of Bridal Veil Fall. Suddenly he saw a rainbow arching over the figure of Ti-sa-yac, who was shining

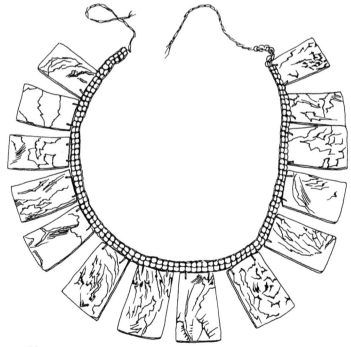

*Abalone necklace*
Miwok

from the water.  She smiled at him and beckoned to him.  With a cry of joy, he sprang into the waterfall and disappeared with his beloved.

The rainbow quivered on the falling water, and the sun went down.

Skinner, *Myths and Legends of Our Own Lands*, vol. II, 259-260.

■

# LEAPING FROG ROCKS
## *Yosemite*
## *(Miwok)*

Long ago, the Yosemites named the three peaks outlined against the north ridge the Leaping Frog Rocks.  Yosemites called them Kom-po-pai-ses, because they look like three frogs sitting on their haunches, ready to spring.  Today in Yosemite National Park you can still see the same formation.

■

The last great chief of the Yosemites was Chief Ten-a-ya.  Constantly he watched from his hideaway mountain lodge, and saw strange white horsemen riding from across the plains to the West.

Often he remembered what the Old Chief his father had said, "Obey my word, Ten-a-ya, and your people shall be as many as the blades of grass.  No enemy tribe shall ever dare to bring war into Yosemite Valley.

"But beware, my son, of the white horsemen coming from across the plains beyond.  If once they cross the western mountains, your tribe will scatter as the dust before the desert wind.  Then the Yosemites will never be the same again.

"Guard your stronghold, Ten-a-ya my son, lest you be the last of the great Chiefs of the Yosemites."

The Old Chief, trembling, had raised his peace pipe above his head and prayed, "Great Spirit Above, be good to my son, Ten-a-ya, Young Chief of the Yosemites."

To the four points of the compass, he turned and prayed:

"To the pines of the north, cold Wind treat him kindly.

"To the rising Sun of the east, Great Sun shine upon his lodge early in the morning.

"To the place where the Sun goes in winter, south wind bless my son, Ten-a-ya.

*Cane whistle*
Miwok

"To the land of the Setting Sun in the west, tenderly carry on the breezes a gentle sleep for him.

"Lowering my pipe I say to you, kind Mother Earth, when you receive my son into your warm bosom, hold him gently forever.

"Let the howl of the coyote, the roar of the bear and the mountain lion, and the sound of the wind swaying the tops of the tall pine trees, be to him a sweet lullaby."

As he remembered the Old Chief's words, Ten-a-ya guarded his mountain retreat like a mother-bear protects her young cub. With great anxiety day after day, he saw the white horsemen coming nearer and nearer from across the plains.

Ten-a-ya watched them take the land that the Great Spirit had made for the Yosemites and the other tribes. Ten-a-ya watched the white men burrow into the earth like moles. He watched them wash the sands and rocks of the rivers, searching for something yellow and shiny. They pastured their cattle upon the sacred hunting grounds of the Yosemites.

Ten-a-ya heard of the strangers stealing Yosemite women and girls for their wives. Nearer and nearer they made their camps, stealing Yosemite supplies.

Because Ten-a-ya was young and strong, he did not fear the white men. In his heart, he hated them for their disregard of what the Great Spirit had created for the Yosemites. Sometimes at night, Ten-a-ya and his braves drove away the white men's horses or killed them for food in place of their own natural game which supply was stolen by the white men.

A feeling of defiance against the white man's encroachment grew among the Yosemite braves. Ten-a-ya grew older with time. White horsemen increased in numbers, arriving at the very walls of Yosemite Valley. Again Ten-a-ya recalled his dying father's words, and Ten-a-ya knew the evil day was drawing near.

The white men climbed the western mountains. They offered gifts in the name of their White Father in Washington, and then made Ten-a-ya their captive. Young Yosemite braves fled from their camps, crossing the North Dome to the camp of the Mono Indians. They were young and could hunt far for food to supply their families. They refused to be herded like cattle in the white man's camp.

Though a captive, in spirit Chief Ten-a-ya remained strong. With native cunning, he watched for a chance and escaped to his mountain stronghold. More and more in his heart, he was growing a strong hatred for the white man.

The children of the Yosemites scattered. They were unable to rally again around Chief Ten-a-ya, because the white horsemen pursued him into his mountain retreat. Day and night, signal fires burned upon the mountaintops.

When messengers from the White Father entered Yosemite Valley, they found it deserted. But five dark figures darted from trees to rocks at the base of the jagged spur of the northern rock wall of Yosemite Valley.

A swollen river lay between the enemy and the five Indian scouts. With this protection, the scouts came into the open and taunted the white strangers. Then the scouts disappeared up the mountain, leaving no trail visible for white men to follow. Later, however, false promises induced the five scouts to come again to the white men's camp. Three of the scouts were sons of Ten-a-ya.

One brother was killed when he became a hostage. Another brother escaped only because of the bad aim of a white stranger.

When Ten-a-ya realized that it was useless to resist further, he surrendered to the messengers of the White Father in Washington. They had stolen his lands and his families, and they would not let the Yosemites live in peace in their homeland.

Ten-a-ya came down the mountain by his secret path from Le-ham-i-te, the canyon of the Arrowwood. His first sight was that of his oldest son's dead body. He spoke no word. That night he secretly carried the young chief's body to a sacred burial place.

Angered at the loss of his son, once more Ten-a-ya tried to escape and gather his tribe together, but he was captured a second time. In grief, he turned his bare chest toward his captors and cried:

"Kill me, White Chief, kill me as you have killed my sons and my people. You have brought sorrow to my heart and to the Yosemites. Kill me—and when I am dead, my spirit will rise up and call the spirits of our dead Yosemites to avenge the deaths you have caused. Our spirits will follow your footsteps forever.

"You will not see me or other Yosemites, but we will follow you wherever you go. You will know it is the spirit of Ten-a-ya and his people. You will come to fear us. Someday you will be sorry. This message is from our Great Spirit Above."

Ten-a-ya's prophecy came true. When the white men crossed the western mountains they encountered many problems and hardships because they had not made friends with the native people in the beginning. Yosemites scattered and never came together again as a tribe. Ten-a-ya was the last great Chief of the Yosemites.

Because the three sons of Ten-a-ya were captured at the base of the northern mountain wall, the three peaks were named to honor the "Three Brothers." Because their posture still resembles the "Three Leaping Frogs," they are also called Kom-po-pai-ses.

Smith, *Yosemite Legends*, 57-64.

■

# THE LEGEND OF THE GEYSERS
## *Ashochimi*
## *(Pomo-Wappo)*

Long, long ago, the peaceful Ashochimi Indian tribe inhabited a rich and luxuriant valley on both sides of a river, now known as the Russian River north of San Francisco.

With ample hunting and fishing, with crops of wild clover, wild oats, acorns, roots, and berries, they lived a happy and contented life of abundance—until Spaniards and Mexicans arrived, establishing their settlements.

The Ashochimis were compelled to hunt for adequate game farther and farther away from their homeland, because their traditional hunting grounds were overtaken by the intruders.

■

One day, Guavo and Kolo, two young Ashochimi hunters, caught sight of an unusually large grizzly bear. They shot their barbed arrows into the monstrous animal's side. The bear dropped instantly as if dead. But the hunters knew the tricks of the grizzly, that he would fall to the ground at the slightest wound, pretending he was dead.

Again the young hunters fired their flint-headed arrows and struck the bear. With four arrows in him, the grizzly got to his feet and staggered into the underbrush, leaving a trail of blood.

Guavo and Kolo pursued at a safe distance, with their arrows ready. They knew it would be only a matter of time until they could claim their prize.

Up the canyon, the grizzly bear led the two young hunters, pausing occasionally to rest.  Guavo and Kolo were amazed at its strength, as mile after mile the bear struggled on, never wavering from its direct course through the canyon.

Most of the way was timbered with low chaparral, but, suddenly, ahead the hunters saw an open grassy spot where the grizzly bear came to a halt.  To Guavo and Kolo the animal seemed to writhe in pain.  They let out a victory whoop at the sight of their dying quarry.  But the startled grizzly bear gave forth one more life-effort as he plunged forward into a ravine below.

*Elkhorn dagger*
Pomo

Guavo and Kolo ran to the edge of the cliff, where they saw the lifeless body of the grizzly at the bottom of the gorge.  At first in their excitement, they did not notice hundreds of minute jets of steam coming out of the hillside.  They did not at first hear the hoarse rushing sound that filled the canyon with a continuous noise.

Guavo and Kolo ran to the dead grizzly.  They halted in amazement when they suddenly realized they were on the brink of a "witches' cauldron" in the midst of seething steam spouts.  They wondered if the geysers had been there before the grizzly bear died.

They took one horrified look at the steaming hillsides, they took one breath of the sulfurous vapor, they took one terrified glance at the trembling earth beneath them.  Scared, Guavo and Kolo ran as fast as they could back to their village.

Chief Asho and his council listened skeptically as the two young hunters told their story:

"After the grizzly bear died, the ground began to smoke," said Guavo.

"Water boiled and bubbled without fire," said Kolo.

"Everywhere steam came out of holes in the ground," said Guavo.

"Choking smells came from the steam," said Kolo.

"Where we stood, the ground shook and trembled," said Guavo.

Because the two young hunters were known among their tribe to be truthful, Chief Asho said, "Take twenty young braves with you and show them the way to the place you have told us about."

All was true. There lay the dead grizzly bear beside the black, bubbling, steaming water.

"The grizzly's evil spirit brought forth the strange hot steam to heal his wounds," declared the tribal Medicine Man. "Before he died, the bear must have known this to be his healing place."

They skinned the bear and cut up parts of the meat for all of the braves to carry back to their tribe. Guavo and Kolo were awarded the skin as their prize, and the tribe prepared a huge fire to roast the bear meat for a feast.

Medicine Man thought the healing steam jets might help their sick people. He led the tribal men and built platforms over the steaming area, then placed their invalids upon them.

But that night, strange sounds arose in the darkness and the earth trembled violently. Medicine Man remembered stories of evil spirits within grizzly bears, and became concerned that those evil spirits were trying to take charge of the geysers.

"All is not good," he warned his people. "Go back to your village and stay there."

Soon thereafter, a strange plague appeared among the tribal men.

"We must help the sick and dying," said Medicine Man. "But I am afraid for you to return to the medicinal springs, because the angry bear's spirit has caused this pestilence."

Finally, a gray-haired, beloved Ashochimi sculptor appeared before Chief Asho.

"With my special tools, I can carve a stone guardian high above the canyon, whose good spirit will appease any angry spirits below," he said as he pleaded for permission.

"Go ahead. We anxiously await the completion of your stone guardian," replied Chief Asho.

Day after day the old sculptor worked alone. He chiseled at the hard rock until it resembled a human face. Each day he carved from dawn until the light of day was nearly gone. The people watched from a distance, eagerly awaiting the time when they could return for healing at the geysers.

"Only one more day of work on the rocky head," announced the old sculptor. But that evening he did not return to the village. A terrible earthquake occurred, toppling many cliffs, and it continued shaking throughout the night.

When the sun arose the next morning, the old sculptor had disappeared; however, the stone face on the great rock was finished and stood alone above the geysers. New springs jetted forth everywere farther down the river. Medicine Man led the men of the tribe to examine the new springs.

"It is safe now," Medicine Man announced bowing reverently toward the stone guardian of the canyon. "Let us build new platforms of willow boughs and bring the sick."

This they did. Steam vapors encircled and healed the invalids of the Ashochimi tribe miraculously. All the people rejoiced at the blessing of good health.

There above them, they were always mindful of the sculptured stone face that guarded all Indians from the wrathful spirit of the dead grizzly bear. They also were mindful of their loving sculptor who gave his life in sacrifice.

Guavo and Kolo were accorded special places of honor among the young braves of their tribe for their discovery of the geysers.

Powers, *Tribes of California*, 200-203.

■

# BEFORE THIS LAND

## *Luiseño*

Another tribe of Mission Indians in San Diego County of California are the Luiseños, who derive their name from the San Luis Rey Mission established in about 1770 by the Franciscan Junipero Serra. Many cultural similarities existed between them and the Diegueños. Under American rule in 1846, the Indians were driven deeper into desert and mountain country, far back from the ocean.

Today, descendants of those first Luiseños still thrive on their reservation in San Diego County.

■

Long, long ago, the Luiseño Indian tribe lived at the ocean side, by the setting-sun. They loved their life there, feeding on the many seafood available with little effort. Their life was leisurely, crops were plentiful, all seemed serene and their tribe prospered.

The Luiseños worshiped their Great Spirit, the Sun-God. Always they did what was commanded of them by the Great Spirit. Their tribal leader and war-god, Uu-yot, was responsible to the Sun-God for the

*Basket*
Luiseño

welfare of his people. Luiseños were loyal and obedient to both Uu-yot and the Sun-God.

One day, Sun-God willed the Luiseños to move eastward and settle in the land of the rising-sun. Many boats were made by the young braves, and the Luiseño tribe began their voyage to find a new home. Uu-yot led the fleet eastward through heavy mist and fog up the San Luis River.

To help keep the boats together, the Luiseños sang their sacred songs to each other while they traveled. At last they reached a beautiful canyon area with wide meadows and woods on either side of the river. They camped and rested, finding the land good. Plenty of acorns from the nearby oak trees were on the ground, providing their favorite dish of *weewish*, a kind of mush made by grinding acorn pulp in a stone metate. Weewish made delicious patty-cakes cooked over a fire or on hot rocks. Besides, the tribal children were kept busy collecting acorns for storage, a good winter food supply.

After several days of rest at this natural homelike campground, Uu-yot declared this to be a good homeland for them to settle upon permanently. All the Luiseños were happy, and agreed. Immediately, the people set to work establishing their family homes, creating a village.

That very evening the entire tribe gathered around a large campfire and participated in a tribal thanksgiving ceremonial led by Uu-yot. A large feast followed, which was prepared by the women of the tribe in gratitude for their new land. Much dancing and singing continued into the night, a "home-warming" affair.

On the following days, garden land was prepared by young braves. Corn and root seeds were planted by all the families for a community garden. Others hunted for wild rabbits, deer, and other small game, as well as fishing the river for food supplies. Uu-yot gave thanks each day to sun-God for the many blessings bestowed upon his tribe, the Luiseños.

Later and without warning, a period of darkness and storms descended upon the area, with sharp lightning flashes and roaring crashes of thunder. Torrential rains fell upon the land. The river overflowed, creating a dangerous situation for the tribe. Uu-yot led his people to higher ground and all were saved. They prayed to the Great Spirit to quiet the forces of nature that again they might live in peace and safety.

Uu-yot gathered his tribesmen to smoke the sacred tobacco in the ceremonial circle, appeasing the Great Spirit and his gods of wrath.

Soon thereafter, a thin line of light broke overhead through the black ominous sky and moved eastward. Next morning, out of the east, the Sun arose again, spreading widely its light, life, and warmth. The Luiseños were grateful and returned to their homes to clean up the debris left by the storm.

Jones, *So Say the Indians*, 26-27.

■

# TALES OF LAKE TAHOE
## *Washo*

*Tah-hoe* (Tä'-ho') is some Indians' pronunciation of their name for the beautiful lake that forms twenty-one miles of the boundary between California and Nevada. Mark Twain wrote of it when he was there: "We plodded on, and at last the lake burst upon us, a noble sheet of blue water...walled in by a rim of snow-clad peaks that towered aloft full 3,000 feet higher still."

The cave mentioned in the second story is on the shore near present-day Glenbrook, Nevada.

■

Long, long ago, our people used to say, Lake Tahoe was the home of the water babies. If they wanted to cross the lake or fish in the lake, they had to prepare by making a basket sealed well with pitch. In it, they put corn, bread, and pine nuts. After each basket was full, the owners would put the cover on it and sink it in the lake.

By doing this, they believed that the water babies helped them to get across safely and to have luck while fishing. But if they didn't take a basket of food, they believed that the water babies would become very angry. Sometimes people did not return from their trips because they were drowned by the will of the water babies.

In Lake Tahoe stood a tall pine tree with a mass of large branches at its top. In these branches was the nest of an enormous bird that ate human beings. The bird's winter home was a cave on the east shore of the lake.

One day it carried a man into its nest and left him sitting there while it ate. The man covered his head with his blanket made of rabbit skin and peered out through the holes in it. Each time the giant bird took a bite, the man could see into its huge mouth and down into its gullet. He threw an arrowpoint into the bird's mouth, and the bird swallowed it along with the meat it was chewing  The arrowpoint was made from some kind of volcanic rock that is poisonous.

Repeatedly, the man threw an arrowpoint into the bird's mouth. Soon it began to tremble, and in a short time it died from the poison of the arrowpoints.

Then the man cut off the bird's wings and tied them together. He climbed down the tree, placed the huge wings on the water like a boat, and sat on them. The wind soon after carried him to the other shore of Lake Tahoe.

Powers, *Tribes of California*, 388.

Curtis, *The North American Indian*, vol. XV, 150-151.

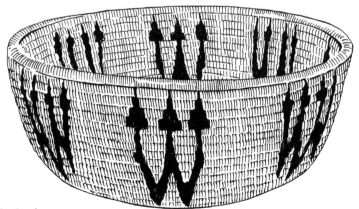

*Basket bowl*
Washo

■

# THE LEGEND OF THE FIRST PEARL FISH HOOK
### Hawaii

Grandmothers of long ago passed along stories of the old ways of the Hawaiian Islands. As with other people living close to the earth and relying upon the resources of land and sea, Hawaiians were continually aware of the creative forces, including gods and goddesses, in their daily living. To these they turned for blessings and ceremonials of thanksgiving.

■

Here is one of these legends, as recited by a wise storyteller:

Ka'eha was a fisherman of Kona on Hawaii. He stood beside his dying father, his heart heavy with sorrow. The old man opened his eyes and spoke: "Do not be sad, my son. I have lived long, and my time has come to die. Throw my bones into the sea, and the gods will give you a good gift."

Ka'eha obeyed his father's dying words. When he returned to the place where he had thrown the bones, he found them gone. He looked carefully for the gift his father had promised and found a shell of pearl. He took it up and looked long at its beauty. Then he separated the halves and tossed one to the sea. From the other he carved an *aku* hook.

That was the first pearl *aku* hook and it proved a good gift indeed. It was a sacred hook which seemed to call these fish. With it Ka'eha became a great fisherman, and his fame went all about these islands.

One day when he was fishing, a great *aku* leaped from the sea. It took the hook, and Ka'eha pulled with all his strength, eager to land that great fish. But his line broke, and the *aku* swam away carrying the sacred hook.

For days Ka'eha was filled with sadness. Then hope came. Perhaps some other fisherman had caught that fish and found the hook! He journeyed all about Hawaii, but heard nothing of the hook that he had lost.

Finally he went to other islands, but had no news until he came to windward Oahu. There, as he paddled near the shore, he saw white-capped terns dipping and circling over a house just as they dip and circle over a school of *aku*. "My hook is there!" he thought, and beached his canoe.

"These are the houses of a chief," he was told.

"Then I shall visit him," Ka'eha thought, for he too was of chiefly family.

He was made welcome and stayed for many days. Always the white-capped birds circled and dipped above the house where fishing gear was kept. But nothing was said of *aku* fishing. Ka'eha heard nothing of a sacred hook. "Perhaps the chief does not know its powers," he thought. "If only he would go *aku* fishing!"

But something very different happened. Ka'eha married the chief's daughter and settled down as son-in-law of the chief. Had he forgotten the pearl hook? Much time passed.

Then one day the chief said, "Tomorrow, O Ka'eha, my men go *aku* fishing with Kaneiki, my son. I have heard that you too are a fisherman. Will you go?"

All the young man's longing for his sacred hook returned, but he answered quietly, "Yes, I will go."

"Good!" said the chief. "Then tomorrow you shall be head fisherman. Be ready at the rising of the morning star."

But Ka'eha thought, "I must make sure that we take the sacred hook. He did not rise before dawn, but lay upon his mats, waiting.

"Ka'eha!" He heard the voice of Kaneiki outside his sleeping house. His brother-in-law was ready to start. He had a hook. That Ka'eha knew. Ka'eha knew also that this was not the sacred hook, so he lay as if still sleeping.

"Ka'eha!" The call came again. Kaneiki was angry that the young man was not ready and chanted:

> The paddles make a rattling sound
> And the bails of the fishermen too,
> O Crab Claws!

The name Crab Claws angered Ka'eha, for it meant one who talks much and does nothing. However, he did not show his anger, but chanted quietly:

> A white shell is the hook of Kaneiki,
> A lifeless thing, a lifeless thing to use.
> Where is the many-colored hook?
> Take that worthless hook back to your father.
>     Kaneiki.

The brother-in-law looked at the white shell in his hand. "Ka'eha lies in his sleeping house," he thought. How does he know what shell I have? He must be very wise." And Kaneiki went to get another hook.

"Come now!" Ka'eha heard the call once more. "I have a good hook for you."

But Ka'eha knew that this still was not his sacred hook. "It is useless!" he called in answer. "Only the many-colored hook will catch *aku* today."

Again and again this happened. Kaneiki could find no hook that pleased his brother-in-law, and at last the chief's hook bowl was empty. What should he do? Suddenly he remembered a hook found some time ago in the stomach of a big fish. The chief had stuck that hook in the thatch of the house where fishing gear was kept. "It is an old and useless hook," he had said.

"That is the only hook left," Kaneiki thought. "I shall take it."

Ka'eha met him at the door of his sleeping house. "That is the one!" he cried, taking the hook. Tears came to his eyes as he looked at this gift from his father and the gods. He put it carefully into a small gourd box which he wore on a cord about his neck. "Today we shall have good fortune in our fishing," he said. "Let us go."

They reached the landing place. "Remember, I am head fisherman," Ka'eha said. "We shall take this double canoe, and the paddlers must be strong men able to save it if it swamps."

The men listened with wonder. Of course they were good paddlers! But the sky was clear, and there was no sign of storm. Soon the canoe was launched, and the men paddled fast. Others had gone *aku*-fishing when first the morning star arose. Those early ones must not get all the fish!

"Look!" someone cried. "There are the other canoes! There the birds circle and dip. Let us paddle swiftly! Any moment the great fish may sound!" They paddled with all their might.

"Here!" called Kaneiki. "We are among the *aku*."

"Paddle farther," Ka'eha commanded, and the men turned to stare at him.

"The fish are here," repeated Kaneiki.

"Today, I am head fisherman," Ka'eha reminded him. "Paddle farther out."

Wondering greatly, the men obeyed. On and on they paddled until Oahu was only a dim gray line upon the ocean. "This is the place," Ka'eha said at last.

The others looked about. No white-capped birds! No *aku*! Again they stared at Ka'eha. What was he thinking of?

"Listen to my commands," the young man said. "Turn the canoe and paddle toward the shore. Paddle with all your might. Do not once look back. When I shout, leap into the sea."

Wondering greatly, the men obeyed. They did not see Ka'eha take the sacred fishhook from his gourd, but they heard the rush of *aku* following the canoe. They felt them splash into it. They felt the canoe sinking beneath the weight of fish. "Leap overboard!" They heard Ka'eha's shout, and leaped into the ocean, just as the canoe filled and swamped.

The paddlers were strong men, at home in the sea. They splashed the water from the canoe and bailed. Wondering greatly, they scrambled in once more. They had no fish, for Ka'eha had put the sacred hook back into its box, and the *aku* had all swum away. Silently the men paddled toward the shore.

As they came near Oahu and could see the breaking surf, Ka'eha repeated his commands: "Paddle toward shore with all your strength. Do not once look back. When I shout, be ready to leap into the sea." Again the rush and splash of *aku*! Again, the men leaped from the swamping boat. Again they emptied the canoe, then paddled toward the reef.

When they were over the reef, Ka'eha spoke once more. "Paddle steadily," he said. "Here I shall fish."

Again the men stared in wonder, and Kaneiki said, "It is useless to fish here. It is true that small fish swim over the reef, but not the great *aku*. To fish for *aku* here is useless, O Ka'eha!"

"Today I am head fisherman," the young man told them once again. "Paddle over the reef without looking back. Be ready to leap when I call to you." He took out his sacred hook and watched as the *aku* came rushing through the shallow water to splash into the canoe. "Leap quickly!" he shouted to the men as he put away his hook.

The paddlers leaped into the water just in time to prevent their boat's sinking to the coral. They waded to the beach, pushing the full canoe. The chief came, and a great crowd of servants and common people. All stared in wonder at the huge, silvery fish. "Never have I seen such a catch!" the chief exclaimed.

"Let these fish be shared," Ka'eha said. "This is my last command. Let the chief feast, and let common men feast also. This is a great day, for my sacred *aku* hook has returned to me." He took just two fish—one for his wife and one to offer in the *heiau* to the spirit of his father.

A long moment of silence told the master the deep interest of those who listened. At last Malu took out the pearl hook which Aukai had given him. He took it from an inner fold of his *malo* where he had kept it close to his body and very safe. "What of this, O master?" he asked.

"Ka'eha found a pearl shell. Do you remember? One part he returned to the sea. From that came many hooks, and this is one. This hook has been in my family for years. It brings good fortune in *aku* fishing. I have no son and give the hook to you, O Malu. Some day you will be head fisherman."

Malu could not speak, but Aukai knew his joy in the gift.

The good time went on—hula, riddles, games. When at last the guests went home, no one was empty-handed. Each had a bundle of food as well as some other gift. This had been a day of sharing, a happy memory for everyone, and for Keao and Malu a time never to be forgotten.

Caroline Curtis, *Life in Old Hawaii.*

■

# THE HULA SCHOOL
## *Hawaii*

Much of the information and customs of the ancient Hawaiian people have been absorbed by more modern influences. However, through their stories told from one generation to the next, we are able to glimpse the interests of boys and girls growing up in those times. This story of the Hula School is a good example of learning that brought happiness to the participants, and enjoyment to others, as Hula Teams displayed their skills and talents to larger groups.

■

## *Laka, Goddess of the Hula*

Keao and 'Ilima were watching children playing in the sand. Suddenly 'Ilima spoke. "I was playing in the sand that way when I heard the call of drums. It was long ago, and I was very small, but the call of the drums drew me as a fisherman draws in the fish. I ran. People were crowded together watching something. I slipped through the crowd to see. You know how a child can slip in where there seems to be no room.

"It was a hula. Men and women were dancing to the beat of drums. There was my grandmother—my own dear grandmother. Perhaps I had seen the hula before. I do not know. But this one I remember; the dancers with moving arms and swirling *pa'u*, the shine of sunlight on leis and bracelets, the tinkle of anklets, and Grandmother softly tapping the drum with her finger tips.

"That night I crawled into her lap. 'Teach me, Grandmother,' I said. 'I want to be a dancer.'

"She did teach me in the years that followed. There is much a child can learn. She said, 'I am too old and heavy to dance and gesture,' but she was not. To me she was beautiful.

"'What are you seeing, Grandmother?' I asked one day. She was looking beyond me, and I turned to look. Only breadfruit trees touched by the wind. "What are you seeing!' I asked again.

"'Laka, my goddess.'

"'Where!' My eyes searched the breadfruit grove.

"'In my mind, Grandchild. I see her as I once saw her in the forest.' Then Grandmother told me about Laka, godess of the hula. 'She is also the goddess of the wild plants which grow in the forest.'

"'She is my goddess,' I said. Every day I prayed to her. Whenever women went to the forest I went with them. I looked for Laka everywhere.

"'Some day you will see her.' Grandmother told me.

"One day I was in the lower forest helping women who were gathering berries to make dye. Rain came, and the women ran into a cave, but I stayed to watch the rain. It was only a light, misty rain. Sunshine sparkled on it and made a rainbow. Then I saw her!" 'Ilima's voice was almost a whisper, and Keao leaned close to listen. "Her *pa'u* was swirling mist. Her anklets were shiny raindrops. She was dancing a hula I did not know. Oh, Keao, I cannot tell you how lovely she was, how graceful!

"Then the misty rain was gone, and the women called me to gather berries. Laka was gone too, but the memory of her is still clear in my mind.

"That night I told Grandmother. 'She has chosen you, 'Ilima, Grandmother said earnestly. You are to be a hula dancer.' After that I worked harder than ever to learn the chants and gestures.

"'When can I train with a hula group?' I asked.

"'We shall ask Wahi.'

"But Wahi, the hula master, said I was too young. 'The training of the *halau* is very hard. You know that,' he said to Grandmother. 'Wait until your grandchild is older and stronger.'

"We have waited. It is three years since Wahi taught the hula in this district. Grandmother has heard that he will come this year. If only he will take me!" Keao saw the longing in her friend's eyes. She heard the longing in her voice. She did not answer, but in her heart she prayed.

A few days passed. Then 'Ilima found Keao making ready to beat *kapa.* Keao jumped up when she saw her friend, for "Ilima's eyes were shining. "Wahi has chosen you!" she cried. "I knew he would. I prayed."

"Can you come, Keao? I have something for you to see."

Keao looked at the bark and *kapa* beater. She did not like to leave her work. But Ana, her mother, said, "Go, Keao. This is a great day for 'Ilima. When she enters the *halau* you two cannot be together. Go with her today."

'Ilima took her friend's hand and urged her along the beach to the place where an old woman sitting under a *hau* tree was braiding sennit. Her hair was white and her face wrinkled, but shining with happiness. "'Ilima has told you," she said.

"I didn't have to tell," 'Ilima answered. "She knew by just looking at me. May I show her—you know what, Grandmother?"

The old woman took a *kapa*-wrapped bundle from the top of her *pa'u*. The girls were on their knees beside her as 'Ilima unwrapped the bundle. "Shells!" Keao exclaimed. "Such beautiful red-striped shells and all the same size! I have never seen shells like those, 'Ilima."

"They are anklets. See. They are strung on coconut fiber. Tell Keao about them, Grandmother."

"You know that I was a hula dancer, Keao," the old woman began. "Once the troupe I was in danced before a visiting chiefess. I danced one hula alone to the rhythm of sharkskin drums. When I had finished, the chiefess said, 'That is a hula dear to my heart, for it is like sunshine on rippling water. Here is something for you to wear next time you dance,' and she gave me these rare shells.

"They were my dearest treasure, and I wore them many times. When I was too old and heavy to dance and gesture I learned to play the instruments. Now I am very old.

"Yesterday Wahi said, 'The grandchild should have bracelets or anklets that have been used before. Have you something you have worn, something that will give her the blessing of our goddess?'

"So I brought out these shells. They are 'Ilima's now for she is my dearest treasure."

The two young women looked thoughtfully at the anklets and Keao said, "The sunlight shines on them as it shines on a lei of feathers. The color glows."

Grandmother put the shells away. "Until tomorrow," 'Ilima whispered. Then she added, "Tell us about the *halau* Grandmother. Tell us what Kanoe is doing."

"An altar will be built in the *halau*," the grandmother explained, "an altar to Laka. Kanoe was the one chosen to get branches for the altar as well as vines and flowers to trim it. He went into the forest at dawn and as he went he prayed. His work is sacred. It must be done in silence and with prayer. Tell Keao what he must gather, Grandchild."

"He is getting *koa* branches." 'Ilima was speaking now. Her eyes seemed to be looking into the dark *kao* forest as she went on. "'Koa' means 'unafraid.' The *koa* branches are a prayer that we shall never be afraid even when we dance before a crowd."

"What else must he gather?" the grandmother asked.

"*Lehua* in the lower forest, sweet smelling *maile*, *'ie'ie*, *palai* fern and *halapepe*," 'Ilima answered. "He must repeat a special prayer for each.

And *pili* grass," she added quickly. "That is very important for '*pili*' means to 'cling.' The *pili* grass is a prayer that chants and gestures may cling to us through all our lives.

"You tell what happens next, Grandmother."

"When Kanoe comes back to the *halau* Wahi will sprinkle the vines and branches with purifying water. He and Kanoe will build an altar to Laka, an altar made of the sacred branches and trimmed with vines and flowers. They will pray Laka to send her spirit into that altar. If you and the others try earnestly Laka will be pleased. Her spirit will stay in the altar, and vines and branches will be green and full of life."

There was a long silence. Keao was thinking, "Tomorrow 'Ilima will be there. She will see. O Laka," she prayed silently, "bless my friend. Help her to be a good hula dancer."

Then 'Ilima spoke, "And tonight, Grandmother? Tell Keao about that."

"Tonight Wahi will stay alone in the *halau*. He will pray Laka to bless his teaching. He will pray that he may remember every chant and gesture, that he may teach with patience and with wisdom. He will pray for all his pupils; that you may work earnestly and remember, that your voices may be rich and true, your bodies graceful, your hearts unafraid and reverent.

"Wahi will also pray for new wisdom. He will ask the goddess to come to him in a dream and teach him a hula he did not know or call to mind one he had forgotten."

Again the three were silent, thinking. Perhaps all three were praying. There was no movement but the sunlight dancing through *hau* leaves.

At last the old woman picked up the coconut fibers which had fallen in her lap. Keao watched her quick fingers as she braided. Though she was old, her hands were not stiff, but beautiful in movement. "Her voice too is strong and sweet," the young woman thought. "It is because of her hula training."

Aloud she said, "I think our district has the best dancers on this island."

"That is something we must never think," the old woman told her. "Chants and gestures taught in one hula school are different, sometimes different only in little ways. But each is good. I still remember the words of my master, 'Never find fault with the teaching of another school. All knowledge does not come from one.'"

"That is what my mother said about *kapa* making," Keao remembered. "'Patterns and dyes may be different, but all work done with prayer and skill is good.'"

Then she asked, "Do you know any stories about the hula?"

"I think the art was brought from far Kahiki by our ancestors," the old woman told her. "Girls of Hawaii taught it to Hi'iaka, and she and other sisters of Pele danced in the fire pit. Then La'a came. Do you know that story, Keao?"

"I have heard it, but tell it once more so we shall be sure to remember it."

"La'a was a son of Moikeha, the voyager," Grandmother began. "He came from far Kahiki. As his canoe sailed along the coast of Hawaii by night La'a softly beat his drum.

"The sound was new and beautiful.

"'What is it?' people asked, and others answered, 'It is the great god, Ku.' At daybreak they paddled out with offerings of food for the god.

"Sometimes La'a stopped at a landing place. Then hula teachers gathered, for they had heard the voice of La's drum. He taught them hulas. Though he beat the drum, he kept it hidden. 'What is it?' they asked each other. 'Its tone is rich and beautiful. If only we could make drums like that!'

"A hula master on Oahu followed the canoe. 'That drum's voice is most beautiful!' he thought. 'I have nothing with such a deep tone. I must see the drum!' So he ran, following the canoe. Sometimes he ran along the beach. Sometimes the trail was on the cliff above.

"As the hula teacher ran, he listened to the rhythms of the drum. They were new to him, and he must learn them. So he beat each one with his hands on his chest until it was fixed in his mind.

"When at last the canoe landed the hula master was there to greet La'a. 'I heard your drum,' he said. 'It sounds like one of mine. I wonder whether they are the same.'

"La'a brought out his drum. The man saw it was larger than any he had known before. It was made from a section of a breadfruit log, hollowed and covered with sharkskin. The sharkskin was laced on with sennit. 'Yes,' said the hula master, 'as I thought, it is much like mine.'

"Soon these words came true for the hula teacher made a drum like that of La'a. On it he played the rhythms he had learned. Since that day the sharkskin drum has been used through all Hawaii."

As 'Ilima came to the *halau*, the house where the hula dancers were to be trained, she felt cold with excitement. She joined others who were chosen for the training. Some were older men and women who had been dancers and would now be trained to play the rhythm instruments. Some were young men and women of 'Ilima's own age. All were people she knew, but today they seemed strange.

At the door of the *halau*, Wahi, the hula master, sprinkled them with purifying water. Once inside, 'Ilima looked about. The *halau* was larger than a sleeping house, but smaller than she had expected.

On the east side was the altar. 'Ilima knew it must be on the side of the rising sun. Placing the altar on the east was a prayer for life, health, and for growth in dancing.

There was time for short rests and for food, but not for games and idleness. The pupils could never forget that they were in the presence of their goddess. They could never be careless in speech or act.

Food was brought to the door by relatives. These people did not enter the *halau*, for it was sacred. Certain kinds of food were *kapu* to those who learned the hula, and these were never brought. The name of one *limu* meant "to hide." It was *kapu*, for eating it might make the memory of chant or gesture hide from those who tried to learn.

One morning as the pupils came from the bathing pool they noticed the master's face. "It is shining," 'Ilima thought.

"Wahi has had a dream," someone whispered. And it was so. The master told them that he had tried for many months to remember a certain hula learned in childhood. "But it had flown," he said. "Last night, as I slept, I saw our goddess, Laka. She danced the hula I longed for. Every gesture, every word was clear."

As 'Ilima learned the hula she seemed to see the goddess dancing. "Laka is in me," the young woman thought again, and danced and chanted easily. That hula was indeed a sacred thing.

One morning Wahi said, "Soon our district chief will send for this hula troupe to dance before his household. That is your graduation. I have asked Ka-ipo, a great hula master, to watch your work and tell us how it can be made better. Yesterday a message came from him. I think he will be with us today."

Many had heard of Ka-ipo. It would be an honor to have him watch their work. There was excitement in the *halau* and in 'Ilima's heart a little fear.

Just as the pupils were taking their places for a dance they heard a voice chanting the password. Wahi's face lighted with joy. The drums were hushed, and everyone listened eagerly as Wahi chanted the reply giving permission to enter.

Ka-ipo was old and white-haired, but straight and handsome. Wahi sprinkled him with purifying water. The old man went to the altar and lifted his voice in prayer. How strong and rich his tones!

> Thy blessing, O Laka,
> On me, the stranger,
> And on these within the *halau*.
> Teacher and pupils.
> O Laka, bless the dancers
> When they come before the people.

Then Wahi took Ka-ipo in his arms. Their faces touched, and their eyes filled with tears of joy. But they did not wail aloud, for they were in the presence of the goddess.

Wahi seated the old master on a mat to watch. Ka-ipo did not interrupt a dance, but after each told how it could be improved. "In this place your breathing was not right," he might say. "Fill your lungs and do not stop for breath until the phrase is finished." After another chant, "Your tone is not that of the bamboo rattles. Listen!" He struck a rattle. "Do you hear the light song of wind blowing through reeds in a marshy place? The music of your voices must be as light as the note of the bamboo."

That night 'Ilima went to her mats tired with the effort of the day, yet happy. The old man's words had made the hula even more full of beauty and worship than before.

Ka-ipo stayed for several days while pupils worked their hardest on dance and chant. At last he said, "It is well." That was all, but coming from the master it was praise enough. 'Ilima knew—everyone knew— the troupe was ready for graduation. A few days later came the chief's command to dance before his household. The time had come!

Just after midnight, when no one was about, the pupils went to the ocean to bathe. Oh, how good to feel its waves once more! At the door of the *halau* Wahi sprinkled each one with purifying water as he had done every time they entered. Then he himself went to bathe. When he returned they danced and chanted, then slept a little while.

At daybreak the pupils were wakened by their teacher's tapping on the sharkskin drum. 'Ilima was wide awake at once. This was the day!

All bathed in the pool just as they had each morning. They chanted as they dressed, but the *pa'u* each put on was new and beautiful. They gathered about the altar and chanted prayers to Laka.

A long ceremony of prayers and chants followed the morning meal. The pupils watched as vines and branches were taken from the altar and replaced with fresh ones. They listened as Wahi talked to them. "Be true to what you have learned in this *halau*," he said. "Then the chants will be yours through all your lives."

And now, for the first time since entering the *halau*, the pupils visited their homes. The men might shave. Everyone might trim hair and nails. They were given fresh leis made by their families. For a moment 'Ilima held her grandmother in her arms. Each knew that understanding and love had grown between them.

The time at home was short. Soon all returned to the *halau* to be sprinkled once more with purifying water and to chant reverently:

> Laka sits in her shady grove.
> An offering we give to you.
> O Laka, let it be well,
> Well with us all,
> O giver of all things.

As the chant ended the pupils crowded to the altar and heaped their leis upon the block of *lama* wood where the spirit of Laka rested.

The many prayers were answered. Quietly the hula troupe went to the chief's home. The audience was there, sitting or lying about the large mat made ready for the dancers. The program was long. Chants and instruments changed, but always the voices carried the tone of instruments used—drums, gourd rattles, sticks, small stones. It seemed to 'Ilima that the spirit of Laka had driven fear from eveyone. The praise which followed the program was not praise for the dancers and musicians. It was not praise for Wahi, but for Laka, their goddess.

That night when graduation was over Wahi took all the sacred things to Kanoe's canoe. He took the branches which had made the altar, the vines and every *pa'u* and lei worn by a dancer, even bits of food from the feast shared with the goddess. Wahi and Kanoe paddled to deep ocean and reverently dropped everything into the starlit waves. Wahi prayed, and the two watched the sacred things disappear. They were safe. No careless hands could touch them, no careless feet step on them.

As she lay in the sleeping house 'Ilima heard the dip of a paddle. "Perhaps it is Wahi and Kanoe returning," she told herself. "Our training is finished." There was a bit of sadness in the thought. Then came another, "Soon *Makahiki* will begin. Our hula troupe will dance in this district and in others." With a thankful prayer to Laka the young woman fell asleep.

Caroline Curtis, *Life in Old Hawaii*.

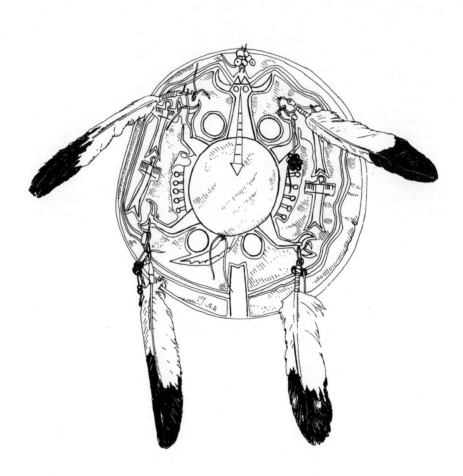

*Buffalo-hide shield*
Arapaho

# PART THREE

# FROM
# THE
# GREAT
# PLAINS

*"Westward Ho!" applied equally to the movement of North American Indians as well as to white settlers of the western Great Plains.*

*Into North and South Dakota, Nebraska, Wyoming, Montana and Colorado they spread. Many tribes followed the hunt for wild horses and buffaloes and gave up their agricultural pursuits for a period. With horses and guns, certain tribes became warlike in defense of their territories against the whites.*

*Smallpox epidemics killed thousands of Indians, wiping out villages and almost whole tribes in the middle 1800s. Several tribes united to strengthen their numbers, and lived together on reservations assigned to them by the government of the United States.*

*Tribes repesented by these stories became part of this western migration. The Hidatsa, Mandan, and Arikara, reduced in numbers, moved to Fort Berthold, North Dakota, which later became their reservation in 1880. In 1900 they became "American Citizens."*

*Cheyenne, meaning "people of alien speech," of the Algonquian language group, left Minnesota and adopted a nomadic life. They, too, joined the westward movement as far as the North Platte and Yellowstone rivers. At the treaty signing of 1851 in Fort Laramie, Wyoming, the tribe separated into two parts: the Northern Cheyenne settled in Montana, the Southern Cheyenne in Oklahoma.*

*Western migration enlarged many tribes: Ute, Acoma, Arapaho, Blackfeet, Piegan, and the powerful Dakota-Sioux who practiced the Ghost Dance Religion and became involved in wars with the U.S. military.*

*Plains Indian toy horse with beaded leather saddle*
Cheyenne

■

# ORIGIN OF THE BUFFALO
## *Cheyenne*

The Cheyenne tribe moved frequently:  In South Dakota they
lived along the Cheyenne River and in the Black Hills.  But bands of
their tribe were known in every western state.  Before 1700 a large
group settled on the Minnesota River, and some Cheyennes visited
LaSalle's Fort in Illinois in 1680.  Between 1780 and 1790, their
settlements were attacked by Chippewas while Cheyenne men were
away hunting.  Escapees settled on the Missouri River near other
Cheyennes.

■

Long ago, a tribe of Cheyenne hunters lived at the head of a rushing
stream, which eventually emptied into a large cave.

Because of the great need for a new food supply for his people, the
Chief called a council meeting.

"We should explore the large cave," he told his people.  "How many
brave hunters will offer to go on this venture?  Of course, it may be very

dangerous, but we have brave hunters." No one responded to the Chief's request.

Finally, one young brave painted himself for hunting and stepped forth, replying to the Chief, "I will go and sacrifice myself for our people."

He arrived at the cave, and to his surprise, First Brave found two other Cheyenne hunters near the opening, where the stream rushed underground.

"Are they here to taunt me," First Brave wondered? "Will they only pretend to jump when I do?"

But the other two braves assured him they would go.

"No, you are mistaken about us. We really do want to enter the cave with you," they said.

First Brave then joined hands with them and together they jumped into the huge opening of the cave. Because of the darkness, it took some time for their eyes to adjust. They then discovered what looked like a door. First Brave knocked, but there was no response. He knocked again, louder.

"What do you want, my brave ones?" asked an old Indian grandmother as she opened her door.

"Grandmother, we are searching for a new food supply for our tribe," First Brave replied. "Our people never seem to have enough food to eat."

"Are you hungry now?" she asked.

"Oh, yes, kind Grandmother, we are very hungry," all three braves answered.

The old grandmother opened her door wide, inviting the young braves to enter.

"Look out there!" she pointed for them to look through her window.

A beautiful wide prairie stretched before their eyes. Great herds of buffalo were grazing contentedly. The young hunters could hardly believe what they saw!

The old grandmother brought each of them a stone pan full of buffalo meat. How good it tasted, as they ate and ate until they were filled. To their surprise, more buffalo meat remained in their stone pans!

"I want you to take your stone pans of buffalo meat back to your people at your camp," said the old grandmother. "Tell them that soon I will send some live buffalo."

"Thank you, thank you, thank you, kind Grandmother," said the three young Cheyenne braves.

When the young hunters returned to their tribe with the gifts of buffalo meat, their people rejoiced over the new, good food. Their entire tribe ate heartily from the old grandmother's three magic pans, and were grateful.

When the Cheyennes waked at dawn the next day, herds of buffalo had mysteriously appeared, surrounding their village! They were truly thankful to the old Indian grandmother and to the Sky Spirits for their good fortune.

Voth, "Origin of Buffalo," 45.

■

# HOW THE BUFFALO HUNT BEGAN
## *Cheyenne*

The following tales were collected at the Cheyenne Agency in Oklahoma in 1899, a task undertaken by the American Museum of Natural History. Oral and written recordings were made in English from translations and writings of the Cheyenne Indians. These versions are only slightly altered to retain the character and flavor of the original.

■

The buffalo formerly ate man. The magpie and the hawk were on the side of the people, for neither ate the other or the people. These two birds flew away from a council between animals and men. They determined that a race would be held, the winners to eat the losers.

The course was long, around a mountain. The swiftest buffalo was a cow called Neika, "swift head." She believed she would win and entered the race. On the other hand, the people were afraid because of the long distance. They were trying to get medicine to prevent fatigue.

All the birds and animals painted themselves for the race, and since that time they have all been brightly colored. Even the water turtle put red paint around his eyes. The magpie painted himself white on head, shoulders, and tail. At last all were ready for the race, and stood in a row for the start.

They ran and ran, making some loud noises inplace of singing to help themselves to run faster. All small birds, turtles, rabbits, coyotes, wolves, flies, ants, insects, and snakes were soon left far behind. When they approached the mountain the buffalo-cow was ahead; then came the magpie, hawk, and the people; the rest were strung out along the way. The dust rose so quickly that nothing could be seen.

All around the mountain the buffalo-cow led the race, but the two birds knew they could win, and merely kept up with her until they neared the finish line, which was back to the starting place. Then both birds whooshed by her and won the race for man. As they flew the course, they had seen fallen animals and birds all over the place, who had run themselves to death, turning the ground and rocks red from the blood.

The buffalo then told their young to hide from the people, who were going out to hunt them; and also told them to take some human flesh with them for the last time. The young buffaloes did this, and stuck that meat in front of their chests, beneath the throat. Therefore, the people do not eat that part of the buffalo, saying it is part human flesh.

From that day forward the Cheyennes began to hunt buffalo. Since all the friendly animals and birds were on the people's side, they are not eaten by people, but they do wear and use their beautiful feathers for ornaments.

Another version adds that when coyote, who was on the side of buffalo, finished the race, the magpie who even beat the hawk, said to coyote, "We will not eat you, but only use your skin."

Grinnell, "How the Buffalo Hunt Began," 161-162.

■

# EAGLE WAR FEATHERS

## *Cheyenne*

■

A long, long time ago the Cheyenne warriors had not learned yet how to use eagle for their war ornaments. One of their men climbed a high mountain; there he lay for five days, crying, without food. Some powerful being, he hoped, would see him and come to him, to teach him something great for his people.

He was glad when he heard a voice say, "Try to be brave, no matter what comes, even if it might kill you. If you remember these words, you will bring great news to your people, and help them." After a time he heard voices, and seven eagles came down, as if to fly away with him. But he was brave, as he had been told, though he continued to cry and keep his eyes closed. Now the great eagles surrounded him. One said, "Look at me. I am powerful, and I have wonderfully strong feathers. I am greater than all other animals and birds in the world."

This powerful eagle showed the man his wings and his tail, and he spread all his feathers as wide as possible. He shows him how to make war headdresses and ornaments out of eagle feathers.

"Your people must use only eagle feathers, and it would be a great help to them in war and bring them victories," eagle said.

Since no loose feathers were about, the seven eagles shook themselves, and plenty of feathers fell to the ground. The Cheyenne picked them up and gratefully took them home to his tribe. On that day, eagle feathers were seen for the first time by the Cheyenne and they knew where they came from.

*Eagle-feathered warbonnet*
Cheyenne

The man showed his people how to make war ornaments from the eagle feathers, as he had been told. From that day onward, the man became a great warrior in his tribe, and their leader in war parties.

He became so successful his people named him Chief Eagle Feather and he wore his Eagle Feather Warbonnet, as he led the Cheyennes with dignity and pride.

Grinnell, "Eagle War Feathers," 163-164.

■

# ENOUGH IS ENOUGH
## *Cheyenne*

■

One Cheyenne man of long ago had a pointed leg. By running and jumping against trees he made his leg stick in them. When he said the magic word, he dropped again to the ground. Sometimes on a hot day he would stick himself high on the tree trunk for greater shade. However, he knew he could not do this trick more than four times in one day.

A white man came along, saw him perform, and cried out, "Brother, sharpen my leg!" Cheyenne man said, "That's not too hard. I can sharpen your leg." So the white man stood on a large log, and with an axe the Cheyenne sharpened his leg. "But you must remember never to perform your trick more than four times in one day, and keep exact count."

White man then went down toward the river and saw a large tree growing on the bank. Toward this he ran, jumped, and thrust his leg into the tree, where it stuck. He called himself back to the ground. Again he jumped against another tree, but only counted one. The third time he only counted two. The fourth time, birds and animals stood by and watched as the white man jumped high and pushed his leg on the tree, up to his knee. But he only counted three.

Then coyotes, wolves, and other animals came to see him. Some asked, "How did the white man learn the trick?" They begged him to show them, so they could stick themselves to trees at night. The white man became even prouder from all of this admiration, and the fifth time he ran harder, jumped higher, and half his thigh entered the tree and there he stuck fast. Then he counted four.

He called and called to bring himself down to the ground again, but he still stuck fast. He called out all night and the next day—but nothing helped him. He asked his animal friends to find the Cheyenne who had taught him the trick, but no one knew whom to look for. The white man had forgotten the secret of freeing himself, and after many days stuck in the tree, he starved to death.

Grinnell, "Enough Is Enough," 169.

■

# FALLING-STAR

## *Northern Cheyenne*

More than fifty versions of a story about a Star-Husband have
been recorded from many Indian tribes across the United States.

■

One day in the long ago, two young Indian girls were lying on the
grass outside their tepee on a warm summer evening. They were
looking up into the sky, describing star-pictures formed by their imag-
inations.

"That is a pretty star. I like that one," said First Girl.

"I like that one best of all—over there," Second Girl pointed.

First Girl pointed to the brightest star in the sky and said, "I like the
brightest one best of all. That is the one I want to marry."

That evening they agreed to go out the next day to gather wood. Next
morning they started for the timbered area. On their way they saw a
porcupine climb a tree.

"I'll climb the tree and pull him down," said First Girl. She climbed
but could not reach the porcupine.

Every time she stretched her hand for him, the porcupine climbed a
little higher. Then the tree started growing taller. Second Girl below
called to her friend, "Please come down, the tree is growing taller!"

"No," said First Girl as the porcupine climbed higher and the tree
grew taller. Second Girl could see what was happening, so she ran back
to the camp and told her people. They rushed to the tree, but First Girl
had completely disappeared!

The tree continued to grow higher and higher. Finally, First Girl
reached another land. She stepped off the tree branch and walked upon
the sky! Before long she met a kindly looking middle-aged man who
spoke to her. First Girl began to cry.

"Whatever is the matter? Only last night I heard you wish that you
could marry me. I am the Brightest-Star," he said.

First Girl was pleased to meet Brightest-Star and became happy again
when she got her wish and married him. He told her that she could dig
roots with the other star-women, but to beware of a certain kind of white
turnip with a great green top. This kind she must never dig. To do so
was "against the medicine"—against the rules of the Sky-Chief.

*Pipe*
Cheyenne

Every day First Girl dug roots. Her curiosity about the strange white turnip became so intense that she decided to dig up one of them. It took her a long, long time. When she finally pulled out the root, a huge hole was left. She looked into the hole and far, far below she saw the camp of her own people.

Everything and everyone was very small, but she could see lodges and people walking. Instantly she became homesick to see her own people again. How could she ever get down from the sky? She realized it was a long, long way down to earth. Then her eyes fell upon the long tough grass growing near her. Could she braid it into a long rope? She decided to try, every day pulling more long grass and braiding more rope.

One time her husband Brightest-Star asked, "What is it that keeps you outdoors so much of the time?"

"I walk a great distance and that makes me tired. I need to sit down and rest before I can start back home."

At last she finished making her strong rope, thinking by now it must be long enough. She tied one end of the rope to a log that she rolled across the top of the hole as an anchor. She let down the rope. It looked as though it touched the ground.

She lowered herself into the hole, holding onto the braided rope. It seemed to take a long time as she slowly lowered herself until she came to the end of the rope. But it did not touch the earth! For a long while she hung on dangling in midair and calling uselessly for help. When she could hold on no longer, she fell to the ground and broke into many pieces. Although she died, her unborn son did not die, because he was made of star-stone and did not break.

A meadowlark saw what happened and took the falling-star baby to her nest. There the lark kept him with her own baby birds. When they were older, Falling-Star crept out of the nest with the little birds. The stronger the birds grew, the stronger grew Falling-Star. Soon all of them could crawl and run. The young birds practiced their flying while Falling-Star ran after them. Then the young birds could fly anywhere they wished, while Falling-Star ran faster and faster to keep up with them.

"Son, you had better go home to your own people," said Mother Meadowlark. "It is time for us to fly south for the winter. Before long, the weather here will be very cold."

"Mother Meadowlark," asked Falling-Star. "Why do you want me to leave you? I want to go with you."

"No, Son," she replied. "You must go home now."

"I will go if Father Meadowlark will make me a bow and some arrows."

Father Meadowlark made a bow and pulled some of his own quills to feather the arrows. He made four arrows and a bow for Falling- Star. Then he started Falling-Star in the right direction toward his home, downstream.

Falling-Star traveled a long time before he reached the camp of his people. He went into the nearest lodge owned by an old grandmother.

"Grandmother," he said. "I need a drink of water."

"My grandson," she said to him, "only the young men who are the fastest runners can go for water. There is a water-monster who sucks up any people who go too close to it."

"Grandmother, if you will give me your buffalo-pouch and your buffalo-horn ladle, I will bring you water."

"Grandson, I warn you that many of our finest young men have been destroyed by the water-monster. I fear that you will be killed, too." But

*Pipe bowl*
Cheyenne

she gave him the things he asked for. He went upstream and dipped water, at the same time keeping watch for the monster.

At the very moment Falling-Star filled his bucket, the Water-monster raised its head above the water. His mouth was enormous. He sucked in his breath and drew in Falling-Star, the bucket, water, and the ladle. When Falling-Star found himself inside the monster's stomach, he saw all the other people who had ever been swallowed. With his Star-stone, he cut a hole in the animal's side. Out crawled all the people, and Falling-Star rescued his pouch and ladle for his grandmother, taking her some cool, fresh water.

"My grandson, who are you?" she asked, marveling at his survival.

"Grandmother, I am Falling-Star. I killed the monster who has caused our people much suffering, and I rescued all the people who had been swallowed."

The old woman told the village crier to spread the good news that the monster was dead. Now that Falling-Star had saved the camp people there, he asked the grandmother, "Are there other camps of our people nearby?"

"Yes, there is one farther downstream," she said.

Falling-Star took his bow and arrows and left camp. The fall of the year had now arrived. After traveling many days, he reached the other camp. Again he went into an old woman's lodge where she sat near her fire.

"Grandmother, I am very hungry," he said.

"My son, my son, we have no food. We cannot get any buffalo meat. Whenever our hunters go out for buffalo, a great white crow warns the buffalo, which drives them away.

"How sad," he said. "I will try to help. Go out and look for a worn-out buffalo robe with little hair. Tell your chief to choose two of his fastest runners and send them to me."

Later, the old woman returned with the robe and the two swift runners. Falling-Star told them his plan. "I will go to a certain place and wait for the buffalo. When the herd runs, I will follow, disguised as a buffalo in the worn-out robe. You two runners chase me and the buffalo for a long distance. When you overtake me, you must shoot at me. I will pretend to be dead. You pretend to cut me open and leave me there on the ground."

When the real buffalo arrived, the white crow flew over them screaming, "They are coming! They are after you! Run, run!" The buffalo herd ran, followed by a shabby-looking bull.

The two swift runners chased the old bull according to plan. All kinds of birds, wolves, and coyotes came toward the carcass from all directions. Among them was the white crow. As he flew over Falling-Star in disguise, he called out shrilly, "I wonder if this is Falling-Star?"

Time after time the crow flew over the carcass, still calling, "I wonder if this is Falling-Star?" He came closer and closer with each pass. When he was close enough, Falling-Star sprang and grabbed the legs of the white crow. All of the other birds and animals scattered in every direction.

When Falling-Star brought the captive white crow home to the grandmother, she sent word for the chief.

"I will take the white crow to my lodge. I will tie him to the smoke hole and smoke him dead," said the chief.

From that moment on, the good Cheyennes were able to kill many buffalo and they had plenty of buffalo meat for all their needs.

The people in gratitude gave Falling-Star a lovely lodge-home and a pretty Indian maiden waiting there to become his wife. They remained all of their lives with the Northern Cheyenne Indian tribe.

Grinnell, "Falling-Star," 308-312.

■

# BUFFALO AND EAGLE WING

## *Unknown*

This story was written years ago by a pupil at the Haskell Institute, a school for Indian boys and girls. He had heard his grandfather tell it. The boy's exact tribe is unknown, although it was one from the Great Plains.

■

A long time ago there were no stones on the earth. The mountains, hills, and valleys were not rough, and it was easy to walk on the ground swiftly. There were no small trees at that time either. All the bushes and trees were tall and straight and were at equal distances. So a man could travel through a forest without having to make a path.

At that time, a large buffalo roamed over the land. From the water, he had obtained his spirit power—the power to change anything into some other form. He would have that power as long as he only drank from a certain pool.

In his wanderings, Buffalo often traveled across a high mountain. He liked this mountain so much that one day he asked it, "Would you like to be changed into something else?"

"Yes," replied the mountain. "I would like to be changed into something nobody would want to climb over."

"All right," said Buffalo. "I will change you into something hard that I will call 'stone.' You will be so hard that no one will want to break you, and so smooth that no one will want to climb you."

So Buffalo changed the mountain into a large stone. "And I give you the power to change yourself into anything else as long as you do not break yourself."

Only buffaloes lived in this part of the land. No people lived here. On the other side of the mountain lived men who were cruel and killed animals. The buffaloes knew about them and stayed as far away from them as possible. But one day Buffalo thought he would like to see these men. He hoped to make friends with them and persuade them not to kill buffaloes.

*Parfleche*
Sioux

So he went over the mountain and traveled along a stream until he came to a lodge. There lived an old woman and her grandson. The little boy liked Buffalo, and Buffalo liked the little boy and his grandmother. He said to them, "I have the power to change you into any form you wish. What would you like most to be?"

"I want always to be with my grandson. I want to be changed into anything that will make it possible for me to be with him, wherever he goes."

"I will take you to the home of the buffaloes," said their guest. "I will ask them to teach the boy to become a swift runner. I will ask the water to change the grandmother into something, so that you two can always be together."

So Buffalo, the grandmother, and the little boy went over the mountain to the land of the buffaloes.

"We will teach you to run swiftly," they told the boy, "if you will promise to keep your people from hunting and killing buffaloes."

"I promise," said the boy.

The buffaloes taught him to run so fast that not one of them could keep up with him. The old grandmother could follow him wherever he went, for she had been changed into Wind.

The boy stayed with the buffaloes until he became a man. Then they let him go back to his people, reminding him of his promise. Because he was such a swift runner, he became a leader of the hunters. They called him Eagle Wing.

One day the chief called Eagle Wing to him and said to him, "My son, I want you to take the hunters to the buffalo country. We have never been able to kill buffaloes because they run so very fast. But you too can run fast. If you will kill some buffaloes and bring home the meat and the skins, I will adopt you as my son. And when I die, you will become chief of the tribe."

Eagle Wing wanted so much to become chief that he pushed from his mind his promise to the buffaloes. He started out with the hunters, but he climbed the mountain so fast that they were soon left far behind. On the other side of the mountain, he saw a herd of buffaloes. They started to run in fright, but Eagle Wing followed them and killed most of them.

Buffalo, the great one who got his power from the water, was away from home at the time of the hunt. On his way back he grew so thirsty that he drank from some water on the other side of the mountain not from his special pool. When he reached home and saw what the hunter had done, he became very angry. He tried to turn the men into grass, but he could not. Because he had drunk from another pool, he had lost his power to transform.

Buffalo went to the big stone that had once been a mountain.

"What can you do to punish the hunter for what he has done?" he asked Stone.

"I will ask the trees to tangle themselves so that it will be difficult for men to travel through them," answered Stone. "I will break myself into many pieces and scatter myself all over the land. Then the swift runner and his followers cannot run over me without hurting their feet."

"That will punish them," agreed Buffalo.

So Stone broke itself into many pieces and scattered itself all over the land. Whenever the swift runner, Eagle Wing, and his followers tried to run over the mountain, stones cut their feet.  Bushes scratched and bruised their bodies.

That is how Eagle Wing was punished for not keeping his promise to Buffalo.

Clark, "Buffalo and Eagle Wing."

■

# THE SUN DANCE
## *Hidatsa*

The Hidatsa Tribe were a part of the Siouan family, also related to the Crow Indians, who lived in Montana on the Missouri River. The Sun Dance of the Hidatsa is similar to that of other tribes. Primarily, it is a prayer to the Sun-God for a Dancer's secret wishes: for his deliverance from his troubles, for supernatural aid, and for beneficent blessings upon all of his people.

■

For many moons this particular Dancer had dreamed of the Chief's daughter becoming his wife. He had a vision of himself performing the Sun Dance in supplication for his secret wish. The vision prompted him to call his tribe together for a Sun Dance. Then the Dancer went to a high place alone, declaring to the Sun-God:

"In the coming summer, I shall build your lodge. I shall stand in the holy place. I shall kill buffalo and take the hides for you. I shall dance for you to be worthy of my beloved that I may have her for my wife. I shall dance for you so that I may have visions to help protect me from my enemies, so that my people may grow strong, so that no disease may come, so that the buffalo may be plentiful, so there will be an abundance of rain throughout the year."

The young Dancer called upon his Mother and his Grandmother, saying, "Please tell all of your relatives that I shall perform the Sun Dance."  They spread the news and the tribal men gathered buffalo hides. These they brought to the tribal women for curing. The Dancer provided the feasts for all who came to the celebration of his Sun Dance.

When everything was in readiness, the Dancer took a buffalo robe to the Priest, one of his Father's clansman who was experienced in presiding over the Sun Dance Ceremony. The Priest represented the Sun-God. Before him the Dancer placed his buffalo robe and offered his pipe,

*Elk horn rake*
Hidatsa

saying, "Wise One, I have come to you for guidance. I wish to obtain the blessings of the Sun-God."

The Priest accepted the pipe and replied, "I am glad, my son, that you have come to me. I will aid you in this ceremony."

When the public announcement was made that the Sun Dance was to be given, the clansmen of the Dancer's Father asked for a scalp and left hand taken from an enemy. Sometimes both of these items were offered freely by a relative or purchased for a high price.

Before raising the sun-pole, a fresh buffalo head with a broad center strip of the back hide and tail were fastened with strong thongs to the top crotch of the sun-pole. Then the pole was raised and set firmly in the ground, with the buffalo head facing toward the setting-sun.

The sacred lodge was built by the Dancer and his clansmen. Men who owned medicine bundles brought them into the lodge of the Priest. The Dancer furnished each man with a buffalo robe upon which to lay his sacred bundle. The Dancer selected a favorite bundle that might be a red fox skin, for example, and for which the owner might ask the Dancer for a token.

The tribal Singer took the red fox skin and held it toward the burning incense. Then he touched it to the body of the Dancer and to that of his mother and Grandmother. Then he replaced it in front of its former owner. In this manner, the Dancer bought many of the medicine bundles and paid what the owners asked, in addition to his gifts of buffalo robes upon which rests each medicine bundle.

By this time, the Singer had learned the sacred songs and the manner of painting that each medicine required. The Singer taught the Dancer the secrets of each medicine that the Dancer bought. Some protect against enemies, some are good luck in contests, and some are for success in love and in hunting. When the Dancer had bought what he desired, the men went out, carrying his gift of the buffalo robe.

After construction of the Sun-Lodge, the Priest took the enemy scalp and left hand and raised them to the North Wind, South Wind, East Wind, and West Wind, saying, "I have often taken these in combat. May you have protection against your enemy always," giving them to the Dancer.

Young men, who are the Fasters and have their flesh pierced, arrived and went into the Sun-Lodge. Each carried his medicine bundle and an armful of sage. They crossed to the south side of the lodge, and each chose a place for his sage. They hung their medicine bundles on short sticks stuck in the ground in front of their sage.

The Dancer took the bundles that he brought and piled them on a buffalo skull. The Singer began the chants of mystery in a slow, measured rhythm. The incense was then burned. The Dancer trembled from excitement. The Priest took white paint, holding it in the incense smoke for a moment and smeared it over the body of the Dancer and drew a white circle around his face.

To complete dressing the Dancer, the Priest hung a medicine hoop on his back, held by a cord around his neck. On his head, the Priest placed a band of jackrabbit skin, with the head dropping over his left ear. An eagle-down feather was tied to the Dancer's scalplock, pointing backward. A whistle made of eagle-bone was hung around the Dancer's neck.

Meanwhile, the Fasters opened their medicine bundles, burned incense, painted themselves, and adorned themselves as they were taught by their elders and Guardian Spirits. Those having no medicine smeared themselves completely with white paint. Each Faster had an eagle-bone whistle hung from his neck and carried a shield and a lance.

The Singer painted himself and placed raven feathers in his hair. He arranged himself in front of the buffalo skin suspended from the sun-pole. He extended his arms toward it, rubbing his body as if receiving some special power from the buffalo.

Medicine-men arranged themselves south of the entrance to the Sun-Lodge. The old women of the tribe who prepared the spot for the Sun Dance, together with the medicine-women, sat on the north side. All come to pray and to fast. The relatives of the young male Fasters entered, carrying food. Each Faster took a bowlful of the food to a clansman of his father.

Then came the challenge to the Fasters' bravery. They appraoched the Priest and the Singer. Two small slits were cut in the shoulder skin of each young man presenting himself. Through the slotted skin, a leather thong was threaded with a wooden pin attached to the end, preventing the thong from pulling out of the slotted skin.

The other ends of these thongs were attached to the top of the sun-pole (similar to a Maypole). The Priest and Singer twirled each Faster four times, his feet barely touching the ground. Then the Faster swung free, twisting and circling around the sun-pole. But he dared not touch the thong with his hands. Any attempt to break the taboos was frowned upon by all his people as a lack of courage and endurance.

When the Faster finally broke loose from the sun-pole, he fell to the ground. Priest and Singer placed him gently on his bed of healing sage. There he remained and fasted from two to four days.

Any Dancer must first have been a Faster in an earlier Sun Dance. The Dancer danced back and forth continuously toward the sun-pole in the circle as long as a Faster was attached to the sun-pole. The Dancer sprang from the ground with his legs rigid and his feet together, his eyes fixed upon the buffalo head, and blew his eagle-bone whistle in rhythm with the beating drum.

The Dancer's mind was intent upon his desire to win his secret wish, the Chief's daughter, and to become a strong leader of his tribe. During his dance he prayed silently for those visions. He continued his dance until he fell from exhaustion. There he stayed until his visions appeared, or until the fourth day of the fast, if necessary.

The young Fasters lay upon their beds of sage. They have dreams and visions, which they related to the Priest. If they were sufficient, the Faster left the Sun-Lodge, because his supplications were answered by the Sun-God.

Near the doorway, the medicine-men still fasted and sought visions. Some of the younger boys of the tribe dragged buffalo heads through the village for fun.

If it was seen that a Faster cannot break away from the sun-pole and might be in danger, he was cut loose honorably. At the end of the fourth day, only a few Fasters still seeking visions remained.

The exhausted Dancer was taken to his lodge. If he or any Fasters wished to continue the Sun Dance, the Sun-Lodge was permitted to stand for them. Otherwise, it was torn down. Only the sun-pole with the buffalo head on top was left to mark the spot of the traditional Sun Dance.

The Dancer and all of the Fasters recovered honorably from their sacred experience.

In due time, the Chief of the Hidatsa tribe declared that the Dancer had won his daughter in marriage.

The Dancer went to the high ground, and in gratitude prayed and praised the Sun-God for the many blessings bestowed upon him and his beloved wife, and upon his tribe.

Curtis, *The North American Indian*, vol. iv, 152-155.

■

# THE CORN CEREMONY
## *Hidatsa*

The Corn Ceremony was held in the spring or early summer as a prayer to the spirits to grant bountiful harvests and strength to the tribe.

■

A man who in the preceding autumn had witnessed the ceremony in a dream, climbed to the top of his lodge. There he made a vow to the Corn Spirit, whose name, *Kadhutetash* means "Old Woman Who Never Dies."

"Hear me, Old Woman Who Never Dies," the man said in a loud voice. "I shall give a great feast in your honor for four reasons. I want to live to see another season. I want my people to become strong and

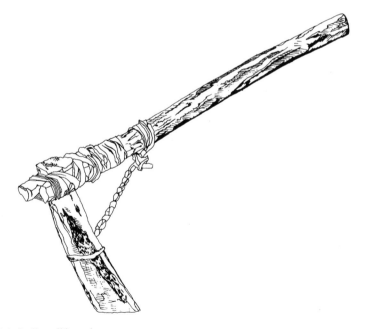

*Prairie Indian elkhorn hoe*
Hidatsa

prosperous. I want our harvest to be bountiful. And I want our children to become as abundant as the flowers in the spring."

All of his people would hear him, and he would hear a murmur of approval throughout all the village. He then began to collect robes, clothing, horses, and other things of value, to be given away as presents or exchanged as medicine bundles.

When everything was in readiness, he took a gift and a pipe to a man whom, he believed, had greater supernatural strength than himself. He requested this man to act as priest in the Corn Ceremony. If the man accepted the invitation and smoked the pipe, he became the Medicine Maker, the chief medicine man of the ceremony. The Medicine Maker soon went to the lodge of the Singer, who knew all the songs and secrets of the ceremony. When the Medicine Maker offered him a robe and invited him to participate in the Corn Ceremony, the Singer gladly accepted. They then smoked the pipe together.

When the Medicine Maker had left the lodge, the Singer dressed and painted himself. Taking a piece of charcoal, he made three motions, as if he were painting his face. The fourth time, he drew a mark across his face as he sang:

"I am walking. I am walking."

The words meant that he was still following the instructions that the Old Woman Who Never Dies gave to the first priests of the first Corn Ceremony. He then placed a necklace of corn ears about his neck as he sang, "Yellow, Yellow," meaning "corn." Taking an ear of corn in his hand, he chanted:

"I am standing. I am walking."

Putting on a cap of the head-skin of his medicine animal—the kit-fox, for example—he sang:

"Kit-fox is walking. Kit-fox is walking."

When he was ready to depart, he addressed Old Woman Who Never Dies by singing:

"Young Woman, your fire-smoke I see;
I am coming. It is here."

The Singer then went to the lodge of the Medicine Maker, where those who were to participate in the ceremony were seated. They had been invited because their medicines were various birds that were thought to be the children of Old Woman Who Never Dies, and were therefore particularly appropriate for this ceremony. Their medicine bundles were laid in the center of the lodge.

The Medicine Maker burned incense, and then all started for the lodge of the man who had made the vow. He was called the *votary*. The Medicine Maker led the group, carrying the head of a deer. The others followed, with the Singer in the center.

As they approached his lodge, the votary came forth with a pipe, which he offered to the Medicine Maker. He took a few whiffs and then returned the pipe. This stopping and smoking occurred four times before the group reached the votary's lodge.

In the place of honor in his lodge, a very fine buffalo skin had been spread as an altar. Upon it the Medicine Maker placed the deer's head he had carried. The Singer sat behind it, and at his right sat the Medicine Maker, the votary and his wife, and the other participants. Buffalo robes had been spread in front of the positions taken by the assisting medicine men. Each of them placed his medicine bundle upon his particular robe.

The Medicine Maker raised the deer's head and touched the body of the votary's wife with it. Then each of the medicine men touched her body with his bundle and laid it in front of the altar, on robes that had been spread out for that purpose. This part of the ceremony was to give to the woman the strength and the power contained in the medicine bundles.

The votary and his wife then seated themselves on the side of the lodge at the left of the Singer. The Singer said to the votary, "Bring a live coal from the fire in the center of the lodge and lay it on an earthen bowl."

Near it was a special bowl that was considered a symbol of Old Woman Who Never Dies. From it, the Singer took a handful of sage. After making a slow motion toward each of the Four Winds, the Singer lowered the sage to the hot coal, made four circles over it, and let the handful of sage fall.

The Medicine Maker waved a large bundle of sage over the smoke. Everyone was silent. The Singer took up the bowl in which the incense burned and passed it back and forth over the medicine bundles. As he passed it, he sang, again and again:

> Sage is good.
> Sage is good.

When he had set the bowl down, all the people stretched their hands toward it and rubbed themselves as if they were receiving its power. The votary filled a pipe and handed it to the medicine man at the end of the row. After inhaling a puff or two, he passed it to the one seated at his left.

When all had smoked, the Singer raised one of the medicine bundles, perhaps the raven, and sang as its owner came forward:

> Raven is walking.  Raven is walking.
> *Pedhifska didahuft.*
> Raven is walking.

The Raven man took the bundle from the Singer's hands and danced backward and forward between the altar and the fireplace. He held the bundle in his hands and swung it back and forth and from side to side. As he danced, he and the Singer chanted:

> Raven is dancing back and forth.
> Raven is dancing back and forth.

The Medicine Maker brought choice bits of meat and pretended to feed the Raven bundle!  The votary then gave it back to him, and he returned to his seat.  His wife gathered up the presents offered to his medicine by the votary.

The Singer thus called, in the correct order, each of the medicine men, and learned the songs as he had learned the Raven songs. When all these songs had been repeated, the votary and his wife brought food and placed it before the altar. The Singer chanted the prayer to The One Who First Made All Things:

> *Madhidift, Ifdihkawahidith.*
> I am walking in your path.

The votary brought a dish of choice parts of meat and laid it before the Singer.  He sang:

> "Old Woman Who Never Dies, I am walking in your path."

Lifting the dish, he extended it to the Four Winds and then threw the meat among the medicine men while he sang:

> I take; I offer; it is done.

This was allegorical of the feeding of her birds by Old Woman Who Never Dies. The people scrambled for the food, chirping like blackbirds, ravens, and chickadees.  The votary and his wife distributed the remainder of the food among the participants and the spectators. When the feast was finished, the owners of the medicine bundles advanced to receive them, while the Singer chanted:

I am walking; I have finished.
The land is green,
The land is yellow,
The land is gray.

The Medicine Maker took a bundle of sage and waved it toward the Four Winds and toward the door, as if to rid the lodge of evil spirits. The Singer brushed himself with sage, removed his cap and his necklace of corn ears, and then washed his face with water brought by the votary. His last song was this:

*Kadhakowift; huft—*
It is done; come—.

This song meant that the vow had been fulfilled and asked the Corn Spirit to answer the prayers for a bountiful harvest.

Curtis, *The North American Indian, vol. iv, 149-152.*

■

# AN ADDRESS TO MOTHER CORN
## *Arikara*

The Arikaras came from the south, many years ago, to the Missouri River in what is now North Dakota and the Fort Berthold Reservation in South Dakota, where they live today. With them, they brought not only reliance on corn as their most important agricultural crop, but also their appreciation of it as a divine gift. The Great Spirit Above gave them corn and they show their gratitude every year in their ceremonies.

■

In these religious ceremonies, corn was honored and referred to in the endearing and also the highly respectful title of "Mother Corn." At a certain time in the ritual, one of the leaders of the tribe made an address to Mother Corn in the following words, or in words with similar effect.

"In ancient time the Great Spirit Above sent Mother Corn to our people to be their friend and helper, to give them support and health and strength. She has walked with our people on the long and difficult

*Cooking pot*
Arikara

path that they have traveled from the faraway past, and now she marches with us toward the future.

"In the dim, distant past days, Mother Corn gave food to our ancestors. As she gave it to them, she now gives it to us. And as she was faithful and bountiful to our forefathers and to us, so will she be faithful and bountiful to our children. Now and in all time to come, she will give to us the blessings for which we have prayed.

"Mother Corn leads us as she led our fathers and our mothers down through the ages. The path of Mother Corn lies ahead, and we walk with her, day by day. We go forward with hope and confidence in the future, just as our ancestors did during all the past ages. When the lonely prairie stretched wide and fearful before us, we were doubtful and afraid. But Mother Corn strengthened and encouraged us.

"Now Mother Corn's return makes our hearts glad. Give thanks! Give thanks to Mother Corn! She brings us a blessing. She brings us peace and plenty. She comes from the Great Spirit Above, who has brought us good things."

Throughout the address and the elaborate ceremony that preceded and followed it, a stalk of corn stood before the altar, representing the spirit of Mother Corn.

About sunset, the staff of corn was dressed like a woman and carried at the head of a religious procession to the brink of the nearby river. White people call it the Missouri River; the Arikaras always called it the Mysterious Waters. With reverence, they placed the stalk in the water so that it might float along as a symbol of their affection for Mother Corn.

Gilmore, *Prairie Smoke*, 172-174.

■

# THE BUFFALO DANCE
## *Mandan*

Since 1700 the Mandan tribe maintained their camp in North Dakota, where they belonged to the Siouan linguistic family. Mandans lived at a strategic point on the Missouri River between Heart River and the Little Missouri Rivers, N.D. Their traditions resemble those of more eastern tribes. They became historically famous when Captains Lewis and Clark chose the site of Mandan settlement to build their first winter camp of 1804-05. There Captain Lewis hired Sacagawea and her husband Charbonneau to join the expedition as interpreters. Sacagawea was Shoshone and was able to get horses from the Shoshones to cross the Rocky Mountains. Later, in 1806, the explorers arrived at the Mandan village on their return from the Pacific Ocean. In 1837, the Mandans were nearly wiped out by smallpox, and later moved to Fort Berthold, N.D.

■

Not too long ago, the buffalo was the principal source of food and clothing for the Mandan Indian tribe.

For these reasons, each year their tribe held a feastival to honor the buffalo. It became the chief celebration, a feast for all, marking the time for the buffalo's return. The buffalo-hunting season followed.

The most exciting event of the festival was the Buffalo Dance. Eight men participated, wearing buffalo skins on their backs and painting themselves black, red, and white. Dancers endeavored to imitate the buffalo on the prairie.

Each dancer held a rattle in his right hand, and in his left a six-foot rod. On his head, he wore a bunch of green willow boughs. The season for the return of the buffalo coincided with the willow trees in full leaf.

Another dance required only four tribesmen, representing the four main directions of the compass from which the buffalo might come. With a canoe in the center, two dancers, dressed as grizzly bears who might attack the hunters, took their places on each side. They growled and threatened to spring upon anyone who might interfere with the ceremony.

Onlookers tried to appease the grizzlies by tossing food to them. The two dancers would pounce upon the food, carrying it away to the prairie as possible lures for the coming of the buffaloes.

During the ceremony, the old men of the tribe beat upon drums and chanted prayers for successful buffalo hunting.

By the end of the fourth day of the Buffalo Dance, a man entered the camp disguised as the evil spirit of famine. Immediately he was driven away by shouts and stone-throwing from the younger Mandans, who waited excitedly to participate in the ceremony.

When the demon of famine was successfully driven away, the entire tribe joined in the bountiful thanksgiving feast, symbolic of the early return of buffalo to the Mandan hunting-grounds.

Spence, *Myths of North American Indians*, 134-135.

■

# SUN DANCE MOUNTAIN
## *Dakota-Sioux*

The Sun Dance was an important religious ceremony performed by many North American Indian tribes. It was of most importance and most spectacular among the Plains Indians. "It reached its fullest development among the Teton band of Dakota Sioux, who regarded the sun as the greatest manifestation of the mysterious, all-pervading power *waka taka*....The ceremony was held usually during the summer solstice."

■

Near the northwest corner of the Black Hills of South Dakota stands Sun Dance Mountain. Its forbidding cliffs look tall against the western sky. At the foot of this strange mountain, the Dakota-Sioux Indians of the area held their annual dance in honor of their sacred Sun God.

Many, many years ago, a wise old warrior said to a beautiful maiden, "If you will marry a brave that is pleasing to the Sun God, you will bring good fortune to yourself and to all of our people."

The beautiful maiden had many wooers, and knew many young men who had ponies and gold and who would like to marry her. But she really favored one who had nothing to offer her except his love. She promised him that when he had the blessing of the sun, she would marry him.

So the young brave started forth to seek the Sun and get his blessing. After many months of search and difficulties, he found the Sun God and

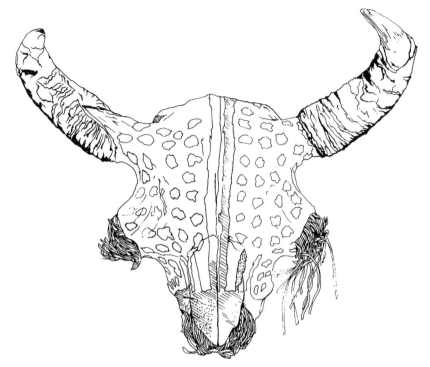

*Plains Indian Sun Dance buffalo skull*
Dakota-Sioux

received his blessing. He then returned to his beloved, and they were married.

After the marriage ceremony, the people of the young brave held dance at the foot of the mountain. Many different kinds of dances were performed, including the Sun Dance. The Sun Dancers danced all the day under the scorching sun. Some of them had no food and no water all day. Some pierced their ears, so that they would bleed while they danced.

They made these sacrifices in order to obtain the favor of the Great Spirit Above. This dance, honoring the marriage of the beautiful maiden to the young brave who had been blessed by the Sun, became an annual affair.

The dances that were held at the base of Sun Dance Mountain were revered by the Indians for a long, long time.

Kurath, *Standard Dictionary of Folklore, Mythology, and Legend*, vol. 2, 1088-1089

Price, *Black Hills: Land of Legend*, 42-43.

■

# ORIGIN OF THE PRAIRIE ROSE
## Dakota-Sioux

■

Long, long ago, when the world was young and people had not come out yet, no flowers bloomed on the prairie. Only grasses and dull, greenish gray shrubs grew there. Earth felt very sad because her robe lacked brightness and beauty.

"I have many beautiful flowers in my heart," Earth said to herself. "I wish they were on my robe. Blue flowers like the clear sky in fair weather, white flowers like the snow of winter, brilliant yellow ones like the sun at midday, pink ones like the dawn of a spring day—all these are in my heart. I am sad when I look on my dull robe, all gray and brown."

A sweet little pink flower heard Earth's sad talking. "Do not be sad, Mother Earth. I will go upon your robe and beautify it."

So the little pink flower came up from the heart of the Earth Mother to beautify the prairies. But when the Wind Demon saw her, he growled, "I will not have that pretty flower on my playground."

He rushed at her, shouting and roaring, and blew out her life. But her spirit returned to the heart of Mother Earth.

When other flowers gained courage to go forth, one after another, Wind Demon killed them also. And their spirits returned to the heart of Mother Earth.

At last Prairie Rose offered to go. "Yes, sweet child," said Earth Mother, "I will let you go. You are so lovely and your breath so fragrant that surely the Wind Demon will be charmed by you. Surely he will let you stay on the prairie."

So Prairie Rose made the long journey up through the dark ground and came out on the drab prairie. As she went, Mother Earth said in her heart, "Oh, I do hope that Wind Demon will let her live."

When Wind Demon saw her, he rushed toward her, shouting: "She is pretty, but I will not allow her on my playground. I will blow out her life."

So he rushed on, roaring and drawing his breath in strong gusts. As he came closer, he caught the fragrance of Prairie Rose.

"Oh—how sweet!" he said to himself. "I do not have it in my heart to blow out the life of such a beautiful maiden with so sweet a breath. She must stay here with me. I must make my voice gentle, and I must sing sweet songs. I must not frighten her away with my awful noise."

*Bone beads*
Sioux

So Wind Demon changed. He became quiet. He sent gentle breezes over the prairie grasses. He whispered and hummed little songs of gladness. He was no longer a demon.

Then other flowers came up from the heart of the Earth Mother, up through the dark ground. They made her robe, the prairie, bright and joyous. Even Wind came to love the blossoms growing among the grasses of the prairie. And so the robe of Mother Earth became beautiful because of the loveliness, the sweetness, and the courage of the Prairie Rose.

Sometimes Wind forgets his gentle songs and becomes loud and noisy. But his loudness does not last long. And he does not harm a person whose robe is the color of Prairie Rose.

Gilmore, *Prairie Smoke: A Collection of Lore of the Prairies*, 48-49, 200-203.

■

# THE HERMIT, OR THE GIFT OF CORN
## *Dakota-Sioux*

Corn entered widely into the mythology and religious practices of North American Indian tribes of the Southwest, Southeast, Plains, and Eastern woodlands. Corn gods in different regions are personified as Corn Mother, Corn Maidens, and even Corn Grandfathers as in this story of the hermit. Various parts of the corn plant are used ritually such as husks, pollen, kernels, and whole ears. Major tribal ceremonies are held prior to corn planting and after the harvest.

■

Alone in a deep forest, far from the village of his people, lived a hermit. His tent was made of buffalo skins, and his robe was made of deerskin. Far from the haunts of any human being, this old hermit was content to spend his many years.

All day long, he wandered through the forest, studying the different plants and collecting roots. The roots he used as food and as medicine. At long intervals some warrior would arrive at his tent and get medicinal roots from him for the tribe. The old hermit's medicine was considered far superior to all others.

One day, after a long ramble in the woods, the hermit came home so tired that, immediately after eating, he lay down on his bed. Just as he was dozing off to sleep, he felt something rub against his feet. Awakening with a start, he noticed a dark object. It extended an arm toward him. In its hand was a flint-pointed arrow.

"This must be a spirit," thought the hermit, "for there is no human being here but me."

A voice then said, "Hermit, I have come to invite you to my home."

"I will come," the old hermit replied. So he arose, wrapped his robe around him, and started toward the voice.

Outside his door, he looked around, but he could see no sign of the dark object.

"Whatever you are, or wherever you be," said the hermit, "wait for me. I do not know where to go to find your house."

He received no answer, nor did he hear any sound of someone walking through the brush. Reentering his tent, he lay down and was soon fast asleep.

The next night he again heard the voice say, "Hermit, I have come to invite you to my home." The hermit walked out of his tent to find the person with that voice, but again he found no one. This time he was angry, because he thought that someone was making sport of him. He determined to find out who was disturbing his night's rest.

The next evening he cut a hole in the tent large enough to stick an arrow through. Then he stood by the door, watching. Soon the dark object came, stopped outside the door, and said, "Grandfather, I came to——" But he never finished his sentence. The old hermit had shot his

*Plains Indian ladle*
Dakota-Sioux

arrow. He heard it strike something that produced a sound as though he had shot into a sack of pebbles.

Early the next morning the hermit went out and looked at the spot near where he thought his arrow had struck some object. There on the ground lay a little heap of corn, and from this little heap a small line of corn lay scattered along a path. The old hermit followed this path into the woods.

When he reached a small mound, the trail ended. At its end was a large circle from which the grass had been scraped off clean.

"The corn trail stops at the edge of this circle," the old man said to himself. "So this must be the home of whatever invited me."

He took his big bone axe and knife and proceeded to dig down into the center of the circle. When he got as far down as he could reach, he came to a sack of dried meat. Next, he found a sack of turnips, then a sack of dried cherries, and then a sack of corn.

Last of all was another sack, empty except for one cup of corn. In the other corner was a hole where the hermit's arrow had pierced the sack. From this hole the corn had been scattered along the trail, which had guided the old man to the hiding place.

From this experience the hermit taught his people how to keep their provisions while they were traveling.

"Dig a pit," he explained to them, "put your provisions into it, and cover them with earth."

By this method, the Sioux used to keep provisions all summer. When fall came, they would return to their hiding place. When they opened it, they would find all their provisions as fresh as they were the day they had been placed there.

The people thanked the old hermit for his discovery of this method of preserving their food. And they thanked him for his discovery of corn, the first they had seen. It became one of the most important foods the Indians knew.

McLaughlin, *Myths and Legends of the Sioux*, 101-103.

■

# THE LEGEND OF STANDING ROCK

## *Dakota-Sioux*

The Dakota-Sioux are one of the most famous tribes in North America. They belong to the Siouan linguistic family, known since about 1600. They spread from Mississippi to Minnesota, Wisconsin, Iowa, North and South Dakota, Montana, Nebraska, and Wyoming. Gold discoveries in the Black Hills caused a rush of miners to the region, who existed in warlike conflict with the Dakota-Sioux, leading to General Custer's defeat at Little Big Horn, June 25, 1876.

■

Years ago, a man from the Dakota-Sioux tribe married a girl from the Arikara tribe. After they had one child, the man brought another wife to their home. The first wife pouted because she was jealous. When time came for their people to break camp, she refused to move from her place. After their tent was taken down, she sat there, on the ground, with her baby on her back. Her husband and the rest of their people moved on.

At noon, her husband stopped the line of people and said to his two brothers, "Go back to your sister-in-law. Tell her to come on. We will wait for you here. But hurry! I fear that she may become desperate and kill herself."

The two rode off and in the evening arrived at their last camping place. The woman still sat on the ground. The elder brother said to her, "Sister-in-law, we have come to get you. The camp is waiting for you. Get up and join us."

When she did not answer, brother-in-law put out his hand and touched her lightly on her head. She had turned into stone!

The two brothers lashed their ponies and rode back to camp. They told their story, but were not believed. "She has killed herself," said her husband, "and my brothers will not tell me."

The whole village broke camp and returned to the place where they had left the woman. There she sat, a block of stone in the form of a woman. Her husband's people were very excited. They chose a pony, a handsome one, made a new travois, and placed the stone in its carrying net. Pony and travois were beautifully painted and then decorated with streamers of various colors. The stone was considered holy, and was given a place of honor in the center of the camp.

Whenever the people moved and made a new camp, the stone and travois were taken with them. For years the stone woman traveled with that group. It stands today in front of the Standing Rock Indian Agency in South Dakota.

McLaughlin, *Myths and Legends of the Sioux*, 40-41.

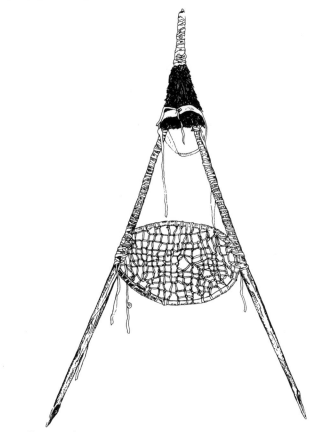

*Plains Indian travois*
Dakota-Sioux

■

# THE MYSTERIOUS BUTTE
## *Dakota-Sioux*

■

One time, long ago, when a young man was out hunting, he came to a steep hill. Its east side suddenly dropped off in a precipitous bank. As he stood on that bank he noticed, at the base, a small opening. Examining it closely after going down the slope, he found that the opening was really large enough for a horse or a buffalo to walk through. On each side of this opening he was surprised to see figures of several different animals carved in the wall.

When he entered, he was amazed to see scattered on the floor before him many pipes, bracelets, and other things that people use as ornaments. They seemed to have been offerings to some great spirit.

Passing through this first room, he entered the second and found it so dark that he could not see his hands in front of him. He was frightened. He hurriedly left the place, returned home, and told what he had seen.

The Chief, hearing the young man's story, immediately selected four of his most daring warriors to go with the young man to find out whether or not he was telling the truth. When they reached the place, the young man refused to go inside because on each side of the entrance, the carved figures had been changed!

The four who entered saw that in the first room everything was exactly as the young man had described it. So was their first glimpse of the second room—so dark that they could not see anything. But they continued walking, feeling their way along the walls. At last they found another entrance—or exit. This one was so narrow that they had to squeeze through it sideways. Again they found their way along the walls until they found another opening. This one was so low that they had to crawl on their hands and knees in order to go into the next room.

It was the last one. Entering it, they were surprised by a very sweet odor coming from the opposite direction. Crawling on their hands and knees, and feeling around with their fingers, they found a hole in the ground. Through that hole came the sweet odor. The four warriors hurriedly held a council and decided to return at once to the camp and report what they had learned.

When they reached the first chamber, one young man said, "I am going to take these bracelets to show that we are telling the truth."

"No!" the other three exclaimed promptly. "You are in the abode of some Great Spirit. Some accident may happen to you for taking something that is not yours."

"Aw! You fellows are like old women!" He took a beautiful bracelet and placed it on his left wrist.

When the men reached the village, they reported what they had seen. The one wearing the bracelet shows it, to prove that they had told the truth.

In a short time, these four men were out preparing traps for wolves. As usual, they raised one end of a heavy log and placed a stick under it to hold it up. About five feet from the log, they placed a large piece of meat and covered the space between meat and log with poles and willows. At the spot where they placed the stick, they left a hole large enough to admit the body of a wolf. A wolf would smell the meat and be unable to reach it and because of the poles and willows, the men felt sure, would crowd itself into the hole. Then it would work itself forward in order to get the meat. When its movement pushed down the stick, the log would trap the wolf under its weight.

When the young man wearing the bracelet followed this procedure with a large piece of meat, the log caught the wrist on which he wore the bracelet. Unable to release himself, he called loud and long for help. Hearing his call, his companions hurried to assist him. When they lifted the log, they found that the man's wrist had been broken.

"Now you have been punished," they said. "You have been punished for taking the bracelet out of the chamber of this mysterious butte."

Some time later, a young man who went to the butte saw engraved on the wall the figure of a woman holding a pole in her hand. With it she was holding up a large amount of meat that had been laid across another pole. It had been broken in two from the weight of so much meat. On the wall, on all sides of the figure of the woman, were the footprints of buffalo.

The next day an enormous herd of buffalo came near the village, and a great many were killed. The women were very busy cutting up and drying the meat. More buffalo meat was at one camp than was at any other. When one of the women was hanging meat upon a long tent pole, the pole broke in two. So she had to hold the meat up with another pole, just as in the engraving the young man had seen on that mysterious butte.

Even after that, the people paid weekly visits to this butte, and would read there the signs that would govern their plans. The butte has been considered the prophet of the band of Sioux who told this story for generations and generations.

McLaughlin, *Myths and Legends of the Sioux*, 104-107.

■

# ORIGIN OF THE SIOUX PEACE PIPE
## *Dakota-Sioux*

■

Long, long ago, two young and handsome Sioux were chosen by their band to find out where the buffalo were. While the men were riding in the buffalo country, they saw someone in the distance walking toward them.

As always they were on the watch for any enemy. So they hid in some bushes and waited. At last the figure came up the slope. To their surprise, the figure walking toward them was a woman.

When she came closer, she stopped and looked at them. They knew that she could see them, even in their hiding place. On her left arm she carried what looked like a stick in a bundle of sagebrush. Her face was beautiful.

One of the men said, "She is more beautiful than anyone I have ever seen. I want her for my wife."

But the other man replied, "How dare you have such a thought? She is wondrously beautiful and holy—far above ordinary people."

Though still at a distance, the woman heard them talking. She laid down her bundle and spoke to them. "Come. What is it you wish?"

The man who had spoken first went up to her and laid his hands on her as if to claim her. At once, from somewhere above, there came a whirlwind. Then there came a mist, which hid the man and the woman. When the mist cleared, the other man saw the woman with the bundle again on her arm. But his friend was a pile of bones at her feet.

The man stood silent in wonder and awe. Then the beautiful woman spoke to him. "I am on a journey to your people. Among them is a good man whose name is Bull Walking Upright. I am coming to see him especially.

"Go on ahead of me and tell your people that I am on my way. Ask them to move camp and to pitch their tents in a circle. Ask them to leave an opening in the circle, facing the north. In the center of the circle, make a large tepee, also facing the north. There I will meet Bull Walking Upright and his people."

The man saw to it that all her directions were followed. When she reached the camp, she removed the sagebrush from the gift she was carrying. The gift was a small pipe made of red stone. On it was carved the tiny outline of a buffalo calf.

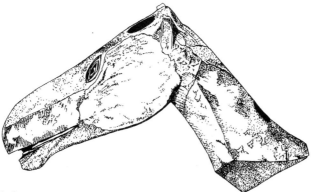

*Horsehead pipe*
Sioux

The pipe she gave to Bull Walking Upright, and then she taught him the prayers he should pray to the Strong One Above. "When you pray to the Strong One Above, you must use this pipe in the ceremony. When you are hungry, unwrap the pipe and lay it bare in the air. Then the buffalo will come where the men can easily hunt and kill them. So the children, the men, and the women will have food and be happy."

The beautiful woman also told him how the people should behave in order to live peacefully together. She taught them the prayers they should say when praying to their Mother Earth. She told him how they should decorate themselves for ceremonies.

"The earth," she said, "is your mother. So, for special ceremonies, you will decorate yourselves as your mother does—in black and red, in brown and white. These are the colors of the buffalo also.

"Above all else, remember that this is a peace pipe that I have given you. You will smoke it before all ceremonies. You will smoke it before making treaties. It will bring peaceful thoughts into your minds. If you will use it when you pray to the Strong One above and to Mother Earth, you will be sure to receive the blessings that you ask."

When the woman had completed her message, she turned and slowly walked away. All the people watched her in awe. Outside the opening of the circle, she stopped for an instant and then lay down on the ground. She rose again in the form of a black buffalo cow. Again she lay down, and then arose in the form of a red buffalo cow. A third time she lay down, and arose as a brown buffalo cow. The fourth and last time she had the form of a spotlessly white buffalo cow. Then she walked toward the north into the distance and finally disappeared over a far-off hill.

Bull Walking Upright kept the peace pipe carefully wrapped most of the time. Every little while he called all his people together, untied the bundle, and repeated the lessons he had been taught by the beautiful woman.  And he used it in prayers and other ceremonies until he was more than one hundred years old.

When he became feeble, he held a great feast.  There he gave the pipe and the lessons to Sunrise, a worthy man.  In a similar way the pipe was passed down from generation to generation.  "As long as the pipe is used," the beautiful woman had said, "Your people will live and will be happy.  As soon as it is forgotten, the people will perish."

McLaughlin, *Myths and Legends of the Sioux*, 72- 74.

■

# LEGEND OF THE THUNDER GOD
## *Dakota-Sioux*

The Black Hills of South Dakota, "with more than a thousand square miles of mysterious, haze-shrouded peaks, peaceful flowering valleys, turbulent streams and gold-ribbed cliffs, have been aptly termed 'the Happy Hunting Ground of the Dakotas.'"

■

When the Thunder God spoke among the people of the Black Hills, the Medicine Man called together the frightened warriors.  They were huddled in the lodges of their camp along the Belle Fourche River.  He told them this story:

"You who now listen will not be harmed.  It is said that the Evil Spirit once became so angry at the Red People that he caused the mountains to vomit fire and hot stones to terrify them.  Their lodges and their children were destroyed.  The Great Spirit had compassion, put out the fire, and chased the Evil Spirit away.

"But when they returned to their wickedness, the Great Spirit permitted the Evil Spirit to return to the mountains and again vomit forth fire.  When again the Red People became good and made sacrifices to the Great Spirit, He chased away the Evil Spirit and kept him from disturbing the people.

"For forty snows, they were undisturbed, except occasionally.  Sometimes the Great Spirit would warn them, through thunder, that if they should return to their wickedness He would have them punished.  Again He would have the mountains vomit forth fire and hot stones, and thus destroy them.  Even today He occasionally warns us.

"So return now to your lodges, and do not be afraid. The Red People now will come to no harm."

Price, *Black Hills: Land of Legend*, 44.

■

# A Teton Ghost Story
## *Dakota-Sioux*

Long ago there was a large band of Dakota-Sioux Indians who had spread to a village in the present Jackson Hole Basin of Grand Teton National Park in Wyoming.

■

The Teton band flourished, and its people were healthy and strong because they ate plenty of buffalo meat. Usually when they camped for the night, a crier would go among the lodges and call:

"There will be many buffalo tomorrow. Be on the alert!"

One day after the Tetons returned to their camp from a hard buffalo hunt, a young man announced that he wished to marry the most beautiful girl in the tribe, the Chief's daughter.

Her father said, "I will not give you my permission until you bring me many horses." So the young Indian set out in search of many wild horses, hoping to please the Chief and win his beautiful daughter for his bride.

While the young brave was away, his tribe abandoned their regular campsite and moved elsewhere. Later, the young Indian returned to the deserted camp with several captured horses. As it was late in the day, he thought he would take shelter nearby in a solitary lodge.

At first, he could not find a doorway into the lodge, because the sides were covered halfway up with sod. Finally, he managed to make an entrance. Inside were four high posts that had been driven into the ground.

The posts supported a kind of burial bed. On the bed lay a woman whose clothes were ornamented with elk's teeth. She turned her head, looking down at the young Teton brave. He immediately recognized her as a member of his tribe—but now she was a Woman Ghost! They stayed there for a long time and she became his wife.

One day he said to himself, "I think I will go on a buffalo hunt." Although he did not speak aloud, the Ghost Woman knew his thoughts and said, "You are hungry for buffalo meat? Mount your horse and ride back to the bluffs.

"When you come to the buffalo herd, rush into the center of them and shoot the fattest one. Bring home the hide and buffalo meat. Roast the meat and bring me a share before you eat yours."

The young Teton Indian brave left and followed Ghost Woman's instructions. When he reached the valley, he came to a large herd of buffalo. He charged his horse at full speed into the middle of them and shot the fattest one. He skinned it and cut up the meat, carrying the robe and meat upon his packhorse. He skewered a large piece of meat and roasted it until it was cooked enough, then he took it to Ghost Woman, who was standing in the center of the lodge.

Her husband was startled to see her standing there. Rows and rows of beautiful beadwork decorated her leather clothing. Already knowing what the young brave was thinking she said, "Please do not be afraid of me!"

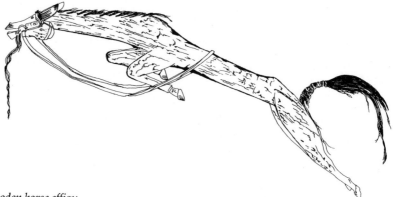

*Wooden horse effigy*
Sioux

From that time on, they talked freely and planned what they would like to do. The young Indian brave said, "Why don't we begin our life together like our parents did when they were first married?"

But the Ghost Woman replied, "No, no, that would never do, because we will need to pitch our tent during the day and travel by night." The young brave wondered about this arrangement.

That is how it happened that they traveled at night. Ghost Woman walked ahead with her head covered, never saying a word to her husband as they traveled. Her legs were invisible. She made no noise as she floated along, ghostlike.

Whenever the young Teton Indian brave thought about anything, Ghost Woman already knew what it was that he had in his mind. Is this why the Teton Indians say, "Beware of Ghosts because Ghosts know all things."

They say Ghosts know when the winds blow and which ones. Ghosts know when there will be snow. Ghosts know when there will be thunder and lightning. Ghosts are glad when the winds blow, because they can float along more swiftly as they travel from place to place.

This is the way Teton Ghost Woman and the young Teton brave lived. Their tribal people never found them again. The Chief's daughter wondered why her young brave never returned to her.

Finally, the young brave also became a Teton Ghost, floating along with the Teton Ghost Woman, every night, forever.

J. O. Dorsey, "Teton Ghost Story," 71-72.

■

# How Medicine Man Resurrected Buffalo

## *Arapaho*

The Arapaho tribe were unusual as they occupied many different regions while migrating westward. They lived for some time in the Red River Valley of Minnesota and North Dakota territories before they crossed the Missouri River and settled in Wyoming. There they divided into the Northern Arapaho and Southern Arapaho. The latter settled on a reservation in Oklahoma, while the Northern Arapaho joined the Shoshones on the Wind River Reservation in Wyoming. In the early 1800s, the Arapaho were famous for raiding other tribes and white settlements on the Great Plains.

■

At one time an Arapaho Medicine Man named Black-Robe wanted very much to be able to make magic because his people were very hungry. How could he lure the buffaloes back to the Arapaho hunting grounds? Buffalo meat was their principal food.

Black-Robe decided to ask Cedar-Tree for his help. "Go west and hunt buffalo for our people. Try very hard to find at least one buffalo."

Cedar-Tree hunted hard as he was asked to do. After a long time, he saw some black objects at a distance. "Could they be buffaloes?" he wondered.

Encouraged, he walked faster, but as he drew closer he was less sure the black objects were buffaloes. Suddenly, he saw the black things fly toward the sky. By then, Cedar-Tree seemed certain the objects were oversized ravens.

Disappointed, he returned to his village, reporting to Black-Robe what he had seen. The Medicine Man scolded him for not believing that what he had seen were buffaloes.

"If you had only believed strong enough, the buffaloes would not have changed to ravens," said Black Robe.

By now the Arapahoes were desperately hungry. One woman on the verge of starving made soup from the soles of her moccasins. The next day her uncle, Trying-Bear, set out early to hunt for anything edible. He had no weapons. Fortunately, on the way he met Black-Robe who loaned him a bow and some arrows.

"Tomorrow morning, I will come to your tent to learn of your success," said Black-Robe. "You must even try to find a dried buffalo, if not a live one."

After hunting a long time to the northwest, Trying-Bear finally found a dried buffalo. He ran home swiftly to tell his people. Black-Robe painted his white pony black and wrapped a black buffalo robe about himself. He stuck his lucky eagle-feather in his hair, mounted his black pony, and took off in a rush to find the dried buffalo.

"Follow me, Trying Bear," Black-Robe called.

Because he wanted to see what Black-Robe would do with the dried buffalo, Trying-Bear followed rapidly. Medicine Man arrived about midday at the place of the dead buffalo. He dismounted, took aim with his magic eagle-feather, and threw it straight at the carcass. Immediately, a live buffalo jumped to its feet!

Black-Robe turned and saw Trying-Bear. "Shoot it!" commanded Medicine Man. Trying-Bear shot it dead.

"Let's skin it and carry everything eatable back to our people," said Black-Robe.

A feast of thanksgiving and rejoicing followed. Black-Robe had saved his people from starvation. Arapahoes still love to tell this story of how their Medicine Man resurrected the dead buffalo with his magic eagle-feather-medicine!

Voth, "How Medicine Man Resurrected Buffalo," 44.

■

# THE BUFFALO ROCK

## *Blackfeet*

The buffalo rock, as called by the Blackfeet Indians, was usually a fossil shell of some kind, picked up on the prairie. Whoever found one was considered fortunate, for it was thought to give a person great power over buffalo. The owner put the stone in his lodge, near the fire, and prayed over it. This story reveals not only the use of such a rock, but also a common method of hunting buffalo before the Indians had horses.

■

There was once a very poor woman, the second wife of a Blackfeet. Her buffalo robe was old and full of holes; her buffalo moccasins were worn and ripped. She and her people were camped not far from a cliff that would be a good place for a buffalo drive. They were very much in need of buffalo, for they were not only ragged but starving.

One day while this poor woman was gathering wood, she heard a voice singing. Looking around, she found that the song was coming from a buffalo rock. It sang, "Take me. Take me. I have great power."

So the woman took the buffalo rock. When she returned to her lodge, she said to her husband, "Call all the men and have them sing to bring the buffalo."

"Are you in earnest?" her husband asked.

"Yes, I am," the woman replied. "Call the men, and also get a small piece of the back of a buffalo from the Bear Medicine man. Ask some of the men to bring the four rattles they use."

The husband did as his wife directed. Then she showed him how to arrange the inside of the lodge in a kind of square box with some sagebrush and buffalo chips. Though it was the custom for the first wife to sit next to her husband, the man directed his second wife to put on the dress of the other woman and to sit beside him. When everything was ready, the men who had been summoned sat down in the lodge beside the woman and her husband. Then the buffalo rock began to sing, "The buffalo will all drift back. The buffalo will all drift back."

Hearing this song, the woman asked one of the young men to go outside and put a great many buffalo chips in line. "After you have them in place, wave at them with a buffalo robe four times, and shout at them in a singsong. At the fourth time, all the buffalo chips will turn into buffaloes and go over the cliff."

The young man followed her directions, and the chips became buffaloes. At the same time, the woman led the people in the lodge in the singing of songs. One song was about the buffalo that would lead the others in the drive. While the people were chanting it, a cow took the lead and all the herd followed her. They plunged over the cliff and were killed.

Then the woman sang,

> More than a hundred buffalo
> Have fallen over the cliff.
> I have made them fall.
> And the man above the earth hears me singing.
> More than a hundred buffalo
> Have fallen over the cliff.

And so the people learned that the rock was very powerful. Ever since that time, they have taken care of the buffalo rock and have prayed to it.

Michelson, "Piegan Tales," 246-247.

■

# THE WISE MAN OF CHIEF MOUNTAIN
## *Blackfeet*

Chief of the Mountains is grim, rugged, and majestic. Indeed, these are very good reasons for the Blackfeet Indians to have named the awesome peak, Chief Mountain. It is located in Montana, in the northeastern corner of Glacier National Park.

Tribal historian Yellow Wolfe of the Blackfeet tribe always enjoyed telling the following story about Chief Mountain and the people who once lived in its shadow.

■

Two members of the Blackfeet tribe were Wise Man and his wife. Their people called him Wise Man because he always seemed to know how to do everything right.

At that time, the Blackfeet wore the plainest kinds of clothes. Wise Man thought about this for a long time. One day he said to his wife, "Let

*Rawhide rattle*
Blackfeet

us go away for a while. I wish to make some things that I have been planning for a long time."

Wise Man and his wife packed their travois, which was drawn by dogs, and moved to the base of the Inside Lakes. There they made their camp. He hunted and killed enough game for him and his wife and their dogs before beginning work on his plan.

First, he climbed to the high ridge between the lakes and Little River, where he dug an eagle trap. Beside the pit, he laid a deer and slashed its body to attract an eagle. When all was ready, Wise Man jumped into the pit and covered it with willow sticks and grass to make a blind. He waited for an eagle to come. Several eagles, with their wings swishing the air, sailed down upon the deer.

While the eagles ate at the deer, Wise Man reached up cautiously, snatched the legs of an eagle, and pulled it down into the pit. By repeating this method, he caught a large number of eagles. These he tied together, dragging them to his camp. There, he removed their tail feathers, their fluffy plume feathers, and other useful feathers that would help his plan.

As winter arrived, weasels appeared, and Wise Man hunted them. This was more difficult than trapping eagles but he set many snares and caught about a hundred weasels.

*Eagle headdress*
Blackfeet

Wise Man made himself an eagle headdress and hung white weasel fur skins upon it. Along the seams of his shirt sleeves and leggings, he hung more weasel skins. Adorned with his newly decorated clothes, he presented himself to his wife.

"Oh, you look brave and handsome!" she said. "Your new clothes with feathers and furs are the most beautiful ones I have ever seen!"

"I'm glad you like them," he replied. "Now I want to make something special for you."

Wise Man put away his new clothes, and dressed for hunting. He started out to look for elk. From these animals, he collected the skins, tusks, and teeth. He sewed them in decorative rows on the front and back of his wife's new dress. Both of them thought it most attractive.

"Now we have a fine new appearance," she said. "Shall we go home to Chief Mountain and show our people what you have accomplished?"

"Not yet," answered Wise Man. "Something is lacking, and I must discover what it is. I shall ask the Great Spirit to show me what more I must do."

On the very next day, when Wise Man walked through the timber, he found a dead porcupine. Its quills were scattered around on the ground. He examined them, thinking how he could dye the quills different colors. If he could, his wife's new dress would be even more beautiful, he thought. He shot another porcupine for its quills, and carried the animal home to cook.

"I know the yellow moss growing on pine trees will stain anything yellow," his wife suggested. "The color will not fade or wash off. I'm sure you can find other dyes for different colors, too."

He found green in another wood, and red in the juice of a certain plant. So Wise Man dyed the quills three colors—yellow, green, and red. He flattened the quills somewhat and sewed them side by side on the leather clothes, making different designs. He took a long time with his work. Finally, he had enough for his shirt and leggings, as well as for the neck, the front, and the back of his wife's new dress.

Each of them were so pleased with the colorful and charming appearance of the other that they hugged and danced together for joy.

At last, Wise Man felt satisfied with the way his plan had developed. They broke camp and started home to their people near Chief Mountain. When they came within sight of their tribe, they put on their newly decorated clothes.

When their friends saw them approaching they did not at first believe they were Wise Man and his wife. But when they came closer, their people recognized them. All of the tribe crowded about Wise Man and his wife, staring, touching, and asking many questions about how their clothes were made.

Wise Man showed all of the people at Chief Mountain how he created the new ornaments. Immediately, the people began to gather the materials to make decorated clothes for themselves.

Since that time, the Blackfeet Indians have become very well known for their handsome and colorful dress. Wise Man became a strong leader in his tribe. He was acclaimed for discovering how to make everything more beautiful. This is why his people loved him and always called him Chief Wise Man of the Blackfeet tribe.

Schultz, *Blackfeet Tales of Glacier National Park*, 235.

*Porcupine quill medicine wheel*
Blackfeet

■

# ORIGIN OF THE SWEAT LODGE
## *Piegan*

The Piegan tribe was southernmost at the headwaters of the Missouri River in Montana, a subtribe belonging to the Siksika Indians of North Saskatchewan in Canada. Piegans were of the Algonquian linguistic family, but warlike toward most of their neighboring tribes, since they had horses for raiding and were supplied with guns and ammunition by their Canadian sources. Piegans also displayed hostility toward explorers and traders. Several smallpox epidemics decimated their population. Now they are gathered on reservations on both sides of the border.

■

A girl of great beauty, the Chief's daughter, was worshipped by many young handsome men of the Piegan tribe. But she would not have any one of them for her husband.

One young tribesman was very poor and his face was marked with an ugly scar. Although he saw rich and handsome men of his tribe rejected by the Chief's daughter, he decided to find out if she would have him for her husband. When she laughed at him for even asking, he ran away toward the south in shame.

After traveling several days, he dropped to the ground, weary and hungry, and fell asleep. From the heavens, Morning-Star looked down and pitied the young unfortunate youth, knowing his trouble.

To Sun and Moon, his parents, Morning-Star said, "There is a poor young man lying on the ground with no one to help him. I want to go after him for a companion."

"Go and get him," said his parents.

Morning-Star carried the young man, Scarface, into the sky. Sun said, "Do not bring him into my lodge yet, for he smells ill. Build four sweat lodges."

When this was done, Sun led Scarface into the first sweat lodge. He asked Morning-Star to bring a hot coal on a forked stick. Sun then broke off a bit of sweet grass and placed it upon the hot coal. As the incense arose Sun began to sing, "Old Man is coming in with his body; it is sacred," repeating it four times.

Sun passed his hands back and forth through the smoke and rubbed them over the face, left arm, and side of Scarface. Sun repeated the ceremony on the boy's right side, purifying him and removing the odors of earthly people.

Sun took Scarface into the other three sweat lodges, performing the same healing ceremony. The body of Scarface changed color and he shone like a yellow light.

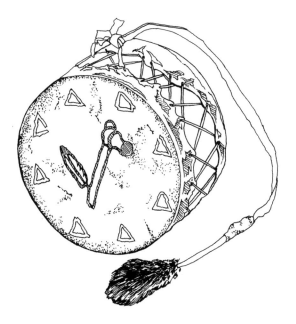

*Drum*
Piegan

Using a soft feather, Sun brushed it over the youth's face, magically wiping away the scar. With a final touch to the young man's long, yellow hair, Sun caused him to look exactly like Morning-Star. The two young men were led by Sun into his own lodge and placed side by side in the position of honor.

"Old Woman," called the father. "Which is your son?"

Moon pointed to Scarface, "That one is our son."

"You do not know your own child," answered Sun.

"He is not our son. We will call him Mistaken-for-Morning-Star," as they all laughed heartily at the mistake.

The two boys were together constantly and became close companions. One day, they were on an adventure when Morning-Star pointed out some large birds with very long, sharp beaks.

"Foster-Brother, I warn you not to go near those dangerous creatures," said Morning-Star. "They killed my other brothers with their beaks."

Suddenly the birds chased the two boys. Morning-Star fled toward his home, but Foster-Brother stopped, picking up a club and one by one struck the birds dead.

Upon reaching home, Morning-Star excitedly reported to his father what had happened. Sun made a victory song honoring the young hero. In gratitude for saving Morning-Star's life, Sun gave him the forked stick for lifting hot embers and a braid of sweet grass to make incense. These sacred elements necessary for making the sweat lodge ceremony were a gift of trust.

"And this my sweat lodge I give to you," said the Sun. Mistaken-for-Morning-Star observed very carefully how it was constructed, in his mind preparing himself to one day returning to earth.

When Scarface did arrive at his tribal village, all of his people gathered to see the handsome young man in their midst. At first, they did not recognize him as Scarface.

"I have been in the sky," he told them. "Behold me, Morning-Star looks just like this. The Sun gave me these things used in the sweat lodge healing ceremony. That is how I lost my ugly scar."

Scarface explained how the forked stick and sweet grass were used. Then he set to work showing his people how to make the sweat lodge. This is how the first medicine sweat lodge was built upon earth by the Piegan tribe.

Now that Scarface was so very handsome and brought such a great blessing of healing to his tribe, the Chief's beautiful daughter became his wife.

In remembrance of Sun's gift to Scarface and his tribe, the Piegans always make the sweat lodge healing ceremony an important part of their annual Sun Dance Celebration.

Curtis, *The North American Indian*, vol. vi, 59-60.

■

# PUMA AND THE BEAR

## *Ute*

A series of Ute legends was collected by A. L. Kroeber in 1900 from the Uintah Utes in Northeastern Utah. These oral recordings were made from English-speaking native Americans. Similar stories seem widespread among various tribes. For example, "Rolling Rock" was told almost everywhere, while "Bungling Host" drew on mythological ideas from other North American Indians. Most of the specific Ute tales seem original with perhaps only slight resemblance to those of other tribes.

■

One day Puma took his son hunting with him. The Bear came to Puma's tent and saw his wife there, and immediately fell in love with her. "I wish to have her for my wife," he thought. Then he went in to where she was sitting. In only a short time, he proposed that she run away with him. She consented and ran away with the Bear.

When Puma returned, he could not find his wife. "I wonder if she could have eloped with that Bear?" he mused. At first he and his son saw no tracks, but eventually they picked up the couple's trail. Angry by now, Puma followed the Bear tracks.

A high wind began to blow, obliterating most of the tracks. The next day Puma found them again and followed on. "Perhaps they are in that

*Tipi*
Ute

cedar wood," he thought. As he moved closer, he heard voices and recognized his wife's and the Bear's.

He sent his son to circle the wood, approaching from the other side of the wood to force the Bear out toward Puma. The woman said "Puma is very strong." "But I am stronger," said the Bear, seizing a cedar tree and pulling it from the ground. "He is stronger than that," said the woman.

The Bear had his moccasins off when Puma's son attacked. Quickly the Bear put on his moccasins, but in his haste he put them on the wrong feet. Then, not knowing who was coming behind him, he ran forward into Puma. The two grappled and Puma threw the Bear to the ground. The Bear rose up again and charged at Puma, who thrust the Bear down against a rock and broke the Bear's back.

Then Puma sent his wife away into the woods, letting her know that he did not want her for his wife again. Puma and his son left on another hunting trip to find a new wife and home for themselves.

Kroeber, "Puma and the Bear," 252, 274.

■

# PORCUPINE HUNTS BUFFALO

## *Ute*

■

In olden days when mostly animals roamed this earth, a Porcupine set out to track some buffalo. He asked the buffalo chips, "How long have you been here on this trail?" He kept on asking, until finally one answered, "Only lately have I been here."

From there Porcupine followed the same path. The farther he went, the fresher the tracks. He continued until he came to a river; there he saw a buffalo herd that had crossed the ford onto the other side.

"What shall I do now?" thought Porcupine as he sat down. He called out, "Carry me across!" One of the buffalo replied, "Do you mean me?" Porcupine called again, "No, I want a different buffalo." Thus he rejected each member of the herd, one after another, as each asked. "Do you mean me?"

Finally the last and best one in the herd said, "I will carry you across the river." The buffalo crossed the river and said to porcupine, "Climb on my back." Porcupine said, "No, I'm afraid I will fall off into the water." Buffalo said, "Then climb up and ride between my horns." "No," replied Porcupine. "I'm sure I'll slide off into the river."

Buffalo suggested many other ways to carry him, but Porcupine protested. "Perhaps you'd rather ride inside of me?" offered the buffalo. "Yes," said Porcupine, and let himself be swallowed by the buffalo.

"Where are we now?" asked Porcupine. "In the middle of the river," said the buffalo, After a little while, Porcupine asked again. "We have nearly crossed," said the buffalo. "Now we have emerged from the water; come out of me!" Porcupine said, "No, not yet, go a little farther."

Soon the buffalo stopped and said, "We have gone far enough, so come out." Then Porcupine hit the buffalo's heart with his heavy tail. The buffalo started to run, but fell down and died right there. Porcupine had killed him. Others in the herd tried to hook Porcupine, but he sat under the buffalo's ribs, where he could not be hooked. Soon the herd tired and ran on their way.

Porcupine came out and said aloud, "I wish I had something to butcher this nice big buffalo with." Now, Coyote was sleeping nearby, and woke up and heard him. Coyote went to Porcupine and said, "Here is my knife for butchering." So they went together to the side of the buffalo.

"Let him butcher who can jump over it," said Coyote. Porcupine ran and jumped, but only partway over the buffalo. Coyote jumped over it without touching the dead animal, so he began to butcher, cutting up the buffalo.

After a little time, he handed the paunch to Porcupine and said, "Go wash it in the river, but don't eat it yet." Porcupine took it to the river, washed it, then he bit off a piece. When Coyote saw what Porcupine had done, he became very angry with him and went after him, "I told you not to eat any of the paunch." Coyote picked up a club and killed Porcupine and placed him beside the buffalo, and went to his home. Then he told his family, "I have killed a buffalo and I have killed a porcupine. Let us go and carry them home."

Before Porcupine had come out of the buffalo, he said magic words, "Let a red pine grow here fast." Then at once red pine began to grow under the meat and under Porcupine. It grew very tall and fast. All of the meat and Porcupine rested at the top of the red pine tree, high in the air, Porcupine magically coming alive again.

Coyote and his family arrived and were surprised that all of the meat was gone. They began to hunt for it. "I wish they would look up," said Porcupine. Then the smallest child looked up and said "Oh!" The family looked up and saw Porcupine sitting on top of the meat in the tall red pine tree.

Coyote said, "Throw down a piece of the neck, we are very hungry."

"Yes," said Porcupine. "Place that youngest child a little farther away. "Yes," they responded and took him to one side.

"Now make a ring and all hold hands upward," said Porcupine. So the family joined hands and held them up. Porcupine threw down several pieces of the buffalo meat, killing Coyote and those in the ring. Porcupine then threw down the rest of the buffalo meat, and climbed down the tree.

He took charge of the young coyote and fed him all the meat he desired. Porcupine took all the meat he could carry to his home. He and the young coyote became good friends and helped each other hunt buffalo together for a long, long time.

Kroeber, "Porcupine Hunts Buffalo," 270-272.

■

# COYOTE VS. DUCK
## *Ute*

■

Coyote became disturbed because he had a sick daughter. He thought Duck had done something against his children in order to make them sick. So Coyote determined to bring harm to Duck. He met Duck at a certain place and ordered that Duck should run to a point with his eyes closed. This Duck did. When he opened them again, he found himself in the hole of a big rock, a little cave high on the face of a cliff. There was no way out for Duck.

Coyote took Duck's wife and children, whom he treated badly. In time, Coyote had more children from this woman, and these he took good care of.

Duck tried constantly to get out of the cave, without success. At last Bat camped nearby, and every day, when he went to hunt rabbits, his children could hear someone crying. They told Bat, and he flew upward to look. On his way he killed rabbits and hung them on his belt. Finally he found Duck, who was very weak from lack of food.

"Who is there?" asked Bat. "I am Duck." Bat asked, "How did you come up here?" Duck said, "Coyote caused me to lose my way with my eyes closed. He got rid of me in order to steal my wife." Then Bat said "Throw yourself down." Duck was afraid to try. So Bat told him, "Throw down a small rock." This Duck did and Bat caught it on his back. He said, "That is exactly the way I will catch you. You will not be hurt."

Duck still feared that Bat would not catch him. Bat continued to urge him to let himself fall. Several times Duck almost let himself go, but drew back. At least he thought, "Suppose I am killed; I shall die here anyway; I am as good as dead now."

Duck closed his eyes as Bat commanded, and let himself fall. Bat caught him gently and put Duck safely on the ground. Bat then took Duck to his home and said, "Do not use the fire-sticks that are near my fireplace, but use those stuck behind the tent poles, at the sides of the tent."

Then he entered, and Duck saw the sticks at the sides of the tent, but only thought them to be fine canes, too handsome for stirring the fire. He saw a number of sticks laying around that were charred on the ends. He took one of these and stirred the embers. Oh, how the sticks cried. All the other sticks called out, "Duck has burned our younger brother."

These sticks were Bat's children, and they all ran away. Duck became frightened at what he had done, and went out and hid in the brush. Bat came and called to him, "Come back! You have done no harm."

For a long time Duck seemed afraid that Bat would punish him. Then he thought, "I've already been as good as dead, so I have nothing more to fear, even if they should kill me." Duck went back into the tent. But Bat did not hurt him and gave him plenty of rabbit meat to eat. Soon Duck was strong again.

Duck said to Bat, "Coyote took my wife and children; I think I shall go and look for them." Believing him to be strong enough, Bat encouraged him to go. Duck went to his old camp, but he found it deserted. He followed tracks leading from it, and after a while found some tracks other than his own children's.

"I think Coyote has got children from my wife," he thought, and he became very angry. Coyote came along with Duck's wife. She was carrying a very large basket. Inside were Coyote's children, well kept; but Duck's children sat on the outer edge of the basket. Nearly falling off. These were dirty and miserable.

Duck caught the basket with a finger and pulled it back. "What are you doing, children?" the woman said. "Don't do that; you must not catch hold of something and hold me back." Duck continued to pull at the basket. At last she turned to look at the children and saw Duck. He said to her, "Why do you take care of Coyote's children, while my children are dirty and uncared for? Why do you not treat my children properly?"

The woman was ashamed and did not answer. Then he asked her, "Where will you camp now?" When she told him, he said to her, "Go to the place where Coyote told you to camp, but when you put up the shelter, make the grass very thin on one side and very thick on the side on which you are, so I can reach Coyote."

The woman arrived at the camping place. Coyote asked, "To whom have you been talking now?" She replied, "I have not met nor talked with anyone. Why do you always ask me that?" She then put up the shelter as Duck had directed her. Immediately Duck began to blow. He blew softly, but again, again, and again, until he made it freezing cold.

Coyote could not sleep. He thrust his spear through the sides of the shelter in all directions and nearly speared the Duck. Coyote said to his wife, "I knew that you met someone. It must have been Duck, who is making it so cold." Duck continued to blow and blow. At last Coyote burrowed himself down into the fireplace ashes, hoping to warm himself there. But it was of no use. Coyote froze to death before morning.

Duck let all of Coyote's children go free where they wished. Then he took his wife and his children back to their old home, where they had lived before all of the disruption began.

Kroeber, "Coyote vs. Duck," 272-274.

■

# TWO FAWNS AND A RABBIT
## *Ute*

■

Two young Fawns sat on the ground talking about their condition. They were two boys without a mother. "We used to have a deer for our mother," they said. Rabbit came to them and said "I'm hungry. I've traveled without eating, and I've come a long way."

The Fawns said, "We have nothing to eat here; our food is not here." Where is it?" asked Rabbit. "It is not here, I say to you again," said one Fawn.

Rabbit said, "Tell me where it is, I am hungry and I want to eat." He continued talking about the Fawns' food for a long time. But they concealed from him how they obtained it.

Then Rabbit said, "I think you both are too lazy to get the food. Show me the path and I will go after it; I will cut off enough for all of us and bring it here."

"But we never eat here," the Fawns said. Rabbit said, "You boys do not know me. I am your grandfather. You did not recognize me; that is why you hid your food from me." The one boy nudged the other and whispered to him, "I think he is our grandfather; I will tell him where we eat."

For a while, the other boy said nothing. Then he spoke up and said, "What we eat is not on the ground; our food is far up in the sky; and we eat at a certain time. When we ask for our food, something always comes down from the sky; it is white like a cloud. At the end of the cloud it's like a person; it has an eye, a mouth, and it watches us. It comes only at a certain time. If we ask before time, it will think someone else wants our food. But when it's time for us to ask for it, we will hide you out of sight." Then they hid him.

One ran toward the East, the other toward the West; then they ran toward each other. When they met, they cried like young animals at play. They circled about, met each other again, crying, and gradually came nearer to the tent. Something white came down from the sky. Rabbit saw it coming. It looked like a cloud with a face above it; like a man sitting on their food.

The boys took up dull knives, and when the food arrived, they cut off a piece. They cut more than usual, so there would be enough for their grandfather. Then the cloud flew upward as fast as lightning.

The Fawn boys cut up their food and called Rabbit to come out and eat with them. The food tasted good and sweet, and Rabbit wanted more and asked the boys to make the thing come again. The Fawns said, "But it only comes at set times." Rabbit replied, "I will live with you, for your food is very good." He made a burrow in the brush nearby and watched.

The food did come down again. The person riding on it looked around like an antelope watching. Rabbit took a bow and arrow from his quiver. Just before the cloud came low enough for the boys to cut off another piece of food, Rabbit shot at the manlike object on the cloud. The white object fell down in a heap.

"I thought that was what it would do," said the older brother to the younger, as if blaming him. Rabbit said to them, "Well, my grandchildren, I will leave you now. You have something to eat and it will last you a long time. After you have consumed all of it, you will go to the mountains and eat grass and become Deer."

Kroeber, "Two Fawns and a Rabbit," 275-276.

■

# Two Grandsons
## *Ute*

■

A man lived on a large rock with his two grandsons. "You had better go hunting and bring home something for us to eat. I am hungry. Go to the hills, sit on top, and watch in all directions; then you may find something," Grandfather said.

The two grandsons went off and watched in the brush. An elk came directly at them. One boy said, "I see an elk, let's kill it." The other said, "My older brother, let us run away. I am afraid." The older said, "No. Sit still. It is an elk. I shall shoot it as our grandfather directed." The other said, "No. I am afraid."

When the older was about ready to shoot, his younger brother fled, crying, "Let's run away. I am frightened." Then the elk started back. The older one said, "What is it? Are you crazy? I was nearly ready to shoot that elk." The younger still said, "I was frightened; but I understand now it is an elk. Let us go after it; it cannot have gone far."

When they neared the elk again, the younger brother wanted to turn to shoot at it. The older brother wanted him to stay behind, but did not persuade him. When ready to shoot, the younger again ran off shouting, and the elk escaped. The older brother scolded him harshly. The younger one said, "I was afraid that it would jump on me. I became too frightened."

The younger brother begged the older boy not to send him back home, as the older brother wished. When they approached the elk another time, he again asked his older brother to allow him a shot, saying, if he missed, the other could be ready and still try to kill the elk. But the same thing happened as before.

The older brother became very angry with his younger brother. It was not yet sunset, but the younger persuaded the older to again go after the elk; so they went around ahead of it. Older brother tied the arms, legs, and mouth of his brother. The elk came close. Younger one tried to scream. At the same time the older brother shot and killed the elk.

Younger brother tossed and thrashed about, trying to scream and flee. "Are you crazy? I have killed the elk," said the older. "Have you truly?" asked the younger. Then the older loosened his brother and showed him the dead elk. "What kind of Deer is it?" asked the younger. "It's an elk," replied the older one. "Hurry! Get some brush for a fire. Let's skin it and go home quickly. There may be bad persons coming about here."

"I'll get some brush presently," said the younger. "Make the fire quickly," said his brother. "I want to roast some meat and eat it, then go home. Be quick." "No, I want to rest now," said the younger. He would not help his older brother. So the older one alone skinned the game and cooked some of the meat. Then he said, "Let's go home now. There may be some bad things about. I am frightened."

"No, I am afraid to go. I cannot go home. Let us stay here all night; there is nothing bad about," said the younger. Then the older urged him no more and said, "Let us sleep in a cedar tree. Make a bed there." The younger agreed and made a bed in the top of the cedar after they had buried the meat for safekeeping. Then they slept.

In the middle of the night the younger one said, "I am hungry. I will go down and eat." The older one awoke and said, "What in the world is the matter with you? Sleep now, eat tomorrow." But the younger one insisted on going down to eat. Finally the older one said, "Very well." So, the younger brother went down, made a large fire, and cooked a whole shoulder of the elk. He began to eat and enjoy himself. He heard cries from far-off in all directions. The younger brother said, "What is it? Is someone approaching? Come here then and eat with me." The older brother remained in the cedar tree.

Someone came to the opposite side of the fire. It was a large man. The younger brother said, "Come, friend, eat; I have good food; sit down there." No answer came from the man. "Here is something to eat," said the boy, holding elk meat out to the man. He did not take it. He did not answer even when he was repeatedly spoken to. Then the boy hit him on the head and knocked him down. When he went closer until he stood by the man's head, suddenly the man reached out and caught him in a violent grip.

"Oh, Oh! Let me go!" cried the boy. The man continued to hold his legs in a tight grip. "Let me go! Older brother, come and help me, this stranger is holding me down." But the older brother was angry at being disturbed so he did not come down from the tree.

The man squeezed the younger boy harder, then picked him up and carried him away. The older brother, half-awake, heard his brother's cries grow weaker and weaker as the distance grew greater. Then there were no more cries.

In the morning the older brother came down from the cedar tree. Crying aloud for his brother, he followed the tracks. They led him to a lake and right down into the water. He could go no farther. He went back, dug up the elk meat, and went home, telling the whole experience to his grandfather.

His grandfather said, "Tomorrow we will go and see that place." The older son went with his grandfather to the lake and watched it. Grandfather said, "Wait here while I go down. I will follow the tracks."

He did not come back until noon, then emerged carrying a dead man, and laid him down.

"Is this the man who killed your brother? Deep in the water I found him. I am going back again, wait here," said the grandfather. He did not return until sunset and said, "This is another man. I entered his house and killed him. Now open his mouth and look between his teeth."

The boy saw a little meat between the teeth. His grandfather said to him, "Take a stick and pick out the meat from his teeth. The boy did so and made a little pile of it. Then the old man told him to cut open the dead man. When the boy had done so, his grandfather asked, "Do you see any bones or other parts? Pick them out."

The boy did as he was told, and then did the same to the other man. They put the meat and bones into a hollow stone and carried them home. They left it standing outside, at a short distance from the tent. Then they slept.

Early in the morning his grandfather called, "He is shouting, Wuwuwuwu! Do you hear him?"

"Yes," said the older brother. They both answered with a loud shout. Then younger brother came walking from the woods, saying, "Grandfather, older brother, I have risen from the meat!"

All three clasped each other warmly, happy to be together again— grandfather and his two grandsons.

Kroeber, "The Two Grandsons," 278-280.

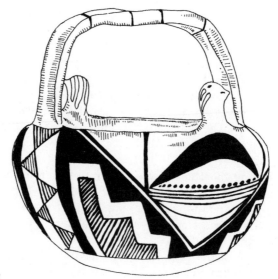

*Pueblo pottery*
Acoma

■

# THE ORIGIN OF SUMMER AND WINTER
## *Acoma*

The oldest tradition of the Acoma and Laguna people indicates they lived on some island off the California Coast. Their homes were destroyed by high waves, earthquakes, and red-hot stones from the sky. They escaped and landed on a swampy part of the coast. From there they migrated inland to the north. Wherever they made a longer stay, they built a traditional White City, made of white-washed mud and straw adobe brick, surrounded by white-washed adobe walls. Their fifth White City was built in southern Colorado, near northern New Mexico. The people were finally obliged to leave there on account of cold, drought, and famine.

■

The Acoma chief had a daughter named Co-chin-ne-na-ko, called Co-chin for short, who was the wife of Shakok, the Spirit of Winter. After he came to live with the Acomas, the seasons grew colder and colder. Snow and ice stayed longer each year. Corn no longer matured. The people soon had to live on cactus leaves and other wild plants.

One day Co-chin went out to gather cactus leaves and burn off the thorns so she could carry them home for food. She was eating a singed leaf when she saw a young man coming toward her. He wore a yellow shirt woven of corn silk, a belt, and a tall pointed hat; green leggings made of green moss that grows near springs and ponds; and moccasins beautifully embroidered with flowers and butterflies.

In his hand he carried an ear of green corn with which he saluted her. She returned the salute with her cactus leaf. He asked, "What are you eating?" She told him, "Our people are starving because no corn will grow, and we are compelled to live on these cactus leaves."

"Here, eat this ear of corn, and I will go bring you an armful for you to take home with you," said the young man. He left and quickly disappeared from sight, going south. In a very short time, however, he returned, bringing a large bundle of green corn that he laid at her feet.

"Where did you find so much corn?" Co-chin asked.

"I brought it from my home far to the south," he replied. "There the corn grows abundantly and flowers bloom all year."

"Oh, how I would like to see your lovely country. Will you take me with you to your home?" she asked.

"Your husband, Shakok, the Spirit of Winter, would be angry if I should take you away," he said.

"But I do not love him, he is so cold. Ever since he came to our village, no corn has grown, no flowers have bloomed. The people are compelled to live on these prickly pear leaves," she said.

"Well," he said. "Take this bundle of corn with you and do not throw away the husks outside of your door. Then come tomorrow and I will bring you more. I will meet you here." He said good-bye and left for his home in the south.

Co-chin started home with the bundle of corn and met her sisters, who had come out to look for her. They were very surprised to see the corn instead of cactus leaves. Co-chin told them how the young man had brought her the corn from his home in the south. They helped her carry it home.

When they arrived, their father and mother were wonderfully surprised with the corn. Co-chin minutely described in detail the young man and where he was from. She would go back the next day to get more corn from him, as he asked her to meet him there, and he would accompany her home.

"It is Miochin," said her father. "It is Miochin," said her mother. "Bring him home with you."

The next day, Co-chin-ne-na-ko went to the place and met Miochin, for he really was Miochin, the Spirit of Summer. He was waiting for her and had brought big bundles of corn.

Between them they carried the corn to the Acoma village. There was enough to feed all of the people. Miochin was welcome at the home of the Chief. In the evening, as was his custom, Shakok, the Spirit of Winter and Co-chin's husband, returned from the north. All day he had been playing with the north wind, snow, sleet, and hail.

Upon reaching the Acoma village, he knew Miochin must be there and called out to him, "Ha, Miochin, are you here?" Miochin came out to meet him. "Ha, Miochin, now I will destroy you."

"Ha, Shakok, I will destroy you," replied Miochin, advancing toward him, melting the snow and hail and turning the fierce wind into a summer breeze. The icicles dropped off and Shakok's clothing was revealed to be made of dry, bleached rushes.

Shakok said, "I will not fight you now, but will meet you here in four days and fight you till one of us is beaten. The victor will win Co-chin-ne-na-ko."

Shakok left in a rage, as the wind roared and shook the walls of White City. But the people were warm in their houses because Miochin was there. The next day he left for his own home in the south to make preparations to meet shakok in combat.

First he sent an eagle to his friend Yat-Moot, who lived in the west, asking him to come help him in his fight with Shakok. Second, he called all the birds, insects, and four-legged animals that live in summer lands to help him. The bat was his advance guard and shield, as his tough skin could best withstand the sleet and hail that Shakok would throw at him.

On the third day Yat-Moot kindled his fires, heating the thin, flat stones he was named after. Big black clouds of smoke rolled up from the south and covered the sky.

Shakok was in the north and called to him all the winter birds and four-legged animals of winter lands to come and help him. The magpie was his shield and advance guard.

On the fourth morning, the two enemies could be seen rapidly approaching the Acoma village. In the north, black storm clouds of winter with snow, sleet, and hail brought Shakok to the battle. In the south, Yat-Moot piled more wood on his fires and great puffs of steam and smoke arose and formed massive clouds. They were bringing Miochin, the Spirit of Summer, to the battlefront. All of his animals were blackened from the smoke. Forked blazes of lightning shot forth from the clouds.

At last the combatants reached White City. Flashes from the clouds singed the hair and feathers of Shakok's animals and birds. Shakok and Miochin were now close together. Shakok threw snow, sleet, and hail that hissed through the air of a blinding storm. Yat-Moot's fires and smoke melted Shakok's weapons, and he was forced to fall back. Finally he called a truce. Miochin agreed, and the winds stopped, and snow and rain ceased falling.

They met at the White Wall of Acoma. Shakok said, "I am defeated, you Miochin are the winner. Co-chin-ne-na-ko is now yours forever." Then the men each agreed to rule one-half of the year, Shakok for winter and Miochin for summer, and that neither would trouble the other thereafter. That is why we have a cold season for one-half of the year, and a warm season for the other.

Pradt, "Shakok and Miochin, The Origin of Summer and Winter," 88-90.

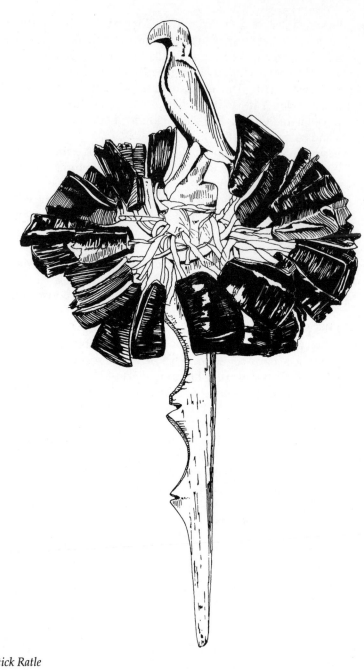

*Stick Ratle*
Chippewa

# PART FOUR

## FROM THE CENTRAL REGION

*Homelands for these tribal stories were chiefly states of the Middle West. But a series of treaties in the 1790s and early 1800s culminated in the loss of many Indian lands to the whites. Tribes then moved westward and northward. Chippewa and Illini occupied Wisconsin, Illinois, and northern Michigan.*

*Ottawa, meaning "to trade," were known as the middlemen in transactions between those living in northern Michigan and those in southern Canada, whose principal city was named Ottawa in 1854. In 1858, Ottawa was selected as the capital city of Canada by Queen Victoria. Most famous of the Ottawa was Chief Pontiac.*

*Winnebago, meaning "people of the filthy water," lived on the south side of Green Bay in Wisconsin. They were the mother tribe of the Chippewas and Iowas, whose names mean "sleepy ones" and "dusty noses." The Iowas stayed mostly in their own territory, now the state of Iowa. A large group of Chippewas came from the East to Mackinaw in northern Michigan and to the shores of lake Superior; they drove out the Dakotas and then spread over northern Minnesota. Chippewa also means "roast until puckered up," referring to the way the seams of their moccasins pucker when held too close to fire.*

*Illini lived in the Illinois village of Michigamea, meaning "Big Water." When driven out by the Chickasaw, they settled in northern Arkansas on a large lake now called Big Lake. In Nebraska lived the Pawnee, known for wearing elk bone on their heads, a mark of hunters. Helpful to the United States Army, they served as scouts. While horse hunting in about 1541, they aided Francisco Coronado's exploration of the Southwest when he also encountered the Wichitas in Kansas territory.*

■

# ARCH ROCK ON MACKINAC ISLAND

## Ottawa

Arch Rock is a natural rock bridge above the eastern shoreline of Mackinac Island in northern Michigan. From certain angles, the arch, which is about 150 feet above the lake, appears to be suspended in the air. This mythical explanation of its origin was recorded in 1850.

■

Many, many winters ago, the sun descended into an immense hole every evening, as soon as the stars appeared in the sky. This hole was thought to be somewhere off in the distant west.

One time a chief of the Ottawa nation committed a shameful act. It was so shameful that the Master of Life was greatly offended and angered. In punishment, he sent a powerful wind upon the earth. The rocky hills trembled because of the wind, and the waters surrounding the hills roared with a dreadful roar.

For one whole day this turmoil lasted. Even the sun was disturbed. It shot through the heavens with an unsteady motion, and when it reached the center of the sky, it stood still. It seemed to be astonished at the wickedness of the chief.

All the people of the Ottawa nation were greatly alarmed. While they stood gazing at the sun, they saw it gradually change to the color of blood. Then they were horrified to see it fall from the sky. With a terrifying noise, it struck the eastern shore of Mackinac Island.

When the frightened Indians dared to look again, they saw that some rocks had been hollowed out so as to make an arch. It hung high above the waters of the lake. The sun had gone through the opening and on down below the surface of the earth. Next morning it came out of the earth in the east, and then made its usual journey across the heavens.

Many winters have passed since that awful day when the sun stood still and fell from the sky. But even now, not even the bravest Ottawa people will walk over that arched rock. Indeed, they seldom dare to approach the place.

Lanman, "Indian Legends," 115-116.

■

# THE GREAT SERPENT AND THE GREAT FLOOD

## Chippewa-Ojibwa

From Maine and Nova Scotia to the Rocky Mountains, Indians told stories about the Great Serpent. The man who recorded this story more than a century ago considered the serpent to be "a genuine spirit of evil." Some version of the story of the Great Flood of long ago, as recounted here, is told around the world.

Nanabozho (Nunà-bōzō, accented on bozo) was the hero of many stories told by the Chippewa Indians. They used to be a large tribe living on the shares of Lake Superior, in what are now the states of Minnesota and Wisconsin and the province of Ontario.

■

One day when Nanabozho returned to his lodge after a long journey, he missed his young cousin who lived with him. He called the cousin's name but heard no answer. Looking around on the sand for tracks, Nanabozho was startled by the trail of the Great Serpent. He then knew that his cousin had been seized by his enemy.

Nanabozho picked up his bow and arrows and followed the track of the serpent. He passed the great river, climbed mountains, and crossed over valleys until he came to the shores of a deep and gloomy lake. It is now called Manitou Lake, Spirit Lake, and also the Lake of Devils. The trail of the Great Serpent led to the edge of the water.

Nanabozho could see, at the bottom of the lake, the house of the Great Serpent. It was filled with evil spirits, who were his servants and his companions. Their forms were monstrous and terrible. Most of them, like their master, resembled spirits. In the center of this horrible group was the Great Serpent himself, coiling his terrifying length around the cousin of Nanabozho.

The head of the Serpent was red as blood. His fierce eyes glowed like fire. His entire body was armed with hard and glistening scales of every color and shade.

Looking down on these twisting spirits of evil, Nanabozho made up his mind that he would get revenge on them for the death of his cousin.

He said to the clouds, "Disappear!"

And the clouds went out of sight.

"Winds, be still at once!" And the winds became still.

When the air over the lake of evil spirits had become stagnant, Nanabozho said to the sun, "Shine over the lake with all the fierceness you can. Make the water boil."

In these ways, thought Nanabozho, he would force the Great Serpent to seek the cool shade of the trees growing on the shores of the lake. There he would seize the enemy and get revenge.

After giving his orders, Nanabozho took his bow and arrows and placed himself near the spot where he thought the serpents would come to enjoy the shade. Then he changed himself into the broken stump of a withered tree.

The winds became still, the air stagnant, and the sun shot hot rays from a cloudless sky. In time, the water of the lake became troubled, and bubbles rose to the surface. The rays of the sun had penetrated to the home of the serpents. As the water bubbled and foamed, a serpent lifted his head above the center of the lake and gazed around the shores. Soon another serpent came to the surface. Both listened for the footsteps of Nanabozho, but they heard him nowhere.

"Nanabozho is sleeping," they said to one another.

And then they plunged beneath the waters, which seemed to hiss as they closed over the evil spirits.

Not long after, the lake became more troubled. Its water boiled from its very depths, and the hot waves dashed wildly against the rocks on its banks. Soon the Great Serpent came slowly to the surface of the water and moved toward the shore. His bloodred crest glowed. The reflection from his scales was blinding—as blinding as the glitter of a sleet-covered forest beneath the winter sun. He was followed by all the evil spirits. So great was their number that they soon covered the shores of the lake.

When they saw the broken stump of the withered tree, they suspected that it might be one of the disguises of Nanabozho. They knew his cunning. One of the serpents approached the stump, wound his tail around it, and tried to drag it down into the lake. Nanabozho could hardly keep from crying aloud, for the tail of the monster prickled his sides. But he stood firm and was silent.

The evil spirits moved on. The Great Serpent glided into the forest and wound his many coils around the trees. His companions also found shade—all but one. One remained near the shore to listen for the footsteps of Nanabozho.

From the stump, Nanabozho watched until all the serpents were asleep and the guard was intently looking in another direction. Then he silently drew an arrow from his quiver, placed it in his bow, and aimed it at the heart of the Great Serpent. It reached its mark. With a howl that shook the mountains and startled the wild beasts in their caves, the

*Wigwam*
Chippewa

monster awoke. Followed by its terrified companions, which also were howling with rage and terror, the Great Serpent plunged into the water.

At the bottom of the lake there still lay the body of Nanabozho's cousin. In their fury the serpents tore it into a thousand pieces. His shredded lungs rose to the surface and coveed the lake with whiteness.

The Great Serpent soon knew that he would die from his wound, but he and his companions were determined to destroy Nanabozho. They caused the water of the lake to swell upward and to pound against the shore with the sound of many thunders. Madly the flood rolled over the land, over the tracks of Nanabozho, carrying with it rocks and trees. High on the crest of the highest wave floated the wounded Great Serpent. His eyes glared around him, and his hot breath mingled with the hot breath of his many companions.

Nanabozho, fleeing before the angry waters, thought of his Indian children. He ran through their villages, shouting, "Run to the mountain-tops! The Great Serpent is angry and is flooding the earth! Run! Run!"

The Indians caught up their children and found safety on the mountains. Nanabozho continued his flight along the base of the western hills, and then up a high mountain beyond Lake Superior, far to the north. There he found many men and animals that had escaped from the flood that was already covering the valleys and plains and even the highest hills. Still the waters continued to rise. Soon all the mountains were under the flood, except the high one on which stood Nanabozho.

There he gathered together timber and made a raft. Upon it the men and women and animals with him placed themselves. Almost immediately the mountaintop disappeared from their view, and they floated along on the face of the waters. For many days they floated. At long last, the flood began to subside. Soon the people on the raft saw the trees on the tops of the mountains. Then they saw the mountains and hills, then the plains and the valleys.

When the water disappeared from the land, the people who survived learned that the Great Serpent was dead and that his companions had returned to the bottom of the lake of spirits. There they remain to this day. For fear of Nanabozho, they have never dared to come forth again.

Squier, "Nanabozho and the Great Serpent," 392

■

# THE FORSAKEN BROTHER
## *Chippewa*

The Chippewa tribe's traditional significance of its name in their own language, "to roast until puckered up," refers to the puckering in seams of moccasins when held too close or too long toward a fire. They were also called Ojibwa, as the band preferred. The Chippewa are one of the two largest divisions of the Algonquin linguistic family. Originally from the Sault Sainte Marie region, they extended along the entire shore of Lake Huron and on both shores of Lake Superior, as well as into the northern interior of North Dakota after separating into Chippewa, Ottawa, and Potawatomi. During the 19th century they gradually gathered upon reservations in the United States and Canada. In 1650, the Chippewa population stood at 35,000. In 1764 at 25,000. They scattered into many states in the Central and Plains regions.

■

One summer evening, scarcely an hour before sunset, the father of a family lay in his lodge, dying. Weeping beside him were his wife and three children. Two of them were almost grown up; the youngest was but a small child. These were the only human beings near the dying man, for the lodge stood on a little green mound away from all others of the tribe.

A breeze from the lake gave the sick man a brief return of strength. He raised himself a little and addressed his family.

"I know that I will leave you soon. Your mother, my partner of many years, will not stay long behind. She will soon join me in the pleasant land of spirits. But, O my children, my poor children! You have just begun life. All unkindness and other wickednesses are still before you.

"I have contented myself with the company of your mother and yourselves for many years, in order to keep you from evil example. I will die content, my children, if you will promise me to love each other. Promise me that on no account will you forsake your youngest brother. I leave him in your charge. Love him and hold him dear."

The effort to speak exhausted the sick man. But taking a hand of each of his older children, he continued his plea. "My daughter, never forsake your little brother! My son, never forsake your little brother!"

"Never, never!" they both exclaimed.

"Never, never!" repeated the father. And then he died, happily sure that his command would be obeyed.

Time wore heavily away. Five long moons passed, and when the sxith moon was nearly full, the mother also died. In her last moments, she reminded the two older children of their promise to their father. Willingly they renewed their promise to take care of their little brother. They were still free from any selfishness.

The winter passed away, and spring came. The girl, the oldest, directed her brothers. She seemed to feel an especially tender and sisterly affection for the youngest, who was sickly and delicate. The older boy, however, already showed signs of selfishness. One day he spoke sharply to his sister.

"My sister, are we always to live as if there were no other human beings in the world? Must I never associate with other men? I am going to visit the villages of my tribe. I have made up my mind, and you cannot prevent me."

"My brother," replied his sister, "I do not say no to what you wish. We were not forbidden to associate with others, but we were commanded never to forsake each other. If we separate to follow our own selfish desires, will we not be compelled to forsake our young brother? Both of us have promised to take care of him."

Making no reply, the young man picked up his bow and arrows, left the wigwam, and returned no more.

For many moons the girl took kindly care of her little brother. At last, however, she too began to weary of their solitude and wished to escape from her duty. Her strength and her ability to provide food and clothing had increased through the years, but so had her desire for company. Her solitude troubled her more and more, as the years went slowly by. At last, thinking only of herself, she decided to forsake her little brother, as the older brother had already done.

One day, she placed in the lodge all the food she had gathered. After bringing a pile of wood to the door, she said to her young brother, "Do not stray far from the lodge while I am gone. I am going to look for our brother. I shall soon be back."

Then taking her bundle, she set off for the villages. She found a pleasant one on the shore of a lake. Soon she became so much occupied with the pleasures of her new life that her affection for her brother gradually left her heart. In time, she was married. For a long time, she did not even think of the sickly little brother she had left in the woods.

In the meantime the older brother had settled in a village on the same lake, not far from the graves of their parents and the solitary home of the little brother.

As soon as the little fellow had eaten all the food left by his sister, he had to pick berries and dig roots. Winter came on, and the poor child was exposed to its cold winds. Snow covered the earth. Forced to leave the lodge in search of food, he strayed far without shelter. Sometimes he passed the night in the crotch of an old tree and ate the fragments left by wolves.

Soon he had to depend for his food entirely on what the wolves did not eat. He became so fearless that he would sit close to them while they devoured the animals they had killed. His condition aroused the pity of the animals, and they always left something for him. Thus he lived on the kindness of the wolves until spring came. As soon as the lake was free from ice, he followed his new friends and companions to the shore.

Now it happened that his brother was fishing in his canoe, far out on the same lake, when he thought he heard the cry of a child. "How can any child live on this bleak shore?" he said to himself. He listened again, and he thought he heard the cry repeated. Paddling toward the shore as quickly as possible, he saw and recognized his brother. The young one was singing,

> My brother, my brother!
> I am now turning into a wolf.
> I am turning into a wolf!

At the end of his song, he howled like a wolf. His brother, approaching, was shocked to find him half a wolf and half a human being. Leaping to the shore, the older brother tried to catch him in his arms. Soothingly he said, "My brother, my brother, come to me!"

But the boy fled, still singing as he ran, "I am turning into a wolf! I am turning into a wolf!" And at the end of his song he howled a terrifying howl.

Conscience-stricken, feeling his love return to his heart, his brother called to him, "My brother, O my brother! Come back to me!"

But the nearer he came to the child, the more rapidly the change to a wolf took place. Still the younger brother sang his song, and still he howled. Sometimes he called on his brother, and sometimes he called on his sister. When the change was complete, he ran toward the wood. He knew that he was a wolf. "I am a wolf! I am a wolf!" he cried, as he bounded out of sight.

The older brother, all the rest of his life, felt a gnawing sense of guilt. And the sister, when she heard what had happened to her little brother, remembered with grief the promise she had solemnly made to their father. She wept many tears and never ceased to mourn until her death.

Jameson, *Winter Studies and Summer Rambles in Canada*, 160-165.

■

# FATHER OF INDIAN CORN
## *Chippewa-Ojibwa*

■

In the long, long ago, a poor Ojibwa Indian lived with his wife and children in a remote part of the present state of Wisconsin. Because he was such a poor hunter, he was not very expert in providing food and supplies for his family.

His children were too young to give him much help. But he was a good man with a kind and contented disposition. He always was thankful to Chief of the Sky Spirits for everything he received to share with his family.

His good disposition was inherited by his eldest son, who had just reached the age when he wanted to pursue his Guardian Spirit Quest. Each young Indian boy looked forward to the time of finding the secret Spirit that would be his guide through his life. Each boy sought to learn his spirit name and what special power would be given him by his Guardian Spirit.

Eldest son had been obedient since early childhood. He seemed pensive, thoughtful of others, mild in manner, and always a joy to his family and to his tribe. At the first indication of spring, tradition told

*Crooked knife*
Ojibwa

him to build a hut somewhere in an isolated place. There, he would not be disturbed during his dream quest. He prepared his hut and himself and went immediately to begin his fast for seven days.

For the first few days, he amused himself walking in the woods and over the mountain trails. He examined trees, plants, and flowers. This kind of physical effort in the outdoors prepared him for a night of sound sleep. His observations of the day filled his mind with pleasant ideas and dreams.

More and more he desired to know how the trees, plants, flowers, and berries grew. Seemingly they grew wild without much help from the Indians. He wondered why some species were good to eat, while others contained poisonous juices. These thoughts came back to him many times as he retreated to his lodge at night. He secretly wished for a dream that would reveal what he could do to benefit his family and his tribe.

"I believe the Chief of Sky Spirits guides all things and it is to him I owe all things," he thought to himself. "I wonder if Chief Sky Spirit can make it easier for all Indians to acquire enough food without hunting animals every day to eat."

"I must try to find a way in my dreams," he pondered. He stayed on his bed the third day of fasting, because he felt weak and faint. Sometimes he thought that he was going to die. He dreamed that he saw a strong, handsome young man coming down from the sky, advancing toward him. He was richly dressed in green and yellow colors. He wore a plume of waving feathers on his head. His every movement was graceful.

"I have been sent to you," said the sky-visitor. "The Sky Chief who made all things in the sky and upon the earth intends for me to be your Guardian Spirit and I have come to test you.

"Sky Chief has observed all that you have done to prepare yourself for your Quest. He understands the kind and worthy secret wish of your heart. He knows that you desire a way to benefit your family and your tribe. He is pleased that you do not seek strength to make war. I have come to show you how to obtain your greatest wish. First, your spirit name shall be Wunzh."

The stranger then told Wunzh to arise and wrestle with him. This was the only way for him to achieve his sacred wish. As weak as he was from fasting, Wunzh wondered how he could ever wrestle the stranger.

He rose to the challenge—determined in his heart to die in the effort if he must. The two wrestled. After some time when Wunzh felt nearly exhausted, the Sky Stranger said, "It is enough for today. I will come again tomorrow to test you some more." Smiling, the visitor ascended in the same direction from which he came.

Next day at the same time, the stranger appeared. Again the two wrestled. While Wunzh felt weaker than the day before, he set his mind and heart to his task. His courage seemed to increase, however, in reverse proportion to his waning physical strength. The stranger stopped just in time before Wunzh dropped to the ground.

"Tomorrow will be your last chance. I urge you to be strong, my friend, as this is the only way for you to achieve your heart's sacred wish," said the sky-visitor.

Wunzh took to his bed with his last ounce of energy. He prayed to the Sky Chief for wisdom and enough strength to endure to the end of his Quest.

The third time they wrestled, Wunzh was so weak that his arms and legs felt like rubber. But his inner determination drove him forward with the kind of endurance necessary to win. The same length of time passed as in the first two wrestling bouts. Suddenly the stranger stopped and declared himself conquered by Wunzh!

Then the sky-visitor entered the lodge for the first time. He sat down beside Wunzh to instruct him in the way he should now proceed to achieve his secret wish.

"Great Sky Chief has granted your desire. You have wrestled manfully. Tomorrow will be your seventh day of fasting. Your father will come to see you and bring you food. As it is the last day of your fast, you will be able to succeed.

"Now I will tell you what you must do to achieve your final victory. Tomorrow we will wrestle once more. When you have prevailed over me for the last time, then throw me down and strip off my clothes. You must clean the earth of roots and weeds and make the ground soft. Then bury me in that very spot, covering me with my yellow and green clothes and then with earth.

"When you have done this, leave my body in the earth. Do not disturb it. Come occasionally to see if I have come to life. Be careful to see that no grass or weeds cover my grave. Once a month, cover me with fresh earth. If you follow what I have told you, you will succeed in your Guardian Spirit Quest. You will help your family and all the Indians by teaching them what I have now taught you," the Sky Stranger concluded as they shook hands and the visitor left.

On the seventh morning, Wunzh's father came with some food.

"My son, how do you feel? You have fasted long enough. It is seven days since you have eaten food. You must not sacrifice your life. The Great Spirit does not require that of you."

"My father, thank you for coming and for the food. Let me stay here alone until the sun goes down. I have my own special reasons."

"Very well. I shall wait for you at home until the hour of the setting-sun," replied the father as he departed.

The Sky Stranger returned at the same hour as before. The final wrestling match began. Wunzh had not eaten the food his father brought. But already he felt a new inner power that had somehow been given to him. Was it Spirit Power from his Guardian Spirit?

Wunzh grasped his opponent with supernatural strength and threw him to the ground. Wunzh removed the beautiful clothes and the plume. Then he discovered his friend was dead.

He remembered the instructions in every detail and buried his Guardian Spirit on the very spot where he had fallen. Wunzh followed every direction minutely, believing his friend would come to life again.

Wunzh returned to his father's lodge at sundown. He ate sparingly of the meal his mother prepared for him. Never for a moment could he forget the grave of his friend. Throughout the spring and into summer he visited the grave regularly. He carefully kept the area clean of grass and weeds. He carefully kept the ground soft and pliable. Soon he saw the tops of green plumes emerging through the earth. He noticed that the more care he gave the plants, the faster the green plumes seemed to grow.

Wunzh concealed his activity from his father. Days and weeks passed. Summer was drawing to a close. Then one day, Wunzh invited his father to follow him to the site of his Quest. He showed his father the graceful-looking plants growing there. They were topped with yellow silken hair and waving green plumes. Gold and green clusters of fruit adorned each side of the stalks.

"Father, these plants are from my dream friend," explained Wunzh. "He is my Guardian Spirit, a friend to all mankind, named Mon- daw-min, meaning 'corn for all Indians.' This is the answer to my Quest, my secret heart's wish. No longer will we need to hunt animals every day for our food. As long as we take care of our corn gift, the earth will give us good food for our living."

Wunzh pulled off the first ear of corn and give it to his father.

"See, my father. This corn is what I fasted for. The Chief of Sky Spirits has granted my Quest. He has sent us this wonderful new food of corn. From now on our people need not depend entirely upon hunting and fishing to survive."

Wunzh talked with his father, giving him all of the instructions he had received from his Guardian Spirit. He showed his father how the corn husks should be pulled off the stalks, and how the first seed must be saved for future plantings. He explained how the ears of corn should be held before the fire only long enough for the outer leaves to turn brown, so that the inside kernels remained sweet and juicy.

The entire family gathered for Wunzh's feast of corn. The father led a prayer of thanksgiving for the bountiful and good gift from the Chief of Sky Spirits. Wunzh felt happy that his Guardian Spirit Quest was successfully completed.

This is how Wunzh became known as the father of Indian corn by the Chippewa and Ojibwa Indian tribes.

Schoolcraft, *North American Indian Legends*, 99.

■

# LEGEND OF THE WHITE PLUME
## *Iowa*

The Iowa tribe belonged to the Siouan linguistic family. While the Iowa seemed to move often they generally remained within the boundaries of the state that still bears their name. In their early history, they located on a western tributary of the Mississippi River, and later moved into the northwestern/Iowa Okoboji Lake district as far as the Red Pipestone Quarry, even to the Big Sioux River. The Red Pipestone Quarry was across the Iowa line in southwest Minnesota. Indians from the entire region traveled to obtain the red stone for their pipes, giving name to the surrounding area and the future site of Pipestone National Monument. In the nineteenth century, they encountered the Dakota warriors and were defeated by Black Hawk in 1821. In about 1850, an Oklahoma tract held by the Iowa was granted to them in severalty. Other Iowans were allotted lands extending from the Platte River of Missouri through western Iowa up to Dakota country.

■

Long ago, near what is now Iowa City, lived a flourishing Iowa Indian tribe. The Chief of the Iowas was very proud of his two beautiful daughters. He was secretly hoping for one of them to marry the handsome hero White Plume, so called because he always wore one in his black hair.

One day, the Chief smeared his daughters' faces with charcoal and took them into the woods for them to fast and pray that one of them might attract the White Plume. The girls were most unhappy, crying until all the animals heard them and came running to find out what was the matter.

Each animal in turn asked, "Am I the one you are looking for?"

*Catlinite pipe bowl*
Iowa

"What do you do for a living?" they asked. "What animals do you kill for your food?" In this way they learned the nature of the animals. When the girls said, "No, you are not the one," that animal ran away.

On another day, a man came wearing a white plume. He announced, "Surely I am the one you are seeking. I hunt for deer, elk, bear, turkey, and all the other good things you like to eat."

Without hesitation, Older Sister decided to marry the man who-wore-the-white-plume. Next morning, Younger Sister said, "You have married the wrong man. Today the real White Plume will come." Older Sister was very cross and declared emphatically that she was certain she had married the true hero, White Plume.

In the middle of that day, birds began to chatter and sing, "White Plume is coming! White Plume is coming!" Even the meadowlarks, whom the Iowas say are really persons in disguise, were broadcasting loudly, "White Plume! White Plume!" Finally White Plume arrived.

"I believe that I am the one you have been seeking," he said to the two sisters.

Older Sister did not believe him, but Younger Sister welcomed him warmly. That same day, the two men each claiming to be White Plume went hunting. The real White Plume killed bear and deer, soon returning with his game.

The other hunter brought back only a few rabbits. Again and again the two men hunted, each returning with the same kind of game as before.

In a few days, the Chief of the Iowas came to visit his daughters. When he judged the results of the hunt, he was convinced that the first man who married Older Sister was an imposter. The Chief believed that the man who was the good provider was the real hero, White Plume.

Older sister began to have some doubts about her husband, and asked, "Why do you not kill larger game for us?" Her husband gave a poor excuse, "I do not think the larger game provide such good meat."

Again the two men hunted together, arriving in a valley where they saw a raccoon. The imposter tricked White Plume into chasing the raccoon into a bog. Now it happened that the imposter had the power to change people; so he changed White Plume into a dog.

Later, when the imposter returned to his lodge with the dog following him, he announced, "I found this dog in the woods. White Plume must have hunted in a different direction."

That night the dog slept in the lodge of Younger Sister. She fed him and made a comfortable place for him to sleep. Next day she took the dog with her into the woods to look for White Plume.

The dog soon killed a sleeping bear and other animals. Together the girl and dog hunted many times, always with success. One day when they were alone in the woods, the dog said to Younger Sister, "Take me to a hollow log and put me in it, then help pull me out at the other end." This she did. From the other end of the log she pulled out the real White Plume!

When the two of them returned to the lodge, the imposter said to the real White Plume, "You must have been lost in the woods." White Plume's answer was casual but pleasant. Later he told his wife, "Sometime, I will even the score."

In a few days, the two hunters started out for more game. White Plume killed a buffalo. They built a campfire, intending to camp there for the night. A sudden snowstorm came upon them. "Watch yourself," said the imposter. "This kind of a moon will burn your clothes."

That evening, they told many stories at the campfire, after which they prepared their blankets for a good night's sleep. Later in the night, White Plume called out to the imposter, but hearing no response, he quietly exchanged his own clothes, which he used for a pillow, with those of the imposter.

Much later in the night, the imposter awoke and stole the clothes from under White Plume's head and tossed them into the fire.

Next morning was bitter cold. White Plume grabbed for his clothes but they were not under his pillow. "Brother, my clothes are gone," he shouted, shivering with cold.

"Did I not tell you that this is the moon that burns your clothes?" said the imposter. Then he reached for his own clothes, only to discover that they were White Plume's clothes! The imposter had burned his own clothes!

Soon they started for home, with White Plume in the lead dragging the frozen buffalo. Somewhere along the way, the imposter must have frozen to death.

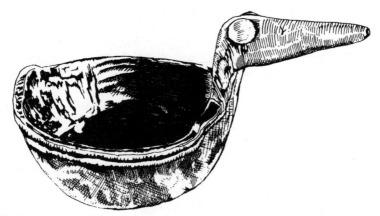

*Effigy bowl*
Winnebago

White Plume returned to his wife and Older Sister. He supplied them well with plenty of meat for the entire winter. Then he told them and the Chief of the Iowas that he was really an eagle.

"When your supplies run low, I shall return. When your Iowa hunters wish plenty of game, always they should wear an eagle's white plume in their hair," said White Plume with this parting blessing. Instantly he became a beautiful large eagle and flew far away.

Skinner, "The Legend of the White Plume," vol. 38, 458.

■

# BOY STOLEN BY THUNDERBIRD
## *Winnebago*

Winnebago were called "people of the filthy water" and even the English called them Stinkards. They belonged to the Siouan family, related to some Iowa, Oto, and Missouri bands, Winnebago of ancient times lived on Green Bay in Wisconsin territory, extending inland to Lake Winnebago. Though they generally maintained peaceful relations with surrounding tribes, in 1671 they were nearly destroyed by Illinois tribe raiders, but recovered from the surprise attack. Winnebagoes thrived upon a delicious native grass they named wild-rice, which grew abundantly in lakes, ponds, and streambeds. These plants, self-seeding in spring and summer and harvested from canoes and barges in fall, maintained their people in good health. They also hunted much game for meat and furs. By treaty in 1825 and 1830 they ceded all of their lands to the federal government in return for a large reservation on the west side of the Mississippi River above the Iowa River. Later, Winnebago moved to another reservation in Minnesota, then to Nebraska where they remain. Winnebago are known as a mother tribe of Siouan linguistic families.

■

Many, many years ago, a young Winnebago Indian orphan boy lived in a small village with his grandmother. He found a friend about his own age. One day, they hunted for hickory wood to make bird arrows, which they used for hunting hawks. Orphan-Boy captured a young pigeon hawk and took it home. Soon, it became his pet bird.

Some time later, Orphan-Boy put a little tobacco in a bundle and tied it around the hawk's neck. It disappeared for a few days, then returned without the tobacco bundle. Again, Orphan-Boy tied another bundle of tobacco around his pet's neck. It disappeared again, but returned to Orphan-Boy as it had before.

When the pet hawk became fully grown, Orphan-Boy suggested that it might want to go away and make a life for itself. So he tied another tobacco bundle around the pigeon hawk's neck, thanking him for staying with him for so long a time. Immediately, the bird flew away and never returned to Orphan-Boy.

Another day, Orphan-Boy and his friend hunted for dogwood to make pointed arrows. They accidentally became separated in a low fog. From above, however, a bad Thunderbird saw Orphan-Boy and swooped down, seizing him in his claws. The huge bird carried him away to its home in the high mountains.

For a long, long time the friend looked for Orphan-Boy. Finally, he gave up searching far and wide. But every day, he faithfully returned to the place where Orphan-Boy had disappeared, mourning still for his lost companion.

When the bad Thunderbird reached its mountainous home, he and his friends tied Orphan-Boy down to the floor. Their purpose was to hold him there until nothing remained in his stomach. Then they planned to devour him.

Little pigeon hawk decided to go and have a look at Thunderbird's prisoner. Imagine his surprise to find that Orphan-Boy, his kind friend, was the prisoner.

Little pigeon hawk left and decided to hunt for some young birds and roast them. Later, he returned, putting some of the meat under his wings and secretly dropping it into Orphan-Boy's mouth. Every day little pigeon hawk brought meat for Orphan-Boy, until the thunderbirds became suspicious of pigeon hawk.

The next day, the bad thunderbirds decided to exclude little pigeon hawk when he came to visit Orphan-Boy. One thunderbird pushed him toward the door, but little pigeon hawk accidentally on purpose fell close to the fire and scorched some of his feathers. He made a great noise and commotion, running to his big brother, Big Black-Hawk, who was Chief of the Thunderbirds.

"What can the matter be, little brother?" asked the Chief. Little pigeon hawk told his big brother the whole story from the beginning. When the Chief heard all, he became very angry.

Immediately, he went to the place where Orphan-Boy was still held down to the floor. The Chief scolded the bad thunderbirds for their wrongdoing. Because they had pushed little pigeon hawk too close to the fire, the Chief announced they could no longer keep Orphan-Boy as

All of the deer in the cave came out and disappeared into the forest. Following them were raccoons, rabbits, and all the other four-footed animals. Last came turkeys, partridges, pigeons, and other winged creatures. They darkened the air as they flew away. Such a noise arose that Kenati heard it at his lodge. To himself he said, "I must go to see what trouble my boys have stirred up."

Kenati went to the mountain, to the place of the large rock. There stood the two boys, but all the animals and birds were gone. Kenati was furious with them, but said nothing. He went into the cave and kicked off the covers of four large jars that stood in the back corner.

Out of the jars swarmed bedbugs, lice, and gants that attached the two boys. they screamed from terror as they tried to beat off the insects. Bitten and stung, the boys dropped to the ground from exhaustion.

When Kenati thought they had learned their lesson, he brushed away the pests. "Now you rascals," he scolded them. "You have always had plenty to eat without working for it. When we needed game, all I had to do was to come up here and take home just what we needed. Now you have let all of the game escape. From now on when you are hungry, you will have to hunt throughout the woods and mountains and then not find enough game."

The two boys went home and asked their mother for something to eat.

"There is no more meat," said Selu. "I will go to the storehouse and try to find something."

She took her basket and went to the two-story provision house set upon poles high above the ground, out of reach of most animals.

Every day before the evening meal, Selu climbed the ladder to the one opening. She always came back with her basket full of beans and corn.

"Let's go and see where she gets the corn and beans," urged Wild Boy to his brother. They followed Selu and climbed up in back of the storehouse. They removed a piece of mud from between the logs and looked through the crack. There stood Selu in the middle of the room with her basket on the floor. When she rubbed her stomach, the basket was half-filled with corn. When she rubbed her legs, the basket was full to the top with beans. Wild Boy said, "Our mother is a witch. Maybe her food will poison us."

When Selu came back to the house, she seemed to know what the boys were thinking. "You think I am a witch?"

"Yes, we think you are a witch," Wild Boy replied.

"When I die, I want you boys to clear a large piece of ground in front of our lodge. Then drag all of my clothes seven times around the inside of the circle. If you stay up all night and watch, next morning you will be rewarded with plenty of corn."

*Booger mask*
Cherokee

Soon thereafter Selu became ill and died suddenly. The boys set to work clearing the ground as she had said. But instead of the whole piece of ground in front of the lodge, they only cleared seven small spots. This is why corn does not grow everywhere in the world.

Instead of dragging Selu's clothing seven times, they only went around the circle twice, outside and inside the circle. The brothers watched all night, and in the morning there were fully grown beans and corn, but only in the seven small spots.

Kenati came home from a long hunting trip. He looked for Selu but could not find her. When the boys came home, he asked them, "Where is your mother?"

"She turned into a witch and then she died," they reported. Kenati was saddened by the news.

"I cannot stay here with you any longer. I will go and live with the Wolf people," he said.

He started on his journey. Wild Boy changed himself into a tuft of bird's down and settled upon Kenati's shoulder to learn where he was going.

When Kenati reached the settlement of the Wolf people, they were having a council in their town-house. He went in and sat down with the tuft upon his shoulder. Wolf Chief asked Kenati what was his business.

"At home I have two bad boys. In seven days, I want you to go and play a game of ball with them."

The Wolf people knew that Kenati wanted them to punish the boys and promised to go in seven days. At that moment the down blew off of Kenati's shoulder and the smoke carried it up and through the smoke hole in the roof. It came down to the ground outside, where Wild Boy resumed his own shape and ran home fast to tell his brother. Kenati did not return but went on to visit another tribe.

The two brothers prepared for the coming of the wolves. Wild Boy the magician told his brother what to do. Together they made a path around the house, leaving an opening on one side for the wolves to enter.

Next, they made four large bundles of arrows. These they placed at four different points on the outside of the circle. Then they hid themselves in the woods nearby and waited for the wolves.

At the appointed time, a whole army of wolves surrounded the house. They came in the entrance the boys had made. When all were within, Wild Boy magically made the pathway become a high fence, trapping the wolves inside.

The two boys on the outside began shooting arrows at the wolves. Since the fence was too high for the wolves to jump over, they were trapped and most were killed.

Only a few escaped through the entrance and made their way into a nearby swamp. Three or four wolves eventually survived. These were the only wolves left alive in the world.

Soon thereafter, some strangers came from a great distance to learn about the brothers' good grain for eating and making bread. Only Selu and her family had the corn secret.

The two brothers told the strangers how to care for the corn and gave them seven kernels to plant the next night on their way home. They were advised that they must watch throughout the night, then the following morning they would have seven ears of corn. This they should do each night, and by the time they reached home, they should have enough corn for all their people to plant.

The strangers lived seven days' distance. Each night they did as the brothers had instructed them. On the last night of the journey, they were so tired that they fell asleep and were unable to continue the whole night's watch. Next morning, the corn had not sprouted and grown as on the previous six nights.

Upon arriving in their own village, they shared all the corn they still had left with their people.  They explained how the two brothers told them the way to make the corn prosper.  They watched over the planting with care and attention.  A splendid crop of corn resulted.  Since then, however, the Cherokee Indians needed to tend their corn only half the year to supply their people.

Kenati never came back to his home.  The two brothers decided to search for him.  Wild Boy sailed a magic disk to the northwind and it returned.  He sailed it to the southwind and it returned, but it did not return from the eastwind.  They knew that was where their father was living.  They walked a long, long time and finally came upon Kenati with a dog walking by his side.

"You bad boys," rebuked Kenati.  "Why have you followed me here?"

"We are men now," they replied.  "We plan to accomplish what we set out to do."  Wild Boy knew that the dog was the magic disk that had not returned, and had become a dog only a few days ago.

Kenati's trail led to Selu, waiting for him at the end of the world where the sun comes up.  All seemed glad to be reunited for the present.

Their parents told the two brothers that they must go to live where the sun goes down.  In seven days, the two boys left for the Land of the Setting-Sun.  There they still live, overseeing the planting and the care of corn.

The brothers still talk about how Selu brought forth the first corn from her seed.  Since that time, the Cherokee tribe refer to her as the "Corn Woman."

Mooney, "The Origin of Game and of Corn," 97-108.

∎

# THE BALL GAME OF THE BIRDS AND THE ANIMALS

## *Cherokee*

The following myth explains the origin of a custom of the Cherokee Indians of North Carolina.  They used to prepare for a popular ball game by holding a dance the night before.  While the drummers beat on their drums, the rest of the people chanted songs.  Before the game, each player asked the help of the bat and of the flying squirrel. For good luck, each player tied a small piece of bat's wing to the stick he would hit the ball with.

■

Long ago, the animals sent a message to the birds. "Let us have a big ball game. We will defeat you in a big ball game."

The birds answered, "We will meet you. We will defeat *you* in a big ball game."

So the plans were made. The day was set. At a certain place, all the animals gathered, ready to throw the ball to the birds in the trees. On the side of the animals were the bear, the deer, and the terrapin or turtle. The bear was heavier than the other animals. He was heavier than all the birds put together. The deer could run faster than the other animals could. The turtle had a very thick shell. So the animals felt sure that they would win the game.

The birds, too, felt sure that they would win. On their side were the eagle, the hawk, and the great raven. All three could fly swiftly. All three had farseeing eyes. All three were strong and had sharp beaks that could tear.

*Lacrosse stick*
Cherokee

In the treetops the birds smoothed their feathers. Then they watched every movement of the animals on the ground below them. As they watched, two small creatures climbed up the tree toward the leader of the birds. These two creatures were but a little bigger than mice.

"Will you let us join in the game?" they asked the leader of the birds.

The leader looked at them for a moment. He saw that they had four feet.

"Why don't you join the animals?" he asked them. "Because you have four feet, you really belong on the other side."

"We asked to play the game on their side," the tiny creatures answered. "But they laughed at us because we are so small. They do not want us."

The leader of the birds felt sorry for them. So did the eagle, the hawk, and the other birds.

"But how can they join us when they have no wings?" the birds asked each other.

"Let us make wings for the little fellows," one of the birds suggested.

"We can make wings from the head of the drum," another bird suggested.

The drum had been used in the dance the night before. Its head was the skin of a groundhog. The birds cut two pieces of leather from it, shaped them like wings, and fastened them to the legs of one of the little fellows. Thus they made the first bat.

The leader gave directions. He said to the bat, "When I toss the ball, you catch it. Don't let it touch the ground.

The bat caught it. He dodged and circled. He zigzagged very fast. He kept t he ball always in motion, never letting it touch the ground. The birds were glad they had made wings for him.

"What shall we do with the other little fellow?" asked the leader of the birds. "We have used up all our leather in making the wings for the bat."

The birds thought and thought. At last one of them had an idea.

"Let us make wings for him by stretching his skin," suggested the eagle.

So eagle and hawk, two of the biggest birds, seized the little fellow. With their strong bills they tugged and pulled at his fur. In a few minutes they stretched the skin between his front feet and his hind feet. His own fur made wings. Thus they made the first flying squirrel.

When the leader tossed the ball, flying squirrel caught it and carried it to another tree. From there he threw it to the eagle. Eagle caught it and threw it to another bird. The birds kept the ball in the air for some time, but at last they dropped it. Just before it reached the ground, the bat seized it. Dodging and circling and zigzagging, he kept out of the way of the deer and other swift animals. At last bat threw the ball in at the goal. And so he won the game for the birds.

Mooney, "Myths of the Cherokee," 286-287.

———, "The Cherokee Ball Play," 575-586.

■

# THE ORIGIN OF MEDICINE
## Cherokee

■

At one time, animals and people lived together peaceably and talked with each other. But when mankind began to multiply rapidly, the animals were crowded into forests and deserts.

Man began to destroy animals wholesale for their skins and furs, not just for needed food. Animals became angry at such treatment by their former friends, resolving they must punish mankind.

The bear tribe met in council, presided over by Old White Bear, their Chief. After several bears had spoken against mankind for their blood-thirsty ways, war was unanimously agreed upon. But what kinds of weapons should the bears use?

Chief Old White Bear suggested that man's weapon, the bow and arrow, should be turned against him. All of the council agreed. While the bears worked and made bows and arrows, they wondered what to do about bowstrings. One of the bears sacrificed himself to provide the strings, while the others searched for good arrow-wood.

When the first bow was completed and tried, the bear's claws could not release the strings to shoot the arrow. One bear offered to cut his claws, but Chief Old White Bear would not allow him to do that, because without claws he could not climb trees for food and safety. He might starve.

The deer tribe called together its council led by Chief Little Deer. They decided that any Indian hunters, who killed deer without asking pardon in a suitable manner, should be afflicted with painful rheumatism in their joints.

After this decision, Chief Little Deer sent a messenger to their nearest neighbors, the Cherokee Indians.

"From now on, your hunters must first offer a prayer to the deer before killing him," said the messenger. "You must ask his pardon, stating you are forced only by the hunger needs of your tribe to kill the deer. Otherwise, a terrible disease will come to the hunter."

When a deer is slain by an Indian hunter, Chief Little Deer will run to the spot and ask the slain deer's spirit, "Did you hear the hunter's prayer for pardon?"

If the reply is yes, then all is well and Chief Little Deer returns to his cave. But if the answer is no, then the Chief tracks the hunter to his lodge and strikes him with the terrible disease of rheumatism, making him a helpless cripple unable to hunt again.

All the fishes and reptiles then held a council and decided they would haunt those Cherokee Indians, who tormented them, by telling them hideous dreams of serpents twining around them and eating them alive. These snake and fish dreams occurred often among the Cherokees. To get relief, the Cherokees pleaded with their Shaman to banish their frightening dreams if they no longer tormented the snakes and fish.

Now when the friendly plants heard what the animals had decided against mankind, they planned a countermove of their own. Each tree, shrub, herb, grass, and moss agreed to furnish a cure for one of the diseases named by the animals and insects.

Thereafter, when the Cherokee Indians visited their Shaman about their ailments and if the medicine man was in doubt, he communed with the spirits of the plants. They always suggested a proper remedy for mankind's diseases.

This was the beginning of plant medicine from nature among the Cherokee Indian tribe a long, long time ago.

Spence, *Myths of the American Indians*, 249-251.

■

# THE HERO WITH THE HORNED SNAKES
## *Cherokee*

■

In ancient times, there lived some very large snakes that glittered nearly as bright as the sun. They had two horns on their heads, and they possessed a magic power of attraction. To see one of these snakes was always a bad omen. Whoever tried to escape from one instead ran directly toward the snake and was devoured.

Only a highly skilled medicine man or hunter could kill a two-horned snake. It required a very special medicine or power. The hunter had to shoot his arrow into the seventh stripe of the snake's skin.

One day a Shawnee Indian youth was held captive by the Cherokees. He was promised his freedom if he could find and kill a horned snake. He hunted for many, many days in caves, over wild mountains, and at last found one high in the Tennessee Mountains.

The Shawnee youth made a large circle of fire by burning pinecones. Then he walked toward the two-horned snake. When it saw the hunter, the snake slowly raised its head. The Shawnee youth shouted, "Freedom or death!"

He then aimed carefully and shot his arrow through the seventh stripe of the horned snake's skin. Turning quickly, he jumped into the center of the ring of fire, where he felt safe from the snake.

A stream of poison flowed from the snake, but was stopped by the fire. Because of the Shawnee youth's bravery, the grateful Cherokees granted him his freedom as they had promised.

Four days later, some of the Cherokees went to the spot where the youth had killed the horned snake. They gathered fragments of snake bones and skin, tying them into a sacred bundle. These they kept carefully for their children and grandchildren, because they believed the sacred bundle would bring good fortune to their tribe.

Also on the same spot, a small lake formed containing black water. Into this water the Cherokee women dipped their twigs used in their basketmaking. This is how they learned to dye their baskets black, along with other colors.

Kate, "The Hero With the Horned Snake," 55.

■

# THE GREEN CORN FESTIVAL

## *Shawnee*

Prior to the Green Corn Festival was the Ceremony held when the first green corn shoots appeared. For the Festival, chanting shamans and warriors circled a cooking fire, carrying cornstalks. These first ears were boiled, removed from the pot, and tied to four tepeelike poles above the fire, as a sacred offering to the Great Spirit. The first ashes were buried, then a large new fire was kindled, cooking corn for the entire village to share in the ensuing feast and dance.

■

No one of the Shawnee people was allowed to eat any corn, even from his own field, until the proper authority was given. When some corn was ready to be eaten, the one who had the authority announced the date for the Corn Feast and Dance.

*Strap-handled and incised pot*
Shawnee

On this occasion, great numbers of roasting ears were prepared, and all the people ate as freely as they desired. After this feast, everyone could have what he wished from that particular field.

This was probably the most highly esteemed Peace Festival among the Shawnees and other corn-growing tribes. It might properly be called the First Fruits Festival, similar to the First Roots Festival and the First Berries Festival held annually by many tribes.

Another Corn Feast was held in the fall, but not so universally as the one when the first corn was ready to be eaten. The first one of each year was held at planting time. It was a feast to secure the blessing of the Great Spirit, so that they might have a bountiful crop.

All of these were religious festivals, and all were accompanied by chants and dancing.

Spencer, "Shawnee Folklore," 319-326.

■

# THE WALNUT-CRACKER
## *Creek*

Creeks became a combined Creek Confederacy of most tribes of the southeastern states who thrived as early as de Soto's time in the early 1500s. Two strong geographical groups, the Upper Creeks and Lower Creeks, each possessed many interesting tribes that gradually increased in size and spread throughout Georgia, Alabama, Florida, Louisiana, Mississippi, and the Carolinas. As whites spread southward along coastal areas, Creeks were driven to the interior areas, especially along the Chattahoochee and Ocmulgee rivers. In the 1700s and 1800s bands of Creek tribes migrated northward, infiltrating tribes of the central, plains, and southwestern areas.

■

A long time ago in western Georgia, among the Southeastern Creek-Hitchiti Indians, lived Walnut-Cracker. His name was given him because he spent most of his time gathering, cracking, and eating walnuts in the same spot.

He always placed walnuts on a large stone and cracked them open, using a smaller stone. For the rest of the day and evening he ate walnuts. This was how Walnut-Cracker lived for many years. When he died, his people buried him at the place where the walnuts grew.

Some time later, a Creek hunter passed that very place and found a large mound of walnuts. As he was hungry, he cracked some and ate the good meat. Later that same evening the hunter returned. He sat down and cracked many walnuts on the large stone.

While the hunter was busy cracking and eating walnuts, a man came out of his nearby lodge. He heard someone at the place where Walnut-Cracker had lived. He listened and plainly heard the cracking noise. Looking closely through the darkness, he saw what looked like a person sitting where Walnut-Cracker always sat.

The man went back into his lodge announcing, "Walnut-Cracker, who died and was buried, now sits at his same place, cracking walnuts on the large stone! Do you think it is his ghost?"

All of the man's family came outside quietly, looking toward Walnut-Cracker's place. There they saw someone cracking walnuts on the large stone, who surely looked like Walnut-Cracker himself.

One of the family was a Lame Man, a good friend of Walnut-Cracker.

"Take me along on your back," he pleaded. "I want to see him again." So he was carried on the back of another who walked quietly toward the ghost.

That is what they thought, and they stopped in fear. But Lame Man whispered, "Please, take me a little farther." His companion took him a little way, then stopped. The hunter did not hear them, because he was cracking walnuts.

"Please take me a little farther," again asked Lame Man. The hunter looked up and saw the people through the shadows. He jumped up, seized his bow and arrows, and ran away!

When the ghost moved, the people ran back to their lodge. The one carrying the Lame Man became frightened and dropped him and left, running back to the lodge. Lame Man, too, jumped up and ran to his people. He was no longer a lame man!

Tribal storytellers say, "He outran the others, beating them to the lodge. He walked perfectly ever after."

As for Walnut-Cracker, no one saw his ghost again!

Swanton, "The Walnut Cracker," 115-116

■

# HOW RABBIT FOOLED ALLIGATOR
## *Creek*

Long ago, the Creek tribe lived mostly in the area of Georgia and Florida. Tribal storytellers loved to relate the following legend over and over to their young people, who loved to hear it again and again.

■

When the animals talked with each other just like people do today, a very handsome alligator lay sunning himself luxuriously on a log in which we now call the Florida Everglades. Then along came Mr. Rabbit, who said to him, "Mr. Handsome Alligator, have you ever seen the devil?"

"No, Mr. Rabbit, but I am not afraid of the devil. Are you?" replied Mr. Alligator.

"Well now, Mr. A., I did see the devil. Do you know what he said about you?" asked Rabbit.

"Now, just what did the devil have to say about me?" Alligator replied.

"The devil said that you are afraid of him," said Rabbit. "Besides, he said you would not even look at him."

"Rubbish," said Alligator. "I know that I am not afraid of the devil, and I am not afraid to look at him. Please tell him so for me the next time you see him."

"I do not think you are willing to crawl up the hill the day after tomorrow and allow me to introduce you to the devil himself," said Rabbit.

"Oh, yes, I am willing and ready to go with you," replied Alligator. "Let us go tomorrow."

"That is just fine with me," replied Rabbit. "But Mr. A., when you see some smoke rising somewhere, do not be afraid. It is a sign that the devil is moving about and will soon be on his way."

"You do not have to worry about me," said Alligator. "I told you I am not afraid of the devil."

"When you see the friendly birds flying about, and the deer running at a gallop, do not be afraid," said Rabbit.

"Don't you be concerned, because I will not be afraid," repeated Alligator.

"If you hear some fire crackling and its comes closer to you, do not be scared," said Rabbit. "If the grasses near you begin to smoke, do not be scared. The devil is only wandering about. Then is the time for you to get a good look at him when the heat is hottest."

After Rabbit's final words of wisdom, he left Alligator sunning himself.

Next day, Rabbit returned and asked Alligator to crawl up the hill, following him. Rabbit led him to the very top and directed him to lie in the tallest grass. Then Rabbit left Alligator, laughing to himself all the way down the hill, because he had led Alligator to the farthest place away from his home in the water.

On his way, Rabbit came to a smoldering stump. He picked up a piece, carrying it back to the high grass, where he made a fire so the wind blew it toward Alligator.

Soon the fire surrounded the place, burning closer and closer to Alligator. Rabbit then ran to a sandy knoll and sat down to watch the fun, chuckling over the trick he had played on Mr. Alligator.

Only a short time passed when the smoke rose in thick spirals, and the birds flew upward and away. Other animals ran for their lives across the field.

Alligator cried out, "Oh, Mr. Rabbit, where are you?"

"You just lie there quietly," replied Rabbit. "It's only the devil prowling about."

The fire began to roar and spread rapidly. "Oh, Mr. Rabbit, what is that I hear?" asked Alligator.

*Southeast Indian alligator basket*
Creek

"That's just the devil breathing hard," replied Rabbit. "Do not be scared. You will see him soon!"

Rabbit became so amused that he rolled and rolled on the sandy knoll and kicked his heels up in the air with glee.

Soon the grass surrounding Alligator caught fire and began to burn beneath him. Alligator rolled and twisted with pain from his burns.

"Do not be afraid now, Mr. Alligator," called Rabbit. "Just be quiet for a little while longer, and the devil will be there for you to get a firsthand look at him."

Alligator could not stand any more toasting! He started to crawl as fast as he could down the hillside toward the water. He wriggled through the burning grass, snapping his jaws, rolling in pain, and choking from the smoke.

Rabbit, upon his sandy knoll, laughed and laughed, jumping up and down with delight at the trick he had played on Alligator.

"Wait a minute, Mr. A. Don't be in such a hurry. You said you were not afraid of the devil," called Rabbit.

By that time Alligator had reached his home in the water, tumbling in to stop the pain of his roasted skin.

Never again did Mr. Handsome Alligator trust that trickster, Mr. Rabbit, or any of his family, ever!

Swanton, "How Rabbit Fooled Alligator," 52-53.

■

# THE CELESTIAL CANOE
## *Alabama*

The Alabama tribe was recognized as early as the 1500s in the chronicles of the Spanish explorer Hernando de Soto, and their relationship with the French dates as far back as the establishment of Fort Toulouse in Alabama in 1717. The tribe's long history was recognized when the state of Alabama took its name and called its principle river the Alabama.

■

Many eons ago, a magic canoe descended from the sky and touched earth near where the Alabama Indian tribe had its camp. Several young women came out of the canoe, singing and laughing. They ran everywhere, enjoying their freedom and playing a game of bounce-ball and catch with each other.

When they tired, they climbed back into their magic canoe, still signing and laughing, and sailed back up to the sky. Another day, they came again the same way as before, singing and dancing, and playing ball. They repeated this performance many times, and always the canoe returned to the same place on earth.

One day, an Alabama Indian youth watched from behind some bushes as the magic canoe descended. During a game, the ball was thrown toward him. A young woman came running after it. When she was near enough, the youth grabbed her hand. The others were frightened and took off in their magic canoe and disappeared into the sky.

The captured woman from the sky became the wife of that same Alabama Indian, and in time they had several children. The father made a large canoe for his family and a smaller canoe for himself.

"Father, we would like to have some fresh meat," the children said one day. "Will you please hunt a deer for us?" The father started through the woods to hunt deer. But in a short time he returned without any game.

The mother said to her children, "Ask your father to go farther away and hunt for a big fat deer this time." Again the children asked their father, and again he went hunting.

While he was away, the mother put the children in the larger canoe with herself, singing the magic song. They rose toward the sky. But the father came running back just in time to pull the canoe down to the ground.

Another time when the father was away, the mother put the children in the large canoe and herself in the small canoe, singing as they rose. At that moment the father came running home, pulling down the large canoe with his children. The mother, singing continuously, disappeared into the sky.

After many weeks, the father missed his wife and the children became lonesome for their mother. Finally, all of them climbed into the large canoe and sang the magic flight song. They sailed upward and away to the sky and through the clouds.

When they arrived in the sky, they came to an old grandmother sitting beside her lodge. The father said to her, "Grandmother, we have come because my children want to see their mother."

"She is yonder, dancing and singing all the time," answered the old grandmother. "If you will please sit down in my lodge, I will cook you some squashes."

When she placed the food before them, they thought to themselves, "This will not be enough." But when they ate one little squash, a larger one magically took its place! They were very hungry and ate for a long time. When they finished, more food was left than when they started to eat. The old grandmother broke an ear of corn and gave the pieces to the children.

The father took his children to another person's house and inquired of their mother. "She stays here, dancing all the time," was the reply. Suddenly the mother danced by, but she did not recognize her family. The next time she danced by, the children threw pieces of corn to attract her attention.

"I smell something earthy," she said. But she danced by on the run again. When she returned, dancing, to the same spot, a small piece of corn hit her feet and she exclaimed, "My children must be here!"

She ran back to them, hugging her entire family. The father then loaded all of them into his canoe and brought his entire family back to earth.

When the family was nicely settled, the father again went hunting. This time the mother took all of her children back to the sky in the magic canoe, singing her song that carried them away. The father never saw his family again, because they became sky people forever.

The father returned to the camp of his Alabama tribe, where he chose another wife, an Indian maiden, whom he felt assured would remain with him on earth.

Swanton, "The Celestial Canoe," 138.

■

# THE MILKY WAY
## Seminole

These Seminole stories were told to their people by Josie Billie, an old Seminole raised in the Big Cypress Swamp of the Everglades. These beliefs he learned from the ancients of his tribe, when he was very young, and later he became the Seminole tribal historian.

■

Ever so long ago, the Breathmaker blew his breath toward the sky and created the Milky Way. This broad pathway in the night sky leads to the City of the West. There is where the souls of good Indians go when they die.

Bad Indian souls stay in the ground where they are buried. When the Seminole Indians walk through the woods and step where a bad person has been buried, they become fearful. Even though the grave is covered with brush, they always seem to know that a bad person is buried there.

The Seminoles say the Milky Way shines brightest following the death of one of their tribe. They believe this is so that the path to the City in the Sky will be lighted brightly for the traveling Seminole.

For a good Indian to be able to walk over the Milky Way, he must first be one whom everyone likes. He cannot be one who talks in an evil manner, or lies and steals. He must be brave at all times and an honor to the Seminoles.

In the Seminole language, *so-lo-pi he-ni* means "spirit way" or "the Milky Way for human souls." And *if-i he-ni* means "dog way" and is the sky-path for the souls of dogs and other animals that die. Spirits never return to earth from the City in the Sky. Seminoles do not believe that ghostly visitors ever come back and visit their people again.

Along the Milky Way lives Rain and Rainbow. The Seminole word for Rainbow means stop-the-rain, and that is what the Rainbow does when it appears.

When the Sun is eclipsed, Seminoles say that toad-frog has come along and taken a bite out of the Sun. Toad-frog continues eating at the Sun until the Sun disappears. Seminole hunters shoot arrows at toad-frogs whenever they see one, preventing eclipses of the Sun or Moon. Seminole hunters like to make a loud clamor to scare the toad-frogs away when they do appear.

Along the Milky Way is Big Dipper, which seems like a boat to the Seminoles. They say it is used to carry the souls of good Seminoles along the Milky Way to the City in the Sky.  The Seminole tribe calls the Morning Star the Tomorrow Star, and the Evening Star is known to them as the Red Star.

Greenlee, "The Milky Way," 138-140.

■

# MEN VISIT THE SKY
## *Seminole*

■

Near the beginning of time, five Seminole Indian men wanted to visit the sky to see the Great Spirit.

They traveled to the East, walking for about a month.  Finally, they arrived at land's end.  They tossed their baggage over the end and they, too, disappeared beyond earth's edge.

Down, down, down the Indians dropped for a while, before starting upward again toward the sky.  For a long time they traveled westward.  At last, they came to a lodge where lived an old, old woman.

"Tell me, for whom are you looking?" she asked feebly.

"We are on our way to see the Great Spirit Above," they replied.

"It is not possible to see him now," she said.  "You must stay here for a while first."

That night the five Seminole Indian men strolled a little distance from the old woman's lodge, where they encountered a group of angels robed in white and wearing wings.  They were playing a ball game the men recognized as one played by the Seminoles.

Two of the men decided they would like to remain and become angels.  The other three preferred to return to earth.  Then to their surprise, the Great Spirit appeared and said, "So be it!"

A large cooking pot was placed on the fire.  When the water was boiling, the two Seminoles who wished to stay were cooked! When only their bones were left, the Great Spirit removed them from the pot, and put their bones back together again.  He then draped them with a white cloth and touched them with his magic wand.  The Great Spirit brought the two Seminole men back to life! They wore beautiful white wings and were called men-angels.

"What do you three men wish to do?" asked the Great Spirit.

"If we may, we prefer to return to our Seminole camp on earth," replied the three Seminoles.

*Chickee*
Seminole

"Gather your baggage together and go to sleep at once," directed the Great Spirit.

Later, when the three Seminole men opened their eyes, they found themselves safe at home again in their own Indian camp.

"We are happy to return and stay earthbound. We hope never to venture skyward again in search of other mysteries," they reported to the Chief of the Seminoles.

Greenlee, "Men Visit the Sky to See God," 143.

■

# ADOPTION OF THE HUMAN RACE
## *Natchez*

Before Europeans arrived in the Great Southeast, between the Atlantic Ocean and the Mississippi River, there were one to two million tribal Indians gathered in their fertile homeland, speaking a variety of languages. The Natchez tribe, on the Gulf Coast, developed skills in contriving numerous kinds of fishing equipment to catch the tremendous quantities and types of fish available to them in fresh and salt waters. Their people had an abundance for themselves and for sale or trade with others.

■

In the very beginning, Moon, Sun, Wind, Rainbow, Thunder, Fire, and Water once met a very old man. This wise old man turned out to be Chief of the Sky Spirits. Thunder asked him, "Can you make the people of the world my children?"

"No, no, no!" Wise Old Man replied. "They cannot be your children, but they can be your grandchildren."

Sun asked Old Man, "Can you make the people of the world my children?"

"No, they cannot be your children" answered Old Man. "But they can be your friends and grandchildren. Your main purpose is to give plenty of light."

Moon asked, "Can you make the people of the world my children?"

"No, no, I cannot do that," Old Man replied. "The people of the world can be your nephews and friends."

Fire asked that the people of the world be made his children.

Wise Old Man replied, "No, I cannot give them to you to be your children, but the people of the world can be your grandchildren. You can be their warmth and give them fire to cook their food."

Wind asked the same question as the others. Wise Old Man told Wind, "No, no, the people of the world cannot be your children, but they can be your grandchildren. You can remove the bad air and all kinds of diseases from the people, and keep them healthy."

Rainbow wanted the people to be his children. "No, they cannot be your children," Wise Old Man explained. "You will always be busy preventing too much rain and floods upon the earth."

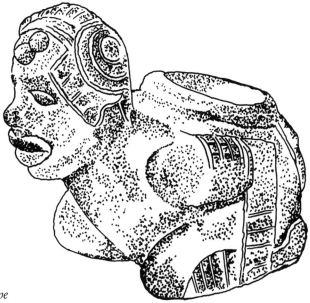

*Effigy pipe*
Natchez

Water asked that human beings be made his children, but Wise Old Man answered, "No, the people of the world can never be your children. When they get dirty, you must always be available to wash them clean. You shall give them long life."

Wise Old Man continued, "I have now told all of you the best ways to guide yourselves and what you can do to help the people of the world. You must always remember that these children of the human race are my children."

Swanton, "Adoption of the Human Race," 240.

*Corn husk mask*
Seneca

# PART SIX

# FROM THE NORTHEAST

*Abnaki or Wabanaki, meaning "those living at the sunrise," was the farthest northeastern Maine tribe. Belonging to the Algonquian linguistic family, they were believed to have immigrated from the South. It is possible that they saw their first white men in 1498 when John Cabot explored the Abnaki territory along the northeast coast.*

*Penobscot and Passamaquoddy tribes were closely related to the Abnaki. When the boundary line between the United States and Canada was established, the Penobscot and Passamaquoddy settled on the southern side. Some of their relatives still lived in Canada. Each of these tribes have a representative in the Maine legislature to speak only on tribal concerns.*

*Iroquois, meaning "we are of the extended house" or "longhouse people," consisted of five strong tribes in the New York State area. The Cayuga, Mohawk, Oneida, Onondaga, and Senecas united to form the large and powerful Iroquois Confederacy in about 1390. The Tuscaroras joined the league in 1715. Influence of the Iroquois League of United Nations spread to other tribes from the eastern shore of Maine to the Mississippi River.*

■

# THE FIRST PEOPLE AND THE FIRST CORN
## Penobscot-Passamaquoddy

This legend was written by a Penobscot Indian, Joseph Nicolar, and was published in 1893. The Passamaquoddy of Maine, as well as the Micmac and Malecite of Nova Scotia, also told this story.

■

Long ago, Klos-kur-beh, the Great Teacher, lived in the land where no people lived. One day at noon, a young man came to him and called him "Mother's brother."

Standing before Klos-kur-beh, he said, "I was born of the foam of the waters. The wind blew, and the waves quickened into foam. The sun shone on the foam and warmed it, and the warmth made life, and the life was I. See—I am young and swift, and I have come to abide with you and to help in all that you do."

Again on a day at noon, a maiden came, stood before the two, and called them "my children." "My children, I have come to abide with you and have brought with me love. I will give it to you, and if you will love me and will grant my wish, all the world will love me, even the very beasts. Strength is mine, and I give it to whosoever may get me. Comfort also is mine, for though I am young, my strength shall be felt over all the earth. I was born of the beautiful plant of the earth. For the dew fell on the leaf, and the sun warmed the dew, and the warmth was life, and that life is I."

Then Klos-kur-beh lifted up his hands toward the sun and praised the Great Spirit. Afterward, the young man and the maiden became man and wife, and she became the first mother. Klos-kur-beh taught their children and did great works for them. When his works were finished, he went away to live in the Northland until it should be time for him to come again.

The people increased until they were numerous. When a famine came among them, the first mother grew more and more sorrowful. Every day at noon she left her husband's lodge and stayed away from him until the shadows were long. Her husband, who dearly loved her, was sad because of her sorrow. One day he followed her trail as far as the ford of the river, and there he waited for her to return.

When she came, she sang as she began to ford the river, and as long as her feet were in the water she seemed glad. The man saw something that trailed behind her right foot, like a long green blade. When she came

*Longhouse*
Iroquois

out of the water, she stooped and cast off the blade. Then she appeared sorrowful.

The husband followed her home as the sun was setting, and he bade her come out and look at the beautiful sun. While they stood side by side, there came seven little children. They stood in front of the couple, looked into the woman's face, and spoke: "We are hungry, and the night will soon be here. Where is the food?"

Tears ran down the woman's face as she said, "Be quiet, little ones. In seven moons you shall be filled and shall hunger no more."

Her husband reached out, wiped away her tears, and asked, "My wife, what can I do to make you happy?"

"Nothing else," she said. "Nothing else will make me happy."

Then the husband went away to the Northland to ask Klos-kur-beh for counsel. With the rising of the seventh sun, he returned and said, "O wife, Klos-kur-beh has told me to do what you asked."

The woman was pleased and said, "When you have slain me, let two men take hold of my hair and draw my body all the way around a field. When they have come to the middle of it, let them bury my bones. Then they must come away. When seven months have passed, let them go again to the field and gather all that they find. Tell them to eat it. It is my flesh. You must save a part of it to put in the ground again. My bones you cannot eat, but you may burn them. The smoke will bring peace to you and your children."

The next day, when the sun was rising, the man slew his wife. Following her orders, two men drew her body over an open field until her flesh was worn away. In the middle of the field, they buried her bones.

*Basket*
Penobscot

When seven moons had passed by and the husband came again to that place, he saw it all filled with beautiful tall plants. He tasted the fruit of the plant and found it sweet. He called it *Skar- mu-nal*—"corn." And on the place where his wife's bones were buried, he saw a plant with broad leaves, bitter to the taste. He called it *Utar-mur-wa-yeh*— "tobacco."

Then the people were glad in their hearts, and they came to the harvest. But when the fruits were all gathered, the man did not know how to divide them. So he sent to the great teacher, Klos- kur-beh, for counsel. When Klos-kur-beh came and saw the great harvest, he said, "Now have the first words of the first mother come to pass, for she said she was born of the leaf of the beautiful plant. She said also that her power should be felt over the whole world and that all men should love her.

"And now that she has gone into this substance, take care that the second seed of the first mother be always with you, for it is her flesh. Her bones also have been given for your good. Burn them, and the smoke will bring freshness to the mind. And since these things came from the goodness of a woman's heart, see that you hold her always in memory. Remember her when you eat. Remember her when the smoke of her bones rises before you. And because you are all brothers, divide among you her flesh and her bones. Let all share alike, for so will the love of the first mother have been fulfilled."

Burlin, *The Indians' Book*, 3-6.

■

# THE ORIGIN OF THE THUNDERBIRD

## *Passamaquoddy*

This tribe, primarily fishermen, was surrounded by lakes, bays, rivers, streams, and the ocean. Passamaquoddies were an old, old tribe, related distantly to the Abnaki and Penobscot. Even today, they still have a representative in the Maine legislature; however, they can speak only on concerns of the tribe.

Passamaquaddy Indians are believers in a power by which a song or chant in one place can be heard in another area many miles away. This power is thought to be the work of *m'toulin* or magic, an important part of their belief. One example gives a strange account of an Indian so affected that he left his home and traveled north to find a cold place. Although barefooted and lightly clothed, he complained he was still too hot. He continued northward seeking colder comfort. One is led to believe that the man must have been insane. To these Indians, insanity is simply the result of magic.

A belief in the magic of the Thunderbird is held by the Passamaquoddy Indians, because he can tame the winds alternating between calm and storms.

■

This is a legend of long, long ago times. Two Indians desired to find the origin of thunder. They traveled north and came to a high mountain. These mountains performed magically. They drew apart, back and forth, then closed together very quickly.

One Indian said, "I will leap through the cleft before it closes. If I am caught, you continue to find the origin of thunder." The first one succeeded in going through the cleft before it closed, but the second one was caught and squashed.

On the other side, the first Indian saw a large plain with a group of wigwams, and a number of Indians playing a ball game. After a little while, these players said to each other, "It is time to go." They disappeared into their wigwams to put on wings, and came out with their bows and arrows and flew away over the mountains to the south. This was how the Passamaquoddy Indian discovered the homes of the thunderbirds.

The remaining old men of that tribe asked the Passamaquoddy Indian, "What do you want? Who are you?" He replied with the story of his mission. The old men deliberated how they could help him.

They decided to put the lone Indian into a large mortar, and they pounded him until all of his bones were broken. They molded him into a new body with wings like thunderbird, and gave him a bow and some arrows and sent him away in flight. They warned him not to fly close to trees, as he would fly so fast he could not stop in time to avoid them, and he would be killed.

The lone Indian could not reach his home because the huge enemy bird, Wochowsen, at that time made such a damaging wind. Thunderbird is an Indian and he or his lightning would never harm another Indian. But Wochowsen, great bird from the south, tried hard to rival Thunderbird. So Passamaquoddies feared Wochowsen, whose wings Glooscap once had broken, because he used too much power.

A result was that for a long time air became stagnant, the sea was full of slime, and all of the fish died. But Glooscap saw what was happening to his people and repaired the wings of Wochowsen to the extent of controlling and alternating strong winds with calm.

Legend tells us this is how the new Passamaquoddy thunderbird, the lone Indian who passed through the cleft, in time became the great and powerfurl Thunderbird, who always has kept a watchful eye upon the good Indians.

Fewkes, "The Origin of the Thunderbird," 265-266.

■

# THE FLYING CANOE
## *Passamaquoddy*

This story was printed in 1901—two years before the Wright brothers traveled by air for 59 seconds. It was told by the Passamaquoddy Indians in the eastern part of the state of Maine and in the province of New Brunswick.

■

Beside a beautiful lake not far from the sea, there lived three brothers. They were young rivals, each trying to do everything better than the others.

Sometimes they were visited by an old woman. She was nearly blind, so crippled that she could hardly walk, and always hungry. But when she had eaten some food, she could do wonderful things, and she could give remarkable power to a person she liked.

Joseph, the youngest of the three young men, treated her very well. Whenever he gave her food, she was grateful. One day after he had fed her, she said to him, "Take your axe and make some moccasins for yourself—some wooden ones. In them you will be able to run as fast as a bird."

Wabanaki "type" canoe (birchbark)

And so Joseph made for himself a pair of wooden moccasins. When he wore them, he could run very fast. In fact, he could run faster than the swiftest animals. He caught game animals and brought home much meat.

His two brothers were jealous because the youngest was a more skillful hunter. They wondered what he had been doing, and they watched him continually. One day they saw him open his birch-bark box and take out his wooden moccasins. Then he disappeared.

The brothers had already noticed certain curious chips where Joseph had been working. So they were very glad when they saw what he took from his box. They gathered together all the wood chips and made moccasins for themselves. In their wooden moccasins they could run even faster than Joseph.

Then Joseph knew that they had learned his secret.

The next time the old woman came for food, he fed her as usual. This time she said, as she thanked him, "Make for yourself a dugout canoe. Then you shall soar across the water like a bird."

So Joseph made a dugout canoe. Using it on the lake, he caught big fish and many birds. Again his brothers were jealous, and again they watched him in all that he did. Finding some chips after he had made his boat, the two older brothers gathered them and built a canoe for themselves. Working together, they made it better than Joseph's. It was a wonderful canoe. In it they went out to sea and speared many whales.

This time Joseph was angry. He called the old woman and fed her well, giving her more food than ever before.

"Now you will make another canoe," she said when she had eaten. "This one will fly in the air. You will really fly like a bird."

And so Joseph made another dugout. When he had finished making it, he carefully picked up all the chips and burned them. Then he took leave of his brothers and sailed off in the air.

He saw many strange lands and many strange people below him. He passed over high mountains and rivers and lakes. He passed over oceans. At last, after much journeying through the air, and after many adventures in other lands, Joseph returned home. There he lived in peace.

Prince, "Notes on Passamaquoddy Literature," vol. XXIII, 381-385 ... and vol. XI, 369-375.

■

# THE LOYAL SWEETHEART

## *Passamaquoddy*

■

Long ago, in a village beside a river, there lived a beautiful girl whom many a young man wished to marry. But she smiled on all alike and encouraged no one. Her name was Blue Flower.

Among her admirers was a young man who was especially skilled in hunting. For many moons he looked upon the girl with longing, but without any hope that he could win her favor.

At last, one autumn, she gave him reason to hope. And so he dared to consult the old woman of the village who carried proposals of marriage. He wanted to know his chances before he departed on the winter's hunt.

To the young man's great joy, the marriage-maker brought back a favorable reply from both the girl and her father. The message made him determined to win even greater fame as a hunter. He wanted to prove to the girl's father that he was indeed worthy of so beautiful a daughter.

"Will you wait for me until we return from he winter's hunt?" he asked her.

The girl gave her consent to his plan and her promise to remain true to him, whatever happened. She added the promise, "If you do not return, I will remain a maiden all my life. I will never marry any other man."

So the young man completed his plans to join the others of the village on the long winter's hunt. On the evening before their departure, he and the girl had a final canoe ride on the river. Then he sang his farewell in this love song of his people:

> Often on a lonely day, my love,
> You look on the beautiful river
> And down the shining stream.
>
> When last I looked upon you,
> How beautiful was the stream,
> How beautiful was the moon,
> And how happy were we!
> Since that night, my fair one,
> I have thought of you always.
>
> Often on a lonely day, my love,
> You look on the beautiful river
> And down the shining stream.
>
> When we paddled the canoe together
> On that beautiful water,
> How fair the mountains looked,
> How beautiful the red leaves
> As the gentle wind whirled them!
>
> After the winter snows,
> When spring has come once more,
> We will paddle again together.
> Then the leaves will be green,
> The mountains fresh and fair.
>
> Often on a lonely day, my love,
> Look on the beautiful river,
> Down the shining stream,
> And know that spring will come.

Next day, the hunters departed. The old men, the women, and the children settled down to finish the autumn's work of preparing for the winter.

Not many days afterward, a war party attacked the village and destroyed it. They carried away as prisoners all the young girls. Among them was the promised bride of the hunter. When the warriors reached their home territory, they persuaded, or forced, many of the young women to become their wives. But Blue Flower refused to submit. The warriors threatened to burn her alive. Still she refused. She preferred death to breaking her promise to her sweetheart.

The warriors complained to their chief and asked that she be burned at the stake. But he would not listen to the cruel counsel of his men. Instead, he gave the girl a longer time in which to make up her mind. Her bravery greatly impressed him. He would save her life now, he thought, and marry her later to one of his best warriors, in order that their children might become a race of heroes.

Weeks passed, and the hunters returned. When they found their village in ashes, they knew which war party had struck. The young hunter, singing his vengeance song, gathered a host of warriors and started northward. They surprised the largest village of their enemy, killed many people, and took others as prisoners.

When the fighting was over, the victors and their friends who had been held captive by the enemy were reunited. There was great rejoicing. Perhaps happiest of all were the young hunter-warrior and Blue Flower, who had remained true to him in spite of threats and promises.

The young man, still thirsting for revenge, wanted to torture and burn the enemy that had been taken prisoners. But his sweetheart stopped him. She reminded him that they had not treated her cruelly.

She was a gentle and peace-loving girl, as well as a loyal sweetheart. In a short time, she became a loyal wife.

Prince, "The Passamaquoddy Wampum Records," 479-495.

■

# ORIGIN OF THE MEDICINE MAN

## *Passamaquoddy*

The first part of this legend strongly reminds one of the biblical story of Moses, which may have been due to the influence of early contacts with Europeans. Note that the mother of the child became pregnant by eating an herb.

In 1884, the writer Charles G. Leland, determined the Medicine Man to be Glooscap, the Good-Spirit. Legend has it that the father of Glooscap is a being who lives under a great waterfall beneath the earth. His face is half-red, and he has a single all-seeing eye. He can give to anyone coming to him the medicine he desires. Glooscap is still busy sharpening his arrows off in a distant place, preparing sometime to return to earth and make war.

Passamaquoddies tell all of their old stories as truth. But of other stories, they speak of them as "what they hear," or hearsay.

■

This is a legend of long, long ago about a Passamaquoddy Indian woman who traveled constantly back and forth and through the woods. From every bush she came to, she bit off a twig, and from one of these she became pregnant. Bigger and bigger she grew, until at last she could not travel, but she built a wigwam near the mouth of a fresh-running stream.

In the night, the woman gave birth to a child. She thought at first that she should kill the child. Finally, she decided to make a bark canoe in which she placed her child. She set it adrift and let it float down the stream. Though the water was rough in places, the child was not harmed, or even wet.

The canoe floated to an Indian village, where it became stranded on the sandy shore near a group of wigwams. One of the women found the baby and brought it to her home. Every morning thereafter, it seemed that a baby of the village died. The villagers did not know what was the matter with their babies.

A neighbor noticed how the rescued child toddled off to the river every night and returned shortly after. She wondered if this could have anything to do with the death of so many babies. Then she saw the child return to its wigwam with a small tongue, roast it, and eat it. Then it lay down to sleep all night.

On the next morning, a report circulated that another child had died. Then the Indian woman was certain she knew who the killer was. She alerted the parents of the dead child and found that the child's tongue had been removed, and the child had bled to death.

Tribal deliberations were held to decide what should be done with the murderer. Some said, cut up the person and throw him into the river. Others said, burn the fragments; this they did after much consultation. They burned the fragments of the wayward child, until nothing but its ashes remained.

Naturally, everyone understood the child was dead. But that night it came back to camp again with a small tongue, which it roasted and ate. The next morning another child was found to have died in the night. The weird child was found sleeping in its usual place, just as before its cremation. He said to everyone that he would never kill any more children, and that now he had become a big boy, in fact.

The big boy announced he would take one of his bones out of his side. This he started to do, and all of his bones spilled out of his body at the same time. He closed his eyes by drawing his fingers over his eyelids, hiding his eyes. He could not move without bones and he began to grow very fat.

He surprised the Passamaquoddies by becoming a great Medicine Man. Anything they desired within reason, he granted. Later, however, his tribe moved away from their old camp. Before they left, they built a fine wigwam for the Medicine Man. So accustomed had they become to call upon his powers that they still returned to make their requests. His tribal members asked him for medicine of all kinds. When he granted their wishes, he asked them, "Turn me over and you will find your medicine beneath me."

A young man came and wished to have the love of a woman, so he asked for a love potion. The Medicine Man said, "Turn me over." The young man turned over the conjurer and found an herb. "You must not give this away or throw it away," said the old man. The young Passamaquoddy went back to his own wigwam.

Soon he was aware that all the young women followed him in the camp, at all times. In fact, he longed to be alone for a change. He did not like to be chased by the women. At last when he became too troubled by the tribal women, he returned to the Medicine Man and gave back the herbal love portion. The young Passamaquoddy left without it.

Another young man went to the conjurer for help. The Medicine Man asked, "What is it you want?" This man said, "I want to live as long as the world shall stand."

"Your request is a hard one to consider, but I will do my best to answer it," replied the Medicine Man. "Now turn me over," and underneath his body was an herb. He said, "Go to a place that is bare of everything, so bare it is destitute of all vegetation, and just stand there." The Medicine Man pointed out this direction for the young man.

The young man went according to the Medicine Man's instructions, but looking back at the conjurer, the standing man saw branches and twigs sprouting all over his own body. He had been changed into a cedar tree, to stand there forever—useless to everyone.

Fewkes, "How a Medicine Man Was Born, and How He Turned a Man into a Tree," 273-275.

■

# THE GIANT AND THE FOUR WIND BROTHERS

## *Penobscot*

Penobscots belonged to the Algonquian linguistic family of Abnakis, Passamaquoddies, Malecites, and Pennacooks. They lived on both sides of Penobscot Bay and up and down the whole area of the Penobscot River. They were visited by Samuel de Champlain in 1604 and numerous later explorers for the next 150 years. Penobscots made peace with the colonials and remained in their own country (not withdrawing to Canada). Conjointly with the Passamaquoddies, the Penobscots have a representative at sessions of the Maine legislature, privileged to speak on native American tribal affairs only.

■

There were four brothers in a family that lived in a huge cave on the top of a high mountain in the present state of Maine. One brother was Northwind, one Southwind, another Westwind, and the other one Eastwind. They were the ones who made all of the winds blow.

Westwind was the youngest, Northwind the oldest, Southwind second oldest, and Eastwind second youngest. To cause the winds, they stood up with their heads above the cave hole and blew. The forthcoming wind occurred according to whichever brother performed—North, South, East, or West.

Westwind was very wild when he blew. Northwind chided him, "No, No! Don't do that! You will raise such high winds that you will destroy our good people, the Penobscots."

When Westwind jumped up again to blow, Northwind again told him, "No! No! Stop or you will kill our mother." So lived the Four Wind Brothers, causing and regulating the winds of the world.

Northwind was always the softest wind, Eastwind a little stronger and harsher, Southwind with strong gusts, but not as much as Westwind the youngest. Whenever the Four Wind Brothers blew the winds, they were not satisfied until each performed in his particular style to perfection.

Often they would say to each other as a warning, "We must try to care for our friends, the Penobscots, so we do not destroy any thing or any one of them."

About this same time, a Giant Beaver had this home on the top of a great rock by the shore of Big Lake. This Giant Beaver, about one hundred feet long, had a very large lodge. Near him lived a Giant Penobscot who liked to hunt for the Giant Beaver. But Giant Penobscot lived in fear of a Monster Eagle, who kept watching all the time for the right moment to snatch and carry Giant Penobscot to its nest.

Monster Eagle was so large that he could pick up a giant man like an ordinary eagle would carry a rabbit, even though the giant was as tall as the tallest tree. At last Giant Penobscot's family was out of food, and he was compelled to go out and hunt. He took his long-handled ice chisel and went in search of the Giant Beaver.

Giant Penobscot succeeded in driving the Beaver from his Lodge, and he cornered him and killed him. After packing the Giant Beaver on his back, Giant Penobscot joyfully started homeward with his prize. Monster Eagle had seen Giant Penobscot from a great height. Down swooped the Eagle, picking up both Giant Beaver and Giant Penobscot, as easily as carrying two rabbits.

Far up on a rocky mountainside, Monster Eagle flew with its prey to its nest, which was thousands of feet above the valley. Monster Eagle's nest was enormous, with many young eagles in it. When Monster Eagle deposited his victims in the nest, he began feeding the dead beaver to his eaglets. Monster Eagle kept Giant Penobscot safely to one side, until all of the beaver had been eaten.

Then Monster Eagle prepared to kill the Giant Penobscot. He quickly flew high into the air and turned sharply, diving straight down to strike Giant Penobscot with his beak, wings, and claws. But Giant Penobscot held upright his sharp ice chisel with the butt end braced against a rocky ledge beside him. Monster Eagle descended violently upon the point of the ice chisel and he died instantly.

Now that Giant Penobscot was free, he wondered how he could get down to earth again before being eaten by the eaglets as they grew larger. He thought and thought, finally deciding to cut out the body of Monster Eagle and crawl inside the feathered skin, using Eagle's wings to glide down from the mountain.

Coincidentally, on this same mountain lived the Four Wind Brothers. Northwind saw Monster Eagle destroy himself. He also observed Giant Penobscot preparing to fly down to earth. Northwind called his three brothers to come and see.

"Let us all blow gently beneath Eagle's wings and help the good Penobscot to land softly upon the earth," said Northwind to his Brother Winds.

Inside Monster Eagle's wings, the Giant Penobscot soared off the mountain. Gently the Four Wind Brothers blew beneath his wings, guiding him while he easily floated to the Penobscot village below.

Meanwhile, when Giant Penobscot's family found that he had disappeared, they knew he must have been carried away by some flying giant, because his tracks led to nowhere.

One of the ancient men of the Penobscot tribe said, "We must all help our brother escape with our good thoughts. We must wish for his safe return by Chief of the Sky Spirits."

When Giant Penobscot floated safely back to his tribe and told his people of his adventure, the Ancient One said, "It was the strength of our wishes to Chief Sky Spirit that brought you back to your people. Now let us have a thanksgiving feast and rejoice."

Gently the Four Wind Brothers passed over the Penobscot Indian village on their happy return to their mountaintop cave.

Speck, "The Giant and the Four Wind Brothers," 74.

■

# THE ORIGIN OF INDIAN SUMMER
## *Penobscot*

■

Long, long ago, the Penobscot Indians used to say, an old man went to the Chief of the Sky Spirits to ask his help. The man's name was Zuni. In the spring, when all of his people were planting their vegetables, Zuni was too ill to do his usual planting. He was ill all summer. During that summer, his people, as usual, gathered their vegetables and dried them for use in winter. But Zuni had none.

So he went to the Chief of the Sky Spirits and said to him, "I have been sick all through the planting and the harvesting seasons. The winter is coming on, and I have no food ready for it. What am I to do?"

"I will help you," was the prompt reply. "Go ahead now. Plant your vegetables as you have always done in the spring. I will see that you have a crop right away."

Zuni went home and immediately put his seeds into the ground. The weather favored him, and almost as soon as he had finished planting, his crops were ready to harvest. In seven days he had as much as any other man in his tribe had. Then winter came.

The Penobscots gave that warm period in the autumn a name that means Indian summer. White people also call it Indian summer.

Speck, "Penobscot Tales," 95-96.

■

# THE WATER FAMINE
## *Penobscot*

In early Penobscot family narrative history, there are a few family groups possessing associated legends as their specific property. In the myth of the water famine, the transformer, Gluskabe, changes certain human beings into aquatic creatures. One of the original families' identity was connected with creatures residing in the water.

■

From this legend we learn of the origin of fish, frogs, and turtles. A long, long time ago, Indians settled up the river. A Monster frog forbade these Indians the use of water. Some died from thirst. Their Spirit Chief, Gluskabe, came to help them. He saw how sickly his people seemed. He asked them, "What is your trouble?"

"The Monster is killing us with thirst. He forbids us water."

"I will make him give you water," Gluskabe replied. The people went with their Chief to see the Monster frog. The Chief said to the Monster, "Why do you abuse our grandchildren? You will be sorry for this treatment of our good people. I will give them water, so all will have an equal share of the water. The benefits should be shared."

Gluskabe suddenly grabbed the Monster frog and broke his back. From thenceforth, all bullfrogs are broken-backed. Even then the Monster did not give up the water. So Gluskabe took an axe and cut down a large yellow birch tree, so that when it fell down, the yellow birch tree killed the Monster frog.

That is how the Penobscot River originated. The water flowed from the Monster frog. All the branches of the yellow birch tree became rivers, and all emptied into the main Penobscot River.

Now, all of the Penobscot Indians were so thirsty, some even near death, that they jumped into the river to enjoy the water inside and outside. Some of them turned into fish; some turned into frogs; some turned into turtles. A few human Penobscots survived. That is the reason they inhabit the whole length of the Penobscot River. This is how they took their family names from all kinds of fish, turtles, and other sea creatures.

Speck, *Penobscot Man, the Life History of a Forest Tribe In Maine.*

■

# THE LEGEND OF THE BEAR FAMILY
## *Penobscot*

The story concerning the Bear family was revealed through a descendant of the original hero of the following tale. He owned a very old powder horn bearing an incised representation of his mother, who was a Bear, seated in the bow of a canoe traveling to the hunting grounds with her husband.

■

Many, many generations ago, a Penobscot, his wife, and their little son started out from their village to go to Canada. They were from Penobscot Bay, bound for a great council and dance to be held at the Iroquois village of Caughnawaga. They went upriver to the point where they had to make a 20-mile portage to reach another river that would take them to the St. Lawrence.

The man started ahead with the canoe on his back, leaving his wife to pack part of the luggage to their first overnight campsite. The little boy ran alongside of her. While she was busy arranging her pack, her son ran on ahead to catch up with his father.

The man had gone so far ahead, the boy became lost. The mother assumed the boy was with his father. When she arrived at the campground, they discovered that their son was with neither of them. They began a search immediately, but they could not find him.

The parents returned home to tell their story to their tribe. All of the men turned out for a wide search party, which lasted for several months without success. In March of the next year, the Penobscots found some sharpened sticks near the river. They concluded that the boy must be alive and had been spearing fish. Footprints of bears were seen, and they thought perhaps the boy had been adopted by a bear family.

In the village, there was a lazy man who did not enter into the search, but lay around idly. Everyone asked him, "Why don't you help hunt for the boy? You seem to be good for nothing."

"Very well, I will," he replied. He went right to the bear's den and knocked with his bow on the rocks at the entrance. Inside, a great noise arose where the father, mother, baby bear, and adopted boy lived. The father-bear went to the entrance, holding out a birch-bark vessel. The lazy man shot at it and killed the bear.

The mother-bear says, "Now I will go." She took another vessel, held it out at the entrance, and also was killed. The baby bear did the same and was killed. All of the bears were laid out dead in the cave. Then the lazy man entered and saw the little boy terribly afraid and huddled in a dark corner, crying for his realtives and trying to hide.

The lazy hunter gently carried him home to the village and gave him to his parents. Everyone gave the lazy man presents: two blankets, a canoe, ammunition, and other good things. He became rich overnight.

The boy's parents, however, noticed that their son seemed to be turning into a bear. Bristles were showing on his upper back and shoulders, and his manners had changed. Finally they helped him to become a real person again, and he grew up to be a Penobscot Indian like his father. He married and had children. Forever after he and all of his descendants were called Bears.

They drew pictures of bears on pieces of birch-bark with charcoal and left them at camps wherever they went. All of their descendants seemed to do this and declare, "I am one of the Bear family."

Speck, *Penobscot Man, the Life History of a Forest Tribe In Maine.*

■

# THE STRANGE ORIGIN OF CORN

## *Abnaki*

The main body of Abnaki was in western Maine, mostly in the valleys of the Kennebec, Androscoggin, and Sacos rivers, and the neighboring coast. They originally emigrated from the Southwest, having encountered John Cabot in 1498; but the Indians had no other dealings with white people at that time. In 1604, Champlain passed along the coast and visited Abnaki bands. In 1607 and 1608 the Plymouth Company made an unsuccessful effort to form a permanent settlement at the mouth of the Kennebec. Later, the Abnaki withdrew to Canada, settling around St. Francis.

■

A long time ago, when the Indians were first made, one man lived alone, far from any others. He did not know fire, and so he lived on roots, bark, and nuts. This man became very lonely for companionship. He grew tired of digging roots, lost his appetite, and for several days lay dreaming in the sunshine. When he awoke, he saw someone standing near and, at first, was very frightened.

But when he heard the stranger's voice, his heart was glad, and he looked up. He saw a beautiful woman with long *light* hair! "Come to me," he whispered. But she did not, and when he tried to approach her, she moved farther away. He sang to her about his loneliness, and begged her not to leave him.

At last she replied, "If you will do exactly what I tell you to do, I will also be with you."

He promised that he would try his very best. So she led him to a place where there was some very dry grass. "Now get two dry sticks," she told him, "and rub them together fast while you hold them in the grass."

Soon a spark flew out. The grass caught fire, and as swiftly as an arrow takes flight, the ground was burned over. Then the beautiful woman spoke again: "When the sun sets, take me by the hair and drag me over the burned ground."

"Oh, I don't want to do that!" the man exclaimed.

"You must do what I tell you to do," said she. "Wherever you drag me, something like grass will spring up, and you will see something like hair coming from between the leaves. Soon seeds will be ready for your use."

The man followed the beautiful woman's orders. And when the Indians see silk on the cornstalk, they know that the beautiful woman has not forgotten them.

Brown, *The Strange Origin of Corn*, 214.

■

# WA-BA-BA-NAL, THE NORTHERN LIGHTS

## *Wabanaki*

Before 1890, Mrs. W. Wallace Brown wrote that folktales among the Wabanaki must have been extensive, for, though these legends were so swiftly dying out, there seemed to be few things in nature for which they had no legend of its life or beginning. They were known as people living at the sunrise in northeastern and northwestern Maine. A large Wabanaki camp was situated in the Kennebec Valley of Maine.

■

Old Chief M'Sartto, Morning Star, had only one son, so different from the other boys of the tribe as to be a worry to Old Chief. The boy would not stay and play with the others, but would take his bow and arrows, and leave home for many days at a time, always going toward the north.

When he came home his family asked, "Where have you been and what did you see?" But he had no reply. At last Old Chief said to his wife, "The boy needs watching. I will follow him when he takes off again."

A few days later, Old Chief followed the boy's trail and they traveled for a long time. Suddenly, Old Chief's eyes closed. He could not hear. A curious feeling came over him. Then he *knew* nothing.

Later, when his eyes opened, he found himself in a strange light country, with no sun, no moon, no stars, but the country was lit by a peculiar brightness. He saw many beings, but all of them different from his own people. They gathered around him and tried to talk, but he did not understand their language.

Old Chief M'Sartto did not know where to go or what to do. He was very well treated by this strange tribe. He watched them play games and became attracted to a wonderful game of ball that he had never seen played before. The game seemed to turn the light into many colors. The players all had lights on their heads and wore very curious kinds of belts, called *Menquan*, or "Rainbow" belts.

In a few days, an old man came and spoke to Old Chief in his own language, asking if he knew where he was. "No," Old Chief replied.

"You are in the country of Wa-ba-ban of the northern lights," the stranger said. "I came here many years ago. I was the only one here

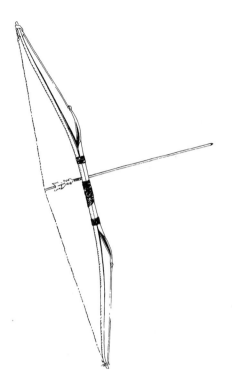

*Bow and arrow*
Abnaki

from the 'Lower Country,' as we usually call it. But now there is a boy who comes to visit us every few days."

"How did you get here, and what tribe did you come from?" Old Chief asked.

"I follow the path called Spirits' Path, through the Milky Way," said the old man.

"That must be the same path I followed to come here," said Old Chief M'Sartto, Morning Star. "Did you have a queer feeling, as if you lost all sense of knowledge when you traveled here?"

"Yes, exactly that kind of sensation," he replied. "I could neither see nor hear."

"We did come by the same path," Old Chief said. "Can you now tell me how I can go to my home at the Wabanaki camp?"

"Yes, the Chief here can direct you."

"Now can you tell me where I can see my son? He's the boy who comes here to visit you."

"Stay here and watch, you will see him playing ball," said the old man, as he left to visit many wigwams to invite everyone out to a ball game.

Old Chief was very glad to hear the news of his son, and soon the ball game began, and many beautiful colors spread out over the playing field.

"Do you see your son playing?" the old man asked.

"Yes, the boy with the brightest light on his head is my son."

The two men then went to see the Chief of the Northern Lights. The old man spoke up and said to him, "The Chief Morning Star of the Lower Country wants to go home and desires to take his son with him."

Chief of Northern Lights called all of his people together to bid good-bye to Old Chief morning Star and his son. Then he ordered two great birds to carry them to their home. When they traveled the Milky Way, Old Chief again felt the same strange feelings he had experienced when going there.

When Old Chief came to his senses again, he found himself near his home. His wife was very glad to see him. Her son had arrived first and told her that his father was safe and would come soon. She paid little notice to that announcement for she had thought that her husband had lost his way.

Now her wigwam was filled with joy again at the sight of her son and Old Chief M'Sartto, Morning Star, returned to Wabanaki.

Brown, "Wa-Ba-Ba-Nal, Northern Lights," 213-214.

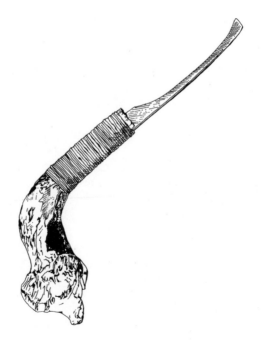

*Crooked knife*
Abnaki

■

# INDIANS AT NIAGARA FALLS
## *Seneca*

The Seneca tribe became one of the five strong tribes of the Iroquois linguistic family in central New York state, forming the Iroquois Nation as early as 1390. Later they obtained guns from the Dutch, giving them a dominating influence over the entire northeast. Senecas lived between Lake Seneca and the Genesee River, about in the middle of the region. Reservations were given to the Iroquois tribes in New York, but later movements of these tribes to Oklahoma were encouraged by the government. The Iroquois Nation attained the highest form of governmental organization reached by any native American tribe.

■

A powerful Seneca Indian tribe lived near Niagara Falls on the Canadian side. For several years, they experienced crop failure from frost. An epidemic followed, killing many of their tribe.

One day a young Seneca girl went into a little cave above the falls to bathe. Suddenly a large rattlesnake attacked her. When she tried to escape, she fell into the rapids, which swept her onto the cataract. By a miracle, the water swirled her into the Cave-of-the-Winds, behind the falls.

There lived the Good Spirit of Thunder and Lightning. It was he who created the mist, which ascended toward the heavens and formed clouds, out of which came the Lightning. Good Spirit told the young girl that also under the waterfall lived Evil Spirit of Famine and Starvation. It was he who caused the crops to fail.

Evil Spirit also controlled a huge Water Serpent that lived in the Niagara River and Lake Erie. Often the Serpent came to the little bay of the river, just above the falls. He cleaned himself there, poisoning the water, which the Senecas used for drinking and cooking.

"Your water is poisoned," said Good Spirit to the girl. "Because of that many of your tribe have died. I want you to return to your people and report to your Chief what I now tell you.

"Your whole tribe must move at once. Your people must pack all of their property and load their canoes. They must go from the Chippewa River up the Niagara River and make a new settlement on Buffalo Creek. There they will grow good crops and enjoy themselves again.

"I know the Evil Spirit will send his Water Serpent after you. Tell your Chief that I will follow the Senecas in a dark cloud. I will send lightning and a thunderbolt upon Water Serpent and kill him, if he does follow you."

Immediately, the young girl went to the Chief of the Senecas and repeated all that Good Spirit had said. The tribe packed and moved as they were directed. Water Serpent followed the canoes.

The Senecas arrived at their new landing site and heard a loud thunderbolt when a lightning flash struck the monster. It thrashed in the water with great force, scooping out a broad basin in Buffalo Creek, which formed the now-famous "horseshoe" of Niagara Falls, according to Seneca storytellers.

After the Senecas had set up a temporary camp, the young girl said, "Can we now send our chiefs to visit Good Spirit and honor him for his kindness to us?"

When the tribal chiefs reached the little bay below Buffalo Creek, they saw the dead Water Serpent. In the village, they saw the Evil Spirit of Famine and Starvation hanging from a high pole. The chiefs thanked the Good Spirit of Thunder and Lightning for the safety of the Seneca Tribe.

Good health and fine crops always have been theirs ever since Chief of the Senecas obeyed the Good Spirit by moving his tribe as directed.

Dow, *Anthology and Bibliography of Niagara Falls*, vol. II, 380-381.

■

# THE SACRIFICE AT NIAGARA FALLS
## *Seneca*

■

*Nee-ah-gah-rah,* meaning "Thundering Waters," is the Iroquois Indian pronunciation of *Niagara.* They believed that the sound of the cataract was the voice of a mighty spirit that dwelt in the waters. In the years gone by, they offered to it a sacrifice every year.

The sacrifice was a maiden of the tribe who was sent over the cataract in a white canoe decorated with fruits and flowers. To be chosen for the sacrifice was considered such a great honor that girls contended for it. In the spirit world, the happy hunting grounds, were special gifts for such a person.

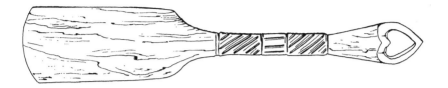

*Corn paddle*
Seneca

Probably the last sacrifice at Niagara Falls was made in 1679, when Lela-wala, the beautiful daughter of Chief Eagle Eye, was chosen for the honor of the sacrifice. That year, the French explorer La Salle was in the area. He had been trying to convert the Senecas to Christianity, and he protested against their plan for the sacrifice.

His Protests were answered by one of the tribal leaders: "Your words witness against you. You say that Christ set us an example. We will follow it. Why should one sacrifice be great and our sacrifice be horrible?"

The maiden's father was a brave warrior and a noble chief. His wife was dead. The only member of his family left was the beautiful Lela-wala, very dear and precious to him. But he showed no sign of the grief he felt and made no protest against the choice of her for the sacrifice.

On the day set for the sacrifice, the tribe gathered on the bank of the river. They enjoyed the games, the singing, and the dancing that always took place on special occasions. Everyone became quiet when the little white canoe came into sight, covered with fruits and flowers given to their chief's daughter.

Shortly after her canoe entered the current, another white canoe darted out from under the trees along the bank of the river. Chief Eagle Eye's grief was so great that he was on his way to join his daughter. With swift and strong movements through the rapids, he was soon beside her.

The two looked at each other once. The crowd lost their calmness and shouted at them, some with frantic despair and some with admiration. Side by side, the canoes plunged over the cataract. The brave maiden and the brave chief were beyond rescue.

"After their death, they were changed into pure spirits of strength and goodness. They live so far beneath the falls that the roaring is music to them." He is the ruler of the cataract; she is the maiden of the mist.

Skinner, *Myths and Legends of Our Land*, vol. I, 61-62.

■

# THREE BROTHERS WHO FOLLOWED THE SUN

## *Seneca*

The Iroquois Nation tribes still retain vestiges of their former adoration of the Sun. They continue to observe certain rites, such as the Sun Dances, which are survivals of more elaborate sun ceremonies of long, long ago.

Among the most popular sun dances of many tribes and bands of Iroquois Indians were the Ostowa-gowa, or the Great Feather Dance. This became a prime religious dance of the Gai'wiu religion of Handsome Lake, the Seneca Prophet. He revolutionized the religious system of the Iroquois of New York and Ontario.

Few of the early folk-beliefs have survived the taboo of the Prophet. These beliefs are difficult to trace, unless one has the Gai'wiu religion of Handsome lake and the Code of Dekanawida, the founder of the Iroquois Confederacy.

The Seneca Sun Ceremony of Thanksgiving is called by any tribal member who dreams that the rite is necessary for the welfare of the community. The ceremony begins promptly at high noon, when three arrows or three musket shots are fired heavenward to notify the Sun of their intention to address him.

After each volley, the people shout their war cries to the Sun—for the Sun loves war. A ceremonial fire is built. In ancient times, fire was started by a pump drill, and more recently by striking a match. The tribal Sun-Priest chants his thanksgiving song while he casts from a husk basket handfuls of native tobacco upon the flames to carry his words upward to the Sun.

The ceremony begins outside of the Long House, where the rising smoke lifts everyone's thoughts and songs to the sun. Immediately after this beginning, the entire assemblage enters the Long House, where costumed Feather Dancers begin their ritualized Sun Dance. The New York Iroquois tribes do not carry effigies of the Sun in their preparation for or in their dance, according to their traditions.

The following Seneca legend was related by Edward Cornplanter, the recognized head preacher of the Gai'wiu of the

Handsome Lake. Cornplanter was a Seneca Indian and a descendant of Gaiant Waka, the Prophet's brother.

In the following legend, there seem to be some modern features, stated Cornplanter. He asserted, however, that the portion relating to the sky and sun are very, very old traditions. He said that he had always heard the upper world described as told in this legend. He then added that the Sun loved the sound of war, and would linger in his morning journey to observe battle activities anywhere, but after he reached midheaven, the Sun traveled on at his usual speed.

■

This legend developed in olden times, when not many people were about. Three brothers who were not married spent their lives hunting. When young they enjoyed the excitement of hunting, but as they grew older they seemed to lose the pleasure of the sport. Youngest brother suggested that for a new experience they walk to the edge of the earth, where the sky comes down and touches the big sea of salt water. At the western side of the salt water, this world is an island.

The other brothers thought the plan sounded like a good one. When everything was ready, they started on their journey. For a good many years they kept going and many things happened to them; however, they always continued straight westward.

Finally, the brothers came to a place where the sun goes under the sky's edge. The sky bends down there, and sinks into the water. For a month, they camped and watched the things that were happening. They noticed just how the sun got under the rim of the sky and disappeared quickly. They saw some men trying to get under the edge of the sky, but it descended too quickly for them, and they were crushed.

The brothers noticed when the sky came up, the water sank lower; and when the sky went into the water, the water rose higher. Youngest brother said he wanted to try to pass under the rim of the sky when the sun slipped under on its sun-road. But eldest brother said he thought the happenings were too evilly mysterious, and he was afraid for them to try.

Without waiting for anyone's opinion, youngest brother ran very quickly under the sky's rim, and found the rim very thick. Second brother followed youngest brother like a flash. They kept on the sun-road with the water on each side of them. Eldest brother watched, and when he saw nothing had injured his brothers, he began to run after them.

The younger brothers turned from their safe place to encourage him, but at that moment the sky came down on the sun-road and crushed

*Headdress*
Seneca

eldest brother. But they did see his spirit shoot by them quickly. The two remaining brothers felt very, very sad.

They discovered that, on the other side of the sky, everything was different. Before them loomed a large hill, which they ascended, and they saw a very large village in the distance. A man came running toward them. As he approached them he called out, "Come!" They realized he was their eldest brother.

"How did you arrive here so quickly, brother?" they asked. "We did not see you come."

"I was too late, and passed by on a spirit road," he replied.

They noticed an old man walking toward them. He was youthful and strong in body, but his hair was long and white. He seemed like a very old man. His face showed wisdom and he bore himself like a chief. "I am the father of the people in the Above-the-Sky-Place," he said.

"Haweni'u is my son. I wish to advise you, because I have lived here a long time. I have always lived here, but Haweni'u was born of the woman on the island. When you see my son, call quickly, 'Nia'we 'ska'no!' If you fail to speak first, he will say, 'You are mine,' and you will be spirits as your brother is."

The three brothers proceeded and came to a high house made of white bark. They walked up the path to the door. A tall man stepped out quickly, and the brothers said the magic words. The great man said, "Doges' I have been watching you for a long time." The brothers entered the house. When inside, the tall man said, "In what condition are your bodies?"

"We have fine bodies," they replied.

"You do not speak the truth," the great man answered. "I am Haweni'u and I know all about your bodies. One of you must lie down, and I will purify him and then the other."

One brother lay down, and Haweni'u placed a small shell to his own lips, and put it on the brother's mouth. He also tapped him on the neck, and sealed the shell with clay. Haweni'u began to skin the brother. He took apart the muscles, and then scraped the bones. He took out the organs and washed them. Then he built the man again. He loosened the clay and rubbed his neck. He did this with both brothers, and they sat up and said, "It seems as if we had slept." Haweni'u said, "Every power of your bodies has been renewed. I'll test you."

The brothers followed Haweni'u to a fine grove of trees surrounded by a thick hedge. All kinds of flowers were blooming outside. "My deer are here," said Haweni'u.

A large buck with wide antlers ran toward them. "He is the swiftest of my runners. Try and catch him," said Haweni'u.

The men ran after the deer and rapidly overtook him. "He has given us good speed," the brothers said. They soon discovered they had many other superior abilities, and the great man tested them all on that day.

They returned to the white lodge, and the brothers saw a messenger running toward them. Upon his wide chest was a great bright ball of light. It was very brilliant. In some unknown language he shouted to Haweni'u and dashed on.

"Do you understand his words, or do you know that man?" asked Haweni'u. "He is the Sun, my messenger. Each day he brings me news. Nothing from east to west escapes his eye. He has just told me of a great war raging between your people and another nation. Let us look down on the earth and see what is happening."

He led them to a high hill in the middle of the country, and looked down through a hole where a tree had been uprooted. They saw two struggling bands of people and all the houses burning. They could hear people crying and shouting their war-cries.

"Men will always do this," said Haweni'u, and then they came back down the hill.

The brothers stayed a very long time in the upper world, and learned so much they could never tell it all at one time. Sometimes they looked down on the earth and saw villages in which no one lived. They seemed to be waiting for people to be born and live there. In the upper world they saw villages, likewise, awaiting the coming of people from below.

Haweni'u told them a good many things, and after a time asked a messenger to lead the brothers to the path that the Sun took when he came out on the earth in the morning. They followed the messenger and came out on the earth. They waited until the Sun had gone over the earth to the west. Again they went under the edge of the sky in the east, and came out in their own country again.

It was night and they slept on the ground. In the morning they saw their village, and it was overgrown with trees. They followed a familar path through the woods, and came upon another village. Their own people were living there. They went into a council-house and talked. They told their story, but no one recognized them except their sister, who was an aged woman by then.

She said, "The war of which you speak took place fifty years ago."

The brothers did not care too much for the earth now, but wished themselves back in the upper world. They were not like the other men, because they never grew tired. They were very strong and could chase animals and kill them with their hands. Nothing could kill the brothers, neither arrow nor disease. After a long time, they were struck by lightning, and they were both killed. Presumably, they were granted their wish, and joined eldest brother in the Above World.

Parker, "Three Brothers Who Followed the Sun," 473-478.

■

# SEEK YOUR FATHER

## *Seneca*

Mrs. Asher Wright served as a Christian missionary to the Senecas for fifty years. She spoke their language perfectly, and recorded these two legends that were related to her by Esquire Johnson, an old Seneca Chief. He described the origin of the twins Good and Evil, and said the Sun was made by the Good-minded twin out of the face of his dead mother, the first earth-woman, who was the daughter of the Sky-woman.

Another version of this Seneca legend, dated 1876, tells practically the same story, but names the Sky-woman as having borne first a daughter, who, without any knowledge of a man, became that earth-mother of the twins Good and Evil. That daughter died giving birth to the twins, and she was buried by her mother, the Sky-woman.

■

Sky-woman said to her grandson the good-mined-spirit, "Now you must go and seek your father. When you find him, you must ask him to give you power."

She pointed to the East and said to him, "He lives in that direction. You must go on and on, until you reach the limits of this huge island. Then continue onward, as you must paddle upon the waters, until you come to a high mountain, which rises straight up out of the water. You must climb this mountain to the summit. There you will see a wonderful being, sitting on the highest peak. You must say to him, 'I am your son.'

"Your father is the Sun, and through you, he is also the father of mankind, because of your earthly origin from my daughter."

Parker, "Seek Your Father," 474-478.

■

# A MASHPEE GHOST STORY

## *Wampanoag*

Nauset or Cape Cod Indians, from the exposed position on the Cape, included the Mashpees of the Wampanoag tribe. Their entire territory came under the observation of many early explorers to the "New World," including Samuel Champlain in 1606, and the English Captain Thomas Hunt in 1614-1615. Hunt kidnapped 27 Wampanoag Indians, all of whom were sold into slavery, a just cause perhaps why five years later the Pilgrims landed and first were met by wary, unfriendly Wampanoags. Later, their Chief Massasoit officially welcomed the Pilgrims at Plymouth and signed a treaty of friendship dated 1621.

This area had escaped a great smallpox epidemic of 1617. The Nausets increased in population as tribal members were driven from their original villages by whites toward 1700. Mashpee village became the principal location of Wampanoags, also referred to as Massasoits after their famous Chief Massasoit. Later, his second son succeeded him and was called King Philip, establishing a strong Indian confederacy. King Philip's war against the whites, 1675-1676, in which the Chief was killed, resulted in the loss of central power of the New England tribes. Long established tribes on Martha's Vineyard also belonged to this Group, derived from the Algonquian linguistic family.

■

One night on Cape Cod at Gay Head, a Mashpee woman and her children were alone in their wigwam. The children were sound asleep in their blankets and their mother sat knitting beside her central fire-pit. As customary, her door-flap was wide open. Suddenly she became aware of someone approaching her doorway, and went to see who it might be.

A sailor stood outside. She asked him, "What do you want?" He replied, "I'd like to come inside and warm myself by your fire, because my clothes are wet and I feel chilled to the bone."

She invited him inside and offered a place for him to sit beside the fire to dry out and warm himself. She placed another log on her fire, then resumed her knitting. As she watched the fire, she noticed that she could see the fire right through the sailor's legs, which were stretched out between her and the fire—as if he were a ghost!

Her fear of him increased, but since she was a brave woman, she kept on with her knitting while keeping a suspicious eye toward the visitor. Finally the sailor turned to the Indian woman and said, "Do you want any money?"

Her first thought was not to answer his question. Then he repeated, "Do you want any money?" She replied, "Yes."

The sailor explained, "If you really want a large amount of money, all you have to do is go outdoors behind your wigwam. Beside a rock there you will find buried a kettle full of money. I thank you for your hospitality. Good night." He went away.

The Mashpee woman did not go outdoors immediately, as she wanted to think about the sailor's proposal. She sat and knitted and thought for a while longer. Still, she felt frightened from the evening's experience and was reluctant to leave her wigwam. More knitting time elapsed. Then she thought, "I might as well go out and see if the sailor spoke the truth—to see if there really is a kettle of money out there."

She took her hoe and went outside to the back of her wigwam, and easily saw the place described by the sailor. She began to dig with her hoe. She realized that every time she struck her hoe into the ground, she heard her children cry out loudly, as if in great pain. She rushed indoors to see what was their trouble. They were soundly sleeping in their blankets.

Again and again she dug with her hoe; each time her children cried out loudly to her; each time she rushed in to comfort them, only to find them soundly asleep as she had left them.

After these episodes had occurred several times, the mother decided to give up digging for the night. She thought she would try again early next morning after bright daylight and her children were awake.

Morning came, but she wondered if she had only dreamed last night's happenings. Her children were eating their breakfast when she went out to the digging place. There was her hoe, standing where she had left it. But she could see that someone else had been there in the meantime, and had finished digging while she slept.

Before her, she saw a big round hole. She knew someone had dug up the hidden treasure. She was too late for the pot of gold promised by the ghostly sailor. But again she thought and wondered, "But was I really too late?"

Again she thought, "That sailor may have been the Evil Spirit in disguise—or even a real ghost. Perhaps he was tempting me to see whether I cared more for my children, or more for the gold?"

Nevertheless, the Mashpee woman and her children continued to live in their village for a long, long time, even without the benefit of the ghost's kettle of gold.

Knight, "Mashpee Ghost Story," 136-137.

■

# Rabbit and Otter, The Bungling Host
## Micmac

Many native American tribes have legends in which various animals display their ways and means of obtaining food from others, sometimes using trickster methods. They return meal invitations and even attempt to provide food of a similar nature and in the manner of the previous host. Sometimes, this leads to trouble.

■

There were two wigwams. Otter lived in one with his grandmother, and Rabbit lived with his grandmother in the other. One day Rabbit started out and wandered over to visit Otter in his camp. When Rabbit entered Otter's wigwam, Otter asked if he had anything to eat at home. "No," replied Rabbit. So Otter asked his grandmother if she would cook something for Rabbit, but she told him she had nothing to cook.

So Otter went out to the pond directly in front of his camp, jumped in, and caught a nice long string of eels. Meanwhile, Rabbit was looking to see how Otter would catch his food. With Otter's great success, Rabbit thought he could do the same.

Rabbit then invited Otter to come over to his camp the next day. His grandmother had already told him that she had nothing to cook for their meal, but asked him to go out and find something. Then Rabbit went out to the same pond where Otter had found the string of eels; but he could get nothing, not one fish, as he could not dive no matter how hard he tried.

In the meantime, his grandmother was waiting. She sent Otter out to find Rabbit, who searched and finally found him at the same pond, soaked and with nothing to show for his efforts.

"What's the matter with you?" he asked.

"I'm trying hard to get us some food," he replied.

So friendly Otter jumped into the pond and again caught a string of fish, this time for Rabbit's grandmother to cook for their dinner. Then Otter went home.

The next day, Rabbit started out to visit Woodpecker. When he reached Woodpecker's wigwam, Rabbit found him at home with his grandmother. She got out her large pot to cook a meal, but said, "We have nothing to cook in the pot." So Woodpecker went out front to a dry tree-trunk, from which he picked a quantity of meal. This he took to his grandmother, and she made a good dinner for them.

Rabbit had watched how Woodpecker obtained his meal, so he invited Woodpecker over to visit him. The very next day Woodpecker arrived at Rabbit's wigwam for a visit. Rabbit asked his grandmother to hang up her pot and cook them some dinner.

"But we have nothing to cook," she replied. So Rabbit went outside with his birch-bark vessel to fill it with meal. He tried to dig out the meal with his nose, as he had seen Woodpecker do. Soon Woodpecker came out to see what caused the delay.

*Quilled box*
Micmac

Poor Rabbit was hurt, with his nose flattened out and split in the middle from trying to break into the wood. Woodpecker left to return to his own wigwam without any dinner. Ever since then, Rabbit has had to carry around his split nose.

Another day, desperate for food, Rabbit thought he would go and steal some of Otter's eels. He got into the habit of doing this every second night. Toward spring, Otter began to wonder where his eels had gone, as his barrel was getting low.

Otter thought he would keep watch and soon found Rabbit's foot tracks, and said to himself, "For that, I am going to kill Rabbit." Now Rabbit knew what was going on in Otter's mind, and when Otter reached Rabbit's camp, he fled.

Otter asked Rabbit's grandmother, "Where has Rabbit gone?"

"I don't know," she replied. "Last night he brought home some eels, then he went away."

"He has been stealing my eels," said Otter. "Now, I'm going to kill him."

So began Otter's search for Rabbit, who guessed Otter would be trailing him. Otter began to gain on Rabbit, who picked up a small chip and asked it to become a wigwam. Immediately, the chip became a wigwam and Rabbit became an old man sitting inside.

When Otter came along and saw the wigwam, he also saw the gray-headed old man sitting inside. He pretended to be blind. Otter did not know that this was Rabbit himself. Out of pity for him, Otter gathered some firewood for the old man and asked if he had heard Rabbit passing by. "No, I have not heard any one today." So Otter continued his search.

Later, Rabbit left his wigwam and started out on another road. Otter could not pick up Rabbit's trail, so he returned to the wigwam. Not only was it empty, but gone entirely. Only a chip remained in its place.

Otter then saw Rabbit's tracks where he had jumped out of the wigwam. This trick made Otter very angry and he cried out, "You won't fool me again." Otter followed the new trail.

When Rabbit sensed Otter was closing in on him, he picked up another chip and wished it to become a house, and there was the house, ready to live in. Otter came along and was supicious as soon as he saw the house with a veranda across the front, and a big gentleman walking back and forth all dressed in white, reading a paper.

This, of course, was Rabbit himself, but Otter did not know it. He asked the big gentleman, "Have you seen Rabbit go this way?" The man appeared not to hear. So Otter asked again. The gentleman replied in Pidgin English a phrase that meant, "Never saw Rabbit." But Otter looked hard at him and noticed the man's feet, which were Rabbit feet. So Otter felt certain this was his prey.

The big gentleman gave Otter some bread and wine, and Otter left hurriedly to again track Rabbit back to the house. He came to the place, but the house was not there. Otter could see the tracks where Rabbit started running away.

"He'll never have a chance to trick me again, that's his last time!" declared Otter.

Rabbit soon came to the head of a bay where there was a very small island, so small that a person could almost jump over it. He jumped onto the island and wished it to become a man-of-war.

Otter came to the same shore and saw the big ship anchored there, and the big gentleman in a white suit walking the deck. Otter called to him, "You can't trick me now! You're the man I want."

Then Otter swam out toward the ship, to board it and to kill Rabbit. But the big gentleman sang out to this sailors, "Shoot him! His skin is worth a lot of money in France."

Speck, *Micmac Tales of Cape Breton Island*, vol. VI, 64-66.

■

# THE ORIGIN OF THE IROQUOIS NATIONS
## *Iroquois*

About 1390, today's State of New York became the stronghold of five powerful Indian tribes. They were later joined by another great tribe, the Tuscaroras from the south. Eventually the Iroquois, Mohawks, Oneidas, Onondagas, and Cayugas joined together to form the great Iroquois Nation. In 1715, the Tuscaroras were accepted into the Iroquois Nation.

■

## *The Five Nations*

Long, long ago, one of the Spirits of the Sky World came down and looked at the earth. As he traveled over it, he found it beautiful, and so he created people to live on it. Before returning to the sky, he gave them names, called the people all together, and spoke his parting words:

"To the Mohawks, I give corn," he said. "To the patient Oneidas, I give the nuts and the fruit of many trees. To the industrious Senecas, I give beans. To the friendly Cayugas, I give the roots of plants to be eaten. To the wise and eloquent Onondagas, I give grapes and squashes to eat and tobacco to smoke at the camp fires."

Many other things he told the new people. Then he wrapped himself in a bright cloud and went like a swift arrow to the Sun. There his return caused his Brother Sky Spirits to rejoice.

## *The Six Nations*

Long, long ago, in the great past, there were no people on the earth. All of it was covered by deep water. Birds, flying, filled the air, and many huge monsters possessed the waters.

One day the birds saw a beautiful woman falling from the sky. Immediately the huge ducks held a council.

"How can we prevent her from falling into the water?" they asked.

After some discussion, they decided to spread out their wings and thus break the force of her fall. Each duck spread out its wings until it touched the wings of other ducks. So the beautiful woman reached them safely.

Then the monsters of the deep held a council, to decide how they could protect the beautiful being from the terror of the waters. One after

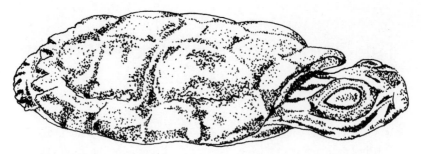

*Soapstone turtle*
Iroquios

another, the monsters decided that they were not able to protect her, that only Giant Tortoise was big enough to bear her weight. He volunteered, and she was gently placed upon his back. Giant Tortoise magically increased in size and soon became a large island.

After a time, the Celestial Woman gave birth to twin boys. One of them was the Spirit of Good. He made all the good things on the earth and caused the corn, the fruits, and the tobacco to grow.

The other twin was the Spirit of Evil. He created the weeds and also the worms and the bugs and all the other creatures that do evil to the good animals and birds.

All the time, Giant Tortoise continued to stretch himself. And so the world became larger and larger. Sometimes Giant Tortoise moved himself in such a way as to make the earth quake.

After many, many years had passed by, the Sky-Holder, whom Indians called *Ta-rhu-hia-wah-ku*, decided to create some people. He wanted them to surpass all others in beauty, strength, and bravery. So from the bosom of the island where they had been living on moles, the Sky-Holder brought forth six pairs of people.

The first pair were left near a great river, now called the Mohawk. So they are called the Mohawk Indians. The second pair were told to move their home beside a large stone. Their descendants have been called the Oneidas. Many of them lived on the south side of Oneida Lake and others in the valleys of Oneida Creek. A third pair were left on a high hill and have always been called the Onondagas.

The fourth pair became the parents of the Cayugas, and the fifth pair the parents of the Senecas. Both were placed in some part of what is now known as the State of New York. But the Tuscororas were taken up the Roanoke River into what is now known as North Carolina. There the Sky-Holder made his home while he taught these people and their descendants many useful arts and crafts.

The Tuscaroras claim that his presence with them made them superior to the other Iroquois nations. But each of the other five will tell you,

"Ours was the favored tribe with whom Sky-Holder made his home while he was on the earth."

The Onondagas say, "We have the council fire. That means that we are the chosen people."

As the years passed by, the numerous Iroquois families became scattered over the state, and also in what is now Pennsylvania, the Middle West and southeastern Canada. Some lived in areas where bear was their principal game. So these people were called the Bear Clan. Others lived where beavers were plentiful. So they were called the Beaver Clan. For similar reasons, the Deer, Wolf, Snipe and Tortoise clans received their names.

Erminnie Smith, *Origin of the Iroquois Nation*, 47.

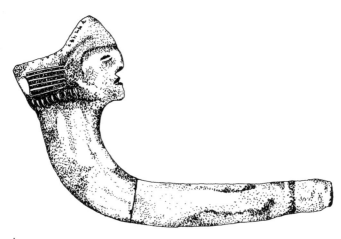

*Clay pipe*
Iroquois

■

# DE-KA-NAH-WI-DA AND HIAWATHA
## *Iroquois*

The Hiawatha in this story is the historic person of the late fourteenth century. He should not be confused with the character in Henry Wadsworth Longfellow's poem, *The Song of Hiawatha*.

In the late nineteenth century, the Iroquois Six Nations Council asked their six hereditary Chiefs to write in English for the first time the traditional oral history of the formation of the League of Five nations. It was formed about 1390, 100 years before Columbus discovered America. (The Tuscaroras joined the League conditionally in 1715.)

The traditional history was dictated by the six ceremonial Chiefs, one from each of these tribes: the Mohawks, Oneidas, Cayugas, Senecas, Onondagas, and the Tuscaroras. Two subchiefs were appointed secretaries, and the typewritten report was prepared by an Indian. On July 3, 1900, the completed history was approved by the Council of the Confederacy.

■

About 1390, an Iroquois mother living near the Bay of Quinte had a very special dream: A messenger came to her and revealed that her maiden daughter, who lived at home, would soon give birth to a son. She would call him De-ka-nah-wi-da (De-käh-a-wēē-dà). When a grown man, he would bring to all people the good Tidings of Peace and Power from the Chief of the Sky Spirits.

De-ka-nah-wi-da was born, as the dream foretold. He grew rapidly. One day he said to his mother and grandmother, "The time has come for me to perform my duty in the world. I will now build my canoe."

When it was completed, and with the help of his mother and grandmother, he dragged the canoe to the edge of the water. The canoe was made of white stone. He got into it, waved good-bye, and paddled swiftly away to the East. A group of Seneca hunters on the far side of the bay saw the canoe coming toward them. De- ka-nah-wi-da stepped ashore and asked, "Why are you here?"

The first man replied, "We are hunting game for our living."

A second man said, "There is strife in our village."

"When you go back," De-ka-nah-wi-da told them, "you will find that peace prevails, because the good Tidings of Peace and Power have come to the people. You will find strife removed. Tell your Chief that De-ka-nah-wi-da has brought the good news. I am now going eastward."

The men on the lakeshore wondered, because the swift canoe was made of white stone. When they returned to their village and reported to their Chief, they found that peace prevailed.

After leaving his canoe on the east shore, De-ka-nah-wi-da traveled overland to another tribal settlement and asked the Chief, "Have you heard that Peace and Power have come to earth?"

"Yes, I have heard," answered the Chief. "I have been thinking about it so much that I have been unable to sleep."

De-ka-nah-wi-da then explained, "That which caused your wakefulness is now before you. Henceforth, you will be called Chief Hiawatha. You shall help me promote peace among all the tribes, so that the shedding of blood may cease among your people."

"Wait," said Hiawatha. "I will summon my people to hear you speak." All assembled quickly.

"I have brought the good tidings of Peace and Power from the Chief of the Sky Spirits to all people on earth. Bloodshed must cease in the land. The Good Spirit never intended that blood should flow between human beings."

Chief Hiawatha asked his tribe for their answer. One man asked, "What will happend to us if hostile tribes are on either side of us?"

"Those nations have already accepted the good news that I have brought them," replied De-ka-nah-wi-da. Hiawatha's tribe then also accepted the new plan of peace.

When the Messenger departed, Hiawatha walked with him for a short distance. "There is one I wish to warn you about because he may do evil to you," confided De-ka-nah-wi-da. "He is a wizard and lives high above Lake Onondaga. He causes storms to capsize boats and is a mischief-maker. I go on to the East."

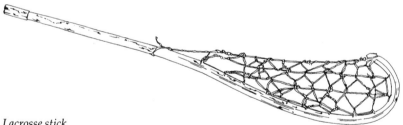

*Lacrosse stick*
Iroquois

Hiawatha had three daughters. The eldest became ill and died. Not long afterward, the second daughter died. All of the tribe gathered to console Hiawatha and to help him forget his great sorrow. One of the warriors suggested a game of lacrosse.

During the game, the last of Hiawatha's daughters went to the spring for water. Halfway there, she saw a beautiful high-flying bird of many bright colors. She called for the people to look at the bird. Then the huge creature swooped down toward her. In fear, she started to run back to her lodge. At the same time, the people came running to see the bird. Hiawatha's daughter was knocked down in the confusion. They did not see her and she was trampled to death.

"Has the wizard sent that bird and caused the death of my daughter?" wondered Hiawatha. Deeper in sorrow, he decided to leave his tribe and go away.

A few days later, he met De-ka-nah-wi-da, who commissioned him a Peacemaker. Henceforth, Hiawatha would spend his time going from village to village and spread the good Tidings of Peace and Power, so that the children of the future would live in peace.

The Mohawk Nation was the first to accept the peace plan, and they invited Hiawatha to make his home with them. One night De-ka-nah-wi-da appeared outside Hiawatha's sleeping room. "It is now urgent," he said softly, "that you come with me. We must go at once to another settlement. I have been there before and I promised to return."

On their way, they came to a large lake. De-ka-nah-wi-da asked Hiawatha to choose between paddling across the rough water and flying over it. Remembering the warning about the wizard, he chose to fly over the lake. De-ka-nah-wi-da used his supernatural power and turned both of them into high-flying birds.

When they reached the opposite shore, they resumed their natural bodies. Then they journeyed to the top of a very high hill to see the one chief, the great wizard, who had not yet accepted the good news of peace. Upon seeing him, Hiawatha was startled—the wizard's head was a mass of writhing snakes. His hands and feet were clawlike and twisted. He used his power to persecute others.

After a long time of discussion and gentle persuasion, Hiawatha noticed that the wizard began to smile! He exclaimed, "I do want to accept your plan of Peace and Power."

At once the wizard began to change. His hands and feet straightened. Hiawatha combed the snakes from his hair. Soon other chiefs arrived to help in the wizard's regeneration.

De-ka-nah-wi-da then asked all the chiefs and their chief warriors and assistants to meet on the shores of Lake Onondaga for a Council. Hiawatha, Chief of the Mohawks, asked the Oneida, Seneca, and Cayuga chiefs to bow their heads with him before the reformed wizard, who was the Onondaga Chief Atotarho (A-tä-tär'-ho). This was their way of showing their acceptance of him and their willingness to follow his leadership when called upon.

The Messenger stood before the Council and explained a plan for the Constitution of the Iroquois League of Peace:

"Let us now give thanks to the Great Chief of the Sky Spirits, for our power is now complete. 'Yo-Hen, Yo-Hen,'" he said, meaning praise and thanksgiving.

The Great Spirit created man, the animals, earth, and all the growing things. I appoint you, Atotarho, Chief of the Onondagas, to be Fire-

Keeper of your new Confederacy Council of the Five United Iroquois Nations.

"Chief Warrior and Chief Mother will now place upon your head the horns of a buck deer, a sign of your authority.

"Hiawatha shall be the Chief Spokesman for the Council. He will be the first to consider a subject and to give his opinion. He shall then ask the Senecas, Oneidas, and the Cayugas for their opinions, in that order. If not unanimous, Atotarho's opinion will be considered next. Hiawatha shall continue the debate until a unanimous decision is reached. If not accomplished within a reasonable time, the subject shall be dropped.

"Let us now make a great white Wampum of shell beads strung on deer sinews. Each bead will signify an event and create a design of memory. We shall place it on the ground before the Fire-Keeper. Beside it we shall lay a large White Wing. With it, he can brush away any dust or spot—symbolic of destroying any evil that might cause trouble.

"We shall give the Fire-Keeper a rod to remove any creeping thing that might appear to harm the White Wampum or your grandchildren. If he should ever need help, he shall call out in his thunderous voice for the other Nations of the Confederacy to come to his aid.

"Each Chief shall organize his own tribe in the same way for the peace, happiness, and contentment of all his people. Each Chief shall sit at the head of his own Council and matters shall be referred to him for final decision.

"In the future, your Annual Confederacy Council Fire shall be held here at the Onondaga village of Chief Atotarho. It will be your Seat of Government.

"Let us now plant a symbolic tree of long leaves destined to grow tall and strong. It will represent your unity and strength. When other nations wish to accept the good Tidings of Peace and Power, they shall be seated within the Confederacy Council. Atop the tall tree will proudly sit an all-seeing eagle to watch and warn you of any danger.

"Let each Chief now bring one arrow to form a bundle of arrows. Tie them together so tightly that they cannot be bent or broken apart. Place the bundle of arrows beside the Council Fire as another symbol of your unity and strength.

"Let us join hands firmly, binding ourselves together in a circle. If a tree should fall upon the circle, your circle cannot be broken. Your people can thus be assured of your unity and peace.

"If a Council Chief should ever want to remove himself as Chief, then his Horns of Authority shall be placed upon the head of his hereditary successor.

"You Chiefs must now decide what you will do with your war weapons," said De-ka-nah-wi-da.

*Hiawatha wampum belt*

Hiawatha then led the thoughtful discussion of the subject. The men agreed to dig a deep chasm where there was a rushing river beneath. Into this river the chiefs and their chief warriors threw all of their armaments of war. Then they closed the chasm forever.

De-ka-nah-wi-da reconvened the Council and stated:

"I charge you never to disagree seriously among yourselves. If you do, you might cause the loss of any rights of your grandchildren, or reduce them to poverty and shame. Your skin must be seven hands thick to stand for what is right in your heart. Exercise great patience and goodwill toward each other in your deliberations. Never, never disgrace yourselves by becoming angry. Let the good Tidings of Peace and Power and righteousness be your guide in all your Council Fires. Cultivate good feelings of friendship, love, and honor for each other always.

"In the future, vacancies shall be filled from the same hereditary tribes and clans from which the first Chiefs were chosen. The Chief Mother will control the chiefship titles and appoint hereditary successors. New Chiefs shall be confirmed by the Confederacy Council before the Condolence Ceremony. At that time, the Horns of Authority shall be placed upon the head of the new Chief.

"All hunting grounds are to be in common. All tribes shall have co-equal rights within your common boundaries. I now proclaim the formation of the League of the Five Iroquois Nations completed. I leave in your hands these principles I have received from the Chief of the Sky Spirits. In the future you will have the power to add any necessary rules for the safety and well-being of the Confederacy.

"My mission is now fulfilled. May your Confederacy continue from generation to generation—as long as the sun will shine, the grass will grow, the water will run. I go to cover myself with bark. I will have no successor and no one shall be called by my name." De-ka-nah-wi-da departed from the Council Fire.

Chief Spokesman and Lawgiver Hiawatha arose before the Council and stated, "Hereafter, when opening and closing the Council Fire, the Fire-Keeper shall pick up the White Wampum strings and hold them high to honor all that has gone before. He will offer praise and thanksgiving to the Great Spirit. In Annual Council, the Chiefs will smoke the Pipe of Great Peace.

"If a chief stubbornly opposes matters of decision before the Council, displaying disrespect for his brother Chiefs, he shall be admonished by the Chief Mother to stop such behavior and to act in harmony. If he continues to refuse, he shall be deposed.

"If a family or clan should become extinct, the Chief's title shall be given to another chosen family within his Nation, and the hereditary title will remain within that family."

All of the Chiefs of that first Council Fire agreed with Hiawatha's plan as a part of their new Constitution.

Chief Fire-Keeper Atotarho arose before the Council with his arms outstretched, holding the White Wampum strings high in praise and thanksgiving to the Holder of the Heavens. Herewith, he closed the historic first Confederacy Council Fire of the Iroquois League of Five Nations. "Yo-Hen, Yo-Hen!" he solemnly concluded, "thank you."

The Five Chiefs then smoked the Pipe of Great Peace!

Scott, *Royal Academy of Canada, Proceedings and Transactions*, 194-246.

Wallace, *White Roots of Peace*.

# Chapter 1

The abduction of April Finnemore took place in the dead of night, sometime between 9:15 p.m., when she last spoke with Theo Boone, and 3:30 a.m., when her mother entered her bedroom and realized she was gone. The abduction appeared to have been rushed; whoever took April did not allow her to gather her things. Her laptop was left behind. Though her bedroom was fairly neat, there was some clothing strewn about, which made it difficult to determine if she had been able to pack. Probably not, the police thought. Her toothbrush was still by the sink. Her backpack was by her bed. Her pajamas were on the floor, so she at least had been allowed to change. Her mother, when she wasn't crying or ranting, told the police that her daughter's favorite blue-and-white sweater was not in the closet. And April's favorite sneakers were gone, too.

The police soon dismissed the notion that she'd simply run away. There was no reason to run away, her mother assured them, and she had not packed the things that would make such an escape successful.

A quick inspection of the home revealed no apparent break-in. The windows were all closed and locked, as were the three doors downstairs. Whoever took April was careful enough to close the door behind them, and lock it on the way out. After observing the scene and listening to Mrs. Finnemore for about an hour, the police decided to have a talk with Theo Boone. He was, after all, April's best friend, and they usually chatted by phone or online at night before going to sleep.

At the Boone home, the phone rang at 4:33, according to the digital clock next to the bed where the parents slept. Mr. Woods Boone, the lighter sleeper, grabbed the phone, while Mrs. Marcella Boone rolled over and began wondering who would call at such an hour. When Mr. Boone said, "Yes, Officer," Mrs. Boone really woke up and scrambled out of bed. She listened to his end of the conversation, soon understood that it had something to do with April Finnemore, and was really confused when her husband said, "Sure, Officer, we can be over there in fifteen minutes." He hung up, and she said, "What is it, Woods?"

"Apparently, April's been abducted, and the police would like to talk to Theo."

"I doubt if he abducted her."

"Well, if he's not upstairs in his room, we may have a problem."

He was upstairs in his room, sound asleep, undisturbed by the ringing of the phone. As he threw on blue jeans and a sweatshirt, he explained to his parents that he had called April the night before on his cell phone and they'd chatted for a few minutes, same as usual.

As they drove through Strattenburg in the predawn darkness, Theo could think of nothing but April and of her miserable home life, her warring parents, her scarred brother and sister, both of whom had fled as soon as they were old enough. April was the youngest of three children born to two people who had no business having a family. Both parents were crazy, according to April herself, and Theo certainly agreed. Both had drug convictions. Her mother kept goats on a small farm outside of town and made cheese, bad cheese in Theo's opinion. She peddled it around town in an old funeral hearse painted yellow, with a pet spider monkey riding shotgun. Her father was an aging hippie, who still played in a bad garage band with a bunch of other leftovers from the 1980s. He had no real job and was often gone for weeks. The Finnemores were in a perpetual state of separation, with talk of divorce always in the air.

April confided in Theo, and told him things he vowed to never repeat.

The Finnemore home was owned by someone else, a rental house April hated because her parents had no interest in maintaining it. It was in an older section of Strattenburg, on a shady street lined with other postwar homes that had seen better days. Theo had been there only one time, for a less-than-successful birthday party April's mother had thrown together two years earlier. Most of the kids who'd been invited did not attend because their parents wouldn't allow it. Such was the Finnemore family reputation.

There were two police cars in the driveway when the Boones arrived. Across the street, the neighbors were on their porches, watching.

Mrs. Finnemore—she went by the name of May and had named her children April, March, and August—was in the living room on a sofa talking to a uniformed officer when the Boones entered, rather awkwardly. Quick introductions were made; Mr. Boone had never met her.

"Theo!" Mrs. Finnemore said, very dramatically. "Someone has taken our April!" Then she burst into tears and reached to hug Theo. He wanted no part of being hugged but went along with the ritual out of respect. As always, she wore a large flowing garment that was more of a tent than a dress, light brown in color and made from what appeared to be burlap. Her long graying hair was pulled into a tight ponytail. Crazy as she was, Theo had always been struck by her beauty. She made no effort at being attractive—quite unlike his mother—but some things you can't hide. She was also very creative, liked to paint and do pottery, in addition to making goat cheese. April had inherited the good genes— the pretty eyes, the artistic flair.

When Mrs. Finnemore settled down, Mrs. Boone asked the officer, "What happened?" He responded with a quick summary of what little they knew at that point.

"Did you talk to her last night?" the officer asked Theo. The cop's name was Bolick, Sergeant Bolick, which Theo knew because he'd seen him around the courthouse. Theo knew most of the policemen in Strattenburg, as well as most of the lawyers, judges, janitors, and clerks in the courthouse.

"Yes, sir. At nine fifteen, according to my phone log. We talk almost every night before going to bed," Theo said. Bolick had the reputation of being a wise guy. Theo wasn't prepared to like him.

"How sweet. Did she say anything that might be useful here? Was she worried? Scared?"

Theo was immediately caught in a vise. He could not

lie to a police officer, yet he could not tell a secret that he'd promised he wouldn't tell. So he fudged a bit by saying, "I don't recall anything like that." Mrs. Finnemore was no longer crying; she was staring intensely at Theo, her eyes glowing.

"What did you talk about?" Sergeant Bolick asked. A detective in plainclothes entered the room and listened carefully.

"The usual stuff. School, homework, I don't remember everything." Theo had watched enough trials to know that answers should often be kept vague, and that "I don't recall" and "I don't remember" were perfectly acceptable in many instances.

"Did you chat online?" the detective asked.

"No, sir, not last night. Just phone." They often used Facebook and text messages, but Theo knew not to volunteer information. Just answer the question in front of you. He'd heard his mother say this to her clients many times.

"Any sign of a break-in?" Mr. Boone asked.

"None," said Bolick. "Mrs. Finnemore was sound asleep in the downstairs bedroom, she heard nothing, and at some point she got up to check on April. That's when she realized she was gone."

Theo looked at Mrs. Finnemore, who again shot him a

fierce look. He knew the truth, and she knew he knew the truth. Trouble was, Theo couldn't tell the truth because he'd made a promise to April.

The truth was that Mrs. Finnemore had not been home for the past two nights. April had been living alone, terrified, with all the doors and windows locked as tightly as possible; with a chair jammed against her bedroom door; with an old baseball bat across the end of her bed; with the phone close and ready to dial 911, and with no one in the world to talk to but Theodore Boone, who had vowed not to tell a soul. Her father was out of town with his band. Her mother was taking pills and losing her mind.

"In the past few days, has April said anything about running away?" the detective was asking Theo.

Oh, yes. Nonstop. She wants to run away to Paris and study art. She wants to run away to LA and live with March, her older sister. She wants to run away to Santa Fe and become a painter. She wants to run away, period.

"I don't recall anything like that," Theo said, and it was the truth because "in the past few days" could mean almost anything; thus, the question was too vague to require a definite answer on his part. He had seen this time and time again in trials. In his opinion, Sergeant Bolick and the detective were being far too sloppy with their questions. So far, they had not been able to pin him down, and he had not told a lie.

May Finnemore was overcome with tears and made a big show out of crying. Bolick and the detective quizzed Theo about April's other friends, any potential problems she was having, how she was doing in school, and so on. Theo gave straight answers, with no wasted words.

A female officer in uniform had entered the den from upstairs, and she sat with Mrs. Finnemore, who was again distraught and overcome. Sergeant Bolick nodded at the Boones and motioned for them to follow him into the kitchen. They did, and the detective joined them. Bolick glared at Theo and in a low voice said, "Did the girl ever mention a relative in prison in California?"

"No, sir," Theo said.

"Are you sure?"

"Sure I'm sure."

"What's this all about?" Mrs. Boone jumped in. She was not about to stand by silently while her son was rudely interrogated. Mr. Boone was ready to pounce, too.

The detective pulled out an 8" x 10" black-and-white photo, a mug shot of a shady-looking character who gave every indication of being a veteran criminal. Bolick went on, "Guy's name is Jack Leeper, a ten-time loser. Distant cousin to May Finnemore, even more distant to April. He grew up around here, drifted away a long time ago, became a career thug, petty thief, drug dealer, and so on. Got busted in California for kidnapping ten years ago, sentenced to life with no parole. Escaped two weeks ago. This afternoon we get a tip that he might be in this area."

Theo looked at the sinister face of Jack Leeper and felt ill. If this thug had April, then she was in serious trouble.

Bolick continued, "Last night around seven thirty, Leeper here walks into the Korean Quick Shop four blocks away, buys cigarettes and beer, gets his face captured on the surveillance cameras. Not the smartest crook in the world. So, we know he's definitely in the area."

"Why would he take April?" Theo blurted, his mouth dry with fear, his knees ready to buckle.

"According to authorities in California, they found some letters from April in his prison cell. She was his pen pal, probably felt sorry for the guy 'cause he's never supposed to get out of prison. So she strikes up a correspondence. We've searched her room upstairs and can't find anything he may have written to her."

"She never mentioned this to you?" the detective asked.

"Never," Theo said. He had learned that with April's weird family there were many secrets, many things she kept to herself.

The detective put away the photo, and Theo was relieved.

He never wanted to see the face again, but he doubted if he could ever forget it.

Sergeant Bolick said, "We suspect that April knew the person who took her. How else can you explain the lack of a forcible entry?"

"Do you think he would hurt her?" Theo asked.

"We have no way of knowing that, Theo. This man's been in prison most of his life. His behavior is unpredictable."

The detective added, "The good thing is that he always gets caught."

Theo said, "If April's with him, she'll contact us. She'll find a way."

"Then, please let us know."

"Don't worry."

"Excuse me, Officer," Mrs. Boone said. "But I thought in a case like this you first investigate the parents. Missing children are almost always taken by one of their parents, right?"

"This is correct," Bolick said. "And we are looking for the father. According to the mother, though, she spoke with him yesterday afternoon and he was with his band somewhere in West Virginia. She feels rather strongly that he is not involved in this."

"April can't stand her father," Theo blurted, then wished he'd remained quiet.

They chatted for a few more minutes, but the conversation was obviously over. The officers thanked the Boones for coming and promised to check back later. Both Mr. and Mrs. Boone said they would be at their office all day if they were needed for anything. Theo, of course, would be in school.

As they drove away, Mrs. Boone said, "That poor child. Snatched from her own bedroom."

Mr. Boone, who was driving, glanced back over his shoulder and said, "Are you okay, Theo?"

"I guess," he said.

"Of course he's not okay, Woods. His friend has just been abducted."

"I can speak for myself, Mom," Theo said.

"Of course you can, dear. I just hope they find her, and soon."

There was a hint of sunlight to the east. As they drove through the residential neighborhood, Theo stared out of his window, searching for the hardened face of Jack Leeper. But no one was out there. Lights in homes were being turned on. The town was waking up.

"It's almost six," Mr. Boone announced. "I say we go to Gertrude's and have her world-famous waffles. Theo?"

"I'm in," Theo replied, though he had no appetite.

"Marvelous, honey," Mrs. Boone said, though all three knew she would have nothing but coffee.

# Chapter 2

Gertrude's was an old diner on Main Street, six blocks west of the courthouse and three blocks south of the police station. It claimed to serve pecan waffles that were famous around the world, but Theo had often doubted this. Did people in Japan and Greece really know about Gertrude and her waffles? He wasn't so sure. He had friends at school who'd never heard of Gertrude's right there in Strattenburg. A few miles west of town, on the main highway, there was an ancient log cabin with a gas pump out front and a large sign advertising DUDLEY'S WORLD-FAMOUS MINT FUDGE. When Theo was younger, he naturally had assumed that everybody in town not only craved the mint fudge but talked about it nonstop. How else could it achieve the status of being world famous? Then one day in class the discussion took an odd turn and found its way to the topic of imports and exports. Theo made the observation that Mr. Dudley and his mint fudge were heavy into exports because they were so famous. It said so right there on the billboard. To his astonishment, only one other classmate had ever heard of this fudge. Slowly, Theo realized that it probably was not as well known as Mr. Dudley claimed it to be. Slowly, he began to grasp the concept of false advertising.

Since then, he'd been very suspicious of such big claims of notoriety.

But on this morning he couldn't dwell on waffles and fudge, famous or not. He was far too occupied with thoughts of April and the slimy figure of Jack Leeper. The Boones were seated at a small table in the crowded diner. The air was thick with bacon grease and strong coffee, and the hot topic, as Theo realized not long after he sat down, was the abduction of April Finnemore. To their right, four uniformed policemen talked loudly about the possibility that Leeper was close by. To their left, a table of gray-haired men spoke with great authority on several subjects, but seemed particularly interested in the "kidnapping," as it was sometimes referred to.

The menu promoted the myth that Gertrude's was indeed the home of "World-Famous Pecan Waffles." In silent protest against false advertising, Theo ordered scrambled eggs and sausage. His father ordered waffles. His mother ordered dry wheat toast.

As soon as the waitress walked away, Mrs. Boone looked Theo squarely in the eyes and said, "Okay, let's have it. There's something else to the story."

Theo was constantly amazed at how easily his mother could do this. He could tell only half of a story, and she immediately looked for the other half. He could offer up a little fib, nothing serious, maybe something just for fun, and she instinctively pounced on it and ripped it to shreds. He could duck a direct question, and she would fire back with three more. Theo suspected she had acquired this skill after years as a divorce lawyer. She often said that she never expected her clients to tell her the truth.

"I agree," said Mr. Boone. Theo couldn't tell if he really agreed, or whether he was just tag-teaming with his wife, which he often did. Mr. Boone was a real estate lawyer who never went to court, and, while he missed little, he was usually a step or two behind Mrs. Boone when it came time to grill Theo about something.

"April told me not to tell anyone," Theo said.

To which his mother responded quickly, "And April is in big trouble right now, Theo. If you know something, let's have it. And now." Her eyes narrowed. Her eyebrows arched. Theo knew where this was headed, and, truthfully, he knew it was better to level with his parents.

"Mrs. Finnemore wasn't at home when I talked to April last night," Theo said, his head low, his eyes darting left and right. "And she wasn't home the night before. She's taking pills and she's acting crazy. April's been living by herself."

"Where's her father?" Mr. Boone asked.

"He's off with his band, hasn't been home in a week."

"Doesn't he have a job?" Mrs. Boone asked.

"He buys and sells antique furniture. April says he'll make a few bucks, then disappear for a week or two with his band."

"That poor girl," Mrs. Boone said.

"Are you going to tell the police?" Theo asked.

Both parents took long sips from their coffee cups. They exchanged curious looks as they pondered this. They eventually agreed that they would discuss it later, at the office, while Theo was at school. Mrs. Finnemore was obviously lying to the police, but the Boones were reluctant to get in the middle of that. They doubted if she knew anything about the abduction. She seemed distressed enough. She probably felt guilty for being away when her daughter was taken.

The food arrived and the waitress refilled the coffee cups. Theo was drinking milk.

The situation was very complicated, and Theo was relieved to have his parents involved and doing their share of the worrying.

"Anything else, Theo?" his father asked.

"Not that I can think of."

His mother said, "When you talked to her last night, was she frightened?"

"Yes. She was really scared and also worried about her mother."

"Why didn't you tell us?" his father asked.

"Because she made me promise not to tell. April has to deal with a lot, and she's very private. She's also embarrassed by her family and tries to protect them. She was hoping her mother would show up at any minute. I guess someone else did."

Theo suddenly lost his appetite. He should've done more. He should've tried to protect April by telling his parents or perhaps a teacher at school. Someone would have listened to him. He could have done something. But, April swore him to silence, and she kept assuring him she was safe. The house was locked; plenty of lights were on, and so forth.

During the drive home, Theo said from the rear seat, "I'm not sure I can go to school today."

"I was waiting for that," his father replied.

"What's your reason this time?" his mother said.

"Well, to start with, I didn't get enough sleep last night. We've been up since, what four thirty?"

"So you want to go home and go to sleep?" his father replied.

"I didn't say that, but I doubt if I can stay awake at school."

"I bet you can. Your mother and I are going to work, and we have no choice but to stay awake."

Theo almost blurted something about his father's daily siesta; a brief power nap at the desk with the door locked, usually around 3:00 p.m. Everyone who worked at the law firm of Boone & Boone knew that Woods was upstairs, shoes off, feet on the desk, phone on Do Not Disturb, snoring away for thirty minutes every afternoon.

"You can tough it out," his father added.

Theo's problem at this moment was his habit of trying to avoid school. Headaches, coughs, food poisoning, pulled muscles, stomach gas—Theo had tried them all and would try them again. He didn't hate school; in fact, he usually enjoyed it once he got there. He made good grades and enjoyed his friends. Theo, though, wanted to be at the courthouse, watching trials and hearings, listening to the lawyers and judges, chatting with the policemen and the clerks, even the janitors. Theo knew them all.

"There's another reason I can't go to school," he said, though he knew this was a battle he would not win.

"Let's hear it," his mother said.

"Okay, there's a manhunt underway, and I need to go help. How often do we have a manhunt in Strattenburg? This is a big deal, especially since it's my close friend they're looking for. I need to help search for April. She would expect me to. Plus, there's no way I can concentrate at school. A total waste of time. I'll think of nothing but April."

"Nice try," his father said.

"Not bad," his mother added.

"Look, I'm serious. I need to be on the streets."

"I'm confused," his father said, though he really wasn't. He often claimed to be confused when discussing things with Theo. "You're too tired to go to school, yet you have enough energy to lead a manhunt."

"Whatever. There's no way I can go to school."

———————

An hour later, Theo parked his bike outside the middle school and reluctantly went inside as the 8:15 bell was ringing. In the main lobby, he was immediately met by three crying eighth-grade girls who wanted to know if he knew anything about April. He said he knew nothing more than what was being reported on the morning news.

Evidently, everybody in town had watched the morning news. The reports showed a school photo of April, and a mug shot of Jack Leeper. There was a strong suggestion that a kidnapping had taken place. Theo didn't understand this. A kidnapping (and he'd checked the dictionary) usually involved a demand for ransom—cash to be paid for the release of the person seized. The Finnemores couldn't pay their monthly bills—how were they supposed to find serious cash to free April? And there was no word yet from the kidnapper. Usually, as Theo remembered from television, the family gets word pretty soon that the bad guys have the child and would like a million bucks or so for a safe return.

Another report from the morning news showed Mrs. Finnemore crying in front of their home. The police were tight-lipped, saying only that they were pursuing all leads. A neighbor said his dog started barking around midnight, always a bad sign. As frantic as the reporters seemed to be that morning, the truth was that they were finding very little to add to the story of a missing girl.

Theo's homeroom teacher was Mr. Mount, who also taught Government. After Mr. Mount got the boys settled, he called the roll. All sixteen were present. The conversation quickly got around to the disappearance of April, and Mr. Mount asked Theo if he'd heard anything.

"Nothing," Theo said, and his classmates seemed disappointed. Theo was one of the few boys who talked to April. Most of the eighth graders, boys and girls, liked April but found her difficult to hang out with. She was quiet, dressed more like a boy than a girl, had no interest in the latest fashions or the weekly teen-gossip magazines, and as everyone knew, came from a weird family.

The bell rang for first period, and Theo, already exhausted, dragged himself off to Spanish.

# Chapter 3

Final bell rang at 3:30, and by 3:31 Theo was on his bike, speeding away from school, darting through alleys and back streets and dodging downtown traffic. He zipped across Main Street, waved at a policeman standing near an intersection and pretended not to hear when the policeman yelled, "Slow it down, Theo." He cut through a small cemetery and turned onto Park Street.

His parents had been married for twenty-five years, and for the past twenty they had worked together as partners in the small firm of Boone & Boone, located at 415 Park Street, in the heart of old Strattenburg. There had once been another partner, Ike Boone, Theo's uncle, but Ike had been forced to leave the firm when he got himself into some trouble. Now the firm had just two equal partners—Marcella Boone on the first floor, in a neat modern office where she handled mainly divorces, and Woods Boone upstairs all alone in a large cluttered room with sagging bookshelves and stacks of files littering the floor and an ever-present cloud of fragrant pipe smoke rolling gently across the ceiling. Rounding out the firm, there was Elsa, who answered the phone, greeted the clients, managed the office, did some typing, and kept an eye on Judge, the dog; there was Dorothy, a real estate secretary, who worked for Mr. Boone and did work that Theo considered horribly boring; and there was Vince, the paralegal, who worked on Mrs. Boone's cases.

Judge, a mutt who was Theo's dog, the family's dog, and the firm's dog, spent his days at the office, sometimes creeping quietly from room to room keeping an eye on things, oftentimes following a human to the kitchen where he expected food, but mostly snoozing on a small square bed in the reception area where Elsa talked to him whenever she typed.

The last member of the firm was Theo, who happily suspected that he was the only thirteen-year-old in Strattenburg with his own law office. Of course, he was too young to be a real member of the firm, but there were times when Theo was valuable. He fetched files for Dorothy and Vince. He scanned lengthy documents looking for key words or phrases. His computer skills were extraordinary and allowed him to research legal issues and dig up facts. But his favorite chore, by far, was dashing off to the courthouse to file papers for the firm. Theo loved the courthouse and dreamed of the day when he would stand in the large, stately courtroom on the second floor and defend his clients.

At 3:40 p.m., on the dot, Theo parked his bike on the narrow front porch of Boone & Boone, and braced himself. Elsa greeted him every day with a fierce hug, a painful pinch on the check, then a quick inspection of whatever he was wearing. He opened the door, stepped inside, and got himself properly greeted. As always, Judge was waiting, too. He bounced from his bed and ran to see Theo.

"I'm so sorry about April," Elsa gushed. She sounded as if she knew the girl personally, which she did not. But by now, as with any tragedy, everyone in Strattenburg knew or claimed to know April and could say only great things about her.

"Any news?" Theo asked, rubbing Judge's head.

"Nothing. I've listened to the radio all day, no word, no sign of anything. How was school?"

"Terrible. All we did was talk about April."

"That poor girl." Elsa was inspecting his shirt, then her

eyes moved down to his pants and for a split second Theo froze. Every day she looked him over quickly and never hesitated to say something like "Does that shirt really match those pants?" or "Didn't you wear that shirt two days ago?" This irritated Theo tremendously and he had complained to both parents, but nothing came of his protests. Elsa was like a member of the family, a second mother to Theo, and if she wanted to quiz him about anything, she did so out of affection.

The rumor was that Elsa spent all her money on clothes, and she certainly gave that appearance. Apparently, she approved of his attire today. Before she had the chance to comment, Theo kept the conversation going with, "Is my mother in?"

"Yes, but she has a client. Mr. Boone is working."

This was usually the case. Theo's mother, when she wasn't in court, spent most of her time with clients, almost all of whom were women who (1) wanted a divorce, or (2) needed a divorce, or (3) were in the process of getting a divorce, or (4) were suffering through the aftermath of a divorce. It was difficult work, but his mother was known as one of the top divorce lawyers in town. Theo was quite proud of this. He was also proud of the fact that his mother encouraged every new client to seek professional counseling in an effort to save the marriage. Sadly, though, as he'd already learned, some marriages cannot be saved.

He bounced up the stairs with Judge at his heels and barged into the spacious and wonderful office of Woods Boone, Attorney and Counselor-at-Law. His dad was behind his desk, at work, pipe in one hand, pen in the other, with papers scattered everywhere.

"Well, hello, Theo," Mr. Boone said with a warm smile. "A good day at school?" The same question five days a week.

"Terrible," Theo said. "I knew I shouldn't have gone. A total waste."

"And why is that?"

"Come on, Dad. My friend, our classmate, has been snatched by an escaped criminal who was sent to prison because he's a kidnapper. It's not like this happens every day around here. We should've been out there on the streets helping with the manhunt, but no, we were stuck in school where all we did was talk about searching for April."

"Nonsense. Leave the manhunt to the professionals, Theo. We have a fine police force in this city."

"Well, they haven't found her yet. Maybe they need some help."

"Help from whom?"

Theo cleared his throat and clenched his jaw. He stared

straight at his father, and got ready to tell the truth. He'd been taught to confront the truth head-on, hold nothing back, just blurt it all out, and whatever followed would be far better than lying or concealing the truth. He was about to say—"Help from us, Dad, April's friends. I've organized a search party, and we're about to hit the streets"—when the phone rang. His father grabbed it, offered his usual gruff "Woods Boone," then began listening.

Theo held his tongue. After a few seconds, his father covered the receiver and whispered, "This might take a while."

"See you later," Theo said as he jumped to his feet and left. He walked downstairs, Judge following close behind, and made his way to the rear of Boone & Boone, to the small room he called his office. He unloaded his backpack, arranged his books and notebooks, and gave every indication that he was about to plunge into his homework. He was not.

The search party he'd organized consisted of about twenty of his friends. The plan was to hit the streets in five units of four bikes each. They had cell phones and two-way radios. Woody had an iPad with Google Earth and GPS apps. Everything would be coordinated, with Theo, of course, in charge. They would comb certain areas of town searching for April, and they would distribute flyers with her face in the center and the promise of one thousand dollars in reward money for information leading to her rescue. They had passed the hat at school and collected almost two hundred dollars from students and teachers. Theo and his friends figured they could get the rest of the money from their parents in the event someone came forward with crucial information. Surely, Theo had argued, the parents would cough up the money, if necessary. It was risky, but there was so much at stake and so little time.

Theo eased out the back door, leaving Judge alone and confused, then sneaked around to the front and hopped on his bike.

# Chapter 4

The search party came together a few minutes before 4:00 p.m., in Truman Park, the largest park of any kind in the city of Strattenburg. The gang met near the main gazebo, a popular place in the heart of the park, a place where politicians made speeches and bands played on long summer evenings and, occasionally, young couples got married. There were eighteen in all; fifteen boys and three girls, all properly helmeted and eager to find and rescue April Finnemore.

Throughout the day at school, the boys had argued and bickered about how a proper manhunt should be conducted. None had ever taken part in such a search, but this lack of experience was not mentioned or acknowledged.

Instead, several of them, including Theo, spoke as if they knew precisely what to do. Another strong voice belonged to Woody, who, because he owned the iPad, felt as though more weight should be given to his ideas. Another leader was Justin, the best athlete in their class and, therefore, the one with the most self-confidence.

There were skeptics in the eighth grade who believed that Jack Leeper had already fled the area with April. Why would he stay in a place where everyone was looking at his face on television? The skeptics argued that any effort to find her was futile. She was gone, hidden in another state, perhaps another country, hopefully still alive.

But Theo and the others were determined to do something, anything. Maybe she was gone, but maybe she wasn't. No one knew, but at least they were trying. Who knows—they might get lucky.

Late in the day, the searchers finally reached an agreement among themselves. They would concentrate their efforts in an old section known as Delmont, near Stratten College, in the northwest part of the town. Delmont was lower income, with more renters than owners, and popular with students and starving artists. The search party figured any kidnapper worth his salt would stay away from the nicer neighborhoods. He would avoid central Strattenburg with its busy streets and sidewalks. He would almost certainly choose an area where strangers came and went with greater frequency. Thus, they had narrowed their search, and from the moment the decision was made, they were convinced that April was stashed away in a back room of some cheap rental duplex, or perhaps gagged and bound and hidden above an old garage in Delmont.

They split into three teams of six, with a girl included a bit reluctantly to each unit. Ten minutes after they gathered in the park, they wheeled into Gibson's Grocery on the edge of Delmont. Woody's team took Allen Street, Justin's, Edgecomb Street. And Theo, who had assumed the role of supreme commander, though he didn't refer to himself in such a manner, led his team two blocks over to Trover Avenue, where they began tacking MISSING flyers on every utility pole they saw. They stopped at a Laundromat and handed flyers to the people washing their clothes. They chatted with pedestrians on the sidewalks and told them to keep a sharp lookout. They talked to old men rocking on porches and nice ladies pulling weeds from flower beds. They pedaled slowly along Trover, taking in each house, each duplex, each apartment building, and as this went on and on, they began to realize that they were not accomplishing much. If April were locked away inside one of the buildings, how were they supposed to find her? They could not peek in. They could not knock on the door and expect Leeper to answer it. They could not yell at the windows and hope she answered. Theo began to realize that their time was better spent handing out flyers and talking about the reward money.

They finished Trover Avenue and moved a block north to Whitworth Street, where they went door-to-door in a shopping center, passing out flyers in a barbershop, a cleaners, a pizza carryout, and a liquor store. The warning on the door of the liquor store plainly forbade the entry of anyone under the age of twenty-one, but Theo didn't hesitate. He was there to help a friend, not buy booze. He marched inside, alone, handed flyers to the two idle clerks at the cash registers, and walked out before they could protest.

They were leaving the shopping center when an urgent call came from Woody. The police had stopped them on Allen Street, and the police were not happy. Theo and his team took off, and a few minutes later arrived at the scene. There were two city police cars and three uniformed officers.

Theo realized immediately that he did not recognize any of the policemen.

"What are you kids doing here?" the first one asked as Theo approached. His bronze nameplate identified him as Bard. "Lemme guess, you're helping with the search?" Bard said with a sneer.

Theo shoved out his hand and said, "I'm Theo Boone."

He emphasized his last name in hopes that one of the officers might recognize it. He'd learned that most of the policemen knew most of the lawyers, and maybe, just maybe, one of these guys would realize that Theo's parents were well-respected attorneys. But, it didn't work. There were so many lawyers in Strattenburg.

"Yes, sir, we're helping you guys search for April Finnemore," Theo went on pleasantly, flashing his braces with a wide smile at Officer Bard.

"Are you the leader of this gang?" Bard snapped.

Theo glanced at Woody, who'd lost all confidence and appeared frightened, as if he were about to be dragged away to jail and perhaps beaten. "I guess," Theo answered.

"So, who asked you boys and girls to join in the search?"

"Well, sir, no one really asked us. April is our friend and we're worried." Theo was trying to find the right tone. He wanted to be very respectful, but at the same time he was convinced they were doing nothing wrong.

"How sweet," Bard said, grinning at the other two officers. He was holding a flyer and he showed it to Theo. "Who printed these?" he asked.

Theo wanted to say, "Sir, it's really none of your business who printed the flyers." But this would only make a tense situation much worse. So he said, "We printed them at school today."

"And this is April?" Bard said, pointing to the smiling face square in the middle of the flyer.

Theo wanted to say, "No, sir, that's another girl's face we're using to make the search even more difficult by confusing everybody."

April's face had been all over the local news. Surely, Bard recognized her.

Theo said, simply, "Yes, sir."

"And who gave you kids permission to tack these flyers on public property?"

"No one."

"You know it's a violation of city code, against the law? You know this?" Bard had been watching too many bad-cop shows on television, and he was working much too hard to try to frighten the kids.

Justin and his team made a silent entry into the fray. They rolled to a stop behind the other bikers. Eighteen kids, three policemen, and several neighbors drifting over to check on things.

At this point Theo should've played along and professed ignorance of the city's laws, but he simply could not do so. He said, very respectfully, "No, sir, it's not a violation of the city code to put flyers on poles used for telephones and electricity. I checked the law online during school today."

It was immediately obvious that Officer Bard wasn't sure what to say next. His bluff had been called. He glanced at his two pals, both of whom seemed to be amused and not the least bit supportive. The kids were smirking at him. It was Bard against everyone.

Theo pressed on, "The law clearly says that permits must be approved for posters and flyers dealing with politicians and people who are running for office, but not for anything else. These flyers are legal as long as they are taken down within ten days. That's the law."

"I don't like your attitude, kid," Bard shot back, puffing out his chest and actually putting a hand on his service revolver. Theo noticed the gun, but wasn't worried about being shot. Bard was trying to play the role of a tough cop, and he was not doing a very good job.

Being the only child of two lawyers, Theo had already developed a healthy suspicion of those people who thought they had more power than others, including policemen. He had been taught to respect all adults, especially those with authority, but at the same time, his parents had instilled in him a desire to always look for the truth. When a person—adult, teenager, child—was not being honest, then it was wrong to go along with their fraud or lie.

As everyone looked at Theo and waited on his response, he swallowed hard and said, "Well, sir, there's nothing wrong with my attitude. And, even if I had a bad attitude, it's not against the law."

Bard yanked a pen and a notepad from his pocket and said, "What's your name?"

Theo thought, I gave you my name three minutes ago, but he said, "Theodore Boone."

Bard scribbled this down in a flurry, as if whatever he was writing would one day carry great weight in a court of law. Everyone waited. Finally, one of the other officers took a few steps toward Bard and said, "Is your dad Woods Boone?" His nameplate identified him as Sneed.

*Finally,* Theo thought. "Yes, sir."

"And your mother's a lawyer, too, right?" Officer Sneed asked.

"Yes, sir."

Bard's shoulders slumped a few inches as he stopped scribbling on his pad. He looked puzzled, as if he was thinking, *Great. This kid knows the law and I don't, plus he's got two parents who'll probably sue me if I do something wrong.*

Sneed tried to help him by asking a pointless question. "You kids live around here?"

Darren slowly raised his hand and said, "I live a few blocks away, over on Emmitt Street."

The situation was sort of a standoff, with neither side sure what to do next. Sibley Taylor got off her bike and walked to a spot next to Theo. She smiled at Bard and Sneed, and said, "I don't understand. Why can't we work together here? April is our friend and we're very worried. The police are looking for her. We're looking for her. We're not doing anything wrong. What's the big deal?"

Bard and Sneed could think of no quick response to these simple questions with obvious answers.

In every class, there's always the kid who speaks before he thinks, or says what the others are thinking but are afraid to say. In this search party, that kid was Aaron Helleberg, who spoke English, German, and Spanish and got himself in trouble in all three. Aaron blurted, "Shouldn't you guys be looking for April instead of harassing us?"

Officer Bard sucked in his gut as if he'd been kicked there, and appeared ready to start shooting when Sneed jumped in. "Okay, here's the deal. You can hand out the flyers but you can't tack them onto city property—utility poles, bus-stop benches, things like that. It's almost five o'clock. I want you off the streets at six. Fair enough?" He was glaring at Theo when he finished.

Theo shrugged and said, "Fair enough." But it wasn't fair at all. They could tack the posters onto utility poles all day long. (But not city benches.) The police did not have the authority to change the city's laws, nor did they have the right to order the kids off the streets by 6:00 p.m.

However, at that moment a compromise was needed, and Sneed's deal was not that bad. The search would continue, and the police could say that they kept the kids in line. Solving a dispute often requires each side to back down a little, something else Theo had learned from his parents.

The search party biked back to Truman Park where it regrouped. Four of the kids had other things to do and left. Twenty minutes after they last saw Bard and Sneed, Theo and his gang moved into a neighborhood known as Maury Hill, in the southeast part of the city, as far away from Delmont as possible. They passed out dozens of flyers, inspected a few empty buildings, chatted with curious neighbors, and quit promptly at 6:00 p.m.

# Chapter 5

The Boone family dinner schedule was as predictable as a clock on the wall. On Mondays, they ate at Robilio's, an old Italian restaurant downtown, not far from the office. On Tuesdays, they ate soup and sandwiches at a homeless shelter where they volunteered. On Wednesdays, Mr. Boone picked up carryout Chinese from Dragon Lady, and they ate on folding trays as they watched television. On Thursdays, Mrs. Boone picked up a roasted chicken at a Turkish deli, and they ate it with hummus and pita bread. On Fridays, they ate fish at Malouf's, a popular restaurant owned by an old Lebanese couple who yelled at each other constantly. On Saturdays, each of the three

Boones took turns choosing what and where to eat. Theo usually preferred pizza and a movie. On Sundays, Mrs. Boone finally did her own cooking, which was Theo's least favorite meal of the week, though he was too smart to say so. Marcella didn't like to cook. She worked hard and spent long hours at the office, and simply did not enjoy rushing home and facing more work in the kitchen. Besides, there were plenty of good ethnic restaurants and delicatessens in Strattenburg, and it made much more sense to let real chefs do the cooking, at least in the opinion of Mrs. Marcella Boone. Theo didn't mind, nor did his father. When she did cook, she expected her husband and her son to clean up afterward, and both men preferred to avoid the dishwashing.

Dinner was always at 7:00 p.m. on the dot, another clear sign of organized people who hurried through each day with one eye on the clock. Theo placed his paper plate of chicken chow mein and sweet-and-sour shrimp on his TV tray and settled on the sofa. He then lowered a smaller plate onto the floor, where Judge was waiting with great anticipation. Judge loved Chinese food and expected to eat in the den with the humans. Dog food insulted him.

After a couple of bites, Mr. Boone asked, "So, Theo, any news on April?"

"No, sir. Just a lot of gossip at school."

"That poor child," Mrs. Boone said. "I'm sure everyone at school was worried."

"That's all we talked about. A total waste. I should stay home tomorrow and help with the search."

"That's a pretty lame effort," Mr. Boone said.

"Did you guys talk to the police about Mrs. Finnemore and explain to them that she's lying about being home with April? That she wasn't home Monday or Tuesday night? That she's a weirdo who's taking pills and neglecting her daughter?"

Silence. The room was quiet for a few seconds, then Mrs. Boone said, "No, Theo, we did not. We discussed it and decided to wait."

"But why?"

His father said, "Because it won't help the police find April. We plan to wait for a day or two. It's still being discussed."

"You're not eating, Theo," his mother said.

And it was true. He had no appetite. The food seemed to stop halfway down his esophagus, where a dull throbbing pain blocked everything. "I'm not hungry," he said.

Later, halfway through a rerun of *Law & Order*, a local newsbreak blasted out the latest. The search for April

Finnemore continued, with the police still tight-lipped about it. They flashed a photo of April, then one of the MISSING posters Theo and his gang had distributed. Immediately after this, there was the same ominous mug shot of Jack Leeper, looking like a serial killer. The reporter gushed, "The police are investigating the possibility that Jack Leeper, after his escape from prison in California, returned to Strattenburg to see his pen pal, April Finnemore."

The police are investigating a lot of things, Theo thought to himself. That doesn't mean they're all true. He had thought about Leeper all day, and he was certain that April would never open the door for such a creep. He had told himself over and over that the kidnapping theory could be nothing but one big coincidence: Leeper escaped from prison, returned to Strattenburg because he lived there many years ago, and got himself caught on videotape at a convenience store at the exact same time that April decided to run away.

Theo knew April well, but he also realized there were many things about her he didn't know. Nor did he want to. Was it possible that she would run away without a word to him? Slowly, he had begun to believe the answer was yes.

He was on the sofa under a quilt, with Judge wedged close to his chest, and at some point, both fell asleep. Theo had been awake since four thirty that morning and was sleep deprived. Physically and emotionally, he was exhausted.

# Chapter 6

The eastern boundary of the city of Strattenburg was formed by a bend in the Yancey River. An old bridge, one used by both cars and trains, crossed over into the next county. The bridge was not used much because there was little reason to travel into the next county. All of Strattenburg lay west of the river, and when leaving the city almost all traffic moved in that direction. In decades past, the Yancey had been a fairly important route for timber and crops, and in Strattenburg's early years the busy area "under the bridge" was notorious for saloons and illegal gambling halls and places for all sorts of bad behavior. When the river traffic declined, most of these places closed and the bad folks went elsewhere. However, enough stayed behind to ensure that the neighborhood would maintain its low reputation.

"Under the bridge" became simply "the bridge," a part of town that all decent people avoided. It was a dark place, almost hidden in the daytime by the shadows of a long bluff, with few streetlights at night and little traffic. There were bars and rough places where one went only to find trouble. The homes were small shacks built on stilts to protect them from high water. The people who lived there were sometimes called "river rats," a nickname they obviously found insulting. When they worked, they fished the Yancey and sold their catch to a cannery that produced cat and dog food. But they didn't work much. They were an idle people, living off the river, living off welfare, feuding with each other over trivial matters, and in general, earning their reputation as quick-tempered deadbeats.

Early Thursday morning, the manhunt arrived at the bridge.

A river rat named Buster Shell spent most of Wednesday evening in his favorite bar, drinking his favorite cheap beer and playing nickel-and-dime poker. When his money was gone, he had no choice but to leave and head home to his irritable wife and his three dirty children. As he walked through the narrow, unpaved streets, he bumped into a man who was going somewhere in a hurry. They exchanged a couple of harsh words, as was the custom under the bridge, but the other man showed no interest in a fistfight, something Buster was certainly ready for.

As Buster resumed his walk, he stopped dead cold. He'd seen that face before. He'd seen it only hours earlier. It was the face of that guy the cops were searching for. What's his name? Buster, half drunk or worse, snapped his fingers in the middle of the street as he racked his brain trying to remember.

"Leeper," he finally said. "Jack Leeper."

By now, most of Strattenburg knew that a reward of five thousand dollars was being offered by the police for any information leading to the arrest of Jack Leeper. Buster could almost smell the money. He looked around, but the man was long gone. However, Leeper—and there was no doubt in Buster's mind that the man was indeed Jack Leeper—was now somewhere under the bridge. He was in Buster's part of town, a place the police preferred to avoid, a place where the river rats made their own rules.

Within minutes, Buster had rounded up a small, well-armed posse, half a dozen men about as drunk as he was. Word was out. The rumor that the escaped convict was in the vicinity roared through the neighborhood. The river people fought constantly among themselves, but when threatened from the outside, they quickly circled the wagons.

With Buster giving orders that no one followed, the search for Leeper sputtered from the start. There was considerable conflict in terms of strategy, and since every man carried a loaded gun, the disagreements were serious. With time, though, they agreed that the one main street that led up the bluff and into town should be guarded. When that was done, Leeper's only chance of escape was either by stealing a boat or going for a swim in the Yancey River.

Hours passed. Buster and his men went door-to-door, carefully searching under the houses, behind the shanties, inside the small stores and shops, through the thickets and underbrush. The search party grew and grew and Buster began to worry about how they might split the reward money with so many people now involved. How could he keep most of the money? It would be difficult. The payment of five thousand dollars to a bunch of river rats would ignite a small war under the bridge.

The first hint of sunlight peeked through the clouds far to the east. The search was running out of gas. Buster's recruits were tired and losing their enthusiasm.

Miss Ethel Barber was eighty-five years old and had lived alone since her husband died years earlier. She was one of the few residents under the bridge who was missing the excitement. When she awoke at 6:00 a.m. and went to make coffee, she heard a faint noise coming from the rear door of her four-room shanty. She kept a pistol in a drawer under the toaster. She grabbed it, then flipped on a light switch. Like Buster, she came face-to-face with the man she'd seen on the local news. He was in the process of removing a screen from the small window on the door, obviously trying to break in. When Miss Ethel raised her gun, as if to shoot through the window, Jack Leeper's jaw dropped, his eyes widened in horror, and he uttered some gasp of shock that she couldn't quite make out. (She had lost most of her hearing anyway.) Leeper then ducked quickly and scrambled away. Miss Ethel grabbed her phone and called 911.

Within ten minutes, a police helicopter was hovering near the bridge and the SWAT team was moving silently through the streets.

Buster Shell was arrested for public drunkenness, unlawful possession of a firearm, and resisting arrest. He was handcuffed and taken to the city jail, his dreams of reward money dashed forever.

They soon found Leeper, in an overgrown ditch near the street that led to and from the bridge. He had circled back and was evidently trying to leave the area. Why he went there in the first place would remain a mystery.

He was spotted by the helicopter crew. The SWAT team was directed to his hiding place, and within minutes the street was filled with police cars, armed officers of all varieties, sharpshooters, bloodhounds, even an ambulance. The helicopter got lower and lower. No one wanted to miss the fun. There was a van from the television news channel, filming live coverage.

Theo was watching. He was up early because he'd been up most of the night, tossing and flipping in his bed, worrying about April. He sat at the kitchen table, toying with a bowl of cereal, watching the small screen on the counter with his parents. When the camera offered a close-up of the SWAT team dragging someone from the ditch, Theo dropped his spoon, picked up the remote, and increased the volume.

The sight of Jack Leeper was frightening. His clothes were torn and covered with mud. He had not shaved in days. His thick black hair was wild and shooting in all directions. He appeared angry and defiant, yapping at the police and even spitting at the camera. As he neared the street and was surrounded by even more officers, a reporter yelled, "Hey, Leeper! Where's April Finnemore!?"

To which Leeper offered a nasty grin and yelled back, "You'll never find her."

"Is she alive?"

"You'll never find her."

"Oh, my God," Mrs. Boone said.

Theo's heart froze and he couldn't breathe. He watched as Leeper was shoved into the rear of a police van and driven away. The reporter was talking to the camera, but Theo didn't hear his words. He gently placed his head in his hands, and began to cry.

# Chapter 7

First period was Spanish, Theo's second favorite class, just behind Government with Mr. Mount. Spanish was taught by Madame Monique, a young, pretty, exotic lady from Cameroon, in West Africa. Spanish was just one of many languages she spoke. Normally, the sixteen boys in Theo's section were easy to motivate and enjoyed the class.

Today, though, the entire school was in a daze. Yesterday, the halls and classrooms were filled with nervous chatter as the rumors spread about April's disappearance. Was she kidnapped? Did she run away? What's up with her weird mother? Where's her father? These questions and more were tossed up for debate and kicked around with great enthusiasm throughout the day. Now, though, with the capture of Jack Leeper, and the unforgettable words he uttered about April, the students and teachers were in a state of fear and disbelief.

Madame Monique understood the situation. She taught April, too, in a girl's section during fourth period. She tried to engage the boys in a halfhearted discussion about Mexican food, but they were too distracted.

During second period, the entire eighth grade was called into an assembly in the auditorium. Five sections of girls, five of boys, along with all the teachers. The middle school was in its third year of an experiment which separated the genders during classroom instruction, but not during the rest of the day's activities. So far, the experiment was getting favorable reviews. But, because they were separated for most of the day, when they came together at lunch, morning break, physical education, or assembly, there was a bit more electricity in the air and it took a few minutes to calm things. Not today, though. They were subdued. There was none of the usual posturing, flirting, gazing, or nervous chatter. They took their seats quietly, somberly.

The principal, Mrs. Gladwell, spent some time trying to convince them that April was probably all right, that the police were confident she would be found soon and returned to school. Her voice was comforting, her words were reassuring, and the eighth graders were ready to believe any good news. Then a noise—the unmistakable thumping of a low-flying helicopter—passed over the school, and all thoughts immediately returned to the frantic search for their classmate. A few of the girls could be seen rubbing their eyes.

Later, after lunch, as Theo and his friends were in the middle of a halfhearted game of Frisbee football, another helicopter buzzed over the school, obviously going somewhere in a hurry. From its markings, it appeared to be from some branch of law enforcement. The game stopped; the boys stared upward until the chopper was gone. The bell rang, ending lunch, and the boys quietly returned to class.

Throughout the school day, there were times when Theo and his friends were almost able to forget about April, if only for a moment. And whenever these moments occurred, and they were indeed rare, another helicopter could be heard somewhere over Strattenburg—buzzing, thumping, watching—like some giant insect ready to attack.

The entire city was on edge, as if waiting for horrible news. In the cafés and shops and offices downtown, the employees and customers chatted in hushed tones and repeated whatever rumors they'd heard in the past thirty minutes. In the courthouse, always a rich source of gossip, the clerks and lawyers huddled around coffeepots and watercoolers and exchanged the latest. The local television stations offered live reports on the half hour. These breathless updates usually offered nothing new, just a reporter somewhere near the river saying pretty much what he or she had said earlier.

At Strattenburg Middle School, the eighth graders quietly went through their daily schedules, most of them anxious to get home.

Jack Leeper, now wearing an orange jumpsuit with CITY JAIL stenciled in black letters across the front and back, was led to an interrogation room in the basement of the Strattenburg Police Department. In the center of the room, there was a small table, and a folding chair for the suspect. Across the table sat two detectives, Slater and Capshaw. The uniformed officers escorting Leeper removed the handcuffs and ankle chains, then retreated to their positions by the door. They remained in the room for protection, though they were not really needed. Detectives Slater and Capshaw could certainly take care of themselves.

"Have a seat, Mr. Leeper," Detective Slater said, waving at the empty folding chair. Leeper slowly sat down. He had showered but not shaved, and still looked like some deranged cult leader who'd just spent a month or so in the woods.

"I'm Detective Slater, and this is my partner Detective Capshaw."

"A real pleasure to meet you boys," Leeper said with a snarl.

"Oh, the pleasure is ours," Slater said, with equal sarcasm.

"A real honor," Capshaw said, one of the few times he would speak.

Slater was a veteran detective, the highest ranking, and the best in Strattenburg. He was wiry with a slick, shaved head, and he wore nothing but black suits with black ties. The city saw very little in the way of violent crime, but when they did Detective Slater was there to solve it and bring the felon to justice. His sidekick, Capshaw, was the observer, the note taker, the nicer of the two when they found it necessary to play good cop/bad cop.

"We'd like to ask you some questions," Slater said. "You wanna talk?"

"Maybe."

Capshaw whipped out a sheet of paper and handed it to Slater, who said, "Well, Mr. Leeper, as you well know from your long career as a professional thug, you must first be advised of your rights. You do remember this, don't you?"

Leeper glared at Slater as if he might reach across the table and grab his throat, but Slater was not the least bit worried.

"You've heard of the *Miranda* rights, haven't you, Mr. Leeper?" Slater continued.

"Yep."

"Of course you have. I'm sure you've been in many of these rooms over the years," Slater said with a nasty grin. Leeper was not grinning. Capshaw was already taking notes.

Slater continued: "First of all, you're not required to talk to us. Period. Understand?"

Leeper shook his head, yes.

"But if you do talk to us, then anything you say can be used against you in court. Got it?"

"Yep."

"You have the right to a lawyer, to legal advice. Understand?"

"Yep."

"And if you can't afford one, which I'm sure you cannot, then the State will provide one for you. Are you with me?"

"Yep."

Slater slid the sheet of paper close to Leeper and said, "If you sign here, then you agree that I've explained your rights and that you are voluntarily waiving them." He placed a pen on top of the paper. Leeper took his time, read the words, fiddled with the pen, then finally signed his name. "Can I have some coffee?" he asked.

"Cream and sugar?" Slater asked.

"No, just black."

Slater nodded at one of the uniformed officers, who left the room.

"Now, we have some questions for you," Slater said. "Are you ready to talk?"

"Maybe."

"Two weeks ago, you were in prison in California, serving a life sentence for kidnapping. You escaped through a tunnel with six others, and now you're here in Strattenburg."

"You got a question?"

"Yes, Mr. Leeper, I have a question. Why did you come to Strattenburg?"

"I had to go somewhere. Couldn't just hang around outside the prison, know what I mean?"

"I suppose. You lived here once, correct?"

"When I was a kid, sixth grade, I think. Went to the middle school for a year, then we moved off."

"And you have relatives in the area?"

"Some distant kin."

"One of those distant relatives is Imelda May Underwood, whose mother had a third cousin named Ruby Dell Butts, whose father was Franklin Butts, better known out in Massey's Mill as 'Logchain' Butts, and 'Logchain' had a half-brother named Winstead Leeper, 'Winky' for short, and I believe he was your father. Died about ten years ago."

Leeper absorbed all this and finally said, "Winky Leeper was my father, yes."

"So somewhere in the midst of all this divorcing and remarrying, you came to be a tenth or eleventh cousin of Imelda May Underwood, who married a man named Thomas Finnemore and now goes by the name of May Finnemore, mother of young April. This sound right to you, Mr. Leeper?"

"I never had any use for my family."

"Well, I'm sure they're real proud of you, too."

The door opened and the officer placed a paper cup of steaming black coffee on the table in front of Leeper. It appeared to be too hot to drink, so Leeper just stared at it. Slater paused for a second, then pressed on. "We have copies of five letters April wrote to you in prison. Sweet, kid stuff—she felt sorry for you and wanted to be pen pals. Did you write her back?"

"Yep."

"How often?"

"I don't know. Several times, I guess."

"Did you come back to Strattenburg to see April?"

Leeper finally picked up the cup and took a sip of coffee. Slowly, he said, "I'm not sure I want to answer that question."

For the first time, Detective Slater seemed to become irritated. "Why are you afraid of that question, Mr. Leeper?"

"I don't have to answer your question. Says so right there on your little piece of paper. I can walk out right now. I know the rules."

"Did you come here to see April?"

Leeper took another sip, and for a long time nothing was said. The four officers stared at him. He stared at the paper cup. Finally, he said, "Look, here's the situation. You want something. I want something. You want the girl. I want a deal."

"What kind of a deal, Leeper?" Slater shot back.

"Just a moment ago it was Mr. Leeper. Now, just Leeper. Do I frustrate you, Detective? If so, I'm real sorry. Here's what I have in mind. I know I'm going back to prison, but I'm really tired of California. The prisons are brutal—overcrowded, lots of gangs, violence, rotten food—you know what I mean, Detective Slater?"

Slater had never been inside a prison, but to move things along he said, "Sure."

"I want to do my time here, where the slammers are a bit nicer. I know because I've had a good look at them."

"Where's the girl, Leeper?" Slater said. "If you kidnapped her, you're looking at another life sentence. If she's dead, you're looking at capital murder and death row."

"Why would I harm my little cousin?"

"Where is she, Leeper?"

Another long sip of coffee, then Leeper crossed his arms over his chest and grinned at Detective Slater. Seconds ticked away.

"You're playing games, Leeper," Detective Capshaw said.

"Maybe, maybe not. Is there any reward money on the table?"

"Not for you," Slater said.

"Why not? You give me some money, I'll take you to the girl."

"It doesn't work that way."

"Fifty thousand bucks, and you can have her."

"What will you do with fifty thousand bucks, Leeper?" Slater asked. "You're in prison for the rest of your life."

"Oh, money goes a long way in prison. You get me the

money, and you arrange things so I can serve my time here, and we got a deal."

"You're dumber than I thought," Slater said, frustrated.

Capshaw added quickly, "And we thought you were pretty dumb before we got started with this conversation."

"Come on, boys. That gets you nowhere. We got a deal?"

"No deal, Leeper," Slater said.

"That's too bad."

"No deal, but I'll make a promise. If that girl is harmed in any way, I'll hound you to your grave."

Leeper laughed loudly, then said, "I love it when the cops start making threats. It's over, boys. I ain't talking no more."

"Where's the girl, Leeper?" Capshaw asked.

Leeper just grinned and shook his head.

# Chapter 8

Theo preferred not to stay at school after classes and watch the girls play soccer. He himself did not play soccer, not that he had the choice. An asthma condition kept him away from strenuous activities, but even without the asthma he doubted he would be playing soccer. He had tried it as a six-year-old, before the asthma, and never got the hang of it. When he was nine, while playing baseball, he collapsed at third base after hitting a triple, and that ended his short career in team sports. He took up golf.

Mr. Mount, though, loved soccer, had even played in college, and was offering extra credit to students who hung around for the game. Plus, there was an unwritten rule at Strattenburg Middle School that the girls cheered for the boys, and vice versa. Any other time, Theo would have happily watched from the bleachers, taking casual notice of the game but really sizing up the twenty-two girls on the field and those on the bench as well. But not today. He wanted to be elsewhere, on his bike, handing out the MISSING flyers, doing something to aid in the search for April.

It was a terrible day for a game of any kind. The Strattenburg kids were distracted. The players and their fans lacked energy. Even the opposing team, from Elksburg, forty miles away, seemed subdued. When another helicopter flew over ten minutes into the game, every girl on the field paused for a second and looked up in apprehension.

As expected, Mr. Mount gradually made his way over to a group of women. The worst kept secret at school was that Mr. Mount had his eye on Miss Highlander, a stunning seventh-grade math teacher just two years out of college. Every boy in the seventh and eighth grades had a desperate, secret crush on Miss Highlander, and evidently Mr. Mount had some interest as well. He was in his mid-thirties, single, by far the coolest male teacher in the school, and the sixteen boys in his homeroom were aggressively pushing him to pursue Miss Highlander.

When Mr. Mount began to make his move, so did Theo. He assumed correctly that Mr. Mount's attention would soon be focused elsewhere; it was the perfect time for a quiet exit. Theo and three others drifted from the soccer field and were soon on their bikes racing away from the school. Their search party was much smaller, and this was by design. Yesterday's had too many kids, with too many opinions, and too much activity that might be noticed by cops such as Officer Bard. Plus, there had been fewer volunteers during the school day as Theo and Woody got things organized. The sense of urgency that Theo felt was not shared by many of his classmates. They were concerned all right, but many of them thought that searches by kids on bikes were a waste of time. The police had SWAT teams, helicopters, dogs, and no shortage of manpower. If they couldn't find April, the search was hopeless.

Theo, along with Woody, Aaron, and Chase, returned to the Delmont neighborhood and roamed the streets for a few minutes to make sure the police were elsewhere. With no cops in sight, they quickly began passing out MISSING flyers and tacking them to utility poles. They inspected a few empty buildings, looked behind some run-down apartments, picked their way through an overgrown drainage ditch, checked under two bridges, and were making real progress when Woody's older brother called his cell phone. Woody froze, listened intently, then reported to the gang, "They've found something down by the river."

"What?"

"Not sure, but my brother is monitoring his police scanner, said the thing has gone crazy with chatter. All cops are headed down there."

Without hesitation, Theo said, "Let's go."

They sped away, out of Delmont, past Stratten College, into downtown, and as they approached the east end of Main Street, they saw police cars and dozens of officers milling about. The street was blocked; the area under the bridge was sealed off. The air was heavy with tension. And noise—two helicopters were hovering over the river. The downtown merchants and their customers stood on the sidewalks, gawking into the distance, waiting for something to happen. Traffic was being diverted away from the bridge and the river.

As the boys watched, another police car crept up beside them. The driver rolled down his window, then snarled, "What are you boys doing here?" It was Officer Bard, again.

"We're just riding our bikes," Theo said. "It's not against the law."

"Don't get smart with me, Boone. If I see you boys anywhere near the river, I swear I'll take you in."

Theo thought of several quick retorts, all of which

would lead to more trouble. So he gritted his teeth and politely said, "Yes, sir."

Bard smiled smugly, then drove away, toward the bridge.

"Follow me," Woody said as they raced off. Woody lived in a section of town called East Bluff, near the river, on a gentle rise that eventually gave way to the lowlands around the water. It was a notorious place, full of narrow streets, dark alleys, creeks, and dead-end roads. The neighborhood was generally safe, but it produced more than its share of colorful stories of strange events. Woody's father was a noted stonemason who'd lived his entire life in East Bluff. It was a large clannish family, with lots of aunts, uncles, and cousins, all living close to each other.

Ten minutes after their encounter with Officer Bard, the boys were zipping through East Bluff, along a narrow dirt trail that zigzagged high above and beside the river. Woody was pedaling like a madman and making it difficult for the others to keep up. This was his turf; he'd been riding his bike through these trails since he was six. They crossed a gravel road, plunged down a steep hill, shot up the other side, and got serious air before landing back on the trail. Theo, Aaron, and Chase were terrified but too excited to slow down. And, of course, they were determined to keep up with Woody, who was prone to talk trash at any moment. They finally slid to a stop at a small overlook, a grassy area where the river could be seen below through some trees. "Follow me," Woody said, and they left their bikes behind. Clutching a vine, they scampered down the side of a cliff to a rocky landing, and there, below, was the Yancey River. Their view was unobstructed.

A mile or two away, to the north, were the rows of small whitewashed houses where the river rats lived, and beyond them was the bridge, crawling with police cars. On the other side of the river, close to the bridge, an ambulance was just arriving on the scene. Policemen were in boats; several were in full scuba gear. The situation looked tense, almost frantic, as sirens wailed, policemen darted about, and the helicopters hovered low, watching everything.

Something had been found.

The boys sat on the cliff for a long time and said little. The search, or rescue, or removal, or whatever it was called, was proceeding slowly. Each of them had the same thought—that they were watching an actual crime scene in which the victim was their friend April Finnemore, and that she'd been harmed in some terrible way and left at the edge of the river. She was apparently dead, since there was no urgency in getting her out of the water and to a hospital. More police cars arrived, more chaos.

Finally, Chase said, to no one in particular, "Do you think it's April?"

To which Woody abruptly responded, "Who else would it be? It's not every day that a dead body floats into town."

"You don't know who it is or what it is," Aaron said. He usually found some way to disagree with Woody, who had quick opinions about almost everything.

Theo's cell phone buzzed in his pocket. He glanced at it—Mrs. Boone on her office line. "It's my mom," he said nervously, then answered his phone.

"Hi, Mom."

On the other end, his mother said, "Theo, where are you?"

"Just left the soccer game," he said, wincing at his friends. It wasn't a complete fib, but it was also pretty far from the truth.

"Well, it appears as though the police have found a body in the river, on the other side, near the bridge," she said. One of the helicopters, red and yellow with Channel 5 painted boldly on the sides, was obviously sending a live feed back to the station, and the entire town was probably watching.

"Has it been identified?" Theo asked.

"No, not yet. But it can't be good news, Theo."

"This is awful."

"When are you coming to the office?"

"I'll be there in twenty minutes."

"Okay, Theo. Please be careful."

The ambulance was moving away from the river, then onto the bridge, where a line of police cars formed an escort. The procession picked up speed over the river, with the helicopters trailing behind.

"Let's go," Theo said, and the boys slowly climbed up the cliff and left on their bikes.

Boone & Boone had a large law library on its first floor, near the front, close to where Elsa worked, keeping an eye on everything. The library was Theo's favorite room in the building. He loved its rows of thick, important books, its large leather chairs, and its long mahogany conference table. It was used for all sorts of big meetings—depositions, settlement talks, and, for Mrs. Boone, pretrial preparation. She occasionally went to trial in divorce cases. Mr. Boone did not. He was a real estate lawyer who seldom left his upstairs office. He did, though, need the library from time to time to close real estate deals.

They were waiting for Theo in the library. A large flat-screen television was on with the local news, and his parents and Elsa were watching. His mother hugged him when he walked in, then Elsa hugged him, too. He took a seat near the television, his mother on one side, Elsa on the other, both patting his knees as if he had just been rescued from near death. The news report was all about the discovery of a body and its transport to the city morgue where authorities were now doing all sorts of important stuff. The reporter wasn't sure what was happening in the morgue, and she was unable to find a witness willing to talk, so she just prattled on the way they normally do.

Theo wanted to tell everyone that he'd had a bird's-eye view down at the river, but such a statement would make things complicated.

The reporter said the police were working with inspectors from the state crime lab and hoped to know more within a few hours.

"That poor girl," Elsa said, and not for the first time.

"Why do you say that?" Theo asked.

"I beg your pardon."

"You don't know it's a girl. You don't know it's April. We don't know anything, right?"

The adults glanced at each other. Both women continued patting Theo's knees.

"Theo's right," Mr. Boone said, but only to comfort his son.

They flashed a picture of Jack Leeper for the one hundredth time, and gave his background. When it became apparent there was nothing new at the moment, the story grew old. Mr. Boone drifted away. Mrs. Boone had a client waiting in the lobby. Elsa needed to answer the phone.

Theo eventually made his way to his office at the rear of the building. Judge followed, and Theo spent a lot of time rubbing his dog's head and talking to him. It made both of them feel better. Theo put his feet on his desk and looked around his small office. He focused on the wall where his favorite sketch always made him smile. It was an elaborate pencil drawing of young Theodore Boone, Attorney, in court wearing a suit and tie, with a gavel flying by his head and the jurors roaring with laughter. The caption screamed, "Overruled!" At the bottom right-hand corner, the artist had scribbled her name, *April Finnemore*. The drawing had been a gift for Theo's birthday the year before.

Was her career over before it started? Was April dead, a sweet thirteen-year-old kid brutally abducted and killed because there was no one to take care of her? Theo's hands were shaking and his mouth was dry. He closed and locked his door, then walked to the drawing and gently touched her name. His eyes were moist, then he began crying. He dropped to the floor and cried for a long time. Judge settled in next to him, watching him sadly.

# Chapter 9

n hour passed and darkness settled in. Theo sat at his small desk, a card table equipped with lawyerly things—a daily planner, a small digital clock, a fake fountain pen set, his own nameplate carved in wood. Before him was an open Algebra textbook. He'd been staring at it for a long time, unable to read the words or turn the pages. His notebook was open, too, and the page was blank.

He could think of nothing but April, and the horror of watching from a distance as the police fished her body from the backwaters of the Yancey River. He had not actually seen a body, but he'd seen the police and scuba divers surround something and work frantically to remove it. Obviously, it was a body. A dead person. Why else would the police be there, doing what they were doing? There had been no other missing persons in Strattenburg in the past week, or the past year, for that matter. The list had only one name on it, and Theo was convinced that April was dead. Abducted and murdered and thrown in the water by Jack Leeper.

Theo couldn't wait for Leeper's trial. He hoped it would happen soon, just a few blocks away in the county courthouse. He would watch every moment of it, even if he had to skip school. Maybe he would be called as a witness. He wasn't sure what he would say on the witness stand, but he would say whatever it took to nail Leeper, to get him convicted and sent away forever. It would be a great moment—Theo being called as a witness, walking into the packed courtroom, placing his hand on the Bible, swearing to tell the truth, taking his seat in the witness box, smiling up at Judge Henry Gantry, glancing confidently at the curious faces of the jurors, taking in the large audience, then glaring at the hideous face of Jack Leeper, staring him down in open court, fearless. The more Theo thought about this scene, the more he liked it. There was a good chance Theo was the last person to talk to April before she was abducted. He could testify that she was frightened, and, surprisingly, alone. Entry! That would be the issue. How did the attacker get into the house? Perhaps only Theo knew that she had locked all the doors and windows and even jammed chairs under doorknobs because she was so frightened. So, since there were no signs of a break-in, she knew the identity of her abductor. She knew Jack Leeper. Somehow he'd been able to persuade her to open the door.

As Theo replayed his last conversation with April, he became convinced that he would indeed be called by the prosecution as a witness. For a few moments, he visualized himself in the courtroom, then he suddenly forgot about it. The shock of the tragedy returned, and he realized his eyes were moist again. His throat was tight and his stomach ached, and Theo needed to be around another human. Elsa was gone for the day, as were Dorothy and Vince. His mother had a client in her office with the door locked. His father was upstairs pushing paper around his desk and trying to finish some big deal. Theo stood, stepped over Judge, and looked at the sketch April had given him. Again, he touched her name.

They met in prekindergarten, though Theo couldn't remember exactly when or how. Four-year-olds don't actually meet and introduce themselves. They just sort of show up at school and get to know each other. April was in his class. Mrs. Sansing was the teacher. In the first and second grades, April was in another section, and Theo hardly saw her. By the third grade, the natural forces of aging had kicked in and the boys wanted nothing to do with the girls, and vice versa. Theo vaguely recalled that April moved away for a year or two. He forgot about her, as did most of the kids in his grade. But he remembered the day she returned. He was sitting in Mr. Hancock's sixth-grade class during the second week of school when the door opened and April walked in. She was escorted by an assistant principal who introduced her and explained that her family had just moved back to Strattenburg. She seemed embarrassed by the attention, and when she sat at a desk next to Theo, she glanced at him and smiled and said, "Hi, Theo." He smiled but was unable to respond.

Most of the class remembered her, and though she was quiet, almost shy, she had no trouble resuming old friendships with the girls. She wasn't popular because she didn't try to be. She wasn't unpopular because she was genuinely nice and thoughtful and acted more mature than most of her classmates. She was odd enough to keep the others guessing. She dressed more like a boy and wore her hair very short. She didn't like sports or television or the Internet. Instead, she painted and studied art and talked of living in Paris or Santa Fe where she would do nothing but paint. She loved contemporary art that baffled her classmates and teachers alike.

Soon there were rumors about her weird family, of siblings named after the months, of a wacky mother who peddled goat cheese, and of an absentee father. Throughout the sixth grade and into the seventh, April became more withdrawn and moodier. She said very little in class and missed more school days than any other student.

As the hormones kicked in and the gender walls came down, it slowly became cool for a boy to have a girlfriend. The cuter and more popular girls were chased and caught, but not April. She showed no interest in boys and didn't have a clue when it came to flirting. She was aloof, often lost in her own world. Theo liked her; he had for a long time, but was too shy and too self-conscious to make a move. He wasn't sure how to make a move, and April seemed unapproachable.

It happened in gym class, on a cold snowy afternoon in late February. Two sections of seventh graders had just begun a one-hour torture session under the command of Mr. Bart Tyler, a young hotshot physical education teacher who fancied himself as a Marine drill instructor. The students, both boys and girls, had just completed a set of brutal wind sprints when Theo suddenly could not catch his breath. He ran for his backpack in a corner, pulled out his inhaler, and took several puffs of medication. This happened occasionally, and, though his classmates understood, Theo was always embarrassed. He was actually exempt from gym, but he insisted on participating.

Mr. Tyler showed the right amount of concern and led Theo to a spot in the bleachers. He was humiliated. As Mr. Tyler walked away and began blowing his whistle and yelling, April Finnemore left the crowd and took a seat next to Theo. Very close.

"Are you all right?" she asked.

"I'm fine," he answered as he began to think that maybe an asthma attack wasn't so bad after all. She placed a hand on his knee and looked at him with tremendous concern.

A loud voice yelled, "Hey, April, what are you doing?" It was Mr. Tyler.

She coolly turned and said, "I'm taking a break."

"Oh really. I don't recall approving a break. Get back in line."

To which she repeated, icily, "I said I'm taking a break."

Mr. Tyler paused for a second, then managed to say, "And why is that?"

"Because I have an asthma condition, just like Theo."

At that point, no one knew if April was telling the truth, but no one, especially Mr. Tyler, seemed willing to push harder. "All right, all right," he said, and then blew his whistle at the rest of the kids. For the first time in his young life, Theo was thrilled to have asthma.

For the remainder of the period, Theo and April sat knee-to-knee in the bleachers, watching the others sweat and groan, giggling at the less-than-athletic ones, mocking Mr. Tyler, gossiping about the classmates they were not so fond of, and whispering about life in general. That night, they Facebooked for the first time.

A sudden knock on the door startled Theo, followed by his father's voice. "Theo, open up."

Theo quickly stepped to the door, unlocked and opened it. "Are you okay?" Mr. Boone asked.

"Sure, Dad."

"Look, there are a couple of policemen here and they would like to talk to you."

Theo was too confused to respond. His father continued, "I'm not sure what they want, probably just more background on April. Let's talk to them in the library. Both your mother and I will be with you."

"Uh, okay."

They met in the library. Detectives Slater and Capshaw were standing and chatting gravely with Mrs. Boone when Theo walked in. Introductions were made, seats were taken.

Theo was secured with a parent/lawyer on each side. The detectives were directly across the table. As usual, Slater did the talking and Capshaw took the notes.

Slater began, "Sorry to barge in like this, but you may have heard that a body was pulled from the river this afternoon."

All three Boones nodded. Theo was not about to admit that he'd watched the police from a cliff across the river. He was not about to say any more than necessary.

Slater went on, "The crime lab people are at work right now trying to identify the body. Frankly, it is not easy because the body is well, shall we say, somewhat decomposed."

The knot in Theo's chest grew tighter. His throat ached and he told himself not to start crying. April, decomposed? He just wanted to go home, go to his room, lock his door, lie on his bed, stare at the ceiling, then go into a coma and wake up in a year.

"We've talked to her mother," Slater said softly, with great patience and compassion, "and she tells us that you were April's best friend. You guys talked all the time, hung out a lot. That true?"

Theo shook his head but could not speak.

Slater glanced at Capshaw who returned the glance without stopping his pen.

"What we need, Theo, is any information about what

April might have been wearing when she disappeared," Slater said. Capshaw added, "The body at the crime lab has the remains of some clothing on it. It could help with identification."

As soon as Capshaw paused, Slater moved in, "We've made an inventory of her clothing, with her mother's help. She said that perhaps you'd given her an item or two. A baseball jacket of some sort."

Theo swallowed hard and tried to speak clearly. "Yes, sir. Last year I gave April a Twins baseball jacket and a Twins cap."

Capshaw wrote even faster. Slater said, "Can you describe this jacket?"

Theo shrugged and said, "Sure. It was dark blue with red trim, Minnesota colors, with the word TWINS across the back in red-and-white lettering."

"Leather, cloth, cotton, synthetic?"

"I don't know, synthetic maybe. I think the lining on the inside was cotton, but I'm not sure."

The two detectives exchanged ominous looks.

"Can I ask why you gave it to her?" Slater said.

"Sure. I won it in an online contest at the Twins website, and since I already had two or three Twins jackets, I gave it to April. It was a medium, kid's size, too small for me."

"She a baseball fan?" Capshaw asked.

"Not really. She doesn't like sports. The gift was sort of a joke."

"Did she wear it often?"

"I never saw her wear it. I don't think she wore the cap either."

"Why the Twins?" Capshaw asked.

"Is that really important?" Mrs. Boone shot across the table. Capshaw flinched as though he'd been slapped.

"No, sorry."

"Where is this going?" Mr. Boone demanded.

Both detectives exhaled in unison, then took another breath. Slater said, "We have not found such a jacket in April's closet or anywhere in her room, or the house for that matter. I guess we can assume she was wearing it when she left. The temperature was around sixty degrees, so she probably grabbed the nearest jacket."

"And the clothing on the body?" Mrs. Boone asked.

Both detectives squirmed in unison, then glanced at each other. Slater said, "We really can't say at this time, Mrs. Boone." They may have been prohibited from saying anything, but their body language was not difficult to read. The jacket Theo had just described matched whatever they'd found on the body. At least in Theo's opinion.

His parents nodded as if they understood completely,

but Theo did not. He had a dozen questions for the police, but didn't have the energy to start firing away.

"What about dental records?" Mr. Boone asked.

Both detectives frowned and shook their heads. "Not possible," Slater said. The answer provoked all manner of horrible images. The body was so mangled and damaged that the jaws were missing.

Mrs. Boone jumped in quickly with, "What about DNA testing?"

"In the works," Slater said, "but it'll take at least three days."

Capshaw slowly closed his notepad and put his pen in a pocket. Slater glanced at his watch. The detectives were suddenly ready to leave. They had the information they were after, and if they stayed longer there might be more questions about the investigation from the Boone family, questions they did not want to answer.

They thanked Theo, expressed their concerns about his friend, and said good night to Mr. and Mrs. Boone.

Theo stayed in his seat at the table, staring blankly at the wall, his thoughts a jumbled mess of fear, sadness, and disbelief.

# Chapter 10

Chase Whipple's mother was also a lawyer. His father sold computers and had installed the system at the Boone law firm. The families were good friends, and at some point during the afternoon, the mothers decided that the boys needed some diversion. Perhaps everyone needed something else to think about.

For as long as Theo could remember, his parents had held season tickets for all home basketball and football games at Stratten College, a small, liberal arts, Division III school, eight blocks from downtown. They bought the tickets for several reasons: one, to support the local team; two, to actually watch a few games, though Mrs. Boone disliked football and could pass on basketball; and, three, to satisfy the college's athletic director, a feisty man known to call fans himself and badger them into supporting the teams. Such was life in a small town. If the Boones couldn't make a game, the tickets were usually given to clients. It was good business.

The Boones met the Whipples at the ticket window outside Memorial Hall, a 1920s-style gymnasium in the center of the campus. They hurried inside and found their seats—mid-court and ten rows up. The game was three minutes old and the Stratten student section had already reached full volume. Theo sat next to Chase, at the end of the row. Both mothers kept looking at the boys, as if they needed some type of special observation on this awful day.

Chase, like Theo, enjoyed sports, but was more of a spectator than an athlete. Chase was a mad scientist, a genius in certain fields; a violent experimental chemist who'd burned down the family's storage shed with one project and nearly vaporized the family's garage with another. His experiments were legendary and every science teacher at Strattenburg Middle School kept a close eye on him. When Chase was in the lab, nothing was safe. He was also a computer whiz, a techno-geek, a superb hacker, which had also caused some problems.

"What's the line?" Theo whispered to Chase.

"Stratten's favored by eight."

"Says who?"

"Greensheet." Division III basketball games were not favored by gamblers and oddsmakers, but there were a few offshore websites where one could find a line and place a bet. Theo and Chase did not gamble, nor did anyone they knew, but it was always interesting to know which team was favored.

"I hear you guys were down at the river when they found the body," Chase said, careful not to be heard by anyone around them.

"Who told you?"

"Woody. He told me everything."

"We didn't see a body, okay. We saw something, but it was pretty far away."

"I guess it had to be the body, right? I mean, the police found a body in the river, and you guys watched it all."

"Let's talk about something else, Chase. Okay?"

Chase had shown little interest in girls so far, and even less interest in April. And she had certainly shown no interest in him. Other than Theo, April didn't care for boys.

There was a time-out on the court, and the Stratten cheerleaders came tumbling out of the stands, hopping and bouncing and flinging each other through the air. Theo and Chase grew still and watched closely. For two thirteen-year-olds, the brief performances by the cheerleaders were captivating.

When the time-out ended, the teams took the court and the game resumed. Mrs. Boone turned and looked down at the boys. Then Mrs. Whipple did the same.

"Why do they keep looking at us?" Theo mumbled to Chase.

"Because they're worried about us. That's why we're here, Theo. That's why we're going out for pizza after the game. They think we're real fragile right now because some thug who escaped from prison snatched one of our classmates and threw her in the river. My mom said that all parents are sort of protective right now."

The Stratten point guard, who was well under six feet tall, slam-dunked the ball and the crowd went wild. Theo tried to forget about April, and Chase as well, and concentrated on the game. At halftime, the boys went to get popcorn. Theo made a quick call to Woody for an update. Woody and his brother were monitoring a police radio and surfing online, but so far there was no word from the police. No positive identification of the body. Nothing. Everything had gone quiet.

Santo's was an authentic Italian pizza parlor near the campus. Theo loved the place because there was always a crowd of students watching games on the big-screen TVs. The Boones and Whipples found a table and ordered two of "Santo's World-Famous Sicilian Pizzas." Theo didn't have the energy to ponder whether the pizza was indeed so famous. He had his doubts, just as he doubted the famousness of Gertrude's pecan waffles and Mr. Dudley's mint fudge. How could a town as small as Strattenburg have three dishes achieving the status of world recognition?

Theo let it go.

Stratten College had lost the game in the final minute, and it was the opinion of Mr. Boone that their coach had blundered badly by not managing his time-outs better. Mr. Whipple wasn't so sure, and a healthy discussion followed. Mrs. Boone and Mrs. Whipple, both busy lawyers, were soon tired of more basketball talk, and they launched into a private chat about the proposed renovation of the main courtroom. Theo was interested in both conversations and tried to follow them. Chase played a video game on his cell phone. Some fraternity boys began singing in a faraway corner. A crowd at the bar cheered the action on television.

Everyone seemed happy and not the least bit concerned about April.

Theo just wanted to go home.

# Chapter II

Friday morning. After a crazy night of dreams, nightmares, frequent naps, insomnia, voices, and visions, Theo finally gave up and rolled out of bed at 6:30. As he sat on the edge of his bed and pondered what dreadful news the day would bring, he caught the unmistakable aroma of sausage drifting up from the kitchen. His mother prepared pancakes and sausage on those rare occasions when she thought her son and sometimes her husband needed a boost in the morning. But Theo wasn't hungry. He had no appetite and doubted if he would find one anytime soon. Judge, who slept under the bed, poked his head out and looked up at Theo. Both looked tired and sleepy.

"Sorry if I kept you awake, Judge," Theo said.

Judge accepted the apology.

"But then, you have the rest of the day to do nothing but sleep."

Judge seemed to agree.

Theo was tempted to flip open his laptop and check the local news, but he really didn't want to. Then he thought about grabbing the remote and turning on the television. Another bad idea. Instead, he took a long shower, got dressed, loaded his backpack, and was about to head downstairs when his cell phone rang. It was his uncle Ike.

"Hello," Theo said, somewhat surprised that Ike was awake at such an early hour. He was not known as a morning person.

"Theo, it's Ike. Good morning."

"Good morning, Ike." Though Ike was in his early sixties, he insisted that Theo call him simply Ike. None of that uncle stuff. Ike was a complicated person.

"What time are you headed to school?"

"Half an hour or so."

"You have time to run by and have a chat? I have some very interesting gossip that no one knows."

Theo was required by family ritual to stop by Ike's office every Monday afternoon. The visits usually lasted about thirty minutes and were not always pleasant. Ike liked to quiz Theo about his grades and his schoolwork and his future and so on, which was tedious. Ike was quick with a lecture. His own children were grown and lived far away, and Theo was his only nephew. He could not imagine why Ike wanted to see him so early on a Friday morning.

"Sure," Theo said.

"Hurry up, and don't tell anyone."

"You got it, Ike." Theo closed his phone and thought, How odd. But he had no time to dwell on it. And, his brain was already overloaded. Judge, no doubt because of the sausage, was scratching at the door.

Woods Boone had breakfast five days a week at the same table in the same downtown diner with the same group of friends at the same time, 7:00. Because of this, Theo rarely saw his father in the morning. Theo received a peck on the cheek from his mother, who was still in her robe, as they exchanged good morning and compared how they slept. Marcella, when she wasn't tied up in court, spent the early part of each Friday morning getting worked on. Hair, nails, toes. As a professional, she was serious about her appearance. Her husband was not quite as concerned about his.

"No news on April," Mrs. Boone said. The small television next to the microwave was not on.

"What does that mean?" Theo asked as he took a seat.

Judge was standing next to the stove, as close to the sausage as he could possibly get.

"It means nothing, at least for now," she said as she placed a plate in front of Theo. A stack of small round pancakes, three links of sausage. She poured him a glass of milk.

"Thanks, Mom. This is awesome. What about Judge?"

"Of course," she said as she placed a small plate in front of the dog. Pancakes and sausage, too.

"Dig in." She took her seat and looked at the large breakfast sitting in front of her son. She sipped her coffee. Theo had no choice but to eat like he was starving. After a few bites, he said, "Delicious, Mom."

"Thought you might need something extra this morning."

"Thanks."

After a pause in which she watched him closely, she said, "Theo, are you all right? I mean, I know this is just awful, but how are you handling it?"

It was easier to chew than to talk. Theo had no answer. How do you describe your emotions when a close friend is abducted and probably tossed in a river? How do you express your sadness when that friend was a neglected kid from a strange family with nutty parents, a kid who didn't have much of a chance?

Theo kept chewing. When he had to say something, he sort of grunted, "I'm okay, Mom." It was not the truth, but at the moment it was all he could manage.

"Do you want to talk about it?"

Ah, the perfect question. Theo shook his head and said, "No, I do not. That just makes it worse."

She smiled and said, "Okay, I understand."

Fifteen minutes later, Theo hopped on his bike, rubbed Judge's head, and said good-bye, then flew down the Boones' driveway and onto Mallard Lane.

Long before Theo was born, Ike Boone had been a lawyer. He had founded the firm with Theo's parents. The three lawyers worked well together and prospered, until Ike did something wrong. Something bad. Whatever Ike did, it was not discussed in Theo's presence. Naturally curious, and raised by two lawyers, Theo had been pecking away at Ike's mysterious downfall for several years, but he had learned little. His father rebuffed all nosiness with a brusque, "We'll discuss it when you get older." His mother usually said something like, "Your father will explain it one day."

Theo knew only the basics: (1) Ike had once been a smart and successful tax lawyer; (2) then he went to prison for several years; (3) he was disbarred and can never be a lawyer again; (4) while he was in prison, his wife divorced him and left Strattenburg with their three children; (5) the children, Theo's first cousins, were much older than Theo and he'd never met them; and (6) relations between Ike and Theo's parents were not that good.

Ike eked out a living as a tax accountant for small businesses and a few other clients. He lived alone in a tiny apartment. He liked to think of himself as a misfit, even a rebel against the establishment. He wore weird clothes, long, gray hair pulled into a ponytail, sandals (even in cold weather), and usually had the Grateful Dead or Bob Dylan playing on the cheap stereo in his office. He worked above a Greek deli, in a wonderfully shabby old room with rows of untouched books on the shelves.

Theo bounced up the stairs, knocked on the door as he pushed it open, and strolled into Ike's office as if he owned the place. Ike was at his desk, one even more cluttered than his brother Woods's, and he was sipping coffee from a tall paper cup. "Mornin', Theo," he said like a real grump.

"Hey, Ike." Theo fell into a rickety wooden chair by the desk. "What's up?"

Ike leaned forward on his elbows. His eyes were red and puffy. Over the years, Theo had heard snippets of gossip about Ike's drinking, and he assumed that was one reason his uncle got off to a slow start each morning.

"I guess you're worried about your friend, the Finnemore girl," Ike said.

Theo nodded.

"Well stop worrying. It ain't her. The body they pulled from the river appears to be that of a man, not a girl. They're not sure. DNA will confirm in a day or two, but the person is, or was, five feet six inches tall. Your friend was about five one, right?"

"I guess."

"The body is extremely decomposed, which suggests that it spent more than a few days in the water. Your friend was snatched late Tuesday night or early Wednesday morning. If her kidnapper tossed her in the river shortly after that, the body would not be as decomposed as this one. It's a mess, with a lot of missing parts. Probably been in the water for a week or so."

Theo absorbed this. He was stunned, relieved, and he couldn't suppress a grin. As Ike went on, Theo felt the tension ease in his chest and stomach.

"The police are going to make the announcement at nine this morning. I thought you might appreciate a little head start."

"Thanks, Ike."

"But they will not admit the obvious, and that is to

say that they've wasted the last two days with the theory that Jack Leeper took the girl, killed her, and tossed her in the river. Leeper is nothing but a lying thug, and the cops allowed themselves to chase the wrong man. This will not be mentioned by the police."

"Who told you all this?" Theo asked, and immediately knew it was the wrong question because it would not be answered.

Ike smiled, rubbed his red eyes, took a gulp of coffee, and said, "I have friends, Theo, and not the same friends I had years ago. My friends now are from a different part of town. They're not in the big buildings and fine homes. They're closer to the street."

Theo knew that Ike played a lot of poker, and his pals included some retired lawyers and policemen. Ike also liked to give the impression that he had a large circle of shady friends who watched everything from the shadows, and thus knew the street talk. There was some truth to this. The previous year, one of his clients was convicted for operating a small-time drug ring. Ike got his name in the paper when he was called to testify as the man's bookkeeper.

"I hear a lot of stuff, Theo," he added.

"Then who's the guy they pulled from the river?"

Another sip of coffee. "We'll probably never know. They've gone two hundred miles upriver and found no record of a missing person in the past month. You ever hear of the Bates's case?"

"No."

"Probably forty years ago."

"I'm thirteen years old, Ike."

"Right. Anyway, it happened over in Rooseburg. A crook named Bates faked his own death one night. Somehow snatched an unknown person, knocked him out, put this person in his car, a nice Cadillac, then ran it into a ditch and set it on fire. The police and firemen show up and the car is nothing but flames. They find a pile of cremated ashes and figure it's Mr. Bates. They have a funeral, a burial, the usual. Mrs. Bates collects the life insurance. Mr. Bates is forgotten until three years later when he's arrested in Montana outside a bar. They haul him back to face the music here. He pleads guilty. The big question is—who was the guy who got fried in his car? Mr. Bates says he doesn't know, never got the boy's name, just picked him up one night as a hitchhiker. Three hours later, the boy was reduced to ashes. Guess he got in the wrong car. Bates gets life in prison."

"What's the point here, Ike?"

"The point, my dear nephew, is that we may never know who the cops pulled from the river. There's a class of people out there, Theo—bums, drifters, hobos, homeless folk— who live in the underworld. They're nameless, faceless;

they move from town to town, hopping trains, hitchhiking, living in the woods and under the bridges. They've dropped out of society, and from time to time bad things happen to them. It's a rough and violent world they inhabit, and we rarely see them, because they do not wish to be seen. My guess is that the corpse the cops are inspecting will never be identified. But that's really not the point. The good news is that it's not your friend."

"Thanks, Ike. I don't know what else to say."

"I thought you might need some good news."

"It's very good news, Ike. I've been worried sick."

"She your girlfriend?"

"No, just a good friend. She has a weird family and I guess I'm one of the few kids she confides in."

"She's lucky to have a friend like you, Theo."

"Thanks, I guess."

Ike relaxed and put his feet on his desk. Sandals again, with bright red socks. He sipped his coffee and smiled at Theo. "How much do you know about her father?"

Theo squirmed and wasn't sure what to say. "I met him once, at their house. April's mother threw a birthday party for her a couple of years ago. It was a disaster because most of the kids didn't show up. The other parents didn't like the idea of them going to the Finnemores' house. But I was there, me and three others, and her dad was hanging around. He had long hair and a beard and seemed uncomfortable around us kids. April told me a lot over the years. He comes and goes and she's happier when he's not around. He plays the guitar and writes songs—bad songs according to April—and still has the dream of making it big as a musician."

"I know the guy," Ike said smugly. "Or, I should say, I know of him."

"How's that?" Theo asked, not really surprised that Ike knew another strange person.

"I have a friend who plays music with him occasionally, says he's a deadbeat. Spends a lot of time with a ragtag band of middle-aged losers. They take little tours, playing in bars and fraternity houses. I suspect there are some drugs involved."

"That sounds right. April told me he was missing one time for a whole month. I think he and Mrs. Finnemore fight a lot. It's a very unhappy family."

Ike slowly got to his feet and walked to the stereo mounted in a bookcase. He pushed a button, and some folk music began playing quietly in the background. Ike spoke as he fiddled with the volume, "Well, if you ask me, the police need to check out the father. He probably got the girl and took off somewhere."

"I'm not sure April would leave with him. She didn't like him and didn't trust him."

"Why hasn't she tried to contact you? Doesn't she have a cell phone, a laptop? Don't you kids chat nonstop online?"

"The police found her laptop in her room, and her parents would not allow her to have a cell phone. She told me once that her father hates cell phones and doesn't use one. He doesn't want to be found when he's on the road. I'm sure she would try and contact me if she could. Maybe whoever took her won't let her get near a phone."

Ike sat down again and looked at a notepad on his desk. Theo needed to get to school, which was ten minutes away by bike if he hit all the shortcuts.

"I'll see what I can find out about the father," Ike said. "Call me after school."

"Thanks, Ike. And, I suppose this is top secret, right, this great news about April?"

"Why should it be a secret? In about an hour the police will make the announcement. If you ask me, they should've informed the public last night. But, no, the police like to put on press conferences, make everything as dramatic as possible. I don't care who you tell. The public has the right to know."

"Great. I'll call Mom on the way to school."

# Chapter 12

Fifteen minutes later, Mr. Mount got his homeroom quiet and settled, which was not as difficult as usual. The boys were again subdued. There was a lot of gossip, but it was more of the whispered variety. Mr. Mount looked at them, and then said, gravely, "Men, Theo has an update on April's disappearance."

Theo stood slowly and walked to the front of the class. One of his favorite trial lawyers in town was a man named Jesse Meelbank. When Mr. Meelbank had a trial, Theo tried to watch as much as possible. The summer before, there was a long trial in which Mr. Meelbank sued a railroad company for the tragic death of a young woman, and Theo watched nonstop for nine days. It was awesome. What he loved about Mr. Meelbank was the way he carried himself in the courtroom. He moved gracefully, but with a purpose, never in a hurry but never wasting time. When he was ready to speak, he looked at the witness, or the judge or jury, and he paused dramatically before saying the first word. And when he spoke, his tone was friendly, conversational, seemingly off the cuff, but not a single word, phrase, or syllable was wasted. Everyone listened to Jesse Meelbank, and he seldom lost a case. Often, when Theo was alone in his bedroom or office (with the door locked), he liked to address the jury in some dramatic, make-believe case, and he always imitated Mr. Meelbank.

He stood before the class, paused just a second, and when he had everyone's attention, he said, "As we all know, the police found a dead body in the river yesterday. It was all over the news, and the reports suggested that the body was April Finnemore." (A dramatic pause as Theo searched their troubled eyes). "However, I have a reliable source that has confirmed that the body is not April. The body is that of a man about five feet six inches tall, and the poor guy has been in the water for a long time. His body is really decomposed."

Grins everywhere, on every face, even a clap or two.

Because he knew every lawyer, judge, court clerk, and practically every policeman in town, Theo's word carried great weight with his friends and classmates, at least in matters like this. When the topic was Chemistry, music, movies, or the Civil War, he was not the expert and did not pretend to be. But when it came to the law, the courts, and the criminal justice system, Theo was the man.

He continued, "At nine this morning, the police will make this announcement to the press. It's certainly good news, but the fact is, April is still missing and the police do not have many clues."

"What about Jack Leeper?" Aaron asked.

"He's still a suspect, but he's not cooperating."

The boys were suddenly talkative. They asked Theo more random questions, none of which he could answer, and they chatted among themselves. When the bell rang, they scampered off to first period, and Mr. Mount hustled down to the principal's office to repeat the good news. It spread like wildfire through the office and teachers' lounge, and then it spilled into the hallways and classrooms and even the restrooms and cafeteria.

A few minutes before 9:00 a.m., Mrs. Gladwell, the principal, interrupted the classes with an announcement through the intercom. All eighth-grade students were to report immediately to the auditorium for another unscheduled assembly. They had done the same thing the day before when Mrs. Gladwell tried to calm their fears.

As the students filed into the auditorium, a large television was being rolled in by two of the custodians. Mrs. Gladwell hurried everyone to their seats, and when they were seated, she said, "Attention, please!" She had an annoying way of dragging out the word *please* so that it sounded more like "Pleeeeeze." This was often imitated over lunch or on the playground, especially by the boys. Behind her, the screen came to life with a muted broadcast of a morning talk show. She went on, "At nine o'clock, the police are going to make an important announcement in the April Finnemore case, and I thought it would be great if we could see it live and enjoy this moment together. Pleeeeze, no questions."

She glanced at her watch, and then glanced at the television. "Let's put it on Channel twenty-eight," she said to the custodians. Strattenburg had two network stations and two cable. Channel 28 was arguably the most reliable, which meant that it generally made fewer blunders than the others. Theo had once watched a great trial in which Channel 28 was sued by a doctor who claimed a reporter for the station had said false things about him. The jury believed the doctor, as did Theo, and gave him a bunch of money.

Channel 28 was showing another morning talk show, one that started the hour not with the news but with the latest breathtaking details of a celebrity divorce. Thankfully, it was still on mute. The eighth graders waited patiently and quietly.

There was a clock on the wall, and when the minute hand made it to five minutes past nine, Theo began to squirm. Some of the students began to whisper. The celebrity divorce gave way to a bridal makeover, one in which a rather plain and somewhat chubby bride got worked on by all manner of flaky professionals. A trainer tried to whip her into shape by screaming at her. A man with painted fingernails restyled her hair. A real weirdo plastered on new makeup. This went on and on with virtually no improvement. By 9:15, the bride was ready for the wedding. She looked like a different person, and it was obvious, even with no sound, that her groom preferred the version he had originally proposed to.

But by then, Theo was too nervous to care. Mr. Mount eased over to him and whispered, "Theo, are you sure the police will make the announcement?"

Theo nodded confidently and said, "Yes, sir."

But all confidence had vanished. Theo was kicking

himself for being such a loudmouth and know-it-all. He was also kicking Ike. He was tempted to sneak his cell phone out of his pocket and text Ike to see what was going on. What were the police doing? The school, though, had a strict policy regarding cell phones. Only seventh and eighth graders could have them on campus, and calls, texts, and e-mails were permitted only during lunch and recess. If you got caught using your phone at any other time, then you lost your phone. About half of the eighth graders had cell phones. Many parents still refused to allow them.

"Hey, Theo, what's the deal?" Aaron Helleberg asked at full volume. He was seated behind Theo, three seats down.

Theo smiled, shrugged, and said, "These things never run on time."

Once the chubby bride got married, it was time for the morning news. Floods in India were claiming thousands of lives, and London got hit with a freak snowstorm. With the news out of the way, one of the hosts began an exclusive interview with a supermodel.

Theo felt as though every teacher and every student was staring at him. He was anxious and breathing rapidly, and then he had an even worse thought. What if Ike was wrong? What if Ike had believed some bad information and the police were not so sure about the dead body?

Wouldn't Theo look like an idiot? Indeed he would, but that would be nothing if the police had in fact pulled April out of the water.

He jumped to his feet and walked over to where Mr. Mount was standing with two other teachers. "I've got an idea," he said, still managing to appear confident. "Why don't you call the police department and see what's going on?" Theo said.

"Who would I call?" Mr. Mount asked.

"I'll give you the number," Theo said.

Mrs. Gladwell was walking over, frowning at Theo.

"Why don't you call, Theo?" Mr. Mount said, and that was exactly what Theo wanted to hear. He looked at Mrs. Gladwell and said, very politely, "May I step into the hall and call the police department?"

Mrs. Gladwell was pretty nervous about the situation, too, and she quickly said, "Yes, and hurry."

Theo disappeared. In the hall, he whipped out his cell phone and called Ike. No answer. He called the police department, but the line was busy. He called Elsa at the office and asked if she had heard anything. She had not. He tried Ike again, no answer. He tried to think of someone else to call at that awful moment, but no one came to mind. He checked the time on his cell phone—9:27.

Theo stared at the large metal door that led into the auditorium where about 175 of his classmates and a dozen or so teachers were waiting on some very good news about April, news that Theo had brought to school and delivered as dramatically as possible. He knew he should open the door and return to his seat. He thought about leaving, just going someplace in the school and hiding for an hour or so. He could claim that his stomach was upset, or that his asthma had flared up. He could hide in the library or the gym.

The doorknob clicked and Theo stuck the phone to his ear as if in a deep conversation. Mr. Mount came out, looked at him quizzically, and mouthed the words "Is everything okay?" Theo smiled and nodded his head as if he had the police on the line and they were doing exactly what he wanted them to do. Mr. Mount returned to the auditorium.

Theo could (1) run and hide; (2) stop the damage with a little fib, something like—"The announcement by the police has been postponed," or (3) stick with the current plan and pray for a miracle. He thought about throwing rocks at Ike, then gritted his teeth, and pulled open the door. Everyone watched him as he returned. Mrs. Gladwell pounced on him. "What's going on, Theo?" she said, eyebrows arched, eyes flashing.

"It should be any minute now," he said.

"Who did you talk to?" Mr. Mount asked—a rather direct question.

"They're having some technical problems," Theo replied, dodging. "Just a few more minutes."

Mr. Mount frowned as if he found this hard to believe. Theo quickly got to his seat and tried to become invisible. He focused on the television screen, where a dog was gripping two paintbrushes in his teeth and splashing paint on a white canvas while the host howled with laughter. Come on, Theo said to himself, someone save me here. It was 9:35.

"Hey, Theo, any more inside scoop?" Aaron said loudly, and several kids laughed.

"At least we're not in class," Theo shot back.

Ten more minutes passed. The painting dog gave way to an obese chef who built a pyramid out of mushrooms, then almost cried when it all tumbled down. Mrs. Gladwell walked in front of the television, shot a vicious look at Theo, and said, "Well, you need to get back to class."

At that moment, Channel 28 cut in with a BREAKING NEWS graphic. A custodian hit the mute switch, and Mrs. Gladwell hurried out of the way. Theo exhaled and thanked God for miracles.

The Police Chief was behind a podium with a row of uniformed officers behind him. To the far right was Detective Slater in a coat and tie. Everyone looked exhausted.

The chief read from a page of notes, and he gave the same information Ike had delivered to Theo about two hours earlier. They were waiting on DNA testing to confirm things, but they were almost certain the body pulled from the river was not that of April Finnemore. He went into some detail about the size and condition of the body, which they were working hard to identify, and he gave the impression they were making progress. As for April, they were following many leads. The reporters asked a lot of questions, and the chief did a lot of talking, but not much was said.

When the press conference was over, the eighth graders were relieved, but still worried. The police had no idea where April was, or who took her. Jack Leeper was still the prime suspect. At least she wasn't dead, or if she was, they didn't yet know it.

As they left the auditorium and returned to class, Theo reminded himself to be more cautious next time. He had just barely avoided being the biggest laughingstock in school.

During the lunch break, Theo, Woody, Chase, Aaron, and a few others ate sandwiches and talked about resuming their search after school. The weather, though, was threatening and heavy rain was predicted for the afternoon and into the night. As the days had dragged by, there were fewer and fewer among them who believed April was still in Strattenburg. Why, then, should they search the streets each afternoon if no one believed she would be found?

Theo was determined to continue, rain or not.

# Chapter 13

alfway through Chemistry, with rain and wind pounding the windows, Theo was trying to listen to Mr. Tubcheck when he was startled to hear his own name. It was Mrs. Gladwell again, over the intercom. "Mr. Tubcheck, is Theodore Boone in class?" she screeched, startling the boys and Mr. Tubcheck as well.

Theo's heart stopped as he bolted straight up in his chair. Where else would I be at this moment? he thought.

"He is," Mr. Tubcheck responded.

"Please send him to the office."

As Theo walked slowly down the hall, he tried desperately to think of why he was needed in the principal's office. It was almost 2:00 p.m. on Friday afternoon. The week was almost over, and what a miserable week it had been. Perhaps Mrs. Gladwell was still sore over the delayed press conference this morning, but Theo didn't think so. That had turned out well. He had done nothing significantly wrong the entire week, violated no rules, offended no one, successfully completed most of his homework, and so on. He gave up. He really wasn't that worried. Two years earlier, Mrs. Gladwell's oldest daughter had gone through an unpleasant divorce, and Marcella Boone had been her lawyer.

Miss Gloria, the nosy receptionist, was on the phone and waved him toward the big office. Mrs. Gladwell met him at the door and escorted him inside. "Theo, this is Anton," she said as she closed the door. Anton was a skinny kid with extremely dark skin. She continued, "He's in Miss Spence's sixth-grade class." Theo shook his hand and said, "Nice to meet you."

Anton said nothing. His handshake was rather limp. Theo immediately thought the kid was in deep trouble and scared to death.

"Have a seat, Theo," she said, and Theo fell into the chair next to Anton. "Anton is from Haiti, moved here several years ago, and lives with some relatives at the edge of town on Barkley Street, near the quarry." Her eyes met Theo's when she said the word *quarry*. It was not a better part of town. In fact, most of the people who lived there were low income or immigrants, legal and otherwise.

"His parents are working out of town, and Anton lives with his grandparents. Do you recognize this?" she asked as she handed Theo a sheet of paper. He studied it quickly, and said, "Oh boy."

"Are you familiar with Animal Court, Theo?" she asked.

"Yes, I've been there several times. I rescued my dog from Animal Court."

"Can you please explain what's going on, for my benefit and Anton's?"

"Sure. This is a Rule 3 Summons, issued by Judge Yeck from Animal Court. Says here that Pete was taken into custody yesterday by Animal Control."

"They came to the house and got him," Anton said. "Said he was under arrest. Pete was very upset."

Theo was still scanning the summons. "Says here that Pete is an African gray parrot, age unknown."

"He's fifty years old. He's been in my family for many years."

Theo glanced at Anton and noticed his wet eyes.

"The hearing is today at 4:00 p.m. in Animal Court. Judge Yeck will hear the case and decide what to do with Pete. Do you know what Pete did wrong?"

"He scared some people," Anton said. "That's all I know."

"Can you help, Theo?" Mrs. Gladwell asked.

"Sure," Theo said, with some reluctance. Truthfully, though, Theo loved Animal Court because anyone, including a thirteen-year-old kid in the eighth grade, could represent himself or herself. Lawyers were not required in Animal Court, and Judge Yeck ran a very loose courtroom. Yeck was a misfit who'd been kicked out of several law firms, couldn't handle a real job as a lawyer, and was not too happy to be the lowest-ranked judge in town. Most lawyers avoided "Kitty Court," as it was known, because it was beneath their dignity.

"Thank you, Theo."

"But I need to leave now," he said, thinking quickly. "I need some time to prepare."

"You're dismissed," she said.

At 4:00 p.m., Theo walked down the stairs to the basement level of the courthouse, and down a hallway past storage rooms until he came to a wooden door with ANIMAL COURT, JUDGE SERGIO YECK, stenciled in black at the top. He was nervous, but also excited. Where else could a thirteen-year-old argue a case and pretend to be a real lawyer? He was carrying a leather briefcase, one of Ike's old ones. He opened the door.

Whatever Pete had done, he'd done a good job of it. Theo had never seen so many people in Animal Court. On the left side of the small courtroom, there was a group of women, all middle-aged, all wearing tight, brown riding britches and black leather boots up to their knees. They looked very unhappy. To the right, sitting as far away from the women as possible, were Anton and two elderly black people. All three appeared to be terrified. Theo eased over to them and said hello. Anton introduced his grandparents, with names that were foreign and impossible to understand the first time around. Their English was okay, but heavily accented. Anton said something to his grandmother. She looked at Theo and said, "You our lawyer?"

Theo couldn't think of anything else to say but, "Yes."

She started crying.

A door opened and Judge Yeck appeared from somewhere in the rear. He stepped up to the long bench and sat down. As usual, he was wearing jeans, cowboy boots, no tie, and a battered sports coat. No black robe was needed in Kitty Court. He picked up a sheet of paper and glanced around the room. Few of the cases on his docket attracted attention. Most involved people whose dogs and cats had been picked up by Animal Control. So, when a little controversy came his way, he enjoyed the moment.

He cleared his throat loudly and said, "I see here that we have a case involving Pete the Parrot. His owners are Mr. and Mrs. Regnier." He looked at the Haitians for confirmation. Theo said, "Your Honor, I'm with the, uh, the owners."

"Well, hello, Theo. How are you doing these days?"

"Fine, Judge, thanks."

"I haven't seen you in a month or so."

"Yes, sir, I've been busy. You know, classes and all."

"How are your folks?"

"Fine, just fine."

Theo had first appeared in Animal Court two years earlier when he made a last-minute plea to save the life of a mutt no one wanted. He took the dog home and named him Judge.

"Please come forward," Judge Yeck said, and Theo led the three Regniers through the small gate to a table on the right. When they were seated, the judge said, "The complaint was filed by Kate Spangler and Judy Cross, owners of SC Stables."

A well-dressed young man popped up and announced, "Yes, Your Honor, I represent Ms. Spangler and Ms. Cross."

"And who are you?"

"I'm Kevin Blaze, Your Honor, with the Macklin firm." Blaze sort of strutted up to the bench, shiny new briefcase in hand, and placed one of his business cards in front of the judge. The Macklin firm was a group of about twenty lawyers and had been around for years. Theo had never heard of Mr. Blaze. Evidently, Judge Yeck had not either. It was apparent, at least to Theo, that the young lawyer's abundance of self-confidence was not appreciated.

Theo suddenly had a sharp pain in his midsection. His opponent was a real lawyer!

Blaze got his clients, the two women, properly seated at the table on the left side of the courtroom, and when everyone was in place, Judge Yeck said, "Say, Theo, you don't happen to own any part of this parrot do you?"

"No, sir."

"Then why are you here?"

Theo stayed in his chair. In Animal Court, all formalities were dispensed with. The lawyers remained seated. There was no witness stand, no sworn oaths to tell the truth, no rules of evidence, and certainly no jury. Judge Yeck conducted quick hearings and ruled on the spot, and in spite of his dead-end job, he was known to be fair.

"Well, uh," Theo began badly. "You see, Your Honor, Anton goes to my school, and his family is from Haiti, and they don't understand our system."

"Who does?" Yeck mumbled.

"And I guess I'm here as a favor to a friend."

"I get that, Theo, but normally the owner of the pet shows up to argue his or her case or they hire a lawyer. You're not the owner, and you're not a lawyer, yet."

"Yes, sir."

Kevin Blaze jumped to his feet and said sharply, "I object to his presence here, Your Honor."

Judge Yeck slowly turned his attention from Theo and settled it heavily onto the eager face of young Kevin Blaze. There was a long pause; a tense lull in the proceedings in which no one spoke and no one seemed to breathe. Finally, Judge Yeck said, "Sit down."

When Blaze was back in his seat, Judge Yeck said, "And stay there. Don't get up again unless I ask you to. Now, Mr. Blaze, can you not see that I am addressing the issue of Theodore Boone's presence in this matter? Is that not obvious to you? I need no assistance from you. Your objection is useless. It is not overruled, nor is it sustained. It is simply ignored." Another long pause as Judge Yeck looked at the group of women seated behind the table on the left.

He pointed and asked, "Who are these people?"

Blaze, firmly gripping the arms of his chair, said, "These are witnesses, Your Honor."

Judge Yeck was obviously not happy with this response.

"Okay, here's the way I operate, Mr. Blaze. I prefer short hearings. I prefer few witnesses. And I really have no patience with witnesses who say the same things that other witnesses have already said. You understand this, Mr. Blaze?"

"Yes, sir."

Looking at Theo, the judge said, "Thank you for taking an interest in this case, Mr. Boone."

"You're welcome, Judge."

His Honor glanced at a sheet of paper and said, "Good. Now, I suppose we need to meet Pete." He nodded to his ancient court clerk, who disappeared for a moment then returned with a uniformed bailiff holding a cheap, wire birdcage. He placed it on the corner of Judge Yeck's bench. Inside the cage was Pete, an African gray parrot, fourteen inches long from beak to tail. Pete glanced around the strange room, moving only his head.

"I guess you're Pete," Judge Yeck said.

"I'm Pete," Pete said in a clear, high-pitched voice.

"Nice to meet you. I'm Judge Yeck."

"Yeck, Yeck, Yeck," Pete squawked, and almost everyone laughed. The ladies in the black boots did not. They were frowning even harder now, not at all amused by Pete.

Judge Yeck exhaled slowly, as if the hearing might take longer than he wanted. "Call your first witness," he said to Kevin Blaze.

"Yes, Your Honor. I guess we'll start with Kate Spangler." Blaze reshifted his weight and turned to look at his client. It was obvious he wanted to stand and move around the courtroom, and felt constrained. He picked up a legal pad covered with notes, and began, "You are the co-owner of SC Stables, correct?"

"Yes." Ms. Spangler was a small, thin woman in her mid-forties.

"How long have you owned SC Stables?"

"Why is that important?" Judge Yeck interrupted quickly. "Please tell me how that is possibly relevant to what we're doing here."

Blaze tried to explain. "Well, Your Honor, we need to prove that—"

"Here's how we do things in Animal Court, Mr. Blaze. Ms. Spangler, please tell me what happened. Just forget all the stuff your lawyer has told you, and tell me what Pete here did to upset you."

"I'm Pete," Pete said.

"Yes, we know."

"Yeck, Yeck, Yeck."

"Thank you, Pete." A long pause to make sure Pete was finished for the moment, then the judge waved at Ms. Spangler. She began, "Well, on Tuesday of last week, we were in the middle of a lesson. I was in the arena, on foot, with four of my students mounted, when suddenly this bird here came out of nowhere, squawking and making all kinds of noises, just a few feet above our heads. The horses freaked out and bolted for the barn. I almost got trampled. Betty Slocum fell and hurt her arm."

Betty Slocum stood quickly so everyone could see the large, white cast on her left arm.

"He swooped down again, like some crazy kamikaze, and chased the horses as they—"

"Kamikaze, kamikaze, kamikaze," Pete blurted.

"Just shut up!" Ms. Spangler said to Pete.

"Please, he's just a bird," Judge Yeck said.

Pete began saying something that could not be understood. Anton leaned over and whispered to Theo. "He's speaking Creole."

"What is it?" Judge Yeck asked.

"He's speaking Creole French, Your Honor," Theo explained. "It's his native tongue."

"What's he saying?"

Theo whispered to Anton, who whispered right back. "You don't want to know, Your Honor," Theo reported.

Pete shut up, and everyone waited for a moment. Judge Yeck looked at Anton and said softly, "Will he stop talking if he's asked to stop talking?"

Anton shook his head and said, "No, sir."

Another pause. "Please continue," Judge Yeck said.

Judy Cross took over and said, "And then the next day, at about the same time, I was giving a lesson. I had five of my riders on their horses. In the course of any lesson, I yell instructions to my students, such as 'Walk on,' and 'Halt,' and 'Canter.' I had no idea he was watching us, but he was. He was hiding in an oak tree next to the arena, and he started yelling, "'Halt! Halt!'"

Pete, on cue, yelled, "Halt! Halt! Halt!"

"See what I mean? And the horses stopped dead still. I tried to ignore him. I told my students to remain calm and just ignore this guy. I said 'Walk on,' and the horses began their movements. Then he started yelling, "'Halt!' 'Halt!'"

Judge Yeck held up both hands for silence. Seconds passed. He said, "Please continue."

Judy Cross said, "He was quiet for a few minutes. We ignored him. The students were concentrating and the horses were calm. They were in a slow walk, when suddenly he started yelling, 'Canter! Canter!' The horses bolted again and began sprinting all around the arena. It was chaos. I barely escaped getting run over."

Pete squawked, "Canter! Canter!"

"See what I mean," Judy Cross gushed. "He's been

harassing us for over a week. One day he'll drop from the sky like a dive-bomber and frighten the horses. The next day he'll sneak up on us and hide in a tree and wait until things are quiet before he starts yelling instructions. He's evil. Our horses are afraid to come out of the barn. Our students want their money back. He's killing our business."

With perfect timing, Pete said, "You're fat."

He waited five seconds, then did it again. "You're fat." His words echoed around the room and stunned everyone. Most of the people looked at their shoes, or boots.

Judy Cross swallowed hard, closed her eyes tightly, clenched her fists, and frowned as if in great pain. She was a large woman with a wide frame, the kind of body that had always carried extra weight, and carried it badly. It was obvious from her reaction that her weight had presented many complicated issues over the years. It was something she had battled, and lost badly. Being heavy was an extremely sensitive topic for Judy, one she wrestled with every day.

"You're fat," Pete reminded her, for the third time.

Judge Yeck, who was desperately fighting the natural reaction to burst out laughing, jumped in and said, "Okay. Is it safe to assume that your other witnesses are willing to say pretty much the same thing?" The women nodded. Several seemed to be cowering, almost hiding, as if they had lost some of their enthusiasm. At that moment, it would take enormous courage to say harmful things about Pete. What would he blurt out about them, and their bodies?

"Anything else?" Judge Yeck asked.

Kate Spangler said, "Judge, you've got to do something. This bird is costing us our business. We've already lost money. This simply isn't fair."

"What do you want me to do?"

"I don't care what you do. Can you put him to sleep or something?"

"You want me to kill him?"

"Halt! Halt!" Pete screamed.

"Maybe you could clip his wings," Judy Cross chimed in.

"Halt! Halt!" Pete continued, then he resorted to Creole and unleashed a furious string of harsh words at the two women. When he finished, Judge Yeck glanced at Anton and asked, "What did he say?"

Anton's grandparents were chuckling and covering their mouths.

"Really bad stuff," Anton replied. "He doesn't like those two women."

"Got that." The judge raised his hands again and asked for calm. Pete got the message. "Mr. Boone."

Theo said, "Well, Judge, I think it might be helpful if my friend Anton gave you some background on Pete."

"Please do so."

Anton cleared his throat, and began nervously. "Yes, sir. Pete is fifty years old. He was given to my father when he was a little boy in Haiti, a gift from his father, so Pete has been in the family for a long time. When my grandparents came to this country a few years ago, Pete came, too. African gray parrots are some of the smartest animals in the world. As you can see, he knows a lot of words. He understands what others are saying. He can even imitate the voices of humans."

Pete was watching Anton as he spoke, the voice so familiar. He began saying, "Andy, Andy, Andy."

"I'm here, Pete," Anton said.

"Andy, Andy."

A pause, then Anton continued, "Parrots like to have a fixed routine each day, and they require at least an hour out of their cages. Every day at four o'clock, Pete gets out, and we thought he was just hanging around the backyard. I guess not. The stables are about a mile away, and he must have found the place. We're very sorry about this, but please don't hurt Pete."

"Thank you," Judge Yeck said. "Now, Mr. Blaze, what am I supposed to do?"

"Your Honor, it's obvious that the owners cannot control this bird, and it's their duty to do so. One compromise might be that the court orders the owners to have its wings clipped. I've checked with two veterinarians and one wildlife specialist, and they've told me that such a procedure is not unusual, nor is it painful or expensive."

At full volume, Pete yelled, "You're stupid."

There was laughter as Blaze's face turned red. Judge Yeck said, "Okay that's enough. Get him out of here. Pete, sorry old boy, but you must leave the room." The bailiff snatched the birdcage and took him away. As the door closed, Pete was cursing mightily in Creole.

When the room was quiet again, Judge Yeck said, "Mr. Boone, what's your suggestion?"

With no hesitation, Theo said, "Probation, Your Honor. Give us one more chance. My friends here will find a way to control Pete and keep him away from the stables. I don't think they realize what he's been doing, or the problems he's created. They are very sorry for all this."

"And if he does it again?"

"Then a harsher punishment would be in order." Theo knew two things that Kevin Blaze did not. First, Judge Yeck believed in second chances and rarely ordered animals destroyed until he had no other choice. Second, he'd been kicked out of the Macklin law firm five years earlier, so he probably held a bit of a grudge.

In typical Yeck fashion, he said, "Here's what we're going to do. Ms. Spangler and Ms. Cross, I am very sympathetic to your complaints. If Pete shows up again, I want you to video him. Have a cell phone or a camera ready, and catch him on video. Then bring me the video. At that point, Mr. Boone, we will take Pete into custody and have his wings clipped. The owners will be responsible for the costs. There will be no hearing—it will be automatic. Is this clear, Mr. Boone?"

"Just a second, Your Honor." Theo huddled with the three Regniers and they were soon nodding in agreement.

"They understand, Your Honor," Theo announced.

"Good. I hold them responsible. I want Pete kept at home. Period."

"Can they take him home now?" Theo asked.

"Yes. I'm sure the good folks at the animal shelter are ready to get rid of him. Case closed. Court's adjourned."

Kevin Blaze and his clients and the rest of the women in black boots hustled out of the courtroom. When they were gone, the bailiff brought Pete back and handed him over to Anton, who immediately opened the cage and removed the bird. His grandparents wiped tears from their cheeks as they stroked his back and tail.

Theo drifted away and walked to the bench where Judge Yeck was making notes on his docket. "Thanks, Judge," Theo said, almost in a whisper.

"That's a bad bird," Judge Yeck said softly with a chuckle. "Too bad we don't have a video of Pete dive-bombing the ladies on their horses." They both laughed, but quietly.

"Nice job, Theo."

"Thanks."

"Any word on the Finnemore girl?"

Theo shook his head. No.

"I'm very sorry, Theo. Someone told me you're a close friend."

Theo nodded and said, "Pretty close."

"Let's keep our fingers crossed."

"Yeck, Yeck, Yeck," Pete squawked as he left the court-room.

# Chapter 14

Jack Leeper wanted to talk. He sent a note to the jailer, who passed it on to Detective Slater. Late Friday afternoon, they marched Leeper from his cell block and through an old tunnel which led to the police station next door. Slater and his trusty sidekick, Capshaw, were waiting in the same dim and cramped interrogation room. Leeper looked as though he had not bathed or shaved since they had chatted with him the day before.

"Something on your mind, Leeper." Slater began rudely. As always, Capshaw was taking notes.

"I talked to my lawyer today," Leeper said, as if he were now more important because he had a lawyer.

"Which one?"

"Ozgoode, Kip Ozgoode."

As if they had rehearsed, both detectives chuckled and sneered at the name. "If you have Ozgoode, you're dead meat, Leeper," Slater said.

"The worst," Capshaw added.

"I like him," Leeper said. "He seems a lot smarter than you boys."

"You want to talk or swap insults?"

"I can do both."

"Does your lawyer know you're talking to us?" Slater asked.

"Yep."

"So what do you want to talk about?"

"I'm worried about the girl. You clowns obviously can't find her. I know where she is, and as the clock ticks her situation gets worse. She needs to be rescued."

"You're a real sweetheart, Leeper," Slater said. "Snatch the girl, stash her somewhere, and now you want to help her."

"I'm sure you have a deal for us," Capshaw said.

"You got it. Here's what I'll do, and you guys better do it fast because there's one frightened little girl out there. I'll plead guilty to one count of breaking and entering;

get two years in prison, with my time to run at the same time as that mess in California. I stay here and do my time. My lawyer says the paperwork can be done in a matter of hours. We sign the deal, the prosecutor and judge okay it, and you get the girl. Time is crucial here boys, so you'd better make a move."

Slater and Capshaw exchanged a nervous look. Leeper had them. They suspected he was lying because they expected nothing else from him. But what if he wasn't? What if they agreed to his deal and he led them to April?

Slater said, "It's almost six p.m. on Friday afternoon, Leeper. All the judges and prosecutors have gone home."

"Oh, I'll bet you can find them. They'll hustle up if there's a chance of saving the girl."

Another pause as they studied his bearded face. Why would he offer such a deal if he didn't know where she was? Such a plea bargain would be thrown out the window if he couldn't deliver. Plus, they had no other leads, no other suspects. Leeper had always been their man.

"I don't mind having a chat with the prosecutor," Slater said, giving in.

"If you're lying, Leeper, we'll ship you back to California come Monday," Capshaw said.

"Is she still in town?" Slater asked.

"I'm not saying another word until I sign the deal," Leeper said.

As Theo was leaving the courthouse after saving Pete the Parrot, he saw a text message from Ike, who wanted him to run by the office.

Because he got off to a slow start each day, Ike usually worked late, even on Fridays. Theo found him at his desk, piles of papers everywhere, a bottle of beer already opened, and Bob Dylan on the stereo.

"How's my favorite nephew?" Ike said.

"I'm your only nephew," Theo replied as he shook off his raincoat and sat in the only chair that wasn't covered with files and binders.

"Yes, but Theo you'd be my favorite even if I had twenty."

"If you say so."

"How was your day?"

Theo had already learned that a large part of being a lawyer was relishing the victories, especially the ones involving courtroom battles. Lawyers love to tell stories about their weird clients and strange cases, but they thrive on their dramatic wins in court. So Theo launched into the saga of Pete, and before long Ike was roaring with laughter. Not surprisingly, Judge Yeck did not hang out with the more respected lawyers in town, and he and Ike occasionally bumped into one another at a certain bar where some of the misfits liked to drink. Ike thought it was hilarious that Yeck allowed Theo to handle cases like a real lawyer.

When the story was over, Ike changed subjects and said, "I still say the police should be checking out the girl's father. From what I hear, they're still concentrating on Jack Leeper, and I think that's a mistake. Don't you?"

"I don't know, Ike. I don't know what to think."

Ike picked up a piece of paper. "His name is Thomas Finnemore, goes by Tom. His band calls itself Plunder and they've been on the road for a few weeks. Finnemore and four other clowns, most from around here. There's no website. The lead singer is a former drug dealer I met years ago, and I managed to track down one of his current girlfriends. She wouldn't say much, but she thinks they're in the Raleigh, North Carolina, area doing cheap gigs in bars and fraternity houses. She did not act as though she missed her boyfriend that much. Anyway, that's all I could find out."

"So what am I supposed to do?"

"See if you can find Plunder."

Theo shook his head in frustration. "Look, Ike, there's no way April would take off with her father. I've tried to tell you. She doesn't trust him, and she really dislikes him."

"And she was scared, Theo. A very frightened little girl.

You don't know what she was thinking. Her mother had abandoned her. These people are nuts, right?"

"Right."

"No one broke in the house, because her father has a key. He gets her and they take off, for how long no one knows."

"Okay, but if she's with her father, then she's safe, right?"

"You tell me. You think she's safe hanging around with Plunder? Not the best place for a thirteen-year-old girl."

"So I find Plunder, and just hop on my bike and fly down to Raleigh, North Carolina."

"We'll worry about that later. You're a whiz with a computer. Start searching, see what you can find."

What a waste of time, Theo thought. He was suddenly tired. The week had been stressful and he'd slept little. The excitement of Animal Court had sapped whatever energy he had, and he just wanted to go home and crawl into bed.

"Thanks, Ike," he said as he grabbed his raincoat.

"Don't mention it."


Late Friday night, Jack Leeper was once again handcuffed and led from his cell. The meeting took place in a room at the jail where lawyers met with their clients. Leeper's lawyer, Kip Ozgoode, was there, along with Detectives Slater and Capshaw, and a young lady from the prosecutor's office named Teresa Knox. Ms. Knox immediately took charge.

She was all business and didn't appreciate being called from home on a Friday night.

"There's no deal, Mr. Leeper," she began. "You're in no position to make deals. You're facing kidnapping charges, which means up to forty years in prison. If the girl is harmed, then more charges. If she's dead, then your life is really over. The best thing for you is to tell us where she is so she won't be harmed anymore and you won't face additional charges."

Leeper grinned at Ms. Knox but said nothing.

She continued, "This is assuming, of course, that you're not playing games. I suspect that you are. So does the judge. So do the police."

"Then all of you will be sorry," Leeper said. "I'm giving you the chance to save her life. As for me, I'm sure I'll die in prison."

"Not necessarily," Ms. Knox fired back. "You give us the girl, safe and sound, and we'll recommend a twenty-year sentence on the kidnapping charge. You can serve your time here."

"What about California?"

"We can't control what they do in California."

Leeper kept grinning, as if he was enjoying the moment. Finally, he said, "As you say, no deal."

# Chapter 15

The Boone family breakfast on Saturday morning was rather tense. As usual, Theo and Judge dined on Cheerios—orange juice for Theo but not for Judge— while Woods Boone ate a bagel and read the sports page. Marcella sipped coffee and scanned her laptop for news around the world. Not much was said, at least not for the first twenty minutes. The remains of other conversations were still hanging in the air, and a disagreement might flare up at any moment.

The tension had several causes. First, and most obvious, was the general gloominess that had afflicted the family since about 4:00 a.m. Wednesday morning when they were awakened by the police and asked to hurry over to the Finnemore home. As the days passed without April, the mood had only darkened. There were efforts, especially by Mr. and Mrs. Boone, to smile and be upbeat, but all three knew these were futile. Second, but less important, was the fact that Theo and his father would not play their weekly nine holes of golf. They teed off almost every Saturday at 9:00 a.m., and it was the highlight of the week.

The golf was being cancelled because of the third reason for the tension. Mr. and Mrs. Boone were leaving town for twenty-four hours, and Theo insisted he be allowed to stay by himself. It was a fight they'd had before, and Theo had lost before, and he was losing again. He had carefully explained that he knew how to lock all the doors and windows; arm the alarm system; call the neighbors and 911, if necessary; sleep with a chair wedged under his door; sleep with Judge by his side ready to attack, and sleep with a seven-iron golf club in his grip, if necessary. He was thoroughly and completely safe and he resented being treated like a child. He refused to stay with a babysitter when his parents went out for dinner or the movies, and he was furious that they refused to leave him on this little overnight trip of theirs.

His parents wouldn't budge. He was only thirteen and that was too young to be left alone. Theo had already started the negotiating, even pestering, and the door was open to serious discussion on the issue when he was fourteen. But for now, Theo needed the supervision and protection. His mother had arranged for him to spend the night with Chase Whipple, which would have been okay under normal circumstances. However, as Chase had explained, his own parents were going out for dinner Saturday night and leaving the two boys to be watched by Chase's older sister, Daphne, a truly dislikable girl of sixteen who was always at home because she had no social life and therefore felt compelled to flirt with Theo. He had suffered through such a sleepover not three months earlier when his parents were in Chicago for a funeral.

He had protested, griped, sulked, argued, pouted, and nothing had worked. His Saturday night was about to be spent in the basement of the Whipple home with pudgy Daphne chattering nonstop and staring at him while he and Chase tried to play video games and watch television.

Mr. and Mrs. Boone had considered cancelling their trip, in light of April's abduction and the general sense of uneasiness in town. Their plans were to drive two hundred miles to a popular resort called Briar Springs for a few hours of fun with a bunch of lawyers from around the state. There would be afternoon seminars and speeches, then cocktails, then a long dinner with more speeches from wise old judges and dull politicians. Woods and Marcella were active in the State Bar Association and never missed the annual meeting at Briar Springs. This one was even more important because Marcella was scheduled to give a speech on recent trends in divorce law, and Woods was on tap to participate in a seminar on the mortgage foreclosure crisis. Both had prepared their remarks and were looking forward to the afternoon.

Theo assured them he would be fine, and that Strattenburg would not miss them if they left for twenty-four hours. Over dinner Friday evening, they had decided to make the trip. And they had decided that Theo would stay with the Whipple family, in spite of his vocal opposition to such a plan. Theo lost the argument, and though he conceded this to himself he still awoke on Saturday in a foul mood.

"Sorry about the golf, Theo," Mr. Boone said without taking his eyes off the sports page.

Theo said nothing.

"We'll catch up next Saturday by playing eighteen. Whatta you say?"

Theo grunted.

His mother closed her laptop and looked at him. "Theo,

dear, we're leaving in an hour. What are your plans for the afternoon?"

Seconds passed before Theo said, "Oh, I don't know. I guess I'll just hang out here and wait for the kidnappers and murderers to show up. I'll probably be dead by the time you get to Briar Springs."

"Don't get smart with your mother," Woods said sharply, then raised the newspaper to conceal a grin.

"You'll have a great time at the Whipples," she said.

"Can't wait."

"Now, back to my question. What are your plans for the afternoon?"

"Not sure. Chase and I might go the high school game at two, or we might go to the Paramount and watch the double feature. There's also a hockey game."

"And you're not searching for April, right, Theo? We've had this conversation. You boys have no business riding around town playing detectives."

Theo nodded.

His father lowered his newspaper, glared at Theo, and said, "Do we have your word, Theo? No more search parties?"

"You have my word."

"I want a text message every two hours, beginning at eleven this morning. Do you understand?" his mother asked.

"I do."

"And smile, Theo. Make the world a happier place."

"I don't want to smile right now."

"Come on, Teddy," she said with a smile of her own. Calling him Teddy did nothing to brighten his mood, nor did her constant reminders to "smile and make the world a happier place." Theo's thick braces had been stuck to his teeth for two years and he was sick of them. He could not imagine how a blazing mouth full of metal could possibly make anyone happier.

They left at 10:00 a.m. on the dot, on schedule, because they planned to arrive precisely at 1:30 p.m. Marcella's speech was at 2:30 p.m.; Woods's seminar was at 3:30 p.m. As busy lawyers, their lives revolved around the clock, and time could not be wasted.

Theo waited half an hour, then loaded up his backpack and took off to the office. Judge followed him. As expected, Boone & Boone was deserted. His parents rarely worked on Saturday, and the staff certainly did not. He unlocked the front door, disarmed the alarm system, and switched on the lights to the main library near the front of the building. Its tall windows looked onto the small front lawn, then the street. The room had the look and smell of a very important room, and Theo often did his homework there, if the lawyers and paralegals weren't using it. He fixed Judge a bowl of water, and then unpacked his laptop and cell phone.

He'd spent a couple of hours the night before searching for Plunder. He still found it hard to believe that April would leave in the middle of the night with her father, but Ike's theory was better than anything Theo could come up with. Besides, what else did Theo have to do over the weekend?

So far, there was no sign of Plunder. Working in the Raleigh-Durham-Chapel Hill area, Theo had found dozens of music halls, clubs, private party rooms, concert venues, bars and lounges, even wedding receptions. About half had websites or Facebook pages, and not one had mentioned a band called Plunder. He also found three underground weeklies that listed hundreds of possible venues for live music.

Using the office landline, Theo began cold calling, in alphabetical order. The first was a joint called Abbey's Irish Rose in Durham. A scratchy voice said, "Abbey's."

Theo tried to lower his voice as much as possible. "Yes, could you tell me if the band Plunder is playing there tonight?"

"Never heard of 'em."

"Thanks." He hung up quickly.

At Brady's Barbeque in Raleigh, a woman said, "We don't have a band tonight."

Theo, with every question scripted to learn as much as possible, asked, "Has Plunder ever played there?"

"Never heard of 'em."

"Thanks."

He plowed on, chewing up the alphabet, getting nowhere. There was a decent chance that Elsa would question the phone calls when she opened the monthly bill, and if this happened Theo would take the blame. He might even warn Elsa, tell her why he made the calls, and ask her to pay the bill without telling his parents. He would deal with it later. He had no choice but to use the office phone because his mother was a Nazi about his cell phone bill. If she saw a bunch of calls to a bunch of bars in Raleigh-Durham, he would have some explaining to do.

The first whiff of success came from a place called Traction in Chapel Hill. A helpful young man, who sounded no older than Theo, said he thought that Plunder had played there a few months earlier. He put Theo on hold and went to check with someone named Eddie. When it was confirmed that Plunder had passed through, the young man said, "You're not thinking about booking them, are you?"

"Maybe," Theo replied.

"Don't. They can't draw flies."

"Thanks."

"It's a frat band."

At exactly 11:00 a.m., he texted his mother: *Home alone. Serial killer in basement.*

She replied: *Not funny. Love you.*

*Love u.*

Theo plugged away, call after call, with little trace of Plunder.

Chase arrived around noon and unpacked his laptop. By then, Theo had chatted with over sixty managers, bartenders, waitresses, bouncers, even a dishwasher who spoke very little English. His brief conversations convinced him that Plunder was a bad band with a very small following. One bartender in Raleigh, who claimed to "know every band that ever came to town," admitted he'd never heard of Plunder. On three occasions, the band was referred to as a "frat band."

"Let's check out the fraternities," Chase said. "And the sororities, too."

They soon learned that there were a lot of colleges and universities in the Raleigh-Durham area, with the obvious being Duke, UNC, and NC State. But within an hour's drive, there were a dozen smaller schools. They decided to start with the larger ones. Minutes passed as the two pecked away, flying around the Internet, racing to be the first to find something useful. "Duke doesn't have fraternity houses," Chase said.

"What does that mean, in terms of parties and bands?" Theo asked.

"I'm not sure. Let's come back to Duke. You take NC State and I'll take UNC."

Theo soon learned that NC State had twenty-four fraternities and nine sororities, most with an off-campus house as headquarters. It appeared as though each maintained a website, though they varied in quality. "How many frats at UNC?" Theo asked.

"Twenty-two for the boys and nine for the girls."

"Let's go through each website."

"That's what I'm doing." Chase's fingers never stopped moving. Theo was quick with his laptop, but not as quick as Chase. The two raced on, each determined to dig up the first bit of useful intelligence. Judge, who always preferred to sleep under things—tables, beds, chairs—snored quietly somewhere under the conference table.

The websites soon blurred together. They provided information on members, alumni, service projects, awards, calendars, and, most importantly, social events. The photos were endless—party scenes, ski trips, cookouts on the beach, Frisbee tournaments, and formals with the boys in tuxedos and the girls in fancy dresses. Theo caught himself looking forward to college.

The two schools played each other in football, with

kickoff at 2:00 p.m. Theo knew this; in fact, he and Chase had discussed the line. NC State was a two-point favorite. Now, though, the line was not that interesting. The important part of the game was that it gave the fraternities another excuse to party. The game was in Chapel Hill, so evidently the State students had partied and danced on Friday night. The UNC fraternities and sororities were planning the same for Saturday night.

Theo closed another website and grunted in frustration. "I count ten frat parties last night at State, but only four websites give the names of the bands. If you're announcing a party on your website, why wouldn't you say who's going to be playing?"

"Same here," Chase said. "They rarely give the name of the band."

"How many parties in Chapel Hill tonight?" Theo asked.

"Maybe a dozen. Looks like a big night."

They finished the search of all websites at both schools. It was 1:00 p.m.

Theo texted his mother: *With Chase. Ax murderers in hot pursuit. Won't make it. Please take care of Judge. Love.*

A few minutes later she replied: *So nice to hear from you. Be safe. Love Mom.*

# Chapter 16

Theo found a bag of pretzels and two diet drinks in the small kitchen where the Boone & Boone firm waged quiet battles over food. The rules were simple: If you brought food that was not to be shared, then put your initials on it and hope for the best. Otherwise, everything was fair game. Reality, though, was more complicated. The "borrowing" of food from someone's private stash was commonplace, and not entirely frowned upon. Courtesy demanded that if food was borrowed, it should be replaced as soon as possible. This led to all sorts of pranks. Mr. Boone referred to the kitchen as a "minefield" and refused to go near it.

Theo suspected the pretzels and drinks belonged to

Dorothy, a secretary who was eternally trying to lose weight. He made a mental note to replenish her supply.

Chase had suggested they go to the high school at 2:00 p.m. to watch Strattenburg play its first basketball game of the season, and Theo agreed. He was tired of the Internet and considered their work useless. But he had one last idea. "Since the parties were at State last night, let's go through each fraternity there, do a random check of several Facebook pages, and look at photos."

"You said there were ten parties, right?" Chase was crunching on a thick pretzel.

"Yes, with four giving the name of the band. That leaves six parties with unknown bands."

"And what, exactly, are we looking for?"

"Anything that might identify Plunder. Electric lights, a banner, the band's name on the bass drum, anything."

"So what if we find out that the band played at a frat party last night at NC State? Does that mean they're playing tonight at UNC?"

"Maybe. Look, Chase, we're just guessing here, all right? We're throwing darts in the dark."

"You got that right."

"You have a better idea?"

"Not at the moment."

Theo sent Chase the links to three fraternities. "Sigma Nu has eighty members," Chase said. "How many—"

"Let's do five from each fraternity. Pick them at random. Of course, you'll have to use pages with open profiles and no security."

"I know, I know."

Theo went to the page of a Chi Psi member named Buddy Ziles, a sophomore from Atlanta. Buddy had a lot of friends and hundreds of photos, but nothing from a party the night before. Theo plowed ahead, as did Chase, with little being said. Both boys were soon bored by the endless shots of groups of students posing, yelling, dancing, always with a beer in hand.

Chase perked up and said, "I got some shots from last night. A party with a band." He went through the photos, slowly, and then said, "Nothing."

A hundred photos later, Theo stopped cold, blinked twice, and zoomed in. He was on the unsecured Facebook page of an Alpha Nu brother named Vince Snyder, a sophomore from D.C. who had posted a dozen photos from last night's dance. "Chase, come here," Theo said, as if he were watching a ghost.

Chase scurried around behind Theo and leaned in. Theo pointed to the screen. The photo was a typical party shot with a mob of kids dancing. "You see that?" he said.

"Yes, what is it?"

"It's a Minnesota Twins jacket, navy with red-and-white lettering."

In the center was a small dance floor, and whoever took the photo did so with the intent of capturing some friends as they moved to the music. One girl in particular had a very short skirt, and Theo figured that was the reason for the photo. To the left of the dance floor, almost in the middle of the mob, was the lead singer, holding a guitar, mouth open, eyes closed, wailing away, and just beyond him was the point where Theo was pointing. Behind a set of tall speakers, there was a small person who appeared to be watching the crowd. The person was standing sideways, and only the *T* and *W* of the word *TWINS* were visible across the back of the jacket. The person had short hair, and though most of her face was lost in the shadows, there was no doubt in Theo's mind.

It was April.

And as of 11:39 p.m., the time of the photo, she was very much alive.

"Are you sure?" Chase asked, leaning closer, their noses almost touching the screen.

"I gave her that Twins jacket last year after I won it in a contest. It was too small for me. I told the police about it and they said they never found it in her house. They assume she was wearing it when she left." Theo pointed again and said, "Look at the short hair and the profile, Chase, it's gotta be April. Don't you agree?"

"Maybe. I don't know."

"It's her," Theo said. Both boys backed away, and then Theo stood up and walked around the room. "Her mother had not been home for three straight nights. She was scared to death, so she called her father, or maybe he called her. Anyway, he drove through the night, got home, unlocked the door with his key, got April, and away they went. For the past four days she's been on the road, just hanging out with the band."

"Shouldn't we call the police?"

Theo was walking, pacing, thinking, rubbing his chin as he pondered the situation. "No, not yet. Maybe later. Let's do this—since we know where she was last night, let's try and figure out where she'll be tonight. Let's call every fraternity and sorority at UNC, Duke, Wake Forest, and the rest of them until we find out where Plunder is playing tonight."

"UNC is the hot spot," Chase said. "There are at least a dozen frat parties."

"Give me the list."

Theo worked the phone as Chase watched and took notes. At the first fraternity house, no one answered the phone. The second call was to the Kappa Delta sorority house, and the young lady who answered the phone was not sure what their band's name was. The third call went unanswered. At the Delta house, a brother gave the name of another band. And on it went. Theo was growing frustrated again, but he was also thrilled to know that April had not been harmed and he was determined to find her.

The eighth call was magic. A student at the Kappa Theta fraternity house said he knew nothing about a band, was late for the football game, but to hang on a minute. He returned to the phone and said, "Yep, it's a band called Plunder."

"What time do they start playing," Theo asked.

"Whenever. Usually around nine. Gotta run, pal."

The pretzels were gone. The truth was that Theo had no idea what to do. Chase felt strongly that they should call the police, but Theo wasn't so sure.

Two things were certain, at least to Theo. One, the girl in the photo was April. Two, she was with the band and the band would be playing at the Kappa Theta house in Chapel Hill, North Carolina, that night. Instead of calling the police, Theo called Ike.

Twenty minutes later, Theo, Chase, and Judge ran up the stairs to Ike's office. He had been eating lunch in the Greek deli downstairs when Theo called. He and Chase introduced themselves as Theo found the photo of April on Ike's desktop computer.

"That's her," Theo declared. Ike studied the photo carefully, his reading glasses perched on the tip of his nose. "Are you sure?"

Theo gave the history of the jacket. He described her height, hairstyle, and hair color, and pointed at the profile of her nose and chin. "That's April," he said.

"If you say so."

"She's with her father, just like you said, Ike. Jack Leeper had nothing to do with her disappearance. The police have been chasing the wrong man."

Ike nodded and smiled but was not the least bit smug. He continued to stare at his computer screen.

"Chase thinks we should notify the police," Theo said.

"I sure do," Chase said. "Why not?"

"Let me think about it," Ike said as he pushed back his chair and jumped to his feet. He turned on his stereo and walked around the office. Finally, he said, "I don't like the idea of notifying the police, at least not right now. Here's what might happen. The police here would call the police in Chapel Hill, and we're not sure what they would do down there. They would probably go to the party and try and find April. This might be more difficult than you think. Let's assume it's a large party, with lots of students celebrating and drinking and other stuff and anything might happen when the police show up. The police might be smart; maybe they're not. Maybe they have no interest in a girl who's just hanging around while her father plays in a band. Maybe the girl doesn't want to be rescued by the police. A lot of things might happen, and most of them not good. There's no warrant out for the arrest of her father because the police here haven't charged him with anything. He's not a suspect, yet." Ike paced along behind his desk as the boys watched every move and hung on every word. "And without a positive identification, I'm not sure the police here would do anything in the first place."

He fell into his chair and stared at the photo. He frowned, pinched his nose, and rubbed his whiskers.

"I know it's her," Theo said.

"But what if it isn't, Theo?" Ike said gravely. "There's more than one Twins jacket in the world. You can't see her eyes. You know it's April because you really want it to be April. You're desperate for it to be April, but what if you're wrong? Let's say we go to the police right now, and they get excited and call their buddies down in Chapel Hill, who also get excited, and tonight they go to the party and (a) can't find the girl, or (b) find the girl and it's not April. We'd look pretty stupid, wouldn't we?"

There was a long heavy pause as the boys considered

how stupid they would look if they were wrong. Finally, Chase spoke. "Why don't we tell her mother? I'll bet she could identify her own daughter, then it's out of our hands."

"I don't think so," Ike said. "That woman's crazy and she might do anything. It's not in April's best interests to have her mother involved at this point. From what I hear, she's driving the police crazy and they're trying to avoid her."

Another long pause as all three looked at the walls. Theo said, "So what do we do, Ike?"

"The smartest thing to do is to go get the girl, bring her back, then call the police. And it has to be done by someone she trusts, someone like you, Theo."

Theo's jaw dropped, his mouth flew open, but no words came out.

"That's a long bike ride," Chase said.

"Tell your parents, Theo, and get them to drive you down there. You have to confront April, make sure she's okay, and bring her back. Immediately. There's no time to waste."

"My parents aren't here, Ike. They're in Briar Springs for the state bar convention and won't be back until tomorrow. I'm staying with Chase tonight."

Ike looked at Chase and asked, "Could your parents make the trip?"

Chase was already shaking his head. "No, I don't think

so. I can't see them getting involved in something like this. Besides, they're having dinner with some friends tonight and it's a big deal."

Theo looked at his uncle and saw in his eyes the unmistakable twinkle of a kid ready for an adventure. "Looks like you're the man, Ike," Theo said. "And, as you say, there's no time to waste."

# Chapter 17

The adventure immediately faced some serious problems. Theo thought about his parents and whether or not he should tell them. Ike thought about his car and knew it couldn't make the trip. Chase thought about the fact that Theo was supposed to spend the night at his house, and it seemed impossible that his absence would go unnoticed.

As for his parents, Theo did not like the idea of calling them and asking permission to take off to Chapel Hill. Ike thought this was a good plan—Chase was neutral— but Theo resisted. Such a call would ruin their trip, upset their speeches and seminars, and so on, and, besides, Theo figured his parents (especially his mother) would say no. Then he would be faced with the decision to obey, or not. Ike thought he could smooth things out and convince Woods and Marcella that the trip was urgent, but Theo wouldn't budge. He believed in being honest with his parents and he concealed little from them, but this was different. If they brought April back, then everyone, including his parents, would be so thrilled that Theo would likely avoid trouble.

Ike's car was a Triumph Spitfire, a notoriously unreliable old sports car with only two seats, a convertible roof that leaked, tires that were nearly bald, and an engine that made strange sounds. Theo loved the car but often wondered how it managed to putter around town. And, they needed four seats—Ike, Theo, Judge, and hopefully, April. His parents had left in his mother's car. His father's SUV was in the garage, ready to go. Ike decided he could borrow the vehicle from his own brother, especially in light of the importance of their mission.

The most serious problem would be Chase's. He would have to hide Theo's absence from the Whipple home throughout the night. They discussed the possibility of informing Chase's parents. Ike even volunteered to call them and explain what they were doing, but Theo thought it was a bad idea. Mrs. Whipple was a lawyer, too, and had plenty to say about almost everything, and there was no doubt in Theo's mind that she would immediately call his mother and ruin their plans. There was another reason Theo wanted Ike to stay quiet—Ike's reputation among lawyers was not good. Theo could easily imagine Mrs. Whipple freaking out at the thought of Ike Boone racing off with his nephew on some crazy road trip.

At 3:00 p.m., Theo texted his mother: *Still alive. With Chase. Hanging out. Luv.*

Theo expected no response because at that moment his mother was in the middle of her presentation.

At 3:15, Theo and Chase parked their bikes in the Whipple driveway and went inside. Mrs. Whipple was pulling a tray of brownies from the oven. She threw her arms around Theo, welcomed him to their home, said she was so happy to have him as a guest, and so on. She tended to be overly dramatic. Theo sat his red Nike overnight bag on the table, so she couldn't miss it.

As she served them brownies and milk, Chase said they were thinking about going to the movies, then maybe watching the volleyball game at Stratten College.

"Volleyball?" Mrs. Whipple asked.

"I love volleyball," Chase said. "The game starts at six

and should be over around eight. We'll be fine, Mom. It's just at the college."

In truth, the volleyball game was the only sports event on campus that evening. And girls' volleyball at that. Neither Chase nor Theo had ever watched a game, live or on TV.

"What's on at the movies?" she asked, still cutting brownies into squares.

"*Harry Potter,*" Theo said. "If we hustle now, we can catch most of it."

Chase chimed in, "And then we'll go to the game. Is that okay, Mom?"

"I suppose," she said.

"Are you and Dad still going out for dinner?"

"Yes, with the Coleys and the Shepherds."

"What time will you be home?" Chase asked, glancing at Theo.

"Oh, I don't know. Ten or ten thirty. Daphne will be here and she wants to order a pizza. Is that okay?"

"Sure," Chase said. With a little luck, Theo and Ike should be in Chapel Hill by 10:00 p.m. The tricky part would be avoiding Daphne from eight until ten. Chase didn't have a plan, but he was working on it.

They thanked her for the snack and said they were leaving for the Paramount, Strattenburg's old-fashioned movie house on Main Street. After they were gone, Mrs. Whipple carried Theo's overnight bag upstairs to Chase's room and placed it on a twin bed.

At 4:00 p.m., Theo, Ike, and Judge left the Boone home in the SUV. Chase was watching the latest Harry Potter, alone.

MapQuest estimated the travel time at seven hours if one obeyed all speed limits, which was the furthest thing from Ike's mind. As they hurried out of town, Ike said, "Are you nervous?"

"Yes, I'm nervous."

"And why are you nervous?"

"I guess I'm nervous about getting caught. If Mrs. Whipple finds out, then she'll call my mother and my mother will call me and I'm in big trouble."

"Why would you get in trouble, Theo? You're trying to help a friend."

"I'm being dishonest, Ike. Dishonest with the Whipples, dishonest with my parents."

"Look at the big picture, Theo. If all goes well, tomorrow morning we'll be back home with April. Your parents, and everyone else in town, will be thrilled to see her. Under the circumstances, this is the right thing to do. It might be a little misleading, but there's no other way to do it."

"It still makes me nervous."

"I'm your uncle, Theo. What's wrong with me and my favorite nephew taking a little road trip?"

"Nothing, I guess."

"Then stop worrying. The only thing that matters is finding April, and getting her back home. Nothing else is important right now. If it all blows up, I'll have a little chat with your parents and I'll take all the blame. Relax."

"Thanks, Ike."

They were racing down the highway in light traffic. Judge was already asleep on the backseat. Theo's phone vibrated. It was a text from Chase: *This movie is awesome. U guys OK?*

Theo responded: *Yep. OK.*

At 5:00 p.m., he texted his mother: *Harry Potter movie is awesome.*

A few minutes later she answered, *Great. Love Mom.*

They turned onto the expressway, and Ike set the cruise control on seventy-five, ten miles over the limit.

Theo said, "Explain something to me, Ike. The story about April has been all over the news, right?"

"Right."

"Then, wouldn't April or her father or one of the guys in the band see the story on the news and realize what's going on? Wouldn't they know about the big search for April?"

"You would think so. Unfortunately, though, there are a lot of missing children, seems like a new one every other day. And while it's big news around here, maybe it's not big news where they are. Who knows what her father has told his pals in the band. I'm sure they know the family is not too stable. Maybe he's told them that the mother is crazy and he was forced to rescue his daughter, and that he wants it kept quiet until some point in the future. The band members might be afraid to say anything. These guys are not too stable either. It's a bunch of forty-year-old men trying to be rock stars, up all night, sleeping all day, traveling around in a rented van, playing for peanuts in bars and frat houses. They're probably all running from something. I don't know, Theo, it makes no sense."

"I'll bet she's scared to death."

"Scared, and confused. A child deserves better than this."

"What if she doesn't want to leave her father?"

"If we find her, and she refuses to come with us, then we have no choice but to call the police in Strattenburg and tell them where she is. It's that simple."

Nothing seemed simple to Theo. "What if her father sees us and causes trouble?"

"Just relax, Theo. It'll work out."

It was dark at 6:30 when Chase texted again: *Vball girls r cute. Where R U?*

Theo answered: *Somewhere n Virginia. Ike's flying.*

It was dark now, and the hectic week finally caught up with Theo. He began to nod off, and then fell into a deep sleep.

# Chapter 18

L ate in the volleyball game, Chase realized that the only way to avoid Daphne was to avoid his house altogether. He could almost see her sitting in the family room in the basement, watching the big-screen TV, waiting for him and Theo to arrive so she could order an extra-large pizza from Santo's.

When the game was over, Chase rode his bike to Guff's Frozen Yogurt near the city library on Main Street. He ordered one scoop of banana, found an empty booth by the front window, and called home. Daphne answered after the first ring.

"It's me," he said. "And look, we have a problem. Theo

and I stopped by his house to check on his dog, and the dog is real sick. Must've eaten something weird. Throwing up, crapping all over the place; the house is a mess."

"Gross," Daphne gushed.

"You wouldn't believe. Dog poop from the kitchen to the bedroom. We're cleaning up now but it'll take some time. Theo's afraid the dog might be dying, and he's trying to get in touch with his mother."

"That's awful."

"Yep. We may have to take him to the vet emergency room. Poor thing can hardly move."

"Can I help, Chase? I can drive Mom's car over and get him."

"Maybe, but not right now. We gotta get this place cleaned up while we're watching the dog. I'm afraid he'd make a mess in her car."

"Have you guys eaten?"

"No, and food is the last thing we're thinking about right now. I'm about to throw up myself. Go ahead and order the pizza. I'll check in later." Chase hung up and smiled at his frozen yogurt. So far so good.

Judge was still asleep on the rear seat, snoring softly as the miles flew by. Theo came and went, napping occasionally, wide-eyed one moment and dead to the world the next. He was awake when they crossed the state line into North Carolina, but he was asleep when they rolled into Chapel Hill.

His 9:00 p.m. text to his mother read: *Going to sleep. Real tired. Luv.*

He assumed his parents were in the middle of their long dinner, probably listening to endless speeches, and that his mother would not have the chance to reply. He was right.

"Wake up, Theo," Ike said. "We're here." They had not stopped in six hours. The digital clock on the dash gave the time at 10:05. The GPS above it took them straight to Franklin Street, the main drag that bordered the campus. The sidewalks were packed with noisy students and fans. UNC had won the football game in overtime and the mood was rowdy. The bars and shops were crowded. Ike turned onto Columbia Street and they passed some large fraternity houses.

"Parking might be a problem," Ike mumbled, almost to himself. "That must be Frat Court," he said, glancing at the GPS and pointing to an area where several fraternity houses faced each other with parking lots in the center. "I'd guess the Kappa Theta house is somewhere in there."

Theo lowered his window as they eased by in heavy

traffic. Loud music filled the air as several bands played from the houses. People were shoulder-to-shoulder, on the porches, on the lawns, sitting on cars, hanging out, dancing, laughing, moving in packs from house to house, yelling at each other. It was a wild scene, and Theo had never seen anything like it. There was an occasional fight or drug bust at Stratten College, but nothing like this. It was exciting at first, but then Theo thought about April. She was somewhere in the midst of this huge carnival, and she did not belong here. She was shy and quiet and preferred to be alone with her drawings and paintings.

Ike turned onto another street, then another. "We'll have to park somewhere and hike in." Cars were parked everywhere, most illegally. They found a spot on a dark narrow street, far away from the noise. "Stay here, Judge," Theo said, and Judge watched them walk away.

"What's the game plan, Ike?" Theo asked. They were walking quickly along a dark and uneven sidewalk.

"Watch your step," Ike said. "We don't have a game plan. Let's find the house, find the band, and I'll think of something." They followed the noise and were soon entering Frat Court from the back side, away from the street. They moved into the crowd, and if they looked a bit odd, no one seemed to notice—a sixty-two-year-old man with long, gray hair pulled into a ponytail, red socks, sandals, a brown plaid sweater that was at least thirty years old, and a thirteen-year-old kid wide-eyed in amazement.

The Kappa Theta house was a large, white stone structure with some Greek columns and a sweeping porch. Ike and Theo made their way through a thick crowd, up the steps, and around the porch. Ike wanted to scope out the place, check out the entrances and exits, and try to determine where the band was playing. The music was loud, the laughter and yelling even louder. Theo had never seen so many cans of beer in his young life. Girls were dancing on the porch as their dates watched them and smoked cigarettes. Ike asked one of the girls, "Where's the band?"

"In the basement," she said.

They inched their way back to the front steps and looked around. The front door was being guarded by a large young man in a suit who seemed to have the authority to decide who got inside.

"Let's go," Ike said. Theo followed him as they moved toward the front door with a group of students. They almost made it. The guard, or bouncer, or whatever he was, threw out his arm and grabbed Ike by the forearm. "Excuse me!" he said rudely. "You got a pass?"

Ike angrily yanked his arm away and looked as though he might slug the guy. "I don't need a pass, kid," he hissed.

"I'm the manager of the band. This is my son. Don't touch me again."

The other students moved back a few steps and for a moment things were quieter.

"Sorry, sir," the guard said, and Ike and Theo marched inside. Ike was moving quickly, as though he knew the house well and had business there. They walked through a large foyer, then a parlor of some sort, both rooms crowded with students. In another open space, a mob of male students was yelling at a football game on a huge screen, two kegs of beer close by. The music was booming from below, and they soon found a large stairway that gave way to the party room. The dance floor was in the center, packed with students engaged in all manner of frenzied jerking and shuffling, and to the left was Plunder, pounding and screeching at full volume. Ike and Theo drifted down in a throng of people, and by the time they left the stairs, Theo felt like his ears were bleeding from the music.

They tried to hide in a corner. The room was dark, with colored strobe lights flickering across the mass of bodies. Ike leaned down and yelled into Theo's ear. "Let's be quick. I'll stay here. You try and get behind the band and have a look. Hurry."

Theo ducked low and wiggled around bodies. He got bumped, shoved, almost stepped on, but he kept moving along the wall on the far left side. The band finished a song, everybody cheered, and for a moment the dancing stopped. He moved faster, still low, his eyes darting in all directions. Suddenly, the lead singer screamed, then began howling. The drummer attacked and a guitarist lurched in with some thunderous chords. The next song was even louder. Theo passed a set of large speakers, came within five feet of the keyboardist, and then saw April, sitting on a metal box behind the drummer. She had the only safe place in the entire room. He practically crawled around the edge of the small platform and touched her knee before she saw him.

April was too shocked to move, then both hands flew up to her mouth. "Theo!" she said, but he could barely hear her. "Let's go!" he demanded.

"What are you doing here?" she yelled.

"I'm here to take you home."

At 10:30, Chase was hiding beside a dry cleaners, watching from across the street as people were leaving Robilio's Italian Bistro. He saw Mr. and Mrs. Shepherd, then Mr. and Mrs. Coley, then his parents. He watched them drive away, and then wondered what to do next. His phone would ring in a few minutes, and his mother would have a dozen questions. The sick dog routine was about to come to an end.

# Chapter 19

Theo and April inched along the wall, sidestepping weary dancers taking a break from the action, and moved quickly through the semidarkness to a door that opened onto a stairway. There was no chance her father would see them, because he was lost in Plunder's intense version of the Rolling Stones' "I Can't Get No Satisfaction."

"Where are we going?" Theo yelled at April.

"This leads outside," she yelled back.

"Wait! I gotta get Ike."

"Who?"

Theo darted through the crowd, found Ike where he'd left him, and the three made a quick exit down the stairs and onto a small patio behind the Kappa Theta house. The music could still be heard and the walls seemed to vibrate, but things were much quieter outside.

"Ike, this is April," Theo said. "April, this is Ike, my uncle."

"My pleasure," Ike said. April was still too confused to respond. They were alone, in the dark, beside a broken picnic table. Other patio furniture was strewn about. Windows on the back side of the house were broken.

Theo said, "Ike drove me down here to get you."

"But why?" she asked.

"What do you mean, 'Why'?" Theo shot back.

Ike understood her confusion. He took a step forward and gently placed a hand on her shoulder. "April, back home no one knows where you are. No one knows if you're dead or alive. Four days ago you vanished without a trace. No one—including your mother, the police, your friends—has heard a word from you."

April began shaking her head in disbelief.

Ike continued: "I suspect your father has been lying to you. He's probably told you that he's talked to your mother and everything is okay back home, right?"

April nodded slightly.

"He's lying, April. Your mother is worried sick. The

entire town has been searching for you. It's time to go home, now."

"But we were going home in just a few days," she said.

"According to your father?" Ike said, patting her shoulder. "There's a good chance he will face criminal charges for your abduction. April, look at me." Ike placed a finger under her chin and slowly lifted it so that she had no choice but to look at him. "It's time to go home. Let's get in the car and leave. Now."

The door opened and a man appeared. With biker boots, tattoos, and greasy hair, he was obviously not a student. "What are you doing, April?" he demanded.

"Just taking a break," she said.

He stepped closer and asked, "Who are these guys?"

"Who are you?" Ike demanded. Plunder was in the middle of a song, so he obviously wasn't a member of the band.

"He's Zack," April said. "He works for the band."

Immediately, Ike saw the danger and came through with some fiction. He reached out with a big handshake and said, "I'm Jack Ford, my son Max, here. We used to live in Strattenburg, now we're in Chapel Hill. Max and April started kindergarten together. Quite a band you got in there."

Zack shook hands. He was too slow to put together his

thoughts. He frowned, as if thinking caused pain, then he gave Ike and Theo a puzzled look. April said, "We're almost finished. I'll be just a minute."

"Does your dad know these guys?" Zack asked.

"Oh sure," Ike said. "Tom and I go back many years. I'd like to talk to him during the next break, if you could pass that along, Zack."

"Okay, I guess," Zack said, and went inside.

"Will he tell your father?" Ike asked.

"Probably," she said.

"Then we should leave, April."

"I don't know."

"Come on, April," Theo said firmly.

"Do you trust Theo?" Ike asked.

"Of course."

"Then you can trust Ike," Theo said. "Let's go."

Theo grabbed her hand and they began walking quickly away from the Kappa Theta house, from Frat Court, and from Tom Finnemore.

April sat in the backseat with Judge and rubbed his head as Ike zigzagged his way out of Chapel Hill. Nothing was said for a few minutes, then Theo asked, "Should we call Chase?"

"Yes," Ike said. They pulled into an all-night gas station

and parked away from the pumps. "Dial him," Ike said. Theo did so and handed the phone to Ike.

Chase answered his cell phone immediately with, "It's about time."

"Chase, this is Ike. We have April and we're headed back. Where are you?"

"Hiding in my backyard. My parents are ready to kill me."

"Go in the house and tell them the truth. I'll call them in about ten minutes."

"Thanks, Ike."

Ike handed the phone to Theo and asked, "Which of your parents is more likely to answer their cell phone at this time of the night?"

"My mom."

"Then get her on the phone." Theo punched the number and handed it back to Ike.

Mrs. Boone answered with a nervous, "Theo. What's the matter?"

Ike calmly said, "Marcella, this is Ike. How are you doing?"

"Ike? On Theo's phone? Why am I suddenly worried?"

"It's a very long story, Marcella, but no one is hurt. Everybody's fine, and there's a happy ending."

"Please, Ike. What's going on?"

"We have April."

"You what?"

"We have April and we're driving back to Strattenburg."

"Where are you, Ike?"

"Chapel Hill, North Carolina."

"Keep talking."

"Theo found her, and we took a little road trip to get her. She's been with her father the entire time, sort of hanging out."

"Theo found April in Chapel Hill?" Mrs. Boone repeated slowly.

"Yep. Again, it's a long story and we'll fill in the details later. We'll be home early in the morning, I'd guess between six and seven. That is, if I can stay awake all night and drive."

"Does her mother know?"

"Not yet. I was thinking that she should call her mom, tell her what's up."

"Yes, Ike, and the sooner the better. We'll check out now and drive home. We'll be there when you get there."

"Great, Marcella. And, I'm sure we'll be starving."

"Got it, Ike."

They passed the phone back and forth again, and Ike spoke to Mr. Whipple. He explained the situation, assured him everything was fine, heaped praise on Chase for helping find April, apologized for the deception and confusion, and promised to check in later.

Ike pulled over to the pumps, filled the tank, and when he went inside to pay, Theo took Judge for a quick walk. When they were on the road again, Ike said over his shoulder, "April, do you want to call your mother?"

"I guess," she said.

Theo handed her his cell phone. She tried her house, but there was no answer. She tried her mother's mobile, and there was no service.

"What a surprise," April said. "She's not there."

ke had a tall cup of coffee, which he gulped down in an effort to stay awake. Just a few miles out of town, he said, "Okay, kids, here's the deal. It's midnight. We have a long way to go, and I'm already sleepy. Talk to me. I want chatter. If I fall asleep at the wheel, we all die. Understand? Go, Theo. You talk, then, April, it's your turn."

Theo turned and looked at April. "Who is Jack Leeper?"

April had Judge's head in her lap. She answered, "A distant cousin, I think. Why? Who told you about him?"

"He's in Strattenburg, in jail. He escaped from prison in California a week or so ago, and he showed up in town about the time you disappeared."

"His face has been all over the newspapers," Ike said.

"The police thought he snatched you and took off," Theo added.

Back and forth they went, tag-teaming as they told Leeper's story; his mug shots on the front page, his dramatic capture by the SWAT team, his vague threats about hiding April's body, and so on. April, who was overwhelmed by the events of the past hour, seemed unable to digest the entire story. "I've never met him," she mumbled softly, over and over.

Ike slurped his coffee and said, "The newspaper said you wrote him letters. You guys were pen pals. That right?"

"Yes. About a year ago we started writing," she said. "My mother said we are distant cousins, though I could never find him in our family tree. It's not your normal family tree. Anyway, she said he was serving a long sentence in California, and was looking for a pen pal. I wrote him, he wrote back. It was kind of fun. He seemed to be very lonely."

Ike said, "They found your letters in his cell after he escaped. He showed up in Strattenburg, so the police assumed he came after you."

"I can't believe this," she said. "My father told me he talked to my mom, and that he talked to the people at the school, and that everyone agreed that I would be gone for a week or so. No problem. I should've known better."

"Your father must be a pretty good liar," Ike said.

"He's one of the best," April said. "He's never told me the truth. I don't know why I believed him this time."

"You were scared, April," Theo said.

"Omigosh!" she said. "It's midnight. The band is quitting. What will he do when he realizes I'm gone?"

"He'll get a dose of his own medicine," Ike said.

"Should we call him?" Theo asked.

"He doesn't use a cell phone," April said. "Says it makes it too easy for people to find him. I should've left a note or something."

They thought about this for a few miles. Ike seemed refreshed and not at all sleepy. April's voice was stronger and she was over the shock.

"What about that Zack creep?" Theo asked. "Could we call him?"

"I don't know his number."

"What's his last name?" Ike asked.

"I don't know that either. I tried to keep my distance from Zack."

Another mile or two passed. Ike knocked back some coffee and said, "Here's what'll happen. When they can't find you, Zack will replay the story of seeing you with us.

He'll try and remember our names—Jack and Max Ford, formerly of Strattenburg but now living in Chapel Hill—and if he can, then they'll scramble around trying to find our phone number. When they can't find us, they'll assume you're at our house. Just old friends catching up after all these years."

"That's a stretch," April said.

"It's the best I can do."

"I should've left a note."

"Are you really that worried about your father?" Theo asked. "Look at what this guy did. He took you away in the middle of the night, didn't tell a single person, and for the past four days, the entire town has been worried sick. Your poor mother is out of her mind. I don't have much sympathy for him, April."

"I've never liked him," she said. "But I should've left a note."

"Too late," Ike said.

"They found a body on Thursday," Theo said, "and the whole town thought you were dead."

"A body?" she said.

Ike looked at Theo, and Theo looked at Ike, and away they went. Theo began with the story about their search party roaming through Strattenburg, passing out flyers, offering a reward, poking around empty buildings, dodging the police, and, finally, watching from across the river as the police pulled someone from the Yancey River. Ike added a few details here and there.

Theo said, "We thought you were dead, April. Left floating in the river by Jack Leeper. Mrs. Gladwell called us into assembly to try and cheer us up, but we knew you were dead."

"I'm so sorry."

"It's not your fault," Ike said. "Blame your father."

Theo turned around, looked at her, and said, "It's really good to see you, April."

Ike smiled to himself. His coffee cup was empty. They left North Carolina, crossed into Virginia, and Ike stopped for more coffee.

A few minutes after 2:00 a.m., Ike's cell phone vibrated. He fished it out of a pocket and said hello. It was his brother, Woods Boone, calling to chat. He and Mrs. Boone had just arrived home in Strattenburg, and they wanted an update on the road trip. Both kids were asleep, as was the dog, and Ike spoke softly. They were making good time; there was no traffic, no weather, and so far, no radar. Not surprisingly, Theo's parents were extremely curious about how he found April. Marcella picked up on another phone, and Ike told the story of Theo and Chase Whipple playing detectives, tracking down the band—with a bit of Ike's help—then randomly poring over thousands of Facebook photos until they got lucky. Once they confirmed the band was in the area, they started calling fraternities and sororities, and got lucky again.

Ike assured them April was fine. He relayed her version of all the lies her father had told her.

Theo's parents were still in disbelief, but also amused. And they were not really surprised that Theo had not only found April, but went to get her.

When the conversation was over, Ike shifted his weight, tried to stretch his right leg, wiggled here and there in his seat, and then, suddenly, almost fell asleep. "That's it!" he yelled. "Wake up, you two!" He punched Theo on the left shoulder, ruffled his hair, and said at high volume, "I almost ran off the road. You guys want to die? No! Theo, wake up and talk to me. April, it's your turn. Tell us a story."

April was rubbing her eyes, trying to wake up and understand why this crazy man was yelling at them. Even Judge looked confused.

At that moment, Ike hit the brakes and came to an abrupt stop on the shoulder of the road. He jumped out of the SUV and jogged around it three times. An 18-wheeler honked as it roared by. Ike got in, yanked his seat belt into place, then took off.

"April," he said loudly, "talk to me. I want to know exactly what happened when you left with your father."

"Sure, Ike," she said, afraid not to tell the story. "I was asleep," she began.

"Tuesday night or Wednesday morning?" Ike asked. "What time was it?"

"I don't know. It was after midnight because I was still awake at midnight. Then I fell asleep."

"Your mother was not there?" Theo asked.

"No, she was not. I talked to you on the phone, waited and waited for her to come home, then fell asleep. Someone was banging on my door. At first I thought it was a dream, another nightmare, but then I realized it wasn't, and this was even more terrifying. Someone was in the house, a man, banging on my door and calling my name. I was so scared I couldn't think, I couldn't see, I couldn't move. Then I realized it was my father. He was home, for the first time in a week. I opened the door. He asked where my mother was. I said I didn't know. She had not been home the last two or three nights. He started cursing, and he told me to change clothes. We were leaving. Hurry up. And so we left. As we drove away, I thought to myself—Leaving is better than staying. I'd rather be in the car with my father than in the house all alone."

She paused for a second. Ike was wide awake, as was Theo. Both wanted to look back and see if she was crying, but they did not.

"We drove for awhile, maybe two hours. I think we were close to D.C. when we stopped at a motel next to the interstate. We spent the night there, in the same room. When I woke up, he was gone. I waited. He came back with Egg McMuffins and orange juice. While we were eating, he told me he had found my mother, had a long talk with her, and she had agreed that it would be better for me if I stayed with him for a few days, maybe a week, maybe longer. She admitted, according to him, that she was having some problems and needed help. He told me that he had spoken to the principal at the school and she had agreed it would be wise if I stayed away from home. She would help me get extra tutoring if I needed it when I returned. I asked him the name of the principal, and, of course, he didn't know it. I remember thinking how odd, but then it would not be unusual for my father to forget someone's name ten seconds after a conversation with her."

Theo glanced back. April was gazing out the side window, seeing nothing, just chatting pleasantly with an odd smile on her face.

"We left that motel and drove to Charlottesville,

Virginia. The band played that night—Wednesday, I guess it was—at a place called Miller's. It's an old bar that's now famous because it's where the Dave Matthews Band got its start."

"I love that band," Theo said.

"They're okay," Ike said, a wiser voice from an older generation.

"My father thought it was so cool playing at Miller's."

"How'd you get in the bar when you're thirteen years old?" Theo asked.

"I don't know. I was with the band. It's not like I was drinking and smoking. The next day we drove to another town, maybe it was Roanoke, where the band played to an empty house in an old music hall. What day was that?"

"Thursday," Ike said.

"Then we drove to Raleigh."

"Were you in the van with the band?" Ike asked.

"No. My father had his car, as did two other guys. We always followed the van. Zack was the driver and the roadie. My father kept me away from the other band members. These guys fight and bicker worse than a bunch of little kids."

"And drugs?" Ike asked.

"Yes, and drinking, and girls. It's silly and kinda sad to

watch forty-year-old men trying to act cool in front of a bunch of college girls. But not my father. He was by far the best behaved."

"That's because you were around," Ike said.

"I suppose."

"How about a pit stop, Ike?" Theo said, pointing to a busy exit ahead.

"Sure. I need some more coffee."

"Where are we going when we get to Strattenburg?" April asked.

"Where do you want to go?" Ike asked.

"I'm not sure I want to go to my house," she said.

"Let's go to Theo's. His mother is trying to find your mother. I suspect she'll be there, and she'll be thrilled to see you."

# Chapter 21

There were some additional cars in the Boone driveway when Ike rolled up at ten minutes after 6:00 a.m. on Sunday morning. His old Spitfire was right where he'd left it. Beside it was a black sedan, very official looking. And behind the Spitfire was the strangest car in town—a bright-yellow hearse once owned by a funeral home but now the property of May Finnemore.

"She's here," April said. Neither Ike nor Theo could tell if this pleased her or not.

It was still dark when they parked. Judge leaped from the vehicle and ran to the holly bushes beside the porch, his favorite place to relieve himself. The front door flew open, and May Finnemore came sprinting out, already crying and reaching for her daughter. They embraced in the front yard for a long time, and as they did so, Ike, Theo, and Judge eased inside. Theo got hugged by his mother, then said hello to Detective Slater, who'd obviously been invited to join the party. After all the greetings and congratulations, Theo asked his mother, "Where did you find Mrs. Finnemore?"

"She was at a neighbor's house," Detective Slater said. "I knew about it. She's been too afraid to stay at home."

What about leaving April home alone, Theo almost blurted.

"Any word from Tom Finnemore?" Ike asked. "We left in a hurry and did not leave a note."

"Nothing," replied the detective.

"No surprise there."

"You must be exhausted," Mrs. Boone said.

Ike smiled and said, "Well, as a matter of fact, the answer is yes. And quite hungry. Theo and I have just spent the past fourteen hours on the road, with little to eat and no sleep, at least for me. Theo and April managed to nap a bit. The dog, though, slept for hours. What's for breakfast?"

"Everything," Mrs. Boone said.

"How'd you find her, Theo?" Mr. Boone asked, unable to conceal his pride.

"It's a long story, Dad, and I gotta use the restroom first." Theo disappeared and the front door opened. Mrs.

Finnemore and April entered, both in tears, both smiling. Mrs. Boone could not restrain herself and gave April a long hug. "We're so happy you're back," she said.

Detective Slater introduced himself to April, who was exhausted and unsettled and a little embarrassed by all the attention. "It's great to see you, kid," Slater said.

"Thank you," April said softly.

"Look, we can talk later," the detective said as he faced Mrs. Finnemore. "But I need to spend about five minutes with her right now."

"Can't this wait?" demanded Mrs. Boone, taking a step closer to April.

"Of course it can, Mrs. Boone. Except for one small matter that I need to explore now. After that, I'll get out of here and leave you alone."

"No one is asking you to leave, Detective," Mr. Boone said.

"I understand. Just give me five minutes."

Theo returned, and the Boones left the den and headed for the kitchen, where the thick smell of sausage hung in the air. Mrs. Finnemore and April sat on the sofa and the detective pulled a chair close.

He spoke in a low voice. "April, we're thrilled that you're back home, safe and sound. We're looking at the possibility of kidnapping charges. I've discussed it with your mother, and I need to ask you a couple of questions."

"Okay," she said timidly.

"First, when you left with your father, did you agree to do so? Did he force you to leave?"

April looked confused. She glanced at her mother, but her mother was staring at her boots.

Slater continued: "Kidnapping requires evidence that the victim was forced to leave against her will."

April slowly shook her head and said, "I was not forced to leave. I wanted to leave. I was very frightened."

Slater took a deep breath and looked at May, who was still avoiding all eye contact. "All right," he said. "The second question—Were you held against your will? Did you want to leave at any time, but were told you could not do so? With kidnapping, there are rare cases where a victim went away without objection, without force, sort of voluntarily, but then as time passed the victim changed her mind and wanted to go home. But her captor refused. At that point, it became a kidnapping. Is this what happened?"

April crossed her arms over her chest, gritted her teeth, and said, "No. That did not happen to me. My father was lying the whole time. He convinced me that he was in contact with my mother, that things were all right here, and that we would come home. Eventually. He never said when, but it would not be long. I never thought about running away, but I certainly could have. I wasn't guarded or locked up."

Another deep breath by the detective as his case continued to slip away. "One last question," he said. "Were you harmed in any way?"

"By my father? No. He might be a liar and a creep and a lousy father, but he would never harm me, nor would he let anyone else. I never felt threatened. I felt alone, and scared and confused, but that's not unusual for me even here in Strattenburg."

"April," Mrs. Finnemore said softly.

Detective Slater stood and said, "This will not be a criminal matter. It should be dealt with in the civil courts." He walked into the kitchen, thanked all the Boones there, and left. After he was gone, April and her mother joined the Boones around the kitchen table for a hearty breakfast of sausage, pancakes, and scrambled eggs. After the plates were served, the food properly blessed, and everyone had taken a bite or two, Ike said, "Slater couldn't wait to get out of here because he's too embarrassed. The police spent four days playing games with Leeper, and Theo solved the case in about two hours."

"How'd you do it, Theo?" his father demanded. "And I want the details."

"Let's hear it," his mother piped in.

Theo swallowed some eggs and looked around the table. Everyone was looking at him. He smiled, at first a nasty little grin, then a full-blown, ear-to-ear blast of orthodontic metal that was instantly contagious. April, already beyond braces, flashed a beautiful smile.

Unable to suppress it, Theo started laughing.

Detective Slater drove straight to the jail where he met Detective Capshaw. Together they waited in a small holding room while Jack Leeper was startled from his sleep, handcuffed, and practically dragged down the hall in his orange jumpsuit and orange rubber shower shoes. Two deputies hauled him into the holding room and sat him down in a metal chair. The handcuffs were not removed.

Leeper, his eyes still swollen and his face unshaven, looked at Slater and Capshaw and said, "Good morning. You boys are up mighty early."

"Where's the girl, Leeper?" Slater growled.

"Well, well, so you're back. You boys ready to make a deal this time?"

"Yep. We got a deal, a really good deal for you, Leeper.

But first you gotta tell us how far away the girl is. Just give us some idea. Five miles, fifty, five hundred?"

Leeper smiled at this. He rubbed his beard on his sleeve, grinned, and said, "She's about a hundred miles away."

Slater and Capshaw laughed.

"I say something funny?"

"You're such a lying scumbag, Leeper," Slater said. "I guess you'll lie all the way to your grave."

Capshaw took a step forward and said, "The girl's home with her momma, Leeper. Seems she took off with her father and spent a few days on the run. Now she's back, safe and sound. Thank God she never met you."

"You want a deal, Leeper?" Slater said. "Here's your deal. We're dropping all charges here, and we're gonna speed up your shipment back to California. We've talked to the authorities there and they've got a special place for you, as an escapee. Maximum security. You'll never see daylight."

Leeper's mouth opened but no words came out.

Slater said to the deputies, "Take him back." Then he and Capshaw left the room.

At 9:00 a.m., Sunday morning, the Strattenburg Police Department issued a statement to the press. It read: "At approximately six o'clock this morning, April Finnemore returned to Strattenburg and was reunited with her mother. She is safe, healthy, in good spirits, and was not harmed in any way. We are continuing our investigation into this matter and will interrogate her father, Tom Finnemore, as soon as possible."

The news was instantly broadcast on television and radio. It roared through the Internet. At dozens of churches, announcements were made to applause and thanksgiving.

The entire town took a deep breath, smiled, and thanked God for a miracle.

April missed it all. She was sound asleep in a small bedroom where the Boones sometimes kept their guests. She did not want to go home, at least not for a few hours. A neighbor called May Finnemore and relayed the news that their home was under siege from reporters, and said it would be wise to stay away until the mob left. Woods Boone suggested that she park her ridiculous vehicle in their garage; otherwise, someone would likely see it and know precisely where April was hiding.

Theo and Judge took a long nap in their upstairs bedroom.

# Chapter 22

When the students at Strattenburg Middle School returned to class on Monday morning, they expected a little excitement. This would not be a typical Monday. A dark cloud had hung over the school since April's disappearance, and now it was gone. Just a few days earlier everyone presumed her dead. Now she was back, and not only had she been found, she'd been rescued by one of their own. Theo's daring mission to Chapel Hill to pluck her from her father's captivity was quickly becoming a legend.

The arriving students were not disappointed. Before daybreak, half a dozen television vans were parked haphazardly around the wide, circular drive at the entrance of the school. Reporters were all over the place, with photographers waiting for a glimpse of something. This upset Mrs. Gladwell, and she called the police. A confrontation took place; angry words were exchanged; arrests were threatened. The police eventually moved the mob off school property, so the cameras were set up across the street. As this was happening, the buses began arriving and the students witnessed some of the conflict.

The bell rang at 8:15 for homeroom, but there was no sign of Theo and April. In Mr. Mount's room, Chase Whipple briefed the class on his participation in the search and rescue, which was received with rapt attention. On his Facebook page, Theo had posted a short version of what happened, and he gave plenty of credit to Chase.

At 8:30, Mrs. Gladwell again called all eighth graders to assembly. As they filed in, the mood was in stark contrast to the last gathering. Now the kids were lighthearted, laughing, and anxious to see April and forget this experience. Theo and April sneaked into the rear of the school, met Mr. Mount near the cafeteria, and hustled to assembly where they were mobbed by their classmates and hugged by their teachers.

April was anxious and obviously uncomfortable with the attention.

For Theo, though, it was his finest hour.

———

Later that morning, Marcella Boone appeared in Family Court to file a petition asking for the appointment of a temporary legal guardian for April Finnemore. Such a petition could be filed by any person concerned about the safety and well-being of any child. There was no requirement that notice be given to the child or to its parents when the petition was filed, but a temporary guardian would not be appointed unless good cause was shown to the court.

The judge was a large old man with a head full of curly white hair and a white beard and round, rosy cheeks that reminded a lot of people of Santa Claus. His name was Judge Jolly. In spite of his name, he was pious and strict, and because of this, and because of his appearance, he was known, behind his back all over town, as St. Nick.

He reviewed the petition while sitting on the bench, then asked Mrs. Boone, "Any sign of Tom Finnemore?"

Mrs. Boone had spent most of her career in Family Court, and knew St. Nick extremely well. She said, "I have been told that he called his wife last night and they talked for the first time in weeks. Supposedly, he will return home this afternoon."

"And no criminal charges are expected?"

"The police are treating this as a civil matter, not a criminal one."

"Do you have a recommendation as to who I should appoint as temporary guardian?"

"I do."

"Who?"

"Me."

"You're asking to be appointed?"

"That's correct, Your Honor. I know this situation very well. I know this child, her mother, and, to a much lesser extent, her father. I'm very concerned about what will happen to April, and I'm willing to serve as her temporary guardian for no fee."

"That's a good deal for everyone, Mrs. Boone," St. Nick said with a rare smile. "You are hereby appointed. What's your plan?"

"I would like to have an immediate hearing before this Court as soon as possible to determine where April should live for the next few days."

"Granted. When?"

"As soon as possible, Your Honor. If Mr. Finnemore returns today, I'll make sure he is immediately notified of the hearing."

"How about 9:00 a.m. tomorrow?"

"Perfect."

Tom Finnemore arrived home late Monday afternoon. Plunder's tour was over, and so was the band itself. The members had quarreled almost nonstop for two weeks, and they made little money. And they felt as though Tom had dragged them into his family mess by snatching his daughter and keeping her with him. April was just one of the many things they had fought over. Their biggest problem was that they were all middle-aged now, and too old to be playing for peanuts in frat houses and beer halls.

At home, Tom was met by his wife, who said little, and his daughter, who said even less. The women were united in their opposition to his presence, but Tom was too tired to fight. He went to the basement and locked the door. An hour later, a deputy arrived and handed him a summons to court. First thing in the morning.

# Chapter 23

After a few hours of tense negotiations, it was finally decided that Theo could skip school Tuesday morning and go to court. At first his parents said no way, but it became apparent that Theo was not about to back down. April was his friend. He knew a lot about her family. He had indeed rescued her, something he reminded his parents of several times. She might need his support, and so on. Mr. and Mrs. Boone finally got tired of arguing and said yes. But his father warned him about his homework, and his mother warned him that he would not be allowed inside the courtroom. In Family Court, matters dealing with children were always handled behind locked doors.

Theo thought he knew a way around this, and he had

a backup plan in the event St. Nick tossed him out of the courtroom.

The tossing happened rather fast.

In Family Court, all issues were decided by the judges, either St. Nick or Judge Judy Ping. (Ping-Pong as she was known, again behind her back. Most of the judges in the Stratten County Courthouse had a nickname or two.) There were no juries, and very few spectators. Therefore, the two courtrooms used for divorce trials, child custody disputes, adoptions, and dozens of other cases were much smaller than the courtrooms where juries were used and crowds gathered. And it was not unusual for the atmosphere to be tense when Family Court was called to order.

It was indeed tense on Tuesday morning. Theo and Mrs. Boone arrived early, and she allowed him to sit at her table as they waited. She pored over documents while Theo caught up on important matters with his laptop. The three Finnemores entered together. Mr. Gooch, one of an army of old semi-retired deputies who killed time in court as uniformed bailiffs, directed Tom Finnemore to his table on the left side of the room. May Finnemore was sent to hers on the right side of the room. April sat with Mrs. Boone in the center, directly in front of the judge's bench.

Theo thought it was a good sign that the family had arrived together. He would find out later that April rode her bike; her mother drove her yellow hearse, minus the monkey; and her father walked, for the exercise. They met at the front door of the courthouse and came in together.

Down the hall in Criminal Court, Judge Henry Gantry preferred the traditional, somewhat dramatic entry in which the bailiff makes everyone jump to their feet while he barks out, "All rise for the Court!" and so on, as the judge enters with his black robe flowing behind him. Theo preferred this, too, if only for the showmanship. There was an excellent chance he would one day become a great judge, much like Henry Gantry, and he certainly planned to stick to the more formal opening of court.

In what other job can an entire room of people, regardless of their age, job, or education, be required to stand in solemn respect as you enter the room? Theo could think of only three—queen of England, president of the United States, and judge.

St. Nick cared little for formalities. He walked in through a side door, followed by the clerk. He stepped up to the bench, took his seat in a battered leather rocker, and looked around the room. "Good morning," he said gruffly. There were a few mumbled replies.

"Tom Finnemore, I presume?" he asked, looking at April's father.

Mr. Finnemore stood nonchalantly and said, "That's me."

"Welcome home."

"Do I need a lawyer?"

"Keep your seat, sir. No, you do not need a lawyer. Maybe later." Mr. Finnemore sat down with a smirk. Theo looked at him and tried to remember him from the frenzy of the frat party last Saturday night. He was the band's drummer and had been partially hidden by the tools of his trade. He sort of looked familiar, but then Theo had not had the time to examine Plunder. Tom Finnemore was a nice-looking man, respectable in some ways. He was wearing cowboy boots and jeans, but his sports coat was stylish.

"And you are May Finnemore?" St. Nick asked, nodding to the right.

"Yes, sir."

"And Mrs. Boone, you are with April?"

"Yes, sir."

St. Nick glared down at Theo for a few seconds, then said, "Theo, what are you doing here?"

"April asked me to be here."

"Oh, she did? Are you a witness?"

"I could be."

St. Nick managed a smile. His reading glasses were perched far down at the end of his nose, and when he smiled, which didn't happen often, his eyes twinkled and he did in fact resemble Santa Claus. "You could also be a lawyer, a bailiff, or a clerk, couldn't you, Theo?"

"I suppose."

"You could also be the judge and decide this matter, couldn't you?"

"Probably."

"Mrs. Boone, is there any legitimate reason for your son to be in this courtroom during this hearing?"

"Not really," Mrs. Boone said.

"Theo, go to school."

The bailiff stepped toward Theo and gently waved an arm toward the door. Theo grabbed his backpack and said, "Thanks, Mom." He whispered to April, "See you at school," and then took off.

However, he had no plans to go to school. He left his backpack on a bench outside the courtroom, ran downstairs to the snack bar, bought a large root beer in a paper cup, ran back up the stairs, and, when no one was looking, dropped the drink onto the shiny marble floor. Ice and root beer splashed and ran into a wide circle. Theo did not slow down. He jogged down the hall, past Family Court, around a corner to a small room that served as a utility closet, storage area, and napping place of Mr. Speedy Cobb, the oldest and slowest janitor in the history of Stratten County. As expected, Speedy was resting, catching a quick nap before the rigors of the day kicked in.

"Speedy, I dropped a drink down the hall. It's a mess!" Theo said urgently.

"Hello, Theo. What are you doing here?" The same question every time he saw Theo. Speedy was getting to his feet, grabbing a mop.

"Just hanging out. I'm really sorry about this," Theo said.

With a mop and a bucket, Speedy eventually made it down the hall. He scratched his chin and inspected the spill as if the operation would take hours and require great skill. Theo watched him for a few seconds, and then retreated to Speedy's little room. The cramped and dirty place where Speedy napped was next to a slightly larger room where supplies were stored. Quickly, Theo climbed up the shelves, passing rows of paper towels, toilet paper, and sanitizer. Above the top shelf was a crawl space, dark and narrow with an air vent to one side. Below the air vent, some fifteen feet away, was the desk of St. Nick himself. From his secret cubbyhole, known only to himself, Theo could see nothing.

But he could hear every word.

## Chapter 24

St. Nick was saying, "The issue before this Court is the temporary placement of April Finnemore. Not legal custody, but placement. I have a preliminary report from Social Services that recommends that April be placed in foster care until other matters can be resolved. Those other matters might, and I repeat the word *might*, include divorce proceedings, criminal charges against the father, psychiatric evaluations of both parents, and so on. We cannot anticipate all of the legal battles that lie ahead. My job today is to decide where to place April while her parents attempt to bring some order to their lives. This preliminary report concludes with the belief that she is not safe at home. Mrs. Boone, have you had time to read the report?"

"Yes, Your Honor."

"Do you agree with it?"

"Yes and no, Your Honor. Last night, April was at home, with both parents in the house, and she felt safe. The night before, she was at home with her mother, and she felt safe. But last week, on Monday night and Tuesday night, she was at home alone and had no idea where either parent was. Around midnight Tuesday, her father showed up, and because she was terrified, she left with him. Now, we all know the rest of the story. April wants to be at home with her parents, but I'm not sure her parents want to be home with her. Perhaps, Your Honor, we should hear from her parents."

"Precisely. Mr. Finnemore, what are your plans for the near future? Do you plan to stay at home, or leave? Tour again with your rock band, or finally give it up? Get a job, or continue to drift here and there? File for divorce, or get some professional help? A clue here, Mr. Finnemore. Give us some idea of what we can expect from you."

Tom Finnemore hunkered down under the barrage of loaded questions suddenly aimed at him. For a long time, he said nothing. Everyone waited and waited and after a while it appeared as though he had no response. But when he spoke, his voice was scratchy, almost cracking. "I don't know, Judge. I just don't know. I took April last week because she was scared to death and we had no idea where May was. After we left, I called several times, never got an answer, and as time passed I guess I quit calling. It never occurred to me that the whole town would think she had been kidnapped and murdered. It was a big mistake on my part. I'm really sorry."

He wiped his eyes, cleared his throat, and continued: "I think the rock tours are over, kind of a dead-end road, you know. To answer your question, Judge, I plan to be at home a lot more. I'd like to spend more time with April, but I'm not sure about spending time with her mother."

"Have the two of you discussed a divorce?"

"Judge, we've been married for twenty-four years, and we separated the first time after two months of marriage. Divorce has always been a hot topic."

"What's your response to the report's conclusion that April be removed from your home and placed somewhere safe?"

"Please don't do that, sir. I'll stay home, I promise. I'm not sure what May will do, but I can promise this Court that one of us will be at home for April."

"That sounds good, Mr. Finnemore, but, frankly, you don't have a lot of credibility with me right now."

"I know, Judge, and I understand. But, please don't take

her away." He wiped his eyes again and went silent. St. Nick waited, then turned to the other side of the room and said, "And you?"

May Finnemore had a tissue in both hands and looked as though she'd been crying for days. She mumbled and stammered before finding her voice. "It's not a great home, Judge; I guess that much is obvious. But it's our home; it's April's home. Her room is there, her clothes and books and things. Maybe her parents are not always there, but we'll do better. You can't take April out of her home and put her with strangers. Please don't do that."

"And your plans, Mrs. Finnemore? More of the same, or are you willing to change your ways?"

May Finnemore pulled papers out of a file and gave them to the bailiff, who in turn handed each one to the judge, Mr. Finnemore, and Mrs. Boone. "This is a letter from my therapist. He explains that I'm under his care now and that he is optimistic about my improvement."

Everyone read the letter. Though couched in medical terms, the bottom line was that May had emotional problems, and to deal with them she had gotten herself mixed up with various and unnamed prescription drugs. She continued, "He has enrolled me in a rehab program as an outpatient. I'm tested every morning at eight a.m."

"When did you start this program?" St. Nick asked.

"Last week. I went to see the therapist after April disappeared. I'm much better already, I promise, Your Honor."

St. Nick put the letter down and looked at April. "I'd like to hear from you," he said with a warm smile. "What are your thoughts, April? What do you want?"

In a voice much stronger than either parent, April began, "Well, Judge, what I want is something that's impossible. I want what every kid wants—a normal home and a normal family. But that is not what I have. We don't do normal, and I've learned to live with that. My brother and sister learned to live with it. They left home as soon as possible, and they're doing okay out in the world. They survived, and I'll survive, too, if I can have a little help. I want a father who doesn't leave for a month without saying good-bye and without calling home. I want a mother who'll protect me. I can deal with a lot of the crazy stuff, as long as they don't run away." Her voice began to break, but she was determined to finish. "I'm leaving, too, as soon as I can. Until then, though, please don't abandon me."

She looked at her father and saw nothing but tears. She looked at her mother and saw the same.

St. Nick looked at the lawyer and said, "As April's guardian, Mrs. Boone, do you have a recommendation?"

"I have a recommendation, Your Honor, and I have a plan," Marcella Boone said.

"I'm not surprised. Continue."

"My recommendation is that April remain at home tonight and tomorrow night, and then on a nightly basis. If either parent plans to be away from home during the night, that parent must notify me in advance, and I'll notify the Court. Further, I recommend the parents begin marriage counseling immediately. I suggest Doctor Francine Street, who is in my opinion the best in town. I've taken the liberty of setting up an appointment this afternoon at five p.m. Doctor Street will keep me posted on the progress. If either parent fails to show up for counseling, then I will be notified immediately. I will contact Mrs. Finnemore's new therapist and ask to be updated on her progress in rehab."

St. Nick stroked his beard and nodded at Mrs. Boone. "I like it," he said. "What about you, Mr. Finnemore?"

"Sounds reasonable, Your Honor."

"And you, Mrs. Finnemore?"

"I'll agree to anything, Judge. Just please don't take her away."

"Then it is so ordered. Anything else, Mrs. Boone?"

"Yes, Your Honor. I have arranged for April to have a cell phone. If something happens, if she feels threatened or in danger, or whatever, then she can call me immediately. If for some reason I'm not available, she can call my paralegal, or perhaps someone with the Court. Plus, I'm sure she can always find Theo."

St. Nick thought for a second and smiled, then said, "And I'm sure Theo can always find her."

Fifteen feet above, in the dark intestines of the Stratten County Courthouse, Theodore Boone smiled to himself.

The hearing was over.

Speedy was back, shuffling through his cramped room below, mumbling to himself as he put his mop away and accidentally kicked his bucket. Theo was trapped and he really wanted to get out of the building and go to school. He waited. Minutes passed, then he heard the familiar sound of Speedy snoring, fast asleep as usual. Silently, Theo climbed down the shelves and landed on the floor. Speedy was kicked back in his favorite chair, cap pulled down over his eyes, mouth open, dead to the world. Theo eased by and made his escape. He was hustling down the wide hallway, almost to the sweeping staircase when he heard someone call his name. It was Judge Henry Gantry, Theo's favorite judge in the entire courthouse.

"Theo," he called loudly.

Theo stopped, turned, and began walking to the judge.

Henry Gantry was not smiling, though he seldom did. He was carrying a thick file of some sort and he was not wearing his black robe. "Why aren't you in school?" he demanded.

More than once, Theo had played hooky or skipped school to watch a trial, and on at least two occasions he'd been caught red-handed, in the courtroom. "I was in court with my mother," he said, somewhat truthfully. He was looking up. Judge Gantry was looking down.

"Would this have anything to do with the April Finnemore case?" he asked. Strattenburg was not a large city and there were few secrets, especially among the lawyers, judges, and police.

"Yes, sir."

"I hear you found the girl and brought her home," Judge Gantry said with the first hint of a smile.

"Something like that," Theo said modestly.

"Nice work, Theo."

"Thanks."

"Just so you'll know, I've rescheduled the Duffy trial to begin in six weeks. I'm sure you'll want front-row seats."

Theo could think of nothing to say. The first murder trial of Pete Duffy had been the biggest in the town's history, and, thanks to Theo, it had ended in a mistrial. The second promised to be even more suspenseful.

Theo finally said, "Sure, Judge."

"We'll talk about it later. Get to school."

"Sure thing." Theo bounded down the stairs, jumped on his bike, and raced away from the courthouse. He had a lunch date with April. They planned to meet outside the school cafeteria at noon and steal away to the old gym where no one could find them. Mrs. Boone had packed veggie sandwiches, April's favorite and Theo's least favorite, and peanut butter cookies.

Theo wanted to hear every last detail of the abduction.

Read where it all began . . .

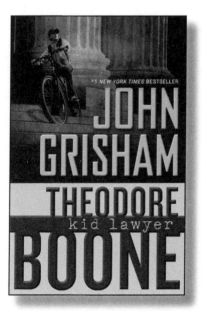

# Chapter 1

Theodore Boone was an only child and for that reason usually had breakfast alone. His father, a busy lawyer, was in the habit of leaving early and meeting friends for coffee and gossip at the same downtown diner every morning at seven. Theo's mother, herself a busy lawyer, had been trying to lose ten pounds for at least the past ten years, and because of this she'd convinced herself that breakfast should be nothing more than coffee with the newspaper. So he ate by himself at the kitchen table, cold cereal and orange juice, with an eye on the clock. The Boone home had clocks everywhere, clear evidence of organized people.

Actually, he wasn't completely alone. Beside his chair, his dog ate, too. Judge was a thoroughly mixed mutt whose

age and breeding would always be a mystery. Theo had rescued him from near death with a last-second appearance in
Animal Court two years earlier, and Judge would always be
grateful. He preferred Cheerios, same as Theo, and they ate
together in silence every morning.

At 8:00 a.m., Theo rinsed their bowls in the sink, placed
the milk and juice back in the fridge, walked to the den, and
kissed his mother on the cheek. "Off to school," he said.

"Do you have lunch money?" she asked, the same
question five mornings a week.

"Always."

"And your homework is complete?"

"It's perfect, Mom."

"And I'll see you when?"

"I'll stop by the office after school." Theo stopped by the
office every day after school, without fail, but Mrs. Boone
always asked.

"Be careful," she said. "And remember to smile." The
braces on his teeth had now been in place for over two years
and Theo wanted desperately to get rid of them. In the
meantime, though, his mother continually reminded him
to smile and make the world a happier place.

"I'm smiling, Mom."

"Love you, Teddy."

"Love you back."

Theo, still smiling in spite of being called "Teddy," flung his backpack across his shoulders, scratched Judge on the head and said good-bye, then left through the kitchen door. He hopped on his bike and was soon speeding down Mallard Lane, a narrow leafy street in the oldest section of town. He waved at Mr. Nunnery, who was already on his porch and settled in for another long day of watching what little traffic found its way into their neighborhood, and he whisked by Mrs. Goodloe at the curb without speaking because she'd lost her hearing and most of her mind as well. He did smile at her, though, but she did not return the smile. Her teeth were somewhere in the house.

It was early spring and the air was crisp and cool. Theo pedaled quickly, the wind stinging his face. Homeroom was at eight forty and he had important matters before school. He cut through a side street, darted down an alley, dodged some traffic, and ran a stop sign. This was Theo's turf, the route he traveled every day. After four blocks the houses gave way to offices and shops and stores.

The county courthouse was the largest building in downtown Strattenburg (the post office was second, the library third). It sat majestically on the north side of Main Street, halfway between a bridge over the river and a park filled with gazebos and birdbaths and monuments to those killed in wars. Theo loved the courthouse, with its air of authority, and people hustling importantly about, and somber notices and schedules tacked to the bulletin boards. Most of all, Theo loved the courtrooms themselves. There were small ones where more private matters were handled without juries, then there was the main courtroom on the second floor where lawyers battled like gladiators and judges ruled like kings.

At the age of thirteen, Theo was still undecided about his future. One day he dreamed of being a famous trial lawyer, one who handled the biggest cases and never lost before juries. The next day he dreamed of being a great judge, noted for his wisdom and fairness. He went back and forth, changing his mind daily.

The main lobby was already busy on this Monday morning, as if the lawyers and their clients wanted an early start to the week. There was a crowd waiting by the elevator, so Theo raced up two flights of stairs and down the east wing where Family Court was held. His mother was a noted divorce lawyer, one who always represented the wife, and Theo knew this area of the building well. Since divorce trials were decided by judges, juries were not used, and since most judges preferred not to have large groups of spectators observing such sensitive matters, the courtroom was small. By its door, several lawyers huddled importantly, obviously not agreeing on much. Theo searched the hallway, then turned a corner and saw his friend.

She was sitting on one of the old wooden benches, alone, small and frail and nervous. When she saw him she smiled and put a hand over her mouth. Theo hustled over and sat next to her, very closely, knees touching. With any other girl he would have placed himself at least two feet away and prevented any chance of contact.

But April Finnemore was not just any girl. They had started prekindergarten together at the age of four at a nearby church school, and they had been close friends since they could remember. It wasn't a romance; they were too young for that. Theo did not know of a single thirteen-year-old boy in his class who admitted to having a girlfriend. Just the opposite. They wanted nothing to do with them. And the girls felt the same way. Theo had been warned that things would change, and dramatically, but that seemed unlikely.

April was just a friend, and one in a great deal of need at the moment. Her parents were divorcing, and Theo was extremely grateful his mother was not involved with the case.

The divorce was no surprise to anyone who knew the Finnemores. April's father was an eccentric antiques dealer and the drummer for an old rock band that still played in nightclubs and toured for weeks at a time. Her mother raised goats and made goat cheese, which she peddled around town in a converted funeral hearse, painted bright yellow. An ancient spider monkey with gray whiskers rode shotgun and munched on the cheese, which had never sold very well. Mr. Boone had once described the family as "nontraditional," which Theo took to mean downright weird. Both her parents had been arrested on drug charges, though neither had served time.

"Are you okay?" Theo asked.

"No," she said. "I hate being here."

She had an older brother named August and an older sister named March, and both fled the family. August left the day after he graduated from high school. March dropped out at the age of sixteen and left town, leaving April as the only child for her parents to torment. Theo knew all of this because April told him everything. She had to. She needed someone outside of her family to confide in, and Theo was her listener.

"I don't want to live with either one of them," she said. It was a terrible thing to say about one's parents, but Theo understood completely. He despised her parents for the way they treated her. He despised them for the chaos of their lives, for their neglect of April, for their cruelty to her. Theo had a long list of grudges against Mr. and Mrs. Finnemore. He would run away before being forced to live there. He did not know of a single kid in town who'd ever set foot inside the Finnemore home.

The divorce trial was in its third day, and April would soon be called to the witness stand to testify. The judge would ask her the fateful question, "April, which parent do you want to live with?"

And she did not know the answer. She had discussed it for hours with Theo, and she still did not know what to say.

The great question in Theo's mind was, "Why did either parent want custody of April?" Each had neglected her in so many ways. He had heard many stories, but he had never repeated a single one.

"What are you going to say?" he asked.

"I'm telling the judge that I want to live with my aunt Peg in Denver."

"I thought she said no."

"She did."

"Then you can't say that."

"What can I say, Theo?"

"My mother would say that you should choose your mother. I know she's not your first choice, but you don't have a first choice."

"But the judge can do whatever he wants, right?"

"Right. If you were fourteen, you could make a binding decision. At thirteen, the judge will only consider your wishes. According to my mother, this judge almost never awards custody to the father. Play it safe. Go with your mother."

April wore jeans, hiking boots, and a navy sweater. She rarely dressed like a girl, but her gender was never in doubt. She wiped a tear from her cheek, but managed to keep her composure. "Thanks, Theo," she said.

"I wish I could stay."

"And I wish I could go to school."

They both managed a forced laugh. "I'll be thinking about you. Be strong."

"Thanks, Theo."

His favorite judge was the Honorable Henry Gantry, and he entered the great man's outer office at twenty minutes after 8:00 a.m.

"Well, good morning, Theo," Mrs. Hardy said. She was stirring something into her coffee and preparing to begin her work.

"Morning, Mrs. Hardy," Theo said with a smile.

"And to what do we owe this honor?" she asked. She

was not quite as old as Theo's mother, he guessed, and she was very pretty. She was Theo's favorite of all the secretaries in the courthouse. His favorite clerk was Jenny over in Family Court.

"I need to see Judge Gantry," he replied. "Is he in?"

"Well, yes, but he's very busy."

"Please. It'll just take a minute."

She sipped her coffee, then asked, "Does this have anything to do with the big trial tomorrow?"

"Yes, ma'am, it does. I'd like for my Government class to watch the first day of the trial, but I gotta make sure there will be enough seats."

"Oh, I don't know about that, Theo," Mrs. Hardy said, frowning and shaking her head. "We're expecting an overflow crowd. Seating will be tight."

"Can I talk to the judge?"

"How many are in your class?"

"Sixteen. I thought maybe we could sit in the balcony."

She was still frowning as she picked up the phone and pushed a button. She waited for a second, then said, "Yes, Judge, Theodore Boone is here and would like to see you. I told him you are very busy." She listened some more, then put down the phone. "Hurry," she said, pointing to the judge's door.

Seconds later, Theo stood before the biggest desk in town,

a desk covered with all sorts of papers and files and thick binders, a desk that symbolized the enormous power held by Judge Henry Gantry, who, at that moment, was not smiling. In fact, Theo was certain the judge had not cracked a smile since he'd interrupted his work. Theo, though, was pressing hard with a prolonged flash of metal from ear to ear.

"State your case," Judge Gantry said. Theo had heard him issue this command on many occasions. He'd seen lawyers, good lawyers, rise and stutter and search for words while Judge Gantry scowled down from the bench. He wasn't scowling now, nor was he wearing his black robe, but he was still intimidating. As Theo cleared his throat, he saw an unmistakable twinkle in his friend's eye.

"Yes, sir, well, my Government teacher is Mr. Mount, and Mr. Mount thinks we might get approval from the principal for an all-day field trip to watch the opening of the trial tomorrow." Theo paused, took a deep breath, told himself again to speak clearly, slowly, forcefully, like all great trial lawyers. "But, we need guaranteed seats. I was thinking we could sit in the balcony."

"Oh, you were?"

"Yes, sir."

"How many?"

"Sixteen, plus Mr. Mount."

The judge picked up a file, opened it, and began reading

as if he'd suddenly forgotten about Theo standing at attention across the desk. Theo waited for an awkward fifteen seconds. Then the judge abruptly said, "Seventeen seats, front balcony, left side. I'll tell the bailiff to seat you at ten minutes before nine, tomorrow. I expect perfect behavior."

"No problem, sir."

"I'll have Mrs. Hardy e-mail a note to your principal."

"Thanks, Judge."

"You can go now, Theo. Sorry to be so busy."

"No problem, sir."

Theo was scurrying toward the door when the judge said, "Say, Theo. Do you think Mr. Duffy is guilty?"

Theo stopped, turned around and without hesitating responded, "He's presumed innocent."

"Got that. But what's your opinion as to his guilt?"

"I think he did it."

The judge nodded slightly but gave no indication of whether he agreed.

"What about you?" Theo asked.

Finally, a smile. "I'm a fair and impartial referee, Theo. I have no preconceived notions of guilt or innocence."

"That's what I thought you'd say."

"See you tomorrow." Theo cracked the door and hustled out.

Mrs. Hardy was on her feet, hands on hips, staring

down two flustered lawyers who were demanding to see the judge. All three clammed up when Theo walked out of Judge Gantry's office. He smiled at Mrs. Hardy as he walked hurriedly by. "Thanks," he said as he opened the door and disappeared.

# Chapter 2

The ride from the courthouse to the middle school would take fifteen minutes if properly done, if one obeyed the traffic laws and refrained from trespassing. And normally this is the way Theo would do things, except when he was running a bit late. He flew down Market Street the wrong way, jumped the curb just ahead of a car, and bolted through a parking lot, used every sidewalk available, then—his most serious offense—he ducked between two houses on Elm Street. Theo heard someone yelling from the porch behind him until he was safely into an alley that ran into the teachers' parking lot behind his school. He checked his watch—nine minutes. Not bad.

He parked at the rack by the flagpole, secured his bike with a chain, then entered with a flood of kids who'd just stepped off a bus. The eight forty bell was ringing when he walked into his homeroom and said good morning to Mr. Mount, who not only taught him Government but was his adviser as well.

"Talked to Judge Gantry," Theo said at the teacher's desk, one considerably smaller than the one he'd just left in the courthouse. The room was buzzing with the usual early morning chaos. All sixteen boys were present and all appeared to be involved in some sort of gag, scuffle, joke, or shoving match.

"And?"

"Got the seats, first thing in the morning."

"Excellent. Great job, Theo."

Mr. Mount eventually restored order, called the roll, made his announcements, and ten minutes later sent the boys down the hall to their first period Spanish class with Madame Monique. There was some awkward flirting between the rooms as the boys mixed with the girls. During classes, they were "gender-separated," according to a new policy adopted by the smart people in charge of educating all the children in town. The genders were free to mingle at all other times.

Madame Monique was a tall, dark lady from Cameroon, in West Africa. She had moved to Strattenburg three years earlier when her husband, also from Cameroon, took a job at the local college where he taught languages. She was not the typical teacher at the middle school, far from it. As a child in Africa, she had grown up speaking Beti, her tribal dialect, as well as French and English, the official languages of Cameroon. Her father was a doctor, and thus could afford to send her to school in Switzerland, where she picked up German and Italian. Her Spanish had been perfected when she went to college in Madrid. She was currently working on Russian with plans to move on to Mandarin Chinese. Her classroom was filled with large, colorful maps of the world, and her students believed she'd been everywhere, seen everything, and could speak any language. It's a big world, she told them many times, and most people in other countries speak more than one language. While the students concentrated on Spanish, they were also encouraged to explore others.

Theo's mother had been studying Spanish for twenty years, and as a preschooler he had learned from her many of the basic words and phrases. Some of her clients were from Central America, and when Theo saw them at the office he was ready to practice. They always thought it was cute.

Madame Monique had told him that he had an ear for

languages, and this had inspired him to study harder. She was often asked by her curious students to "say something in German." Or, "Speak some Italian." She would, but first the student making the request had to stand and say a few words in that language. Bonus points were given, and this created enthusiasm. Most of the boys in Theo's class knew a few dozen words in several languages. Aaron, who had a Spanish mother and a German father, was by far the most talented linguist. But Theo was determined to catch him. After Government, Spanish was his favorite class, and Madame Monique ran a close second to Mr. Mount as his favorite teacher.

Today, though, he had trouble concentrating. They were studying Spanish verbs, a tedious chore on a good day, and Theo's mind was elsewhere. He worried about April and her awful day on the witness stand. He couldn't imagine the horror of being forced to choose one parent over another. And when he managed to set April aside, he was consumed with the murder trial and couldn't wait until tomorrow, to watch the opening statements by the lawyers.

Most of his classmates dreamed of getting tickets to the big game or concert. Theo Boone lived for the big trials.

Second period was Geometry with Miss Garman. It was followed by a short break outdoors, then the class returned to homeroom, to Mr. Mount and the best hour of the day, at least in Theo's opinion. Mr. Mount was in his midthirties, and had once worked as a lawyer at a gigantic firm in a skyscraper in Chicago. His brother was a lawyer. His father and grandfather had been lawyers and judges. Mr. Mount, though, had grown weary of the long hours and high pressure, and, well, he'd quit. He'd walked away from the big money and found something he found far more rewarding. He loved teaching, and though he still thought of himself as a lawyer, he considered the classroom far more important than the courtroom.

Because he knew the law so well, his Government class spent most of its time discussing cases, old ones and current ones and even fictitious ones on television.

"All right, men," he began when they were seated and still. He always addressed them as "men" and for thirteen-year-olds there was no greater compliment. "Tomorrow I want you here at eight fifteen. We'll take a bus to the courthouse and we'll be in our seats in plenty of time. It's a field trip, approved by the principal, so you will be excused from all other classes. Bring lunch money and we'll eat at Pappy's Deli. Any questions?"

The men were hanging on every word, excitement all over their faces.

"What about backpacks?" someone asked.

"No," Mr. Mount answered. "You can't take anything into the courtroom. Security will be tight. It is, after all, the first murder trial here in a long time. Any more questions?"

"What should we wear?"

Slowly, all eyes turned to Theo, including those of Mr. Mount. It was well known that Theo spent more time in the courthouse than most lawyers.

"Coat and tie, Theo?" Mr. Mount asked.

"No, not at all. What we're wearing now is fine."

"Great. Any more questions? Good. Now, I've asked Theo if he would sort of set the stage for tomorrow. Lay out the courtroom, give us the players, tell us what we're in for. Theo."

Theo's laptop was already wired to the overhead projector. He walked to the front of the class, pressed a key, and a large diagram appeared on the digital wide-screen whiteboard. "This is the main courtroom," Theo said, in his best lawyer's voice. He held a laser pointer with a red light and sort of waved it around the diagram. "At the top, in the center here, is the bench. That's where the judge sits and controls the trial. Not sure why it's called a bench. It's more like a throne. But, anyway, we'll stick with bench. The judge is Henry Gantry." He punched a key, and a large formal photo of Judge Gantry appeared. Black robe, somber face. Theo shrank it, then dragged it up to the bench. With the judge in place, he continued, "Judge Gantry has been a judge for about twenty years and handles only criminal cases. He runs a tight courtroom and is well liked by most of the lawyers." The laser pointer moved to the middle of the courtroom. "This is the defense table, where Mr. Duffy, the man accused of murder, will be seated." Theo punched a key and a black-and-white photo, one taken from a newspaper, appeared. "This is Mr. Duffy. Age forty-nine, used to be married to Mrs. Duffy, who is now deceased, and as we all know, Mr. Duffy is accused of murdering her." He shrank the photo and moved it to the defense table. "His lawyer is Clifford Nance, probably the top criminal defense lawyer in this part of the state." Nance appeared in color, wearing a dark suit and a shifty smile. He had long, curly gray hair. His photo was reduced and placed next to his client's. "Next to the defense table is the prosecution's table. The lead prosecutor is Jack Hogan, who's also known as the district attorney, or DA." Hogan's photo appeared for a few seconds before it was reduced and placed at the table next to the defense.

"Where'd you find these photos?" someone asked.

"Each year the bar association publishes a directory of all the lawyers and judges," Theo answered.

"Are you included?" This brought a few light laughs.

"No. Now, there will be other lawyers and paralegals at both tables, prosecution and defense. This area is usually crowded. Over here, next to the defense, is the jury box. It has fourteen chairs—twelve for the jurors and two for the alternates. Most states still use twelve-man juries, though different sizes are not unusual. Regardless of the number, the verdict has to be unanimous, at least in criminal cases. They pick alternates in case one of the twelve gets sick or excused or something. The jury was selected last week, so we won't have to watch that. It's pretty boring." The laser pointer moved to a spot in front of the bench. Theo continued, "The court reporter sits here. She'll have a machine that is called a stenograph. Sorta looks like a typewriter, but much different. Her job is to record every word that's said during the trial. That might sound impossible, but she makes it look easy. Later, she'll prepare what's known as a transcript so that the lawyers and the judge will have a record of everything. Some transcripts have thousands of pages." The laser pointer moved again. "Here, close to the court reporter and just down from the judge, is the witness chair. Each witness walks up here, is sworn to tell the truth, then takes a seat."

"Where do we sit?"

The laser pointer moved to the middle of the diagram. "This is called the bar. Again, don't ask why. The bar is a wooden railing that separates the spectators from the trial area. There are ten rows of seats with an aisle down the middle. This is usually more than enough for the crowd, but this trial will be different." The laser pointer moved to the rear of the courtroom. "Up here, above the last few rows, is the balcony where there are three long benches. We're in the balcony, but don't worry. We'll be able to see and hear everything."

"Any questions?" Mr. Mount asked.

The boys gawked at the diagram. "Who goes first?" someone asked.

Theo began pacing. "Well, the State has the burden of proving guilt, so it must present its case first. First thing tomorrow morning, the prosecutor will walk to the jury box and address the jurors. This is called the opening statement. He'll lay out his case. Then the defense lawyer will do the same. After that, the State will start calling witnesses. As you know, Mr. Duffy is presumed to be innocent, so the State must prove him guilty, and it must do so beyond a reasonable doubt. He claims he's innocent, which actually in real life doesn't happen very often. About eighty percent of those indicted for murder eventually plead guilty, because they are in fact guilty. The other twenty percent go to trial, and ninety percent of those are found guilty. So, it's rare for a murder defendant to be found not guilty."

"My dad thinks he's guilty," Brian said.

"A lot of people do," Theo said.

"How many trials have you watched, Theo?"

"I don't know. Dozens."

Since none of the other fifteen had ever seen the inside of a courtroom, this was almost beyond belief. Theo continued: "For those of you who watch a lot of television, don't expect fireworks. A real trial is very different, and not nearly as exciting. There are no surprise witnesses, no dramatic confessions, no fistfights between the lawyers. And, in this trial, there are no eyewitnesses to the murder. This means that all of the evidence from the State will be circumstantial. You'll hear this word a lot, especially from Mr. Clifford Nance, the defense lawyer. He'll make a big deal out of the fact that the State has no direct proof, that everything is circumstantial."

"I'm not sure what that means," someone said.

"It means that the evidence is indirect, not direct. For example, did you ride your bike to school?"

"Yes."

"And did you chain it to the rack by the flagpole?"

"Yes."

"So, when you leave school this afternoon, and you go to the rack, and your bike is gone, and the chain has been cut, then you have indirect evidence that someone stole your bike. No one saw the thief, so there's no direct evidence. And let's say that tomorrow the police find your bike in a pawnshop on Raleigh Street, a place known to deal in stolen bikes. The owner gives the police a name, they investigate and find some dude with a history of stealing bikes. You can then make a strong case, through indirect evidence, that this guy is your thief. No direct evidence, but circumstantial."

Even Mr. Mount was nodding along. He was the faculty adviser for the Eighth-Grade Debate Team, and, not surprisingly, Theodore Boone was his star. He'd never had a student as quick on his feet.

"Thank you, Theo," Mr. Mount said. "And thank you for getting us the seats in the morning."

"Nothing to it," Theo said, and proudly took his seat.

It was a bright class in a strong public school. Justin was by far the best athlete, though he couldn't swim as fast as Brian. Ricardo beat them all at golf and tennis. Edward played the cello, Woody the electric guitar, Darren the drums, Jarvis the trumpet. Joey had the highest IQ and made perfect grades. Chase was the mad scientist who was always a threat to blow up the lab. Aaron spoke Spanish, from his mother's side, German from his father's, and English, of course. Brandon had an early morning paper route, traded stocks online, and planned to be the first millionaire in the group.

Naturally, there were two hopeless nerds and at least one potential felon.

The class even had its own lawyer, a first for Mr. Mount.